Mental Health Interventions and Services for Vulnerable Children and Young People

also by Panos Vostanis

Homeless Children
Problems and Needs
Edited by Panos Vostanis and Stuart Cumella
ISBN 978 1 85302 595 2

of related interest

A Multidisciplinary Handbook of Child and Adolescent Mental Health for Front-line Professionals
Nisha Dogra, Andrew Parkin, Fiona Gale, and Clay Frake
Foreword by Panos Vostanis
ISBN 978 1 85302 929 5

Shattered Lives
Children Who Live with Courage and Dignity
Camila Batmanghelidjh
ISBN 978 1 84310 603 6

Introducing Mental Health
A Practical Guide
Caroline Kinsella and Connor Kinsella
Foreword by Vikram Patel
ISBN 978 1 84310 260 1

Reaching the Vulnerable Child
Therapy with Traumatized Children
Janie Rymaszewska and Terry Philpot
Foreword by Mary Walsh, co-founder and Chief Executive of SACCS
ISBN 978 1 84310 329 5

The Child's Own Story
Life Story Work with Traumatized Children
Richard Rose and Terry Philpot
Foreword by Mary Walsh, co-founder and Chief Executive of SACCS
ISBN 978 1 84310 287 8

Living Alongside a Child's Recovery
Therapeutic Parenting with Traumatized Children
Billy Pughe and Terry Philpot
Foreword by Mary Walsh, co-founder and Chief Executive of SACCS
ISBN 978 1 84310 328 8

Understanding Attachment and Attachment Disorders
Theory, Evidence and Practice
Vivien Prior and Danya Glaser
ISBN 978 1 84310 245 8

Mental Health Interventions and Services for Vulnerable Children and Young People

Edited by Panos Vostanis

Foreword by Richard Williams

Jessica Kingsley Publishers
London and Philadelphia

Most answers are amazingly simple...if only we would listen to what children are trying to tell us.

To all the children and young people I have met over the years, and whose strength and determination to defeat adversity have never ceased to amaze me. Similarly, to the dedicated carers and practitioners who may also feel powerless at times, but whose commitment and passion ultimately sees children and young people through their difficulties.

First published in 2007
by Jessica Kingsley Publishers
116 Pentonville Road
London N1 9JB, UK
and
400 Market Street, Suite 400
Philadelphia, PA 19106, USA

www.jkp.com

Copyright © Jessica Kingsley Publishers 2007
Foreword copyright © Richard Williams 2007

Library of Congress Cataloging in Publication Data

Mental health interventions and services for vulnerable children and young people / edited by Panos Vostanis ; foreword by Richard Williams.
p. ; cm.
Includes bibliographical references and index.
ISBN 978-1-84310-489-6 (alk. paper)
1. Child mental health services. 2. Youth--Mental health services. I. Vostanis, Panos.
[DNLM: 1. Mental Disorders--therapy. 2. Mental Health Services. 3. Child. 4. Vulnerable Populations. WS 350.2 M549 2008]
RJ499.M4192 2008
618.92'89--dc22

2007021480

British Library Cataloguing in Publication Data

A CIP catalogue record for this book is available from the British Library

ISBN 978 1 84310 489 6

Printed and bound in Great Britain by
Athenaeum Press, Gateshead, Tyne and Wear

Contents

Part III: Applying the Evidence and Therapeutic Principles to Different Welfare and Health Systems, Cultural Contexts and Social Circumstances

List of Tables, Figures and Boxes

Tables

Figures

Boxes

Foreword

> If this particular period in the world's history had to be characterised in any simple way, it might be as one that is more highly, more globally, and more unexpectedly connected than at any time before it. (Watts 2004)

It is my honour and a great pleasure to introduce this book. In it, Panos Vostanis sets out to martial synopses of current knowledge and evidence about vulnerable children. He and his authors rise to the challenge by providing incisive summaries of current knowledge in each of their topic areas. They span policy, science, values, diversity and practice. This book illustrates well that our knowledge of vulnerable children and young people and their needs is expanding rapidly. In his recent book, the sociologist Duncan Watts states that, soon, it will be 'beyond the ability of any one person to learn in a life-time' all of the scientific knowledge that impinges on us. In this scenario, abbreviated accounts that bring us up to date provide an extremely helpful service; this book amply fulfils that role.

I introduce this book to you from a particular perspective. I am keen to see the wisdom contained in books of this kind used to encourage connectedness between governance, strategic and service delivery policies, practice, and people who need to use our services. That connectedness must encourage vision and innovation, but be realistic; it must be informed by evidence but also be reflective of the diversity of people's values that are, inevitably, involved.

The size of that task emerges in Miranda Wolpert's chapter. I was struck by her finding that 'only a handful of countries have an articulated national policy in relation to children and young people'. who have a mental health problem or disorder. Nonetheless, she states that where those policies exist, they are 'preoccupied with trying to focus on the needs of the most vulnerable children'. To my mind, her chapter poses a number of challenges; some are explicit and others are implicit. One of those concerns who is and who is not to be considered 'vulnerable'; the authors of this book take a broad and inclusive view. They set out what we know about a substantial number of children who are considered vulnerable because they have particular attributes or have had certain past and present experiences or are growing up in particular settings or have experienced a combination of these matters. Another question is whether or not services for vulnerable people should be delivered within and by generic services, or by special teams within services for all children, or by discreet and separate services.

In this situation, Duncan Watts might excuse my focus and partiality. He observes that 'real science occurs in the same messy ambiguous world that scientists struggle to clarify, and is done by real people who suffer the same kind of limitations and confusions as anybody else' (Watts 2004). Duncan Watts shows, in respect of other topics, that there is circularity between how we endeavour to solve complex problems and the nature of the problems that are at the core of our work. Altering the context of his statement, I assert that we are all trying to make sense of and intervene effectively and respectfully to help vulnerable children in a world that appears, and is, often, messy and ambiguous. I include in that endeavour scientists, policymakers, commissioners of services, managers, practitioners, but, particularly importantly, children, young people and their families. This book is relevant to all of them.

It reminds us that there are universal challenges in designing and delivering mental health services for vulnerable people. They include: lack of knowledge; stigma; the realities posed in the global world by cultural diversity, population movements and displacement, and challenges posed by having problems with communicating; the poor and unstable living and school circumstances of so many vulnerable children; and the relative frequency of abuse, violence and disaster.

Often, the children and young people who are the focus of this book are described in professional circles as having 'complex' problems. Sometimes, this is an apt description. On other occasions, 'complex' is used as a synonym for having multiple problems. However, the problems faced by other people are all too simple to perceive, but intervening effectively with them is another matter which reveals major challenges.

Together, the authors of this book paint word pictures of some of the most vulnerable children and young people in the twenty-first century society. All too often, they have multiple needs, more severe, persistent and entrenched problems with living that are evolving but, paradoxically, difficult to change. Many of these younger people and their families find difficulties, sometimes great difficulties, in engaging with services that are split across a range of agencies in ways that do not reflect their experiences, needs or preferences. Vulnerable children have problems and needs that spring from them that 'interact with each other, and in interacting…can generate bewildering behavior' (Watts 2004, p.8). Their educational, social, relationship and mental health needs are interconnected but dynamic and the interactions are less static than we tend to think. This calls for services that can respond in equally dynamic and connected ways.

But, we should remind ourselves that, occasionally, even complex problems can have straightforward solutions 'and sometimes understanding can be enough'[1] to change practice and guide our actions to design and run systems to respond effectively to children's needs. This book provides important summaries of the understandings that should underpin our efforts to improve services.

Nonetheless, as this book reveals, simple solutions do not always work. Engaging vulnerable children and young people in therapy provides a good example of the particular awareness and knowledge that is enormously helpful to practitioners. In part, this is because healthcare, social care and education services are also complex human organizational systems. Watts argues, 'connected systems can be at once robust and fragile' (Watts 2004, p.262). Certainly, it is my experience that vulnerable children often reveal the fragilities in otherwise stable services. We, that is professionals, managers and policymakers talk about 'child-centred services', but vulnerable children provide us with uncomfortable evidence of fault lines in their care. Arguably, we have a long way to go before we can claim that our services, even in an age of networked connectedness, are sufficiently child-centred.

In that context, I see the chapters on rights, ethics and cultural diversity as important contributions in assisting us to design and deliver principled services. I also take this opportunity to identify the ethical challenges that are faced by policymakers and commissioners in deciding where and on whom to place their priorities. These tasks require a new form of what I call public health ethics and clarity about good decision-making. Work to develop these approaches is underway.

This book reveals a deep irony. While, our world is increasingly well connected, achieving consistently planned and sufficiently networked services to serve vulnerable children and young people well in co-ordinated and timely ways still remains a challenge. We are all aware of recurrent reports and governments' policies that induce us to work in closer partnerships and of the endeavours of policymakers to re-structure services and the money supply across traditional boundaries with a view to removing those fault-lines in care in response to knowledge of what has gone wrong previously and our awareness of children's needs and preferences. But, on many occasions, and despite the worthiness of these policies, it appears clear that this knowledge, and its moral power, is insufficient on its own to achieve what is needed. In those circumstances, we must also take into account a number of other systemic matters that may act as assets or blocks in achieving change. They include the dynamic natures and interconnectedness of the complex experiences, relationships, values, problems and needs that characterise many vulnerable young children's worlds, our own values, the values and roles of policymakers and the complexity of the co-ordinated healthcare, social care and education systems that are required if we are to mount effective services. This book provides a strong and evidenced starting point from which to begin those enquiries.

Faced with their special knowledge, experience, responsibilities, and frustrations, we can see why some policymakers, commissioners and practitioners advocate establishing separate services for particular groups of children. However, in my opinion, that approach risks not integrating particularly troubled children and young people and their care, though access to services for them might be improved. The approaches we take to translating the wisdom that is contained in this book into service design are, therefore, a challenge too. Professor Vostanis returns to one of the questions I posed earlier in his final chapter. He argues for services for vulnerable children being integrated into and connected with the generality of services. He says while, 'there is now substantial evidence that…children in need are unlikely to…engage with services, unless their characteristics are understood and taken into consideration when care pathways and interventions are set up…[this]…does not imply that these children should be seen separately from generic…services, but…that they should be approached in a different way'.

Panos Vostanis distils core messages from this book about the way forward in his closing chapter. He takes an optimistic tone. Realistically in my opinion, he recommends that we must take on developing international, national and local policies, apply both therapeutic interventions and the roles of preventative programmes, tackle the requirement for evaluation, and recognize the core position of training, if we are to deliver better integrated and more sustainable services in the future.

The contents of this book will be enormously helpful in designing and delivering better services that enable vulnerable children to be approached in ways that reflect the realities of their experiences, needs and preferences. All of these matters impact on whether or not they engage. This book should inform better-integrated plans; it challenges us to renew our endeavours to provide services of broad scope that are more responsive, adaptable and flexible. In my opinion, Panos Vostanis' position also calls on us to consider what we can learn from the emerging science and theory of networks alongside our knowledge of vulnerable children's needs and preferences when we are developing policy and designing services. We are also reminded in Chapter 7 that practitioners also deserve consideration because of the emotional toll that they may face in doing their work.

Panos Vostanis' challenge to us also requires us to be capable of recognizing and working with the diversity of values that are evident in different professions, disciplines, agencies and practitioners and across families. Sometimes people assert that science is values-free. In my opinion, this cannot be so; we reveal values in everything we do including in what we choose to research and how. Furthermore, it is a core tenet of values-based policymaking, commissioning and practice that more science brings with it more choices and, therefore, more arenas in which values are vital matters in decision-making (Williams and Fulford 2007). Inevitably, we all come to the evidence provided by this book from our personal perspectives.

At the outset, Panos Vostanis declares his perspective, his values, and his reasons for choosing to write about children and young people who are vulnerable and the ways in which he sees progress being made. The values of the authors are also palpable from the ways in which they write, what they say and the recommendations they offer. Inevitably, you will have your own reactions to what you read herein. You will be provoked to think about your own values and preferred courses of action. If this book achieves that as well as providing a thorough review of our current knowledge, it offers the basis for better connectedness between knowledge, values, skills, and plans for the future.

Richard Williams,
Professor of Mental Health Strategy, Welsh Institute for Health and Social Care;
University of Glamorgan Honorary Professor of Child and Adolescent Mental Health,
University of Central Lancashire
and Consultant Child and Adolescent Psychiatrist, Gwent Healthcare NHS Trust

References

Watts, D.J. (2004) *Six Degrees: the science of a connected age.* London: Vintage.

Williams, R. and Fulford, K.W.M. (2007) 'Evidence-based and values-based policy, management and practice in child and adolescent mental health services.' *Clinical Child Psychology and Psychiatry 12,* 223–242.

PART I
Evidence, Policy and Legislation

CHAPTER 1

Introduction

Panos Vostanis

Are some children more vulnerable than others? If so, do we really need to think of them in a different context? More importantly, should we be developing different interventions and planning different services at a time when child and adolescent mental health services are slowly taking off around the world in their own right? A recent national UK policy was called *Every Child Matters* (DoH 2003). It may have stated the obvious: that all children and young people are important, and that we should ensure them the best possible help and support to reach their potential; however, it is more likely that the policy was driven by the same principle of this text, that is, neither that some children matter more than others, nor that any policy-makers or practitioners over the years thought otherwise. What it has tried to highlight is a simple public health and welfare philosophy: that some groups of the population have multiple needs, which are not necessarily met by conventional services.

In order to meet the needs of these population groups effectively, we should first understand: why they are particularly vulnerable; why their difficulties can be particularly severe and entrenched, and hence not easy to break; why these difficulties cannot be addressed by any single agency; why they cannot easily engage or access what is on offer, and consequently, how we should best use available evidence and adapt therapeutic frameworks, interventions, and generic services to reach and help these young groups of the population. A number of related approaches and initiatives during the last decade, across societies with different health and social care systems, allow us to be optimistic that we are ready to implement this knowledge and thus generate evidence-based and sustainable service models.

It is, of course, difficult, and ultimately pointless, to categorize children and young people in 'boxes', since they will always overlap on some characteristics and differ on others. Many underlying risk factors will be inter-related, for example children exposed to domestic violence, followed by family disruption, homelessness, and loss of their supportive networks. Also, children and families move between these categories, such as those young people leaving public care who are excluded from education and who become homeless.

Despite this need to remain cautious in using such definitions, some children and young people are inevitably 'more vulnerable' than others, in particular, where the impact of trauma, abuse or neglect, family, and other adversities is chronic and compounded by secondary effects. These, in turn, lead to loss of friends, schooling, stability, and other protective influences for children's development and emotional growth. In addition, the impact of their initial needs on their mental health, that is, maladaptive behaviours, emotional distress, and social relationship difficulties can be followed by school exclusion, offending, sexual exploitation, and substance abuse.

Vulnerable children and young people have several characteristics, and it is essential that these are taken into consideration by practitioners and service-planners. They may have multiple and changing carers, such as foster families and residential staff, and frequently changing circumstances. These characteristics are likely to increase insecurity, lack of trust, and uncertainty for the future. In parallel with the number of carers, there are several agencies involved, often not in co-ordination, and several transfer points, that can increase the sense of despondence and rejection. There are also difficulties in distinguishing between children's mental health, social care, developmental, and educational needs, as these are usually inter-related, and fluctuate concurrently. Children's mobility between geographical areas may adversely determine service responses, and may be compounded by their lack of advocacy, either because of the absence of parents to undertake this fundamental role, or because of the emotional fragility and capacity of their parent(s) to do so.

A number of young client groups fulfil these characteristics to varying degrees. Children in public care (those 'looked after' by local authorities) readily come to mind, with an already large body of therapeutic knowledge on working with foster carers, residential units (children's homes and other residential establishments), and care leavers, although albeit rather limited evidence on their specificity and effectiveness. The number of refugee and asylum-seeking families has steadily increased in recent years within Western societies, with particular concerns for unaccompanied minors in relation to ethical dilemmas, child protection, and successful re-integration in their new communities. Homeless children and young people are a heterogeneous group with several underlying causes and routes to homelessness. On the whole, homeless families are victims of domestic violence or neighbourhood harassment; they have different needs from single young homeless people, with the latter often overlapping with leaving care, the judicial system, and substance misuse. Young offenders may not initially be thought of as a vulnerable group per se. However, there is now strong evidence that a substantial proportion of young people who come into contact with the courts have longstanding adverse family, community, and school experiences, as well as exposure to trauma and abuse. Policies and service objectives have recently reflected the importance of addressing their needs at different levels. Other groups of children and young people do not share all the above patterns, in particular the lack of stability, but can be affected by similar vulnerability factors. Examples constitute children with complex physical and developmental disabilities, and those who have been adopted. For these overarching reasons such groups of children, young people, and their carers are discussed throughout this text, both in relation to specific needs, such as working with foster carers or interventions for young offenders, and when considering issues that are common across these groups, for example stigmatization and ethics.

We are now also in a better position to understand the nature, severity, and complexity of the mental health problems and related needs of vulnerable children. A lot of evidence and conclusions may be drawn from the general child mental health research literature on the cumulative impact of acute stressors and chronic adversities on children's emotional well-being. These have been confirmed by specific evidence on studies with high-risk young groups selected from all the populations previously mentioned, including 'looked-after' children, young offenders, homeless young people, and refugees. The findings from a range of small- or larger-scale designs, descriptive or in-depth studies, using rating scales or detailed interviews, point to the same direction of evidence. This suggests that vulnerable children and young people have significantly higher levels of mental health problems than the general population, including children living in socio-economically deprived, albeit stable, circumstances. These problems are likely to be more severe and entrenched, and are consequently more difficult to manage in isolation from their other developmental, social, and educational needs. In contrast to what places children at risk of mental health problems, there is strikingly less evidence on what protects them from such difficulties, particularly in the face of adversity.

Despite the strong evidence of high levels of mental health and related needs, the reverse – and apparently contradictory – finding has been established for the utilization of mental health and related services by children and young people, predominantly because of poor access and engagement. When looked at in more detail the reasons are closely related to the characteristics of these children, and what makes them vulnerable in the first instance. In other words, vulnerable children often do not conform to existing service structures and operational criteria because of their mobility, lack of consistent adult advocacy, and multiplicity of needs. This paradox has always acted as my personal motive in working with vulnerable children and young people over the years, and for my seeking alternative types of interventions and services which take into consideration these features rather than merely replicate services designed for the general, and mostly stable, population.

The lack of evidence on effective therapeutic interventions for vulnerable young groups is less surprising, since this is still relatively limited for child mental health problems and disorders as a whole, with the possible exception of more structured modalities, such as parent training and cognitive-behavioural therapy. Not withstanding the methodological, pragmatic, and ethical difficulties in designing and evaluating interventions for groups such as looked-after children and young offenders, there are also specific conceptual reasons which, again, relate to the core characteristics of vulnerable children. The indications for thera-peutic work are not as clear as for other children with more homogenous mental health presentations; therapy cannot be considered separately from environmen-tal factors; this interface is not static but can change quickly, irrespective of the therapeutic plan; different agencies can deliver different levels of therapeutic work, but can also construe variable definitions and expectations of therapies. Taking into consideration the wealth of knowledge from the main therapeutic schools (psychodynamic, social learning, attachment, family, cognitive therapies), the current challenge is how to best *translate* and *apply* these modalities for chil-dren, young people and carers who may not often conform to the norms of the generic population in contact with child and adolescent mental health services. This was the key rationale for this book.

Despite the relatively limited and systematic evidence on 'what works best' for different groups of vulnerable children and young people, policies and ser-vices are increasingly being guided by common principles. These include a combination of generic components and lessons learnt from generic services for all children and young people, and their adaptation to the specific needs of the targeted group. Principles consist of joint working between agencies, clear defini-tion of each agency's remit within an integrated care plan, availability of therapeutic interventions at different levels (from prevention to treatment), inter-ventions that allow some flexibility in their delivery, quick response, and accessible as well as engaging services. There are increasing numbers of examples of service initiatives and innovative practice in this direction, as well as emerging new evidence. The challenge now is to incorporate this emerging and diverse body of knowledge and experience when formulating rationalized, consistent, well-resourced, and evidence-based models of interventions and services, rather than the ad hoc delivery of individually driven practice.

Few experts in this field are better positioned than our chapter authors to contribute to existing knowledge on mental health interventions and services for vulnerable children and young people. I have been fortunate to have known and worked with most contributors over the years, in their practice, academic and policy capacities. Having learnt a lot from their sound knowledge and innovative work with vulnerable groups, I am sure that these skills will come across throughout this text, and will be of interest to our readers. Their key messages and rich material should be relevant to all agencies working with vulnerable young clients. I do hope that this will stimulate even further interest in improving practice and services for the benefit of very needy children and young people.

Reference
Department of Health (DoH) (2003) *Every Child Matters.* London: Stationery Office.

CHAPTER 2

Developing a Policy Framework for Vulnerable Children with Mental Health Needs: Challenges and Possibilities

Miranda Wolpert

National policy, in relation to any given area, aims to articulate a vision for future development that helps to prioritize and inform resource allocation on the basis of the latest research findings and expert consensus. At its best, policy can provide a common language that can inspire future service developments, clarify key objectives, and provide a useful framework for assessing progress. At its worst, misguided or poorly formulated policy can lead to poor use of resources, creates confusion, and deadens innovation.

Policy development in relation to the mental health needs of vulnerable children is still in its infancy. Only a handful of countries have an articulated national policy in relation to children and young people with mental health problems. Of 191 countries sampled in 2003, 14 (7%) had produced a policy in this area (WHO 2005). What policy there is in existence is preoccupied with trying to focus on the needs of the most vulnerable children. However, policy-makers struggle with the challenge of how best to conceptualize which children should be deemed most 'vulnerable' in a given context; how best to prioritize competing needs between and within groups; how best to help those once identified; and how to evaluate progress meaningfully.

This chapter explores how policy development in relation to the mental health needs of vulnerable children might start to rise to these challenges, in relation to the following:

- assessing need
- developing evidence-based policy
- creating a framework for assessing progress.

Assessing need

As alluded to earlier, a range of factors can make it appropriate to categorize children as 'vulnerable' because of their circumstances. Children will be defined in national policy as 'vulnerable' or 'in difficult circumstances' depending on their national context, and the particular priorities and preoccupations of the government at that time. Children who are orphaned by AIDS, living in extremes of poverty, and are victims of war or abuse are all likely to be seen as falling into this category currently (WHO 2003). In some countries, children experiencing divorce or who are 'looked after' (in the care of the state) are also viewed in these terms (McAuley, Pecora and Rose 2006).

The size of this population of vulnerable children will vary, depending on the criteria used for inclusion, and these are likely to vary with the values and culture of a given society and change over time. To give some idea of potential numbers, it is estimated that the number of AIDS orphans is currently 14 million (largely concentrated in Africa) and this figure is anticipated to rise to 20 million by 2010 (UNICEF) (WHO 2005). In 2002, 1.8 million children in the USA were reported as abused or neglected (a 46% increase on 1990). In the USA in 2002 12 million children were living below the poverty line (five million living in extreme poverty) (Pecora, Whittaker and Maluccio 2006). In the UK, in 2003, 3.6 million children were living in households which were in need of extra help (the criterion being that the family had normally less than half the national average income) (McAuley *et al.* 2006).

Which vulnerable children should be seen as the highest priority for policy development will clearly be context-dependent, and this decision is likely to be a matter for political debate and decision within a given community. AIDS orphans are likely to be a particular key focus for policy concern in relation to those African countries where this population is most concentrated, but will also be a focus for international policy concern. All those children across the world living in the contexts of war, famine, or abuse are likely to be priorities for policy internationally (WHO 2005). In some of the more economically developed Western countries the particular focus in recent years has been on the needs of children looked after by the state and on children who are living in communities that are thought to have reduced accesses to mainstream services.

Determining which are the most pressing needs for the most vulnerable children in a community is likely to be a key task in terms of policy development. Child mental health needs are increasingly recognized as a crucial aspect of public health policy, but should be considered alongside a range of other needs, including basic needs for food, shelter, and safety. The following basic requirements need to be provided to all children in a community to allow for survival and normal development (Biersteier and Robinson 2000):

- nutrition
- water and sanitation
- child and maternal health services
- early childhood education and basic education
- social welfare developmental services
- child protection measures
- leisure and cultural activities.

National policy needs to ensure these basic needs are met, and address how best to meet them. In some countries, this may make independent child mental health provision an unaffordable luxury when pitted against other basic needs (Robertson *et al.* 2004). It needs to be borne in mind that, whilst 'vulnerable' children are likely to include those with high and complex mental health needs (Belfer 2004), there may be children who are seen as vulnerable because of their traumatic or difficult circumstances who do not have specific mental health needs or for whom other needs take precedence (Robertson *et al.* 2004).

In planning best approaches to help vulnerable children, it is perhaps particularly important to consider the potential negative and even harmful impact of policy that focuses on increased specialist mental health services. Mental health professionals are frequently in danger of assuming that more specialist mental health provision is unquestionably an unalloyed good. The need for more provision must be set in the context of other (sometimes competing) 'needs' raised above, such as the primary need of children to be nourished, sheltered, and protected, but also other key needs such as their need not to be stigmatized or miss education and their need not to receive inappropriate, ineffective, or harmful treatment. At times, an inappropriate mental health focus can be an unhelpful drain on resources (Shooter 2005). One documented example occured when well-meaning voluntary groups entered a country after a disaster to provide interventions for post-traumatic stress disorders (PTSD) that were not linked to other relief efforts and actually interfered with and undermined key initiatives (WHO 2005). Although the costs of not providing effective specialist mental health inputs can be high, it is important to remember there are also costs to providing unhelpful services.

Moreover, it is important to bear in mind that vulnerability to mental health issues may arise from difficult circumstances (such as those referred to above), but vulnerability is also increased to by a range of individual factors such as brain injury, low birth weight, genetic predisposition, low IQ, and irritable temperament (Goodman and Scott 2005). These children, who may not be deemed vulnerable by their social circumstances, also need to be considered as a possible priority focus for policy development in relation to mental health-focused provision.

There is as yet no clear guide to help policy developers in prioritizing between the needs of the different groups, or indeed between competing needs in the same group. The emerging literature on the mental health needs of these groups has not always clarified these issues, and there is sometimes an implicit assumption that once the 'needs' are assessed, all policy-makers and service providers need do is 'meet them'. In fact, even assuming that policy-makers can decide which groups to prioritize and that allocated resources are adequate, how best to meet these needs presents yet further challenges.

Meeting needs: developing evidence-based policy

Increasingly, there is a consensus that policy development needs to be based as far as possible on research and evidence (Davies, Nutley and Smith 2000). The arguments for trying to promote evidence-based public policy and service development are compelling. When the evidence base is not used as the basis for policy development in relation to health provision, for example, it makes it more likely that seemingly plausible but ineffective or harmful, or both, approaches may be introduced or continued, and that new interventions which have been shown to do more good than harm may never be introduced (Gray 2001).

However, as yet, few policies have really grown out of a considered analysis of evidence. A major limiting factor remains the sheer lack of research to draw on. This can be compounded by unwillingness from some policy-makers to build in means of evaluating different approaches at an early enough stage in policy development. For example, Rutter (2006) provides an interesting critique of the lack of randomized, controlled studies as part of the roll-out of 'Sure Start', which is a community programme designed to help promote mental health among some of the more vulnerable communities across the UK.

What research is in existence around what might be ways forwards for policy development in this area is often flawed in design, and the meaning of the outcomes is debatable. For example, the implications to be drawn from the Fort Bragg study in the USA, which sought to examine a model of service provision that was meant to increase access for service users, have been hotly contested (Bickman *et al*. 2000). Perhaps inevitably there is likely to be a complex interaction between the emerging 'evidence base' and the values and priorities of a given country. These may have implications, both for which aspects of the evidence base are (funded to be) explored and for the credence given to any findings that emerge. The current emphasis at a policy level in many countries on service user active involvement in planning service (Street and Herts 2005) may stand as one example of this.

This means that current policy development in this area is still just starting to explore tentatively how to prioritize between different options. For example, a key issue for most countries it likely to be how to balance resource allocation between approaches designed to promote mental and emotional well-being, and prevent the development of problems among the most vulnerable groups, and the need to ensure adequate resources are available to provide services for the most impaired and 'mentally ill' children within these groups. Although there is as yet no easy metric to determine what the ratio should be, the World Health Organization (WHO) has suggested that where resources are particularly limited, priority for funds for child mental health provision should be given to those children with existing difficulties which: occur frequently (and/or have highest cost implications); cause a high degree of impairment and the greatest long-term care/cost consequences; have an evidence base for treatment and (particularly in those countries with the most limited resources) where the difficulties can be dealt with in primary care or universal services such as schools or general practitioners (WHO 2003). In such conditions, the best that can be suggested for promotion is to encourage positive activity in terms of universal service provision that does not require additional resource allocation. How far this should be targeted at the most vulnerable groups remains an issue for discussion.

In countries with greater resources there is more opportunity for policies to support an articulated range of provision. In such countries, child mental health professionals' input is generally starting to be conceptualized as being provided at universal, targeted, and specialist levels. This involves supporting and working alongside universal provision to promote emotional well-being, whether in schools or via primary care health workers. Targeted provision aims to promote emotional well-being in those deemed most vulnerable. Here, specialist mental health professionals will work alongside practitioners from other sectors who take a lead in relation to the needs of these groups as a whole, such as social welfare workers and primary care staff. Specialist provision aiming to support those with diagnosed difficulties can be provided at a local community level, though for more rare conditions, specialized resources may be provided at a regional or even a national level (DfES 2003).

Current policy development across a range of countries emphasizes the need for good working across sectors (such as health, education, and social welfare) to ensure that the most vulnerable children are not 'lost' between services. It may be hypothesized on the basis of the current evidence that integral to creating joined-up services may be the ability for state departments, or their equivalent, to agree joined-up policy. Thus, clear and shared agreements about protocols around information-sharing, prioritized outcomes, and agreed child protection arrangements are crucial, though often sadly lacking. It appears that coherence and collaboration at this level may be more important than service re-organization at the level of service provision, and, indeed, without it any attempt to improve collaboration at the level of front-line service providers will founder (Grimes 2004).

There is a clear policy emphasis on making services not just more extensive and more integrated, but also more accessible to currently excluded groups, many of which are among the most vulnerable in society. For example, in the UK, the vision for child and adolescent mental health (CAMH) services is that they should no longer be based uniquely in health service clinics, to which children and young people are referred and brought for 'treatment' by specialist staff. Increasingly, the delivery of services should mix this approach with more multi-agency and community approaches, for example via common delivery sites in health centres, schools, children's homes or youth centres (DfES 2003; DoH 2004).

In terms of increasing access for the most vulnerable groups, policy-makers have looked to promoting the use of a new workforce above and beyond clinic-based specialist mental health workers. In the developing world and elsewhere, the ability to engage a workforce which also links with relevant belief systems of the community, such as ayurvedic treatment and yoga, may be crucial (Thara, Padmavati and Srinivasan 2004). Where resources are particularly short, policy is likely to support the need for mental health provision to 'piggy-back' on those other sectors with more provision, such as HIV programmes in Africa (Robertson et al. 2004). For example, the walk-in community centre, Empilwent, pioneered a more accessible drop-in approach in South Africa (WHO 2005).

Paediatricians are often a key professional group working with some of the most difficult and complex children with a range of behavioural and psychological needs, in particular in the younger age range. Their role therefore needs to be acknowledged and supported in policy, as they constitute an important resource in many developing countries and also in industrialized countries. In some European countries, such as Austria, Finland, and Germany, links with paediatrics and child mental health are particularly strong (Rydelius 2004). In those parts of the world where there is no community child health service, as in parts of Africa, it is vital to work with other physical health provisions such as those focused on reproductive health, HIV clinics, and general primary care services.

Models of rapid professional training for primary care staff have been piloted. The training up of traditional healers or educational support workers has been promoted as attempts to improve mental health provision where specialist input is lacking (Robertson et al. 2004). However, research highlighting the importance of fidelity to model, in terms of efficacy of interventions, indicates that there may be a necessary threshold of amount of training, combined with ongoing organizational support, for subsequent interventions to be effective (Scott 2004).

Even in the industrialized West, it may be relevant to look to develop new workforces to extend capacity, such as the use of support staff, technicians, graduate students, and volunteers. Models of encouraging family involvement to train as outreach or key workers are now being piloted across both industrialized countries and parts of the developing world (US Department of Health and Human Services 1999). Community-orientated approaches seem to be particularly well received in some communities such as parts of Africa.

Internationally, schools are increasingly recognized as perhaps the most influential place in relation to help-seeking, and much policy focuses on the need to train and educate staff to recognize and work with mental health difficulties (Remschmidt, Belfer and Goodyer 2004). Some promotion programmes in schools are showing positive results in terms of emotional well-being and academic performance, for example the international FRIENDS programme and the 'roots of empathy' in Canada (Wyn *et al.* 2000; Weare and Markham 2005). However, it is recognized that care must be taken not to overload schools, and there is likely to remain a need for more specialist and health-focused provision for some children.

In some countries, such as Switzerland, Hungary, and Egypt, child mental health services are primarily organized under the auspices of education. This has many advantages for younger children in terms of reducing stigma and increasing accessibility, but can increase difficulties of co-ordination for older adolescents and those with more severe mental illness. Countries have dealt with boundary issues in a variety of ways. In Australia and New Zealand, there is a deliberate two-year overlap between youth and adult mental health service provision to encourage flexibility for young people in this transitional age group (18–20 years old). In Finland, inpatient units for under-11s are located, wherever possible, nearer paediatric resources, and those for adolescents nearer adult mental health provision (Piha and Almqvist 1999). There is increased attention internationally to the need for services to be meaningfully linked across a range of sectors, including the criminal justice system, substance abuse services, and religious networks (Belfer 2004).

Monitoring progress

Any policy development in this area needs to consider how to ensure quality of provision, to promote best practice, and to allow for changed practice in light of increased knowledge and future policy priorities. One mechanism of quality assurance is to set standards for key activities. Services may then be evaluated by inspectors to ensure compliance, and a variety of incentives and penalties may be applied. However, real problems are presented by the danger of perverse incentives, as activities can easily become skewed. For example, in an effort to meet waiting list targets, crucial other activities may be neglected.

Policy can support the development of guidelines to shape practice. Different countries have developed systems to sift the evidence and pull together consensus statements to guide and inform practice, for example the National Institute of Clinical Excellence (NICE) in the UK, and the American Psychiatric Association practice parameters in the USA. The danger here is of overprescription on a narrow evidence base, and the possibility that the implementation of poorly understood guidance may be every bit as distorting as inappropriate targets. Some countries have sought to overcome this by stressing that guidance is advisory only. For example, in New South Wales in Australia, care packages for adolescents with severe problems are outlined. These include one 90-minute family-orientated mental health assessment, and six 45-minute family-orientated community contacts. Their aim is to inform service planning, rather than prescribe or proscribe clinical work.

Whilst no country in the world has systematic data gathering for the assessment of CAMH services outcomes at a national level, some encouraging national and international collaborations are emerging, and these are supported by national policy. The CAMHS Outcome Research Consortium (CORC) (chaired by the author) is a collaboration between over half of all services across the UK which are implementing an agreed model of routine outcome and joint ways to present the data in order to inform service providers and users, and service development (Wolpert *et al.* 2005). The approach has parallels with those being employed in Australia, Norway, and the USA (Ohio), and links are being established with these countries. In all cases, a small suite of measures is completed by services users and providers at initial contact and at some time later. Services for vulnerable children face the challenge of applying multiple outcome measures, because of children's interlinked needs regarding their quality of care, social functioning, mental health, housing, education, and physical growth.

Conclusions

It needs to be acknowledged from the outset that policy to meet the needs of vulnerable children is still in the early stages of development. This chapter has presented a brief outline of some the issues that need to be taken into account and some possible ways forwards. It has been argued that it is essential to start with an analysis of the range of anticipated needs which seeks to articulate these different needs, how a given country is going to prioritize between competing needs, and how to draw on the emerging evidence base to develop an approach that best chimes with national priorities and preoccupations. In framing policy in this area, there is likely to be an ongoing tension between the need to make policy general enough to allow innovation, whilst specific enough to allow measurement. The aspiration for the future is that it will become possible to develop policy based on a growing evidence base, underpinned by a comprehensive and fully articulated assessment of needs, and with an explicit consideration of how these are prioritized in line with the core values and priorities of a given society at a given time.

References

Belfer, M. (2004) 'Systems of Care: A Global Perspective.' In H. Remschmidt, M. Belfer, and I. Goodyer (eds) *Facilitating Pathways: Care, Treatment and Preventions in Child and Adolescent Mental Health.* Berlin: Springer-Verlag.

Bickman, L., Lambert, E., Andrade, A. and Penaloza, R. (2000) 'The Fort Bragg continuum of care for children and adolescents: Mental health outcomes over 5 years.' *Journal of Consulting and Clinical Psychology 68,* 710–716.

Biersteier, L. and Robinson, S. (2000) 'Socio-economic Policies: Their Impact on the Children of South Africa.' In D. Dondald and A. Louw, J. (eds) *Addressing Childhood Diversity.* Cape Town: David Philip.

CAMHS Outcome Research Consortium (CORC). Available at: www.annafreudcentre.org/corc.htm, accessed on 10 September 2007.

Davies, H., Nutley, S. and Smith, P. (2000) *What Works: Evidence-Based Policy and Practice in Public Services.* Bristol: The Policy Press.

Department for Education and Skills (DfES) (2003) *Every Child Matters.* London: The Stationery Office.

Department of Health (2004) *The Mental Health and Psychological Well-Being of Children and Young People: Standard Nine of the National Service Framework for Children, Young People and Maternity Services.* London: Department of Health.

Goodman, R. and Scott, S. (2005) *Child Psychiatry.* Oxford: Blackwell.

Gray, M. (2001) *Evidence-Based Healthcare: How to Make Health Policy and Management Decisions.* Edinburgh: Churchill Livingstone.

Grimes, K. (2004) 'Systems of Care in North America.' In H. Remschmidt, M. Belfer and I. Goodyer (eds) *Facilitating Pathways: Care, Treatment and Prevention in Child and Adolescent Mental Health.* Berlin: Springer.

McAuley, C., Pecora, P. and Rose, W. (eds) (2006) *Enhancing the Well-Being of Children and Families through Effective Interventions: International Evidence for Practice.* London: Jessica Kingsley Publishers.

Pecora, P., Whittaker, J. and Maluccio, A. (2006) 'Child Welfare in the US: Legislation, Policy And Practice.' In C. McAuley, P. Pecora and W. Rose (eds) *Enhancing the Well-Being of Children and Families through Effective Interventions: International Evidence for Practice.* London: Jessica Kingsley Publishers.

Piha, J. and Almqvist, F. (1999) 'Child and Adolescent Psychiatry in Finland.' In H. Remschmidt and H. Van Engeland (eds) *Child and Adolescent Psychiatry in Europe: Historical Development, Current Situation, Future Perspectives.* Darmstadt: Steinkopff/Springer.

Remschmidt, H., Belfer, M. and Goodyer, I. (eds) (2004) *Facilitating Pathways: Care, Treatment and Prevention in Child and Adolescent Mental Health.* Berlin: Springer-Verlag.

Robertson, B., Mandlhate, C., El Din, A. and Seck, B. (2004) 'Systems of Care in Africa.' In H. Remschmidt, M. Belfer, and I. Goodyer (eds) *Facilitating Pathways: Care, Treatment and Prevention in Child and Adolescent Mental Health.* Berlin: Springer.

Rutter, M. (2006) 'Is Sure Start an effective preventive intervention?' *Child and Adolescent Mental Health 11*, 135–141.

Rydelius, P. (2004) 'Systems of Care in Europe.' In H. Remschmidt, M. Belfer, and I. Goodyer (eds) *Facilitating Pathways: Care, Treatment and Prevention in Child and Adolescent Mental Health.* Berlin: Springer.

Scott, S. (2004) 'Outcomes of treatment.' In H. Remschmidt, M. Belfer, and I. Goodyer (eds) *Facilitating Pathways: Care, Treatment and Prevention in Child and Adolescent Mental Health.* Berlin: Springer.

Shooter, M. (2005) 'European Psychiatry: Construction, Destruction and Reconstruction'. In R. Williams and M. Kerfoot (eds) *Child and Adolescent Mental Health Services: Strategy, Planning, Delivery, and Evaluation.* Oxford: Oxford University Press.

Street, C. and Herts, B. (2005) *Putting Participation into Practice: A Guide for Practitioners Working in Services to Promote the Mental Health and Well-Being of Children and Young People.* London: Young Minds.

Thara, R., Padmavati, R. and Srinivasan, T. (2004) 'Focus on psychiatry in India.' *British Journal of Psychiatry 184*, 366–373.

US Department of Health and Human Services (1999) *Mental Health: A Report of the Surgeon General.* Rockville, MD: Department of Health and Human Services.

Weare, K. and Markham, W. (2005) 'What do we know about promoting mental health through schools?' *Promotion and Education 12*, 118–122.

Wolpert, M., Bartholomew, R., Domb, Y. and Fonagy, P. (2005) *Collaborating to Improve Child and Adolescent Mental Health Services: CAMHS Outcomes Research Consortium Handbook, Version 1.* London: CAMHS Outcome Research Consortium (CORC).

World Health Organization (WHO) (2003) *Caring for Children and Adolescents with Mental Disorders: Setting WHO Directions.* Geneva: World Health Organization.

WHO (2005) *Atlas of Child and Adolescent Mental Health Resources: Global Concerns – Implications for the Future.* Geneva: World Health Organization.

Wyn, J., Cahill, H., Holdsworth, R., Rowling, L. and Carson, S. (2000) 'Mindmatters, a whole-school approach promoting mental health and well-being.' *Australian and New Zealand Journal of Psychiatry 34*, 594–601.

CHAPTER 3

Vulnerable Children's Rights to Services

Maria Stuttaford

Children's rights to health are enshrined in a multitude of conventions, declarations, and policies. These rights are invoked, and thwarted, individually and collectively, through the judiciary as well as policy and practice. The 'right to health' refers to the highest attainable standard of health (ICESCR 1966), and to the underlying determinants of health (e.g. water, housing, food, and education) as well as health services (UN 2000). Of particular relevance here is Point 23 of General Comment 14 on rights to health, which asserts that:

> States Parties should provide a safe and supportive environment for adolescents, that ensures the opportunity to participate in decisions affecting their health, to build life-skills, to acquire appropriate information, to receive counselling and to negotiate the health-behaviour choices they make. The realization of the right to health of adolescents is dependent on the development of youth-friendly health care, which respects confidentiality and privacy, and includes appropriate sexual and reproductive health services. (UN 2000, Point 23)

The rights of children have been given increasing prominence in recent years. The focus of much work, especially in the UK, has been on the civil and political rights of children (e.g. Alderson 2000; Flekkøy and Kaufman 1997; John 2003; Kiddle 1999). There is increasing application of a human rights framework to socio-economic and cultural rights, including child health, although more often from 'developing' country contexts (e.g. Singh *et al.* 2006), and it is increasingly accepted that civil and political rights and socio-economic and cultural rights are indivisible. Although human rights and child rights grow in importance internationally and are often 'universally' set out, they are not always universally accepted. In addition, the concept of 'childhood' is not universally accepted. For the purposes of the Convention on the Rights of the Child (1989), a child is a human being below the age of 18. However, this age-based approach to childhood is increasingly contested for not recognizing the cultural dimension in definitions of childhood (Aitken 2001). Western norms defining childhood and the idea of rights that have universal applicability are being challenged. A practical manifestation of this is for children who live in mobile populations and seek health in transitory spaces of care. Whilst they move through these spaces, there may not be spaces in which these children can access health and the determinants of health. I begin by summarizing the structures that set out the health rights of children and then go on to consider the agency that is required to make their substantive rights to health a practical reality, before examining in more detail the experiences of young homeless people in relation to how where they live affects on their realization of their rights to mental health. I argue that there are sites in which health rights may be invoked, and thwarted. For children in transitory spaces of care, it is particularly challenging for them to invoke their rights to health.

Conventions, declarations and policies on the rights to health of children

Conventions, declarations, and agreements setting out rights to health of children exist at international, regional, and national levels. For the purposes of this chapter, I outline the key international conventions, and provide examples from Europe and Africa for the regional and national levels.

International level

Internationally, human rights have grown in prominence since the signing of the Universal Declaration of Human Rights (UDHR) in 1948. Subsequently, the International Bill of Human Rights was formed, composed of the UDHR, the International Covenant on Civil and Political Rights (ICCPR 1966), and the International Covenant on Economic, Social, and Cultural Rights (ICESCR 1966). The International Bill of Human Rights sets out that children and young people are entitled to special care and protection (UN 1948, Article 25[2]; ICESCR 1966, Article 10[3]) and that this protection should be afforded without discrimination (ICCPR 1966, Article 24[1]). Following on from this recognition of the special status of children, the key document relating to children has become the Convention on the Rights of the Child (CRC) (1989). Of particular relevance here is Article 24[1], which states that:

> States Parties recognize the right of the child to the enjoyment of the highest attainable standard of health, and to facilities for the treatment of illness and rehabilitation of health. States Parties shall strive to ensure that no child is

deprived of his or her right of access to such health care services. (CRC 1989, Article 24[1])

The Convention also stipulates many conditions and services related to the underlying determinants of health, for example the right to freedom of expression, the right to benefit from social security, the right to education, the right to rest and leisure, and the right to protection from torture and abuse.

An ongoing debate in the field of human rights is the extent to which rights are universal. For example:

> Zimbabweans have now become part of the wider world community, and the government has formally accepted a United Nations Charter on the Rights of the Child, which does not totally agree with some traditional ideas on the authority of parents: the Charter asserts that, in certain circumstances, children have a right to a say in matters concerning their own future…[T]he signing of the United Nations Charter on the Rights of the Child gives some legal protection to children. But, in everyday life, the social pressures of those around you are more relevant than what the remote legal system might decide. (Bourdillon 1993, pp.57–8).

In some traditional African contexts, children do not become adults, and have the same rights as adults, until they are married (Gyekye 1997). This is not dissimilar to pre-industrial Europe, in which marriage signalled the transition to adulthood (Aitken 2001). Notions of childhood and rights of children are often formulated in the global North, and impose Western norms (Aitken 2001) which have implications for the health of children. For example, in Zimbabwe child-headed households are not added to the village register to receive food aid (Chizororo 2006). In London, HIV-positive children of African migrants were found to be balancing the Western principles of rights to information for HIV-positive children, with their traditional cultural beliefs that as children they did not have any rights or autonomy (Chinouya and O'Keefe 2004). The universality of human rights is a contested and rapidly evolving area. Human rights frameworks from Africa, predominantly Islamic countries, Asia, and Latin America are growing in prominence and it will become increasingly important for practitioners to recognize and engage with these as populations become increasingly mobile.

Regional level
At a regional level, there has been an increasing focus on child rights. For example, the Charter of Fundamental Rights of the European Union (EC 2000) states that:

[1] Children shall have the right to such protection and care as is necessary for their well-being. They may express their views freely. Such views shall be taken into consideration on matters which concern them in accordance with their age and maturity. [2] In all actions relating to children, whether taken by public authorities or private institutions, the child's best interests must be a primary consideration. [3] Every child shall have the right to maintain on a regular basis a personal relationship and direct contact with both his or her parents, unless that is contrary to his or her interests. (EC 2000, Article 24)

The African Charter on Human and People's Rights stipulates that the rights of the child, as set out in international declarations and conventions, should be adhered to (OAU 1982), and the African Charter on the Rights and Welfare of the Child (OAU 1990) goes further to note the critical situation of most African children. The latter stipulates that 'Every child shall have the right to enjoy the best attainable state of physical, mental and spiritual health' (OAU 1990, Article 14 [1]). It goes on to set out ways in which this should be achieved, including preventive healthcare; a holistic and broad definition of health; and the participation of children, parents, the wider community, and non-governmental organizations (NGOs) in achieving rights to health for children.

National level

Finally, the rights of children are set out at a national level. For example, the UK Human Rights Act (ISO 1998) sets out rights important for realizing health, for example the right of children to education. The South African Bill of Rights (Constitutional Assembly 1996) sets out not only the conditions for realizing health, but also refers specifically to the rights of children to health: 'Every child has the right to basic nutrition, shelter, basic health care services and social services' (Constitutional Assembly 1996, Article 28[1][c]).

Even if substantive rights to healthcare services and the underlying determinants of health are accepted, these are often tempered by several factors. First, the right to health is the highest attainable standard of health attainable within the resources of the country. Second, and related to this, is that it is accepted that there is a progressive realization of rights to health as a country becomes more able to attain a higher standard of health (Gruskin and Tarantola 2005). In addition to these factors, the ability of individuals and groups to invoke rights will depend on them having an understanding of what rights they are entitled to, as well the skills and resources to access the mechanisms by which rights may be invoked (Mubangizi and Mubangizi 2005). In a review of strategies for achieving the UK's international development targets and the rights of poor people, the Department for International Development (2000) identified several lessons in promoting human rights. It is possible for these lessons to be applied to people living in poverty across the globe, including the UK and the USA, for example. These lessons include: the principles of the UNDHR still remain as aspirations for people living in poverty, rather than a reality; the progressive realization of human rights requires resources and strategic planning for medium- and long-term action; and there are difficulties with relying solely on legal mechanisms for the protection of human rights.

The substantive rights to health for children described above set out procedures, mechanisms, and institutions for enforcing and protecting these rights, for example the UN Committee on the Rights of the Child, the European Court of Human Rights, and the South African Constitutional Court. In addition, international, national, and local public sector and voluntary sector organizations work to advocate and protect children's rights to health. For example, the World Health Organization (WHO 2002) has published a comic book aimed at educating children about their human rights, including the right to health. In light of the fact that rights to health are mediated by factors such as the resources of the country, the skills of people to invoke them, the procedures for protecting and enforcing rights, and in light of the lessons learnt to date for a rights-based approach to health, this chapter focuses on non-legal mechanisms for invoking rights to health for children.

Sites for rights to health of children

The different levels of the structures of rights to health, the different places in which rights to health are upheld, and the different forms of agency (in other words, the different ways in which people take action) for invoking rights to health are here referred to as 'sites for health rights'. In the previous section, it was described how the substantive rights to health for children are set out at the international, regional, and national levels. The procedures for invoking, protecting, and enforcing rights operate in several contexts within and across these levels. Where the agencies are located may be seen as physical sites for health rights, for example courts of law, social services buildings, safe homes, and safe public places. Mediating access to these physical sites are metaphorical landscapes of power. For example, where children live and the extent to which they are involved in decision-making will mediate the extent to which they are able to invoke their rights to health.

In addition to the different levels by which child rights are invoked, there are different levels of agency (or action) – individual agency (actions of individuals) and collective agency (actions of groups). Actions to fulfil, defend, and advocate for child rights are taken in the context of the individual, but also in the context of the collective family (Henricson and Bainham 2005). It is possible to think of individual child rights also being realized in the context of collectives other than the family, for example schools, clinics, grandparents, childminders, foster homes, orphanages, and places of safety.

The structures operating at the international level often focus on the judicial aspects of rights to health, for example the WHO (2003) policy support package on mental health for children and young people is entitled *Mental Health Legislation and Human Rights*. At the regional and national level, policies become increasingly focused on practice. The European Commission Green Paper (EC 2005) on mental health stresses the importance of promoting mental health, including providing school environments and information to students, parents, and teachers on skills for improving mental health. However, regional policies are often too broad to take account of vulnerable children and young people, for example children who are mobile and living in transitory spaces of care, such as homeless shelters, refugee camps, and travellers' sites. Children living in these transitory spaces may enrol in school sporadically or not at all, for which reason alternative sites for addressing mental health needs as well as educating about rights to health need to be considered.

In the UK, the NHS has established long-term improvement strategies, known as National Service Frameworks (NSFs), for key areas of healthcare, including one for 'Children, Young People and Maternity Services'. As part of this NSF, there is a 'Standard on The Mental Health and Psychological Well-being of Children and Young People' which states that:

> All children and young people, from birth to their eighteenth birthday, who have mental health problems and disorders have access to timely, integrated, high-quality, multi-disciplinary mental health services to ensure effective assessment, treatment and support, for them and their families. (DoH 2004)

The NSF recognizes the need to improve equity and the need to develop services for particular groups such as children and young people who are homeless. At the local level, this involves health and local authorities commissioning services informed by a multi-agency assessment of need. However, as with all policies, the extent to which such a framework is implemented varies and depends on a complexity of local factors. At present, access to mental healthcare services is dependent on an individual remaining in one place, for example when awaiting a referral to specialist therapy or treatment. In order for rights to mental health to be realized, alternative sites for rights, both physical and metaphorical, need to be considered.

Rights to health of children in transitory spaces of care

Transitory spaces of care are spaces of health and social care that are in transition, rather than in a geographically fixed location, for example free food distribution points such as soup kitchens (Johnsen, Close and May 2005), multi-purpose drop-in health and social care centres, mobile clinics, and outreach services. It can be argued that transitory spaces of care may also be defined by the experience of the people who use fixed spaces of care. For example, a mental health drop-in service attached to a hostel may be transitory because the people who use the services are themselves transitory.

For children who are vulnerable, such as those who are seeking asylum, refugees, travellers, nomads, boat people, or the homeless, the challenge of invoking rights is all the more complicated by not having a site where they can invoke their right to mental health or not knowing where such a site might be. Their experiences emphasize the way differential access to spaces interacts with social differences and exclusion, and leads to disadvantages in health (Curtis 2004). Public spaces are increasingly becoming regulated and, in doing so, spaces open to homeless people are shrinking (Mitchell 2003). Street-drinking bans, civil injunctions on begging, and anti-social behaviour orders are, on one hand, enforcement interventions for the welfare of street users, but, on the other, they may have a negative impact on the welfare of people with complex health and social care needs (Fitzpatrick 2006). Traveller women reject behavioural explanations for health inequalities, describing rather how structural factors such as poor accommodation and discrimination account for low health outcomes (Hodgins, Millar, and Barry 2005).

In light of the need for transitory spaces of care, especially with access to public spaces shrinking, there is an increasing need to understand what might constitute a therapeutic landscape for people in transition. Gesler (1992) describes therapeutic landscapes as encompassing physical, psychological, and social environments with a reputation for treatment or healing in a physical, mental, or spiritual sense. A community-based alcohol recovery programme can be seen as a therapeutic landscape (Wilton and DeVerteuil 2006).

I have so far referred specifically to rights in a positive sense, that is, the sense of invoking, protecting, and upholding rights. However, an alternative view is to see sites for rights as places where rights are thwarted and abused. Landscapes may not only be therapeutic; they may, in fact, be landscapes of despair (Curtis 2004). In order to illustrate this point, I draw on the voices of young people interviewed as part of a research project evaluating the provision of a mental health service in non-statutory hostels in England (Taylor *et al.* 2006; Taylor *et al.* 2007). For some young people, hostels are therapeutic landscapes, and thereby facilitate them in invoking their rights to mental health. However, for others, hostels are landscapes of despair and thwart their rights to mental health services.

Some young people described the hostels where they were living as having a positive impact on them:

> A lady called N come and done basic skills with me, and I went and seen her a few weeks for about two hours, and I can read like books now, and remember when I couldn't do that like two years ago…and this place has made me very confident, I think, 'cos I stand up for myself now, I didn't used to. I'm very quiet, I won't, I'm not a sociable person, I won't socialize in like a group of 19-year-olds, but I'll stand up to it and I, I connect more with like older people, so. But I have a lot more confidence and I'll stand up for myself. (19-year-old female)

One resident was being evicted for substance use; however, she still described how the experience of the hostel was one of caring:

> Um, [pause] they got the sniffer dogs in and I got caught, so I got given my four weeks' notice. Um, they were really good about helping me find a move-on flat and that, um, had quite a few meetings with G to sort out everything, and when I found a shared house, um, they went through all my housing benefit forms with me, sorted out my benefit; so, yeah, they just like helped me you know what I mean, it was quite cool because it was just like, I thought because of the situation that they just wouldn't care and be like, right get out sort of thing, it's your own fault. But they, well they seemed really quite concerned that I was going to be all right, whether I'd manage or not. (17-year-old female)

Residents explained how moving to a new place was difficult at first, but that after a period time they settled in:

> It was just, I don't know, it felt weird. I wasn't used to having the security guards and the gate and having to share with people that I've never met before, um, it was just like, I don't know. I felt really small, just kind of get lost in this place when you first move in but after about a week or so, all the residents started to be really cool with us and showing us around and talking to us, so that's cool, and the staff were quite good about helping me settle in, so. (17-year-old female)

However, hostels were also described as landscapes of despair:

> It's this building, it's making everybody worse, I swear it is. You've got people coming in here, I was fine, I was normal before I moved in this building, and then like six months down the line and I'm a nervous wreck, I can't even go out of this building and that's because of the staff…And there's other people in there, S, he was all right until he moved in this building. Six months down the line, he's exactly the same. You know, and I swear, if you stay here for longer than six months, you get cursed or something. (21-year-old female)

Where people live, even which room or flat they occupy, and whom they share with, affects the extent to which they access affordable and acceptable food and other underlying determinants of health, for example:

> So, and I kicked up a bit of a stink, 'cos like me and my flatmate got on absolutely brilliantly, we moved from a three-bedroom to a two-bedroom, we got on

absolutely brilliantly and then they just split us up and we're like: 'but why?' You know, we do things together, we do our shopping together, we pay for things together so that we can eat in this building, and they've just split us up, ruining everything. Which means we have to buy our own food, buy our own drinks, if we're short one week, we've got nobody else to fall back on. (21-year-old female)

Several residents described how they felt they were being watched and were under surveillance while at the hostel. This led to a feeling of lack of privacy, with interviewees describing how access to their room was demanded by staff at any time of day and night. Other interviewees said how their levels of anxiety were raised when other hostel residents were raided:

Uh, there's always loads of arguments and that. With people graffiti-ing all over the walls and that, banging on your doors at like three o'clock in the morning and that, and just people who literally want to cause trouble. Like last week the building got smashed off, doors got put through, lights got put through and it was just like not nice to be here at the time. The police came. There was a couple of weeks ago when about eight police come charging in the building and they searched people's rooms and that for armed robbery, I was like crying me eyes out and that, and I had to phone a key worker because like 'cos there was two members of staff on that were new and they weren't, like, they weren't that experienced, like, they were just learning. So they had to phone the key worker and E, so I could talk to him on the phone and I was in a right state. It's just examples like that. When people try and cause trouble for each other and that. (21-year-old female)

These quotes simply serve to illustrate how young people view transitory spaces of care, such as a hostel, in different ways. Whereas for some the hostel is a safe place to gain confidence and skills, for others it is a place of surveillance and anxiety. The experience of invoking rights to mental health varies, depending on the individual and collective experience of the place. Where rights to health are invoked, and thwarted, is as important as how and who invokes them. We need to understand better how sites for rights can be nurtured, especially for children in transitory spaces of care.

Conclusions

The ICESCR (1966) is a legally binding document setting out that the right to health is the right to the highest attainable standard of health. A general comment on the implementation of this Covenant emphasizes that the right to health is not only about the rights to access services, but also rights to the underlying determinants of health. Furthermore, it acknowledges social and mental well-being, as well as physical health and the special care to which children and young people are entitled. Although international, regional and national conventions, declarations and policies set out the substantive rights to health and the judicial structures for invoking and protecting rights, less work has been done on the non-judicial, everyday experiences of vulnerable young people attempting to invoke their rights to mental health. The focus of agencies working at the local, practice level in the area of children's rights have tended to focus on advocating for political and civil rights, for example improving the mechanisms by which children can participate in decision-making. However, there is a need to build on this advocacy role to include social economic and cultural rights such as mental health. Human rights are socially constructed. As such they are malleable and can respond to changing society and contexts. As debates on the universality of human rights and the universality of childhood continue, we should remain open to continue to learn from children as to what mental health rights mean to them and where and how they invoke these rights.

Acknowledgements

The primary data quoted here were collected as part of a research project conducted with Helen Taylor, Bob Broad, and Panos Vostanis. It was funded by the Gatsby Foundation. Thanks to Helen Taylor and Panos Vostanis for their comments on an early version of this chapter.

References

Aitken, S.C. (2001) 'Global crisis of childhood: rights, justice and the unchildlike child.' *Area* *33*, 119–127.

Alderson, P. (2000) *Young Children's Rights: Exploring Beliefs, Principles and Practice.* London: Jessica Kingsley Publishers.

Bourdillon, M. (1993) *Changing Culture in Zimbabwe.* Harare: University of Zimbabwe Press.

Chinouya, M. and O'Keefe, E. (2004) 'Young African Londoners Affected by HIV: Making Sense of Rights.' In D. Fox and A. Scott-Samuel (eds) *Human Rights, Equity and Health.* London: The Nuffield Trust.

Chizororo, M. (2006) Personal communication with PhD student, thesis entitled 'The Social Dynamics and Experiences of Orphaned Child-headed Households in Rural Zimbabwe in the Era of HIV/AIDS Pandemic'. School of Geography & Geosciences, University of St Andrews, 4 October.

Constitutional Assembly (1996) *Constitution of the Republic of South Africa 1996.* Cape Town: South African Constitutional Assembly.

Convention on the Rights of the Child (CRC) (1989) General Assembly Resolution 44/25, UN Document E.C. 12.1999.10. New York, NY: United Nations.

Curtis, S. (2004) *Health and Inequality: Geographical Perspectives.* London: Sage.

Department for International Development (DfID) (2000) *Realizing Human Rights for Poor People: Strategies for Achieving the International Development Targets.* London: Department for International Development.

Department of Health (DoH) (2004) *CAMHS Standard: National Service Framework for Children, Young People and Maternity Services.* London: Department of Health.

European Commission (EC) (2000) *Charter of Fundamental Rights of the European Union.* Brussels: European Commission, 2000/C 364/01.

European Commission (EC) (2005) Green Paper: Improving the Mental Health of the Population Towards a Strategy on Mental Health for the European Union. EC Document COM(2005) 484 final. Brussels: European Commission.

Fitzpatrick, S. (2006) *Enforcement in Street Homelessness Policies in England.* European Observatory on Homelessness Conference, Dundee, March.

Flekkøy, M. and Kaufmann, N. (2000) *The Participation Rights of the Child: Rights and Responsibilities in Family and Society.* London: Jessica Kingsley Publishers.

Gesler, W. (1992) 'Therapeutic landscapes: medical issues in light of the new cultural geography.' *Social Science and Medicine 34,* 735–746.

Gruskin, S. and Tarantola, D. (2005) 'Health and Human Rights.' In S. Gruskin, M. Grodin, G. Annas and S. Marks (eds) *Perspectives on Health and Human Rights.* New York, NY: Routledge.

Gyekye, K. (1997) *Tradition and Modernity: Philosophical Reflections on the African Experience.* New York, NY: Oxford University Press.

Henricson, C. and Bainham, A. (2005) *The Child and Family Policy Divide: Tensions, Convergence and Rights.* London: Joseph Rowntree Foundation.

Hodgins, M., Millar, M. and Barry, M. (2006) '"…It's all the same no matter how much fruit or vegetables or fresh air we get": Traveller women's perceptions of illness causation and health inequalities.' *Social Science and Medicine 62,* 1978–1990.

International Covenant on Economic, Social and Cultural Rights (ICESCR) (1966). General Assembly Resolution 2200A (XXI), UN GAOR, 21st Session, Suppl. 16, at 49, UN Document A/6316. Geneva: United Nations.

International Covenant on Civil and Political Rights(ICCPR) (1966). General Assembly Resolution 2200A (XXI), UN GAOR, 21st Session, Suppl. 16, at 49, UN Document A/6316. New York, NY: United Nations

John, M. (2003) *Children's Rights and Power: Charging Up for a New Century.* London: Jessica Kingsley Publishers.

Johnsen, S., Close, P. and May, J. (2005) 'Transitory spaces of care: serving homeless people on the street.' *Health and Place 11,* 323–336.

Kiddle, C. (1999) *Traveller Children: A Voice for Themselves.* London: Jessica Kingsley Publishers.

Mitchell, D. (2003) *The Right to the City: Social Justice and the Fight for Public Space.* New York, NY: Guilford Press.

Mubangizi, J. and Mubangizi, B. (2005) 'Poverty, human rights law and socio-economic realities in South Africa.' *Development Southern Africa 22,* 277–290.

Organization of African Unity (OAU) (1981) *African Charter on Human and People's Rights.* Accessed on 6 August 2007 at: www.achpr.org/english/_info/charter_en.html

Organization of African Unity (OAU) (1990) *African Charter on the Rights and Welfare of the Child.* CAB/LEG/24.9/49.

Singh, S., Behler, E., Dahal, K. and Mills, E. (2006) 'The state of child health and human rights in Nepal.' *PLoS Medicine 3.*

Taylor, H., Stuttaford, M., Broad, B. and Vostanis, P. (2006) 'Why a "Roof" is not enough: the mental health characteristics of young homeless people referred to a designated mental health service in England.' *Journal of Mental Health 15,* 491–501.

Taylor, H., Stuttaford, M., Broad, B. and Vostanis, P. (2007) 'Listening to service users: young homeless people's experiences of a new mental health service.' *Journal of Child Health Care 11,* 221–230.

The Stationary Office (TSO) *The 1998 Human Rights Act.* London: The Stationary Office.

United Nations (UN) (1948) *Universal Declaration of Human Rights.* General Assembly Resolution 217A (III), UN GAOR, Resolution 71, UN Document A/810. New York, NY: United Nations.

United Nations (UN) (2000) *The Right to the Highest Attainable Standard of Health.* UN Document E/C,12/2000/4 (General Comments). Geneva: United Nations.

Wilton, R. and DeVerteuil, G. (2006) 'Spaces of sobriety/sites of power examining social model alcohol programs as therapeutic landscapes.' *Social Science and Medicine 63, 649–661.*

World Health Organization (WHO) (2002) *The Right to Health.* Geneva: World Health Organization.

World Health Organization (2003) *Mental Health Legislation and Human Rights.* Geneva: World Health Organization.

CHAPTER 4

Ethical Issues
in Working Therapeutically
with Vulnerable Children

Sharon Leighton

The aim of this chapter is to discuss practical ethical dilemmas in working therapeutically with vulnerable children. This is a complex issue which requires both consideration and definition of several concepts. The chapter provides a discussion of some of the issues in order to assist professionals in making therapeutic decisions about vulnerable children.

The usual chapter structure has been reversed and a case study has been placed at the beginning. This decision is based on a desire to provide a practical context for theoretical content. Readers may like to hold the scenario in mind whilst reading the chapter and return to the questions on completion. All the characters are fictitious; they are based on professional knowledge and experience of similar young lives and situations. A child is defined as 'a person under the age of 18' (Children Act 1989) (DfES 1989). This is the definition used in this chapter. The issues of human rights and stigma are covered in other chapters.

Case vignette
The characters
Abdul, aged 14 years, fled from a small Liberian village after seeing his mother raped and murdered and his father bayoneted. He managed to escape to Europe and arrived in the UK in a lorry full of boxes. Abdul is solitary and wary. He does not speak much, partly because his English is limited, and partly because he goes to great lengths to avoid talking about the past. He feels extremely confused, traumatized by fear and grief, and the internal feelings of desperation and terror are mounting.

Beccy, aged 15 years, was sexually abused by her stepfather between the ages of 7 and 11 years. The abuse occurred whilst her mother worked a late shift at a local hospital. Her mother had a history of depression and Beccy always felt a sense of responsibility for her. After the abuse came to light, her mother disowned her, calling her a liar, and remaining loyal to the stepfather. Beccy feels emotionally numb much of the time. She experiences frequent flashbacks, and uses alcohol as a form of self-medication to manage these and the accompanying emotional pain. She feels that it does not matter if she lives or dies.

Jason, aged 13 years, is the only child of a father diagnosed with schizophrenia, who committed suicide 10 years ago, and a mother who he has regularly seen beaten up by his stepfather. Jason has also been regularly beaten up and cruelly taunted by this man. Jason has frequent, unpredictable, and violent rages which take over and lead to violence against people and property. It was in one such rage that he attempted to kill his stepfather and ended up in detention. To Jason, all life seems worthless and he feels no compassion for himself or anyone else.

Anne is the social worker for all three children. She is more comfortable focusing on the legal aspects of a case. However, Anne feels a sense of desperation in relation to each of them and is extremely concerned about their mental health. Although not really sure how specialist child and adolescent mental health (CAMH) services operate, and having heard much criticism about long waiting lists, she refers the children for urgent assessment and therapy.

Sam is a nurse specialist in the local specialist CAMH service. This is a small team of experienced clinicians. Recently a new business manager has been appointed and clinicians are under increasing pressure to justify caseloads, see more referrals, and watch the amount of time allocated to individual cases. Sam and his colleagues feel increasingly uncomfortable with this. The referrals for the three young people have just been allocated to Sam for initial assessment.

Pat is the new CAMH service business manager. Her background is in finance, not mental health. The Trust has several priorities, including reducing waiting lists and costs, which Pat has to impose on the CAMH service team. She feels under increasing pressure from the Trust hierarchy and resented by the CAMH service team. Pat is concerned to discover that these three new referrals imply long-term commitment of expensive resources.

The issue

The aim is to consider the referral of these three vulnerable children to specialist CAMH services for therapeutic intervention. Reflect on the scenario from the perspective of individual players, addressing the following:

1. Clarify what you understand by concepts such as therapeutic intervention, consent, and risk.

2. What are your instinctive feelings about therapeutic intervention in this situation?

3. What do you consider would be the purpose of therapeutic intervention here?

4. What would you hope to achieve by engaging in therapy?

5. Are there possible alternatives to therapy?

6. What are your priorities?

7. Justify your decisions about:

   (a) the potential benefits of therapeutic intervention

   (b) prioritization, by considering:

       (i) your values and beliefs

       (ii) professional knowledge and experience

       (iii) legal issues

       (iv) ethical considerations

       (v) resources.

Philosophical underpinnings of ethical enquiry

The areas to be discussed in this section are vast, and are explored only as far as is feasible within the aims and confines of the chapter.

Utilitarianism and deontology provide the traditional underpinnings of ethical enquiry in healthcare (Edwards 1996). Although they have an important place in the decision-making process through consideration of potential outcomes and duties and motives, there are also limitations (Seedhouse 1998). Utilitarianism aims to focus attention on possible outcomes of proposed interventions, and encourages clarification of priorities. It incorporates the welfare principle of 'the child is paramount' (Children Act 1989) (DfES 1989). However, decisions as to what is in the best interests of the child are inevitably subjective, and all possible consequences of an action cannot be known (Seedhouse 1998), for example effects on trust and the therapeutic relationship of sharing concerns about the safety of a child. The consideration of duties and motives corresponds to the deontological position. This links with recognized healthcare rules (fidelity, veracity) and principles (beneficence, nonmaleficence) (Beauchamps and Childress 1989). When working with children, there could be occasions when these take priority, for example if a child revealed that they were at immediate risk of significant harm and they did not want anyone to know, this would not be possible, as the individual has a duty to minimize harm and protect children from abuse (Children Act 1989) (DfES 1989). However, if a child revealed abuse that happened four years ago and there was no contact with the perpetrator, then the child's right to autonomy and confidentiality may be respected. Deontological theory in its purest form can be too rigid and impossible to achieve (Seedhouse 1998), for example a belief that one must always tell the truth may be harmful in some situations, such as telling a child who is seriously ill after a suicide attempt that her best friend succeeded in her endeavour.

Aristotle viewed deliberation (i.e. 'considered reflection') to be the essence of ethics, since a contemplative process must be undertaken in every case where there are conclusions to be reached about the worth of human activity (Kaufman 1998). Aristotle's considered reflection with its review of existing knowledge, including the opinions and views of ordinary people, leads to the suggestion that moral philosophy be viewed as a process of deliberation, and that 'ethical analysis is a matter of reflecting on evidence and values, with the genuine intent of finding the most reasonable solution to our problems...[but] there are no answers that are truly ethical' (Seedhouse 2005, p.136) and no clear ultimate solutions. Further-more, considered reflection is about generating questions, living with uncertainty and discomfort, and coping with failures and mistakes (Stott *et al.* 2006). There-fore, considered reflection could be more helpful in healthcare decision-making than utilitarianism and deontology, as it encompasses both, whilst recognizing their limitations, and reaching beyond them to include reflection and communication. The discussion now turns to healthcare decision-making.

Decision-making in healthcare

This section focuses on two important aspects of decision-making: the definition of concepts and the influence of individual values on the process. Whilst legal issues, professional codes of conduct, evidence-based practice, and changes in health and social care are clearly important considerations when making decisions, they are not the focus of this discussion.

Defining concepts

Seedhouse (1998) suggests that part of the problem in decision-making arises from difficulty in defining complex concepts. Thus clarification of meaning is an important factor in ethical enquiry. It is vital to clarify what is meant to both self and others in order to be able to make sense of a situation. However, when we do define concepts, it is important to acknowledge that our definitions might not correspond with those of other people. Individuals have different backgrounds, experiences, knowledge and skills, priorities, and frames of reference (Seedhouse 2005).

'Vulnerable children' within the context of this chapter are defined as children 'looked after' by UK local authorities. They include the following:

- Children suffering, or likely to suffer, significant harm if they remain with family and subject to a Care Order (Section 31, Children Act 1989).

- Unaccompanied asylum seeking children and homeless young people who are accommodated at their own or parents' request (Section 20, Children Act 1989).

- Children in police protection or detention, or remanded to the Local authority by the courts (Section 21, Children Act 1989).

Under Sections 20 and 21, parental responsibility remains with the parent(s). This is an interesting idea when applied to unaccompanied asylum-seeking children, as the whereabouts of the parents may not be known. Under Section 31, the local authority has the power to restrict the exercise of parental responsibility by parents (Children Act 1989; DfES 1989). Parental responsibility refers to all rights, duties, powers, responsibilities, authority, which by law the parent of a child has in relation to the child and their property. It includes decisions made about medical treatment.

The local authority owes all three groups of vulnerable children the same duties, as outlined below:

- The safeguarding and promoting of their welfare.

- Consultation with the child when making decisions which affect them.

- Taking into consideration the wishes and feelings of the child in light of their age, as well as the wishes and feelings of parents and other relevant persons.

- Taking into consideration the child's racial origin, religious and cultural background. (Section 22, Children Act 1989)

This includes making referrals to CAMH services for therapeutic work with a child (DoH 2002). However, no indication is given as to the weight that should be attached to children's views (Hamilton 2005).

Seedhouse (1998) proposes that the purpose of healthcare is to raise human potential. Therapy can be perceived as a specific form of healthcare. It is the treatment of disease or disability, with psychotherapy being the treatment of mental and emotional disorders using psychological means, such as counselling. The terms 'psychotherapy' and 'counselling' are often used interchangeably. Generally, psychotherapy deals with more complex emotional and mental health problems (Parry and Cape 2002). Sutton (2001) argues that there could be advantages in a model of therapy which understands the processes of psychotherapy as ones in which we work implicitly and explicitly, from a foundation of respect for the individual's autonomy at their level of developmental competence. Autonomy and competence are concepts which are considered at length later in the chapter.

The influence of individual values

It is important to be aware of our own values and how these influence decision-making. Decisions are not made solely on logical grounds (i.e. evidence-based), but are also influenced by intrinsic factors such as our values, beliefs, and attitudes (Seedhouse 2005). In this context, beliefs are based on our knowledge of the world, whether or not it is accurate, complete or thought through (Collier 1999), for example 'all abused children benefit from therapy'. Values refer to an individual's sense of the worth, desirability, or utility of a person or object (Gross 2001; Woodbridge and Fulford 2004), for example therapy for abused children is crucial. These are extremely complex entities, varying with time and place, and from person to person (Woodbridge and Fulford 2004). Attitudes have much in common with beliefs and values, but are distinguishable in that attitudes can be perceived as consisting of a combination of beliefs and values (Bohner and Wanke 2002; Gross 2001), for example, 'it is essential that all abused children must receive therapy'.

Seedhouse (2005) argues that values-based decision-making, by offering a framework for making decisions, should make the specifics easier as we become aware of our own frames of reference, aims, plans, and the means to achieve these, as well as becoming aware of those of other people, when we attempt to make decisions. Thus, from a service perspective we might be reluctant to offer therapy to a vulnerable child on the grounds that evidence suggests that these children will be highly traumatized and at risk of psychiatric disorder (BMA 2006; Meltzer et al. 2003; Vostanis 2004). Furthermore, complex and lengthy interventions may be necessary (Hunter 2001) whilst resources are limited. In addition, involvement with mental health services further labels an already vulnerable child. A clinician might agree with this, but consider it appropriate to focus on the potential positive effects of learning to establish and maintain trusting relationships on an individual's developing sense of self (Schofield and Beek 2005), and offering a less intensive and more supportive intervention.

An additional benefit of values-based decision-making is tolerance borne of understanding, for example a child's frequent and unpredictable rages in the care home may make more sense if it is known that they suffered longstanding abuse from a parental figure.

Autonomy as a central concept

Beauchamps and Childress (1989) define autonomy as general capacity. Seedhouse (1998) identifies autonomy as being an intrinsic personal quality – the ability to do – which is essential to human dignity, rather than as an abstract principle or a right. In this context, the creation of autonomy is considered fundamental to healthcare. This raises several pertinent questions: how to create and respect autonomy in the context of working therapeutically with vulnerable children, and how to balance this with the duty to safeguard their welfare.

A child's autonomy may be enhanced or diminished through inherent differences, and by what happens to them and how they are treated by others (Reder and Fitzpatrick 1998). For example, a sexually abused child with learning disabilities living in local authority care will have less autonomy than the healthy and talented child of loving parents.

When working with vulnerable children, tensions can exist between the children's entitlement to participate in decisions and to develop autonomously, and their right to have their welfare protected (Dickenson and Jones 1996; Zutlevics and Henning 2005). This raises a question as to what processes are in place to enable children to be listened to, heard, and also protected (Golding *et al.* 2006). Furthermore, at what point is a decision made that a child's wishes are unsafe or clearly against their interests, and therefore overridden (Golding *et al.* 2006)? Emanuel (2002) suggests initial consultation to the social services network, rather than immediate individual psychotherapy, as a way of preventing further harm to vulnerable children. In such circumstances, the 'duty of care' involves working with the wider system first, in order to foster autonomy in the long term, that is, helping a vulnerable child achieve their potential by first providing a secure base and an experience of trustworthy adults.

In order to create and respect the autonomy of vulnerable children, practitioners need to feel that their own autonomy is respected, and that there is space to develop it within the current health and social care context. Practitioners and agencies need protected space within which they can reflect. Without this space, some of the experiences of vulnerable children will continue to be replicated (Emanuel 2002; Stott *et al.* 2006).

The next subsection focuses on the concept of competence. Competence and autonomy are clearly interrelated concepts, which are separated here for ease of discussion.

Competence

There is no standard or agreed definition of the clinical concept of competence. Beauchamps and Childress (1989) define competence as the ability to perform specific tasks. Tan and Jones (2001) define it as a person's ability to consent to treatment. A simple working definition is that a person is competent if they are able to achieve what they set out to achieve. For example, if a child can demonstrate that they understand what is being proposed in terms of therapy, and the potential consequences of receiving or not receiving treatment, then they are competent to make a decision. However, their competence could be improved by providing alternative options to the treatment proposed.

The capabilities of children and adults are undoubtedly different. Nevertheless, understanding of children's capability is shaped by society's understanding of the experience of childhood. Legally imposed age boundaries are used to distinguish the 'evolving capacities' of the child and to represent the transition from child to adult status. Such rigid determination of child status is socially defined and does not automatically represent the level of maturity and competency that an individual holds (Spencer 2000). Kroger (2004) asserts that, for a significant portion of our lives, there is a large discrepancy between cultural expectations, which are often concealed, and our intellectual ability to understand these in areas such as schooling, work, and intimate relationships. Moreover, it has been shown that less than half of all adults reach Piaget's stage of formal operational thought, whilst some children younger than 12 years will have developed some element of this ability (Dickenson and Jones 1996). Therefore, differences in competence are relative rather than absolute, with the majority of adults only competent in small areas of life, and competence being context-specific. Nonetheless, an important distinction made between children and adults is that a child's identity is less firmly formed. Their wishes, intentions, motives, emotions, and values on which they base choices may be less secure (Dickenson and Jones 1996). Additionally, trauma may impinge on a child's feelings and values (Dickenson and Jones 1996) as well as on their developing brain (Le Doux 2002).

> Children's sufficient understanding is deemed a critical factor in determining their capacity to consent to treatment… However, the concept has remained undefined…it should refer not only to the child's cognitive development, but also to the influence of personal and interpersonal conflicts. (Reder and Fitzpatrick 1998, p.103)

Sufficient understanding is more than a cognitive concept, and the meanings which children attribute to issues concerning their future depend on context, past and present experiences, and their emotional and interpersonal circumstances (Reder and Fitzpatrick 1998).

Currently, there is no accurate way to determine when an individual has achieved autonomous capacity. Therefore, in the interests of consistency and fairness, decision-making should include all relevant individuals who have attained the cognitive and volitional capacity to deliberate and act on a set of values (Aiken 2001).

The discussion turns now to the controversial decision-making topic of children and consent.

Consent

The impact of mental disorders on children's current and future ability to consent to treatment has not been investigated (Tan and Jones 2001). Empirical research is needed on current competency to make treatment decisions and the child's developing autonomy. In contrast, there are a lot of reviews on the subject, mainly based on 'opinions', discussing various themes of paediatric consent and children's capacity. These articles do not consider children with learning disabilities, alternative cultures, or different ethnic groups (Tan and Jones 2001).

Informed consent in itself is a complex and contentious concept when applied to children, and to medical treatment (Bartholomew 1996; Goodwin *et al.* 2000; Paul 2004). The law recognizes that as children develop they acquire the capacity to make personal decisions for themselves, including decisions on medical treatment (Bridge 1997). The case of *Gillick v. West Norfolk and Wisbech Area Health Authority* (1985) and S.8(1) of the Family Law Reform Act (ISO 1969) are evidence of this. However, the case of *Gillick v. West Norfolk and Wisbech Area Health Authority* (1985) does not address the issue of mentally disturbed or disordered adolescents, but rather provides unclear guidelines as to what constitutes capacity to consent (Bridge 1997). Additionally, a Gillick-competent child may give consent to assessment or treatment, but can have a refusal overruled by parents or those *in loco parentis* on the grounds of lack of competence (Reder and Fitzpatrick 1998; Goodwin *et al.* 2000; Paul 2004). In contrast, adults deemed competent to consent to treatment are not deemed incompetent if they refuse treatment (Bartholomew 1996; Batten 1996). Furthermore, adults are presumed competent to refuse or consent to medical treatment regardless of mental illness, but, whether or not they are mentally ill, children are deemed incompetent (Dickenson and Jones 1996). As long as someone with parental responsibility for a child consents to treatment on their behalf, a child has no right to refuse consent, whether or not judged competent (Dickenson and Jones 1996), for example social services on behalf of a looked-after child. Despite rulings that capacity and not age is the relevant factor in determining competence, practice indicates that children are presumed incompetent and must prove otherwise, whilst the opposite is true for those aged over 18 (Paul 2004).

The question of the appropriateness of involving children in decisions relating to their healthcare:

> focuses on the dilemmas this involvement poses around issues of competency and autonomy, and the legal implications of respecting the competent child's participation in the consent process; in particular, in situations where their

decision is at variance with that of the professional and/or carer. (Goodwin *et al.* 2000, p.97)

Paul (2004) argues that:

the lack of specific acknowledgement of...(social, political or legal) status,... underlies the inconsistencies within the law and guidance on minors' healthcare decision-making and consent. (Paul 2004, p.309)

She suggests consulting with children and their parents in relation to four different levels of decision-making:

- being informed
- expressing an opinion
- influencing decision-making
- being the main decision-maker.

Moreover, practitioners owe children honesty about the extent and limits of their involvement at all four levels. This includes explaining why any decisions that might result in significant harm or death will be overridden. The application of such a practical approach is considered most likely to maximize children's participation in treatment decisions (Paul 2004). It also helps foster, and respects, the child's autonomy.

The concept of competency in relation to a child's consent to psychiatric treatment can be viewed as a multi-faceted and complex interaction involving:

- the developmental stage of the child and its effect on cognitive ability and rationality
- their social environment and previous experience
- their relationship with the professional, as well as with their family
- information presented to them about the treatment, as well as their understanding of that information
- their mental state at the time of making the decision (Batten 1996; Reder and Fitzpatrick 1998).

Furthermore, these factors exist on a continuum, rendering the application of rigid arbitrary limits inappropriate, for example levels of mental distress may vary – anxiety levels increase when experiencing flashbacks; feelings of paranoia may be transitory.

Tan and Jones (2001) argue that rather than focusing solely on a child's ability to consent a balance is needed between the child's and the system's negotiated consent, and consideration should be made of the impact of emotional and mental disorders on competence to consent. Furthermore, the need to protect children's interests when they are not fully able to do so for themselves, and respecting their autonomy when they are, has to be balanced. Individuals with a serious mental illness raise concerns in professionals as to their ability to be truly autonomous. In such cases the concept of 'compassionate interference' has been advocated (Faith 2002). Verkerk (1999) argues that involuntary treatment can be a means of actually helping patients with serious mental illness to regain their autonomy, particularly when such illness threatens survival. Children given life-sustaining treatment for severe eating disorders without their consent have later been grateful for treatment (Faith 2002). Severely depressed and suicidal vulnerable children may be similarly appreciative.

Informed consent by children needs to be based upon respect for personal autonomy, as it is with adults, taking into consideration whether necessary information to allow informed consent has been understood, rationally processed, and a clear decision communicated, free from coercion (Batten 1996; Goodwin *et al.* 2000; Paul 2004). If it is not, then a message that this may send to the child is, 'you do not really have capacity; or, if you do have capacity, you either do not know what is best for you or are deliberately making a wrong choice. Therefore, for your own good, we will override your decision'. The potential self-concept effects of this on a vulnerable child's self-concept, their trust in others, and in therapy can be harmful.

The next section explores confidentiality, another concept requiring sensitive handling.

Confidentiality

Building up a good working relationship with a child often requires assurance of confidentiality, but sometimes practitioners need to pass information on to others.

No definition exists in statute law in England or Wales regarding confidential relationships (Hamilton 2005). Although some relationships are automatically seen as confidential (e.g. doctor–patient; counsellor–client), the need to protect children from significant harm means that no confidential service for them can guarantee absolute confidentiality (Hamilton 2005). Social services are under a statutory duty to make enquiries where there is reasonable cause to suspect that a child is suffering, or is likely to suffer, significant harm (Children Act 1989) (TSO 1989). Bentovim (1991, p.23) defined significant harm as 'a compilation of significant events, both acute and longstanding, which interact with the child's ongoing development, and interrupt, alter, or impair physical and psychological development'. All agencies in contact with children are required to work in partnership to promote children's welfare and to protect them from abuse and neglect. The safety and welfare of the child is paramount, and necessitates sharing information about suspected abuse with statutory agencies (DoH 1999). Therefore:

> therapy with [vulnerable] children has to take place in a very clear framework of child protection and the best interests of the child. This, on occasions, clashes with the best interests of a therapeutic relationship, which has to give way for the child's overall good. (Hunter 2001, pp.49–50)

During the assessment process, the aims and limits of confidentiality need to be shared with the child (Hamilton 2005). Confidentiality should neither be a cover for collusion, nor an excuse for therapists not to take ordinary adult responsibility in relation to children. Nevertheless, deciding where to draw the line is usually a complex and debatable issue (Hunter 2001). A key factor in deciding whether or not to disclose confidential information is proportionality: is the proposed disclosure a proportionate response to the need to protect the welfare of the child? For example, a disclosure of sexual abuse could depend on whether the abuse is current and whether the alleged perpetrator is around or if the abuse occurred several years ago but there is no current contact. Moreover, the amount of confidential information disclosed, and the number of people to whom it is disclosed, should be no more than is strictly necessary to meet the public interest in protecting the health and well-being of a child (DoH 2003).

A therapeutic relationship necessarily involves trusting the therapist. For a vulnerable child whose trust has been repeatedly abused, this can pose a major challenge. Occasionally children need to be told that trust includes the therapist's judgement to share information with others (Hunter 2001), for example concerns that a child may be coerced by another child in a care home. Furthermore, when working with vulnerable children, the therapist is part of the network and requires clear lines of two-way communication with other adults involved. Knowing that the therapist is aware of what is happening in their life, and is in contact with others in the network, can help provide a secure base for vulnerable children. This may present an opportunity to learn that some adults can be trusted and provide the foundation for establishing secure relationships in the future. It may also help foster autonomy in the long term.

Conclusions

If the purpose of healthcare is defined as maximizing human potential, and autonomy is perceived as an inherent personal quality which is fundamental to healthcare, then working therapeutically with vulnerable children needs to be underpinned by respect for their autonomy at their level of competence. However, a balance is required between the creation of and respect for autonomy, and the duty to safeguard the welfare of vulnerable children.

Ethical enquiry raises more questions than answers. It may be perceived as a process of values-based decision-making which clarifies our own frames of reference, including reflecting on what we mean when we use different words and concepts – our aims, plans and the means to achieve them, as well as considering those of other interested parties. This includes actively involving the child in the decision-making process and considering their wishes.

The final consideration in this chapter is for the reader to return to the case scenario described at the beginning, and reflect on the questions posed.

References

Aiken, W. (2001) 'Moral reflection on adolescent decision making?' *Community Ethics (Special Supplement) 7, 1.*

Bartholomew, T. (1996) *Challenging Assumptions about Young People's Competence: Clearing the Pathway to Policy?* Paper presented at Fifth Australian Family Research Conference. Available at: www.aifs.gov.au, accessed on 16 August 2006.

Batten, D. (1996) 'Informed consent by children and adolescents to psychiatric treatment'. *Australian and New Zealand Journal of Psychiatry 30,* 623–632.

Beauchamp, T. and Childress, J. (1989) *Principles of Biomedical Ethics* (3rd ed). Oxford: Oxford University Press.

Bentovim, A. (1991) 'Significant Harm in Context'. In M. Adcock, R. White and A. Hollows (eds) *Significant Harm.* Croydon: Significant Publications.

British Medical Association (BMA) Board of Science (2006) *Child and Adolescent Mental Health: A Guide for Healthcare Professionals.* London: British Medical Association.

Bohner, G. and Wanke, M. (2002) *Attitudes and Attitude Change.* Hove: Psychology Press.

Bridge, C. (1997) 'Adolescents and mental disorder: who consents to treatment?' *Medical Law International 3,* 51–74.

Collier, A. (1999) *Being and Worth.* London: Routledge.

Department for Education and Skills (DfES) (1989) Children Act 1989. London: The Stationery Office.

Department of Health (DoH) (1999) *Working Together to Safeguard Children: A Guide to Inter-agency Working to Safeguard and Promote the Welfare of Children.* London: Department of Health.

Department of Health (DoH) (2002) *Promoting the Health of Looked After Children.* London: Department of Health.

Department of Health (DoH) (2003) *Confidentiality: NHS Code of Practice.* London: Department of Health.

Dickenson, D. and Jones, D. (1996) 'True wishes: the philosophy and developmental psychology of children's informed consent.' *Philosophy, Psychiatry and Psychology 2,* 287–303.

Edwards, S. (1996) *Nursing Ethics: A Principle-Based Approach.* Basingstoke: MacMillan.

Faith, K. (2002) Addressing Issues of Autonomy and Benificence in the Treatment of Eating Disorders. Available at: www.nedic.ca, accessed on 1 August 2006.

Emanuel, L. (2002) 'Deprivation x 3: "The contribution of organizational dynamics to the 'triple deprivation' of looked-after children".' *Journal of Child Psychotherapy 28,* 2, 163–179.

Family Law Reform Act 1969. London: The Stationary Office.

Golding, K., Dent, H., Nissim, R. and Stott, L. (2006) 'Being Heard: Listening to the Voices of Young People, and their Families'. In K. Golding, H.R. Dent, R. Nissim and L. Stott (eds) *Thinking Psychologically About Children Who Are Looked After and Adopted.* Chichester: Wiley.

Goodwin, M., Bickerton, A., Parsons, R. and Lask, B. (2000) 'Paediatric heart/heart-lung transplantation: a systemic perspective on assessment and preparation.' *International Journal of Psychiatry in Clinical Practice 4*, 93–99.

Gross, R. (2001) *Psychology: The Science of Mind and Behaviour* (4th Ed). London: Hodder & Stoughton.

Hamilton, C. (2005) *Working with Young People: Legal Responsibility and Liability* (6th ed). Colchester: The Children's Legal Centre.

Hunter, M. (2001) *Psychotherapy with Young People in Care: Lost and Found.* Hove: Brunner-Routledge.

Kaufmann, W. (1998) *Aristotle: Nicomachean Ethics.* New York, NY: Dover.

Kroger, J. (2004) *Identity in Adolescence: The Balance between Self and Other* (3rd ed). Hove: Routledge.

LeDoux, J. (2002) *Synaptic Self: How our Brains Become Who we Are.* New York, NY: Penguin.

Meltzer, T., Gatward. R., Corbin. T., Goodman. R. and Ford. T. (2003) *The Mental Health of Young People Looked After by Local Authorities in England.* London: HMSO.

Parry, G. and Cape, J. (2002) 'Psychological Therapies.' In A. Elder and J. Holmes (eds) Mental Health in Primary Care. Oxford: Oxford University Press.

Paul, M. (2004) 'Decision-making about children's mental health care: ethical challenges'. *Advances in Psychiatric Treatment 10*, 301–311.

Reder, P. and Fitzpatrick, G. (1998) 'What is sufficient understanding?' *Clinical Child Psychology and Psychiatry 3*, 103–113.

Schofield, G. and Beek, M. (2005) 'Providing a secure base: parenting children in long-term foster family care.' *Attachment and Human Development 7*, 1, 3–25.

Seedhouse, D. (1998) *Ethics: The Heart of Health Care* (2nd ed). Chichester: Wiley.

Seedhouse, D. (2005) *Values-Based Decision-Making for the Caring Professionals.* Chichester: Wiley.

Spencer, G. (2000) 'Children's competency to consent: an ethical dilemma.' *Journal of Child Health Care 4*, 3, 117–122.

Stott, L., Nissin, R., Dent, H. and Golding, K.S. (2006) 'Travelling Hopefully – the Journey Continues'. In K.S. Golding, H. Dent, R. Nissim, and L. Stott (eds) *Thinking Psychologically about Children who are Looked After and Adopted.* Chichester: Wiley.

Sutton, A. (2001) 'Consent, latency and psychotherapy or "what am I letting myself in for?"' *Journal of Child Psychotherapy 27*, 3, 319–333.

Tan, J. and Jones, D. (2001) 'Children's consent.' *Current Opinion in Psychiatry 14*, 303–307.

The Stationery Office (1989) *The children's Act 1989.* London: The Stationery Office.

Verkerk, M. (1999) 'A care perspective on coercion and autonomy.' *Bioethics 13*, 358–368.

Vostanis, P. (2004) 'The impact, psychological sequelae and management of trauma affecting children.' *Current Opinion in Psychiatry 17*, 269–273.

Woodbridge, K. and Fulford, K. (2004) *Whose Values?* London: The Sainsbury Centre for Mental Health.

Zutlevics, T. and Henning, P. (2005) 'Obligation of clinicians to treat unwilling children and young people: an ethical discussion.' *Journal of Paediatric Child Health 41*, 677–681.

CHAPTER 5

Tackling the Stigma of Mental Health in Vulnerable Children and Young People

Fiona Gale

The severe and pervasive effects of the stigma of mental health are known to affect individuals and families, and can result in intense feelings of shame, social exclusion, and a reluctance to seek help (Wahl 1999). There is an increasing body of knowledge which explores the impact of stigma in children and young people who may have mental health needs. There is potential for the effects of stigma to be so insidious that they can significantly reduce access to children's mental health services and create fear, marginalization, and low self-esteem in children, and diminish the effectiveness of interventions. Stigma can have such a significant effect that there is a potential for mental health problems to increase in severity. Often, the experience of stigma has been described as on a par with the experience of having a mental health problem (Gale 2006).

Certain vulnerable groups of children and young people are known to be at greater risk of mental health problems, especially those groups discussed within this book. These children are also known to experience greater health in-equalities than the rest of the population (DoH 2003) and be subject to discrimination because of their status, and because of the perception that they are 'at-risk'. This can result in children within vulnerable groups experiencing a 'double-bind' of stigma and discrimination which may pose significant barriers to accessing treatment and have a heightened impact on the development of and recovery from mental health problems (Social Exclusion Unit 2004).

This chapter will examine the origins and experiences of the stigma surrounding mental health in relation to vulnerable children and young people with emerging mental health needs. There is a paucity of literature on the effects of stigma in this population; however, this chapter will explore literature that focuses on the context and impact of stigma on children and young people from the general population and will apply it to children from vulnerable groups. It will also determine factors that could contribute to cross-agency service improvements and interventions to tackle stigma.

What is stigma? definitions and concepts

Compounding the complexity of mental health problems and mental illness, and the impact they have on individuals, is the stigma that surrounds them. Stigma operates at a number of levels within individuals, families, education systems, the community, healthcare provision, the media, and within social policy (Hinshaw 2005).

Some research suggests that people who are labelled as being mentally ill, regardless of diagnosis, are stigmatized to a greater degree than those with other health conditions (Weiner, Magnusson and Perry 1988; Corrigan *et al.* 2000).

Defining stigma and its relationship with mental health

The origin of the term 'stigma' reportedly stems from ancient Greek. The term was used to signify a visible mark or brand placed on members of tainted groups, such as slaves or traitors (Goffman 1963). Recently, stigma has been defined as a mark of discredit, disfavour, or disgrace that sets a person, or a group of people, apart from others. The term 'stigma' is often referred to as the negative effects of a label placed on any group (Hinshaw 2005). This label may cover a wide range of experiences including mental illness, physical disability, race, culture, or sexual identity. 'Stigmatization' is the process whereby one aspect of a person is linked by strong attribution to a wide and pervasive dimension of their identity. Stigma is, therefore, the establishment of deviant identities, based on negative stereotyping (Alexander and Link 2003).

With regard to mental illness, Hayward and Bright (1997) highlight the concerning fact that there are 33 synonyms in Roget's *Thesaurus,* for the term 'insane', most of which sound discriminatory or prejudicial, and many of which are still in use in general vocabulary. A great deal of work on defining stigma and its relationship to mental illness was undertaken over 40 years ago; however, the discriminatory aspects still seem prominent when considering contemporary studies on mental health and stigma. The relevance of exploring the impact of stigma relates to the fact that the most disabling context of mental health can be the effect of stigma itself (Page 1995). This effect has been reported to have a severe effect on individuals and the way that they perceive themselves in relation to the rest of the community (Link 1987; Wahl 1999). The recent report on mental health and stigma from the Social Exclusion Unit (2004), suggests that stigma arises from negative stereotypes associated with the symptoms or diagnosis of mental health problems.

In his classic work, *Stigma: Notes on a Spoiled Identity* Goffman (1963) stated that stigma was socially discrediting, permanent, and affected the perceptions of the person as a whole. He suggested that cues which signal stigma are not always readily evident. With this in mind, it seems reasonable to suggest that people with mental illness or mental health needs can 'hide' the tarnish, to some extent, which identifies them with a stigmatized group. Therefore, concerns about being 'discovered' can be seen to continue and contribute to the fear of being discredited by their condition.

Extent of stigma and discrimination

Research exploring people's perceptions of mental health has mostly focused on adult views (Philo *et al.* 1993; Penn *et al.* 1994; Brunton 1997). Studies undertaken with the general public, service users, and professionals seem to show that they have little consensus on the meaning of 'mental health' (MacDonald 1993). An early study (Cumming and Cumming 1957), which examined the attitudes of the general public in relation to mental illness, concluded that most people feared and disliked the mentally ill, and would avoid them at all costs. Such early research is particularly striking when compared to the results of the Social Exclusion Unit consultation (2004), which highlighted that 83 per cent of people with mental health problems reported that stigma was a still serious issue, and 52 per cent had experienced negative attitudes towards mental health in the community. Corrigan (2000) states that stigmatizing views about mental illness do not seem to be limited to the general population. Some research studies which examined attitudes of well-trained professionals, including those from mental health disciplines, showed that they subscribed to prejudicial stereotypes about mental illness (Keane 1990; Lyons and Ziviani 1995).

Mental illness appears to be given a high profile in the media. The common stereotype of the mentally ill patient may be seen as a subject in a wide range of media products, from horror films like *Silence of the Lambs* and *Nightmare on Elm Street* to children's comic books, computer games, and soap operas (Wahl 1995, 2003). Sieff (2003) stated that the media does have a strong impact on perceptions. In the USA, many adults reported that most of their knowledge about mental health and illness came from mass media coverage (Wahl 1995).

The process of stigmatization and mental health

Stigma incorporates a number of processes, and some terms are often used in conjunction with it. Corrigan and Watson (2002) conceptualize stigma in two social-cognitive models. They determine the two processes that take place within society, as 'public stigma' and 'self-stigma'. Public stigma relates to the reaction that the general population has towards people with mental illness, whereas self-stigma relates to the experiences of those people with mental illness, as a response to the stigma process. Both forms of stigma contain three specific terms that are commonly used to describe the processes; these are 'Stereotyping', 'Prejudice' and 'Discrimination' (Box 5.1).

Within this process, stigma is said to emanate from these potential sources, but in particular from the experience of discrimination. People with mental illness will experience all of the key features of the stigma process; they will be officially labelled, shunned, connected to undesirable characteristics, and broadly discriminated against, in all aspects of their lives (Alexander and Link 2003). In relation to Corrigan's (2000) definitions of self-stigma, the person with mental illness assigns the process to themselves, that is, they will apply a negative stereotype to themselves and agree with the prejudicial effects, resulting in low self-esteem. They will then behave in a way that responds to the prejudice, such as avoiding specific social settings, therefore experiencing discrimination.

In addition, to public stigma and self-stigma, is the notion of 'courtesy stigma' (Goffman 1963). Courtesy stigma is defined as a social disapproval for people associated with a stigmatized individual. Families, friends, and even neighbours are possible recipients of the effects of courtesy stigma. People who experience courtesy stigma as a result of their affiliation with an individual can experience varying levels of stigma, which they can regulate through their ability to distance themselves from the person with mental illness (Gray 1993).

It is claimed that the acquisition of stigma is an ongoing process and is related to the responses of others, including family, the community, and professionals (Szasz 1961; Sarlin 1967; Horwitz 1982). The causes of stigmatization are said

---

Box 5.1 Common terms in the stigmatization process

- *Stereotyping* is a process by which members of a group are perceived to have a set of common characteristics or traits (Crocker *et al.* 1998).

- *Prejudice* relates to negative, emotive pre-judgements about members of visible groups (Crocker *et al.* 1998).

- *Discrimination* can be defined as the less-favourable treatment of people, including a reduction in access to both opportunities and resources, which can arise as a result of stigma (Welsh Assembly Government 2002). Discrimination can be applied to persons or groups on the basis of belief, perception, and alleged or other attributed characteristics, rather than actual ones.

to be complex and deeply rooted in cultural attitudes, as a result of entrenched historical ideas or myths about 'madness', and from assumptions about the nature of mental illness.

Corrigan and Watson (2002) suggest that stigmatization occurs between the process of being stigmatized by the public and the effects of self-stigma by the individual. The difference between the two processes seems to be that public stigma results in the individual avoiding the label, whereas self-stigma can result in the individual avoiding treatment. Such processes may also be seen in the behaviour of carers when seeking help for their relative. Thus, the situation of the individual can escalate, which then contributes to the cycle within the stigmatizing process and the excluding effects of stigma.

In his classic work, *Being Mentally Ill: A Sociological Theory,* Scheff (1966) outlined that stereotyped imagery of mental disorder is learnt in early childhood. He states that patterns of social differentiation affect the individual's concept and learning about mental illness. Similar learning patterns have been found in studies undertaken on the acquisition of children's beliefs about race (Goodman 1970), suggesting that stigmatizing attitudes need to be tackled early if there is to be lasting change. Equally, such attitudes can begin to have an impact on individuals from stigmatized or discriminated groups at an early age.

Consequences of stigma

Stigmatization has been shown to have a detrimental effect on mental health, not only after problems have developed, but also possibly at the onset of the problems, or presentation of illness itself (Penn and Wykes 2003). A damaging aspect of stigma is the effect of internalizing stigma on those with mental health problems, including a belief that they were 'spoiled' and of less value than 'normal' people (Green *et al.* 2003). Associated feelings of stigma include guilt and shame, self-protective denial, and a serious reluctance to access help (Kendell 2004).

Stigma can have a disabling impact on the individual's sense of self, including a significantly diminished self-esteem, self-value, and confidence. The effects can be so pervasive that the person with mental illness can become secretive about the illness itself, and selectively avoid those who know about it. Similar responses to stigma have been found to be true of families, or carers of people with mental health problems, who often portray their experience of stigma in the form of shame and self-blame (Link *et al.* 2001). Stigma has also been shown to have an impact on adherence to ongoing contact with help providers (Corrigan 2004).

Mental health stigma in children and young people

Research in social cognition has suggested that the development of mature attributional styles and personality traits is still in progress between the ages of 6 and 12 years (Flavell, Miller and Miller 1993). A national survey of mental health awareness in young people in Scotland concluded that young people of all ages could provide a description for the terms 'mental health' and 'mental illness'. This study found that mental health tended to be described as something positive, whereas mental illness perceptions were largely negative (RAMH Education 1996).

Children as young as six years old have an understanding of everyday language and terms related to mental illness (Cook 1972). These beliefs have been found to be comparable with those of their parents and professionals they have come into contact with. Two studies by Weiss (1986, 1994) outlined that a developmental consequence occurs in the acquisition of beliefs: that attitudes towards the mentally ill have developed and become clear by kindergarten. Weiss (1994) concluded that with maturation children became more psychologically sophisticated and were able to differentiate between the attributes of a range of presentations. Acceptance was more positive if the child had experience of, or contact with, someone with a mental health problem. He also suggested that, with increasing age, children display attitudes and perceptions that progress from a general nature to those resembling adult specificity and differentiation. Wahl (2000) argued that a combination of community, parental and peer beliefs, and media representation is responsible for the development of perceptions in children. Reluctance to access available help may be explained by the stigma attached, as children learn from an early age that people with mental health problems are often perceived as failures (Wahl 2000).

Development of concepts of stigmatization in children

Many studies on the process of stigmatization in children have primarily focused on physical disability, race, ethnicity, and religious groups, rather than examining issues for children from these groups in relation to the effects of mental health stigma. In studies that examined racial attitudes, very young children were found to have developed some negative attitudes, and that as they grew older, they were more likely to possess a negative attitude over a positive one (Goodman 1970). Indicators which relate to the negative acquisition of beliefs and the beginning of the process of stigmatization at an early age suggest that children first display reactions to those who are physically or visually different (Katz 1982). Preference has also been found in young children for able-bodied rather than physically disabled people (Sigleman, Thomas and Whitworth 1986). In this respect children and young people with mental health problems from vulnerable groups could be marginalized because of their perceived 'difference' on two counts.

Wilkins and Velicer (1980) examined the process of stigmatization in children and their attitudes towards three vulnerable groups: those with physical disability; learning disability; and those with mental illness. Children's reactions towards the mentally ill group seemed to receive the most negative association. Although there was no evidence in the study to suggest why this might be, there is an implication that the more negative attitudes towards mentally ill people were learnt within the family and established before entry into the school system. Wahl (2003) supports these theories, suggesting that children acquire understanding about mental health through socialization, by contribution from significant others, and through the mass media.

The concept of mental health stigma in children has also been suggested to evolve from fear and associated personal safety issues. Roberts, Beidleman and Wurtele (1981) explored children's perceptions of medical and psychological disorders in their peers, and found that negative responses to those with mental illness were related to the fear of irrational or aggressive behaviours. Reducing such perceptions of mental illness would require significant investment in developing professionals' and parents' understanding of mental illness for this to be conveyed to children.

A recent qualitative study of 10- and 11-year-olds (Roose and John 2003), suggested that children's concepts of mental health were sophisticated, and that they considered many different behaviours to be an indication of a serious mental health problem. Children were clear about the difference between mental health and physical health problems, and were able to articulate them. There was also evidence of empathy and help-seeking knowledge in relation to those with mental health problems. Wahl (2002) suggests that as children reach their teenage years they begin to understand that behaviours expressed externally could be a result of inner distress. This enables them to form more positive opinions about behaviours related to mental illness, which they had previously deemed to be irrational.

The process of mental health stigmatization in children

The process of stigmatization in adults relates similarly to children. However, there is some evidence that the process regarding children and stigma is less direct, and may be conveyed from experiences communicated from relationships with significant adults (Gale 2006). Hinshaw (2005) suggests four main elements which relate to the process of stigmatization in children, that is, courtesy stigma, labelling effects, effect of parental mental illness, and children's perceptions of mental illness. As a result of courtesy stigma, children associated with people with a mental disorder (e.g. a parent with mental illness) may be shunned by peers, the community and society.

Courtesy stigma can extend in either direction, that is, children can think the same of others in the same situation, or parents may struggle to disassociate themselves from the blame for their child's mental health problem. Labelling can also have effects on the child and can influence peer response towards children with mental health problems (Harris *et al.* 1992), wherein a negative expectation of behaviour can emanate from a non-labelled child about a child with a label or diagnosis. Conversely, some studies have been undertaken which showed that having a diagnosis can be empowering. Some parents reported that once their children had been given a diagnosis they received greater access to more support, and professionals were more empathetic and helpful (Klasen 2000).

Hinshaw's (2005) third domain of stigmatization in children relates to the effect of parental mental illness. Research on risk and resilience factors highlights that parental mental illness can be a causative factor for mental health problems in children, not just from a biological point of view, but in relation to attachment and in the child's experience within society (Kurtz 1996). The fourth area of Hinshaw's model relates to children's perceptions of mental health and illness. This is discussed in the following section.

Children's and young people's perceptions of mental health and illness

Weiss (1980, 1986) studied children's attitudes towards socially stigmatized groups, including people with mental illness. Children in kindergarten were unexpectedly able to make highly discriminated judgements about their preference of stigmatized groups, and people with mental illness were regarded with fear, disgust, distrust, and aversion. Weiss (1985) also found that children took an increasingly parent-like view of those with mental illness and seemed to consider that they may be able do something to help them.

The study by Adler and Wahl (1998) indicated that younger children lacked consistent conceptions of mental illness, with an inability to articulate examples of mental illness. On the whole, those labelled mentally ill were described in more negative terms than those with physical illness. More recently, Wahl (2002) looked at the understanding displayed by young children and found that they were more accurate about mental illness as they approach adolescence.

There have been few studies on the perceptions of children who have been referred to child and adolescent mental health (CAMH) services. A qualitative study with children aged 5–11 years who had mental health needs (Gale 2006) identified that they are able to recognize feelings of stigma and discrimination in relation to mental health, and also that they possessed negative beliefs about people (mainly adults) who have mental health problems. This indicates that the cycle of stigmatization for children with mental health needs can be increasingly pervasive.

A UK study of young people aged between 11 and 17 (Bailey 1999) found that the participants had a wide range of understanding and acceptance of people with mental illness. Overall, they felt that adults could give them constructive solutions for dealing with mental illness, but they also wanted to be part of the process. A study which looked at young people's experiences of mental health services (Laws *et al.* 1999) concluded that young people sometimes believed that the way they were treated in mental health services made them feel worse and was impersonal. They perceived that they were not listened to, and that accessing help for the first time was particularly difficult. They also recalled experiences of being stigmatized, which included feelings of shame, embarrassment, and that their problems were not understood by family and friends. Such experiences should be considered when developing services for vulnerable children.

Listening to Children (Armstrong, Hill and Secker 1999) examined young people's perceptions of mental health. The findings show that understanding about the term 'mental health' was not always clear and consistent. Young people had definitive views about the issues which affected their mental health, wished to be listened to, and believed that professionals should have a clear understanding of mental health and how information is imparted to them.

Durham (2000) looked specifically at Gujarati girls' attitudes towards mental health and contrasted them with those of white British girls. Their perceptions of mental health were similar, with the most distinct difference occurring in the Asian girls' experience of family life, which they appeared to find more acutely distressing. Both groups showed a good empathy for people with mental health issues. Such findings are echoed in the study by Armstrong *et al.* (1999), which included a representative sample from black and minority ethnic groups, suggesting that the differences in attitudes across ethnic groups are minimal.

The impact of mental health stigma on vulnerable children and young people

It is evident from the issues presented above that the impact of mental health stigma on children and young people identified as being vulnerable can be great. Although a number of recent policy developments in England have aimed to reduce inequalities, discrimination and social exclusion (DfES 2004; DoH 2004a, 2004b), it is important to consider specific issues regarding mental health stigma for children and young people in different vulnerable groups.

Black and minority ethnic groups

There is evidence to suggest that mental health problems in children and young people from black and minority ethnic groups (Malek 2004) are at a higher rate than in the general population. In addition, they are considered more likely to experience other risk factors that are associated with the increased occurrence of mental health problems. These specifically relate to discrimination, deprivation, and poor life opportunities (BMA 2006). A report, *Minority Voices: A Guide to Good Practice in Planning and Providing Services for the Mental Health of Black and Minority Ethnic Young People* (Young Minds 2005), suggests that there are specific barriers to children and young people accessing help from mental health services, which could result in an increased experience of stigma. These barriers include:

- the lack of understanding of cultural and religious needs
- a shortage of professionals from a black and minority ethnic (BME) background
- the deficit in staff's knowledge around cultural competence
- the diversity in understanding of what constitutes mental health, across different cultures
- in some cultures the perception of the stigma surrounding mental health is stronger than in others, so could result in reluctance to access mental health services
- language barriers can also result in unnecessary fears about mental health and what it means to the child; where there is limited or no access to translation services, when English is not the first language, this could have specific implications for refugees and asylum seekers; this issue could be exacerbated where children are unaccompanied asylum-seekers
- the perception that children and young people consider the attitudes and practices of health professionals to be racist, adds to the discriminatory aspects associated with mental health problems for the BME population.

Refugees and asylum seekers

The very nature of seeking asylum means that a person has suffered in some way in their country of origin and is looking for protection and safety. Many asylum seekers have suffered or witnessed such atrocities that mental health issues are almost always intrinsically bound with their personal circumstances. However, the cultures of other countries often place more intense stigmas and taboos upon anyone with mental health problems. For this reason, many asylum seekers are said not to mention their mental health needs, as they would not automatically consider them to be an issue or they would fear further exclusion (Save the Children 2007).

Children and young people may have originated from countries where, in addition to witnessing atrocities and violence, their social and cultural differences have been very different (Hodes 2004). Practical problems, such as where to live and the attitudes of the community they are placed in, can cause children to fear to speak out about their mental health needs. They may also be reticent about divulging their experiences, or have been persecuted for their views. Such issues, emanating from the fear of being stigmatized or 'standing out', could severely affect a child's ability to communicate with CAMH service professionals, or even admit that help is required. Given the fears about stigma identified by children in the general population, with mental health needs (Gale 2006), it is easy to recognize the reasons for a heightened reluctance to access help.

Looked-after and adopted children

Children who are looked after in the care of local authorities are likely to have complex health, mental health, and social needs (Dogra *et al.* 2002). One of the major issues raised by professionals caring for looked-after children is their reluctance for children to receive mental health assessments, owing to the labelling and stigma attached to having a mental health disorder (Scott and Lindsey 2003). In addition, there are concerns about the confidence and capacity of practitioners and foster carers to support children with mental health needs. Children have preconceived and stigmatized ideas about CAMH services, which are often based on their poor experiences of health services during their journey into care, and accessing services can be daunting (Grant, Ennis and Stuart 2002).

The experience of going into care or being moved between carers can exacerbate feelings of stigma (BMA 2006), and if the child also develops mental health problems then self-stigma can become two fold. Most of children will have experienced a great deal of discrimination and social exclusion as they are more likely to experience poor life outcomes (Green *et al.* 2005). Many of them struggle with attainment at school, having difficulties with reading, mathematics, and spelling. They are also more inclined to have come to the attention of the police (BMA 2006). As a result, children and young people can often present with more severe mental health problems which have gone unrecognized because of the complexity of their needs. Fear of stigmatization related to mental health can enhance their already poor sense of self, therefore access to services must be timely and involve the young person in decision-making about their care. Recognition of the potential for mental health stigma to increase the severity of needs must be part of the interventions and support given to the young person.

In addition to the issues related to looked-after children, adopted children often have the added dimension of problems related to identity. Not only do these tend to present as mental health problems, they can also become entrenched within the cycle of stigma and self-stigma. Adoptive parents can also struggle to talk about these issues with children, and the origins of mental health problems within the child's biological family may go undiscovered or are not discussed (Mind 2007). The parents of adoptive children can experience stigma related to difficulties in attachment with their child, their fears about being able to deal with challenging behaviour, and anxiety about not being able to cope (Young Minds 2002).

Young offenders

As with other vulnerable groups, young offenders are at high risk of having mental health needs. There is also a higher rate of suicide among young offenders in secure settings (DoH 2004a, 2004b). Although there has been an increase in the UK in CAMH service support to community-based Youth Offending Services (YOS) (Health Care Commission 2006), many young people in secure settings have no access to mental health workers, staff have limited knowledge of mental health issues, and young offenders find it hard to access mental health services. Their lives can be particularly chaotic and their motivation to attend the YOS may often be around the expectations of their order. On this basis they can have limited understanding of their mental health needs, which can often be missed by officers within the YOS or secure setting (Health Care Commission 2006). Many have suffered exclusion in several realms of their lives and they may also be members of a number of vulnerable groups, for example looked-after, black and minority ethnic groups, refugees and asylum seekers, homeless, and so on. This can increase the experience of stigma and discrimination, and being confronted with mental health needs can have a severe impact on an already damaged self-worth and identity. The key is to increase these groups' understanding of mental health and ensure that services are non-stigmatizing, accessible, and designed in partnership with young people where possible.

Physical and learning-disabled children and young people

According to a recent mapping exercise (Young Minds 2002), many CAMH services do not have adequate services for disabled children and young people with mental health needs, especially those with learning disability. Children with a disability can be acutely aware that they are different from others, and can have low self-esteem (Foundation for People with Learning Disabilities 2002). Often, they can find it difficult to achieve independence and social involvement, and this may be combined with feelings of failure. They are also frequently subjected to bullying and are marginalized by peers. Young people with disabilities have reported that their voice is not always heard, that they can be excluded from making decisions about their health needs, and as a result this can mean that it is difficult to get their mental health needs recognized. They can also experience increased public and self-stigma as a result of having mental health needs. Access to CAMH services means having identified care pathways, and being supported by those in universal services. Mental health promotion and a partnership with children, young people, and their families will enable them to express their needs in a safer and non-stigmatizing environment.

Interventions to combat mental health stigma in children and young people

Promoting the understanding of the mental health of vulnerable children and challenging stigma have implications for local implementation within CAMH services across all levels of provision. A model of interventions for tackling stigma in children, young people, and their families is presented in Figure 5.1 (Gale 2006). These can be put into practice within CAMH services locally, and within specific services for vulnerable children, in order to tackle the severe effects of stigma related to mental health. However, whilst the interventions were designed

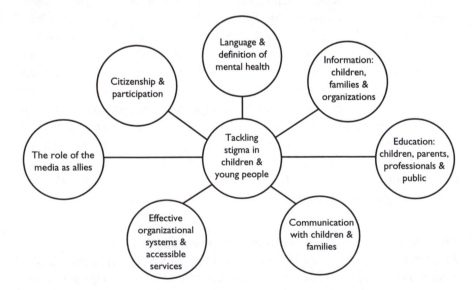

Figure 5.1 A multi-dimensional framework for local intervention: tackling the stigma of mental health in children and young people. Adapted from Gale (2006)

to be implemented across all tiers of CAMH services, they are relevant to vulnerable children and should be considered alongside some of the issues of stigma that affect them. In addition, it is vital that approaches to tackling stigma and raising awareness of child mental health should be recognized and mainstreamed across all children's agencies, not just within healthcare settings.

Agreeing a definition and working towards a common language of mental health

Many studies of stigma outlined in this chapter address the importance of developing a salient definition of mental health. Local services could tackle this by considering their language and terminology, and also through development of standard explanations of mental health, which are age-appropriate and do not inadvertently stigmatise. Children and young people have demonstrated that they are able to hold articulate and sophisticated discussions about mental health (Armstrong *et al.* 1999; Gale 2006), and they are able to contribute to such discussions with professionals. In this respect they could usefully contribute to developing definitions and terminology which promote equality and inclusiveness within CAMH services. Developing a shared understanding of mental health between professionals, and with children and their parents or carers, would be a sound base from which to launch programmes to promote mental health awareness and to challenge stigma.

The diversity of understanding about mental health, especially within black and minority ethnic groups, and the range and level of stigma within different cultures could be reduced if there is an active engagement in mental health promotion and prevention activities. Much policy and guidance about the mental health needs of vulnerable children and young people indicates that inclusive mental health promotion programmes should form the beginning of any CAMH services care pathway. The role of universal services, in particular schools and community groups, is imperative if understanding about mental health is to be developed. Local CAMH services and children's agencies should collaborate to develop a shared understanding with young people and families from vulnerable groups, in order to agree the principles of a good service that is accessible and non-stigmatizing.

Developing information for children and families

Children and young people have highlighted their concerns about seeking help and attending CAMH services. Many of them were uncertain about what would happen when they attended their first appointment. When seeking help, parents and carers have explained that they were not sure where to go or which was the right service for their child's mental health needs (Day, Carey and Surgenor

2006; Gale 2006). These issues can contribute to the mystique and fear which surround CAMH services, concerns about asking for help, and the adverse effects of stigma experienced by children and their parents or carers.

Useful interventions to combat these fears might include the development and dissemination of age-appropriate and user-friendly information about child mental health services. In addition, such information could be used by parents or carers to help them reduce the child's potential anxieties. In many of the reports and studies discussed in relation to vulnerable children, it is evident that they wish to have a voice, and to develop a partnership with professionals when designing their services. In particular, children from black and minority ethnic groups need to have access to culturally and age-appropriate information about CAMH services and their mental health, in their first language. This is best designed with children and families if it is to be useful. One of the main issues throughout the discussion on stigma has related to the fear and reluctance of vulnerable children and young people to access CAMH services. Developing understanding alongside these worries could serve to reduce the additional levels of stigma these groups experience and develop increased understanding of how and when to ask for help.

If CAMH services are to tackle stigma and raise mental health awareness in a strategic way, it is imperative that all services consider how they impart information. Developing material and protocols to ensure that children and young people are informed about their care could be an outcome that is easily achieved, with few resource implications.

Educating children, families, and professionals

As the reform of children's services and CAMH services has indicated the need for the early recognition of child mental health problems, and for increased capacity and knowledge about children's mental health across services, it is necessary to develop robust, local education programmes (DoH 2004a, 2004b; DfES 2004). Such education programmes should be delivered in multiple contexts, across agencies and levels of provision, and include a curriculum on children's mental health and stigma. In addition, the inclusion of knowledge about child mental health and the stigmatization process could be included in training courses available for professionals at a pre-registration and post-graduate level.

Sebuliba and Vostanis (2001) described an inter-agency training and education model around children's mental health for front-line staff, which could be implemented at a local level, and which could include training about the effects of stigma. Such courses could be tailored to include the needs of specific vulnerable groups and delivered in a range of settings, such as children's homes, YOS, secure settings, youth, and community services. Delivering training within services for vulnerable children may build networks and collaborative arrangements to ensure that care pathways are more robust and transparent.

Local services would also need to consider how parents or carers and children can best contribute to education programmes and how they might benefit from them. The citizenship model (Hart 1992) would be a useful framework for the appropriate involvement of vulnerable children and families in the design and delivery of training. Such involvement would be beneficial in empowering children to promote their own mental health, to recognize their mental health needs, and to challenge the negative impact of stigma.

In addition, it is imperative that professionals working with vulnerable children and young people with mental health needs have an understanding of their levels of cultural competence, and that they ensure engagement in training on delivering a culturally competent CAMH service. Some of the literature discussed earlier highlights the need for a staff group with relevant skills and knowledge that reflects the ethnic profile of the population. When recruiting staff it is vital to encourage applications from black and minority ethnic groups, and to ensure that they have knowledge of the issues relating to cultural competence and the effects of stigma on vulnerable groups.

Communicating with children and families

The desire of vulnerable children and young people to act as informed participants in their care has been clearly articulated. Poor communication with children and their families or carers, and between agencies can result in loss of faith in the systems and leaves them feeling unsupported. Children often perceive that they are not listened to and have indicated that they wish to be part of the decision-making process about their problems. Such concerns suggest that services need to consider their relationship with users. Inclusive models of working should be developed to ensure that children and parents or carers are active partners in determining the care process. Within clinical services, agreements or contracts can be developed in partnership with the child and the family or carers to ensure that all parties are clear and have a vehicle to ask questions or challenge assumptions. Such approaches are used in therapeutic relationships, often in family therapy (McDowell 1999), and they can assist parents or carers and children in feeling they are active partners in the process. Also within the therapeutic alliance, in particular between the clinician and child, it would be beneficial for clinicians to develop their awareness of the possible effects of stigma, in combination with the specific aspects of their vulnerabilities, on the child and their family, thus ensuring they take steps to consider the impact of stigma within their practice.

Developing effective organization systems and accessible services
UK policy recommendations for more accessible, responsive, timely, and comprehensive CAMH service provision (DoH 2004b) point to the requirement for the revision of some local organizational structures. Lack of clarity in referral routes and criteria for services for vulnerable children, across levels of provision, uncertainty about their remit, lack of knowledge about community and specialist or targeted services, and ambiguity about joint-agency working can contribute to experiences of self-stigma, shame, and powerlessness.

The development of transparent referral protocols and criteria would contribute to the reduction of stress, confusion, and reluctance associated with seeking help. In conjunction with this, the apparent gap between specialist CAMH services and universal services could be closed by the further development of the Primary Mental Health Worker (PMHW) role, which is located at the interface between specialist and universal services. The role of the PMHW is to support front-line staff by building their knowledge, confidence and capacity to work with vulnerable children with emerging mental health needs (Health Advisory Service 1995; Gale 2003; Gale and Vostanis 2003).

There are many emerging examples of services that have been developed for vulnerable children and young people with mental health needs, at all tiers of provision. Many of these are multi-agency and have clear supporting networks to ensure that children do not fall through gaps (DoH 2006). Local providers and commissioners should consider whether their current configuration of services enables non-stigmatizing provision for vulnerable children, based on a comprehensive assessment of local need.

Partnerships with the local media
Wahl (2003) suggests that the mass media contribute to children's negative attitudes about mental health, therefore adults should actively guard children from being subjected to negative media influences, through rigorous regulation of films, computer games, and other materials. In addition, it may be beneficial for CAMH services to work with local media organizations to impart positive information about children's mental health and help that is available. In this respect, local newspapers, television, and cinema could be supportive in getting information about children's mental health out into the public domain.

Children and young people as partners
The move towards involving vulnerable children, young people, and parents or carers as citizens, partners, and decision-makers requires a co-ordinated and practical approach at a local level. The request from children and young people to

be involved in all aspects of their care requires professionals across the CAMH services tiers to identify opportunities to mainstream this approach. In order to develop a participatory approach, professionals need to understand techniques and processes that promote participation, and to ensure that these are embedded within the service ethos. Street and Herts (2005) outlined a range of participatory activities for CAMH services; however, to design and implement such effective participation plans for children and families requires local services to identify staff and resources. Such an approach should become a fundamental part of effective service delivery to ensure that the participation of children and young people moves from tokenism to partnership.

Conclusions

The stigma of mental health affects vulnerable children and young people on a number of dimensions. They have sophisticated and complex perceptions of mental health and the stigma attached to it. Understanding of mental health is not salient, and in this respect it contributes to experiences of stigma and engagement with the stigmatization process. Experiences of stigma and discrimination pose barriers to seeking help, achieving timely assessment, and responsive intervention for children's mental health problems. This is confirmed by stigmatizing attitudes in society and through unclear care pathways and organizational systems.

Children and young people have advocated for a change in attitude towards mental health, through far-reaching education programmes to improve the understanding of mental health and stigma among children, professionals, organizations, and the general population, and through their active participation in service development and care provision. Children have established that they can develop a positive understanding of health through the school curriculum and through professionals who work with them. They are able to conceptualize positive aspects of mental health and can display empathy for peers who may have problems similar to them. In this respect, they should be key stakeholders in the planning and implementation of collaborative approaches to tackling the stigma of mental health.

References

Adler, A. and Wahl, O. (1998) 'Children's beliefs about people labelled mentally ill.' *American Journal of Orthopsychiatry 68*, 321–326.

Alexander, L. and Link, B. (2003) 'The impact of contact on stigmatising attitudes toward people with mental illness.' *Journal of Mental Health 12*, 271–289.

Armstrong, C., Hill, M. and Secker, J. (1999) *Listening to Children.* London: Mental Health Foundation.

Bailey, S. (1999) 'Young people, mental illness and stigmatization.' *Psychiatric Bulletin 23*, 107–110.

British Medical Association (BMA) (2006) *Child and Adolescent Mental Health: A Guide for Healthcare Professionals.* London: BMA.

Brunton, K. (1997) 'Stigma.' *Journal of Advanced Nursing 26*, 891–898.

Cook, A. (1972) 'An Exploration of Children's Stereotypes of Mental Illness.' Unpublished MPhil Thesis. Leicester: University of Leicester.

Corrigan, P. (2000) 'Mental health stigma as social attribution: Implications for research methods and attitude change.' *American Psychological Association 7*, 48–67.

Corrigan, P. (2004) 'How stigma interferes with mental health care.' *American Psychologist 59*, 614–625.

Corrigan, P. and Watson, A. (2002) 'The paradox of self-stigma and mental illness.' *Clinical Psychology: Science and Practice 9*, 35–53.

Corrigan, P., River, L., Lundin, R., Uphoff, K., Campion, J. and Mathisen, J. (2000) 'Stigmatising attributions about mental illness.' *Journal of Community Psychology 28*, 91–102.

Crocker, J., Major, B. and Steele, C. (1998) 'Social Stigma.' In D.T. Gilbert, S.T. Friske and G. Lindzey (eds) *Handbook of Social Psychology* (4th ed). Boston, MA: McGrew Hill.

Cumming, E. and Cumming, J. (1957) *Closed Ranks: An Experiment in Mental Health Education.* Cambridge, MA: Harvard University Press.

Day, C., Carey, M. and Surgenor, T. (2006) 'Children's key concerns: Piloting a qualitative approach to understanding their experience of mental health care.' *Clinical Child Psychology and Psychiatry 11*, 139–155.

Department of Health (DoH) (2003) *Tackling Health Inequalities: A Programme for Action.* London: DoH Publications.

Department of Health (DoH) (2004a) *National Service Framework for Children, Young People and Maternity Services.* London: DoH Publications.

Department of Health (2004b) *Standard 9: The Mental Health and Psychological Well-Being of Children and Young People.* London: DoH Publications.

Department of Health (DoH) (2006) *Report on the Implementation of Standard 9 of the NSF for Children, Young People and Maternity Services.* London: DoH Publications.

Department for Education and Science (DfES) (2004) *Every Child Matters: Change for Children.* London: DfES.

Dogra, N., Parkin, A., Gale, F. and Frake, C (2002) *A Multidisciplinary Handbook of Child and Adolescent Mental Health for Frontline Professionals.* London: Jessica Kingsley Publishers.

Durham, J. (2000) 'Asian Young People's Attitudes Toward Mental Health.' Unpublished report. Leicester: University of Leicester.

Flavell, J., Miller, P. and Miller, S. (1993) *Cognitive Development* (3rd ed). Englewood Cliffs, NJ: Prentice Hall.

Gale, F. (2003) 'When tiers are not enough: the developing role of the primary mental health worker in child and adolescent mental health.' *Child and Adolescent Mental Health in Prmary Care 1*, 5–9.

Gale, F. (2006) 'Children's and Parents'/Carers' Perceptions of Mental Health and Stigma.' Unpublished PhD thesis: University of Leicester.

Gale, F. and Vostanis, P. (2003) 'The primary mental health worker role in child and adolescent mental health services.' *Clinical Child Psychology and Psychiatry 8*, 227–240.

Foundation for People with Learning Disabilities. (2002) *Count Us In: The Report to the Committee of Inquiring into Meeting the Needs of Young People with Learning Disabilities.* London: Mental Health Foundation.

Goffman, E. (1963) *Stigma: Notes on the Management of a Spoiled Identity.* Middlesex: Pelican Publishing.

Goodman, M. (1970) *Race Awareness in Young Children.* New York, NY: Collier Books.

Grant, A., Ennis, J. and Stuart, F. (2002) 'Looking after health: a joint working approach to improving the health outcomes of looked after and accommodated children and young people.' *Scottish Journal of Residential Care 1*, 23–30.

Gray, D. (1993) 'Perceptions of stigma: The parents of autistic children.' *Sociology of Health and Illness 15*, 102–120.

Green, G., Hayes, C., Dickenson, D., Whittaker, A. and Gilheany, B. (2003) 'A mental health service user's perspective to stigmatization.' *Journal of Mental Health 12*, 223–234.

Green, H., McGinnity, A., Meltzer, H., Ford, T. and Goodman, R. (2005) *Mental Health of Children and Adolescents in Great Britain, 2004.* Basingstoke: Palgrave.

Harris, M., Milich, R., Corbitt, D., Hoover, D. and Brady, M. (1992) 'Self-fulfilling effects of stigmatising information on children's interactions.' *Journal of Personality and Social Psychology 63*, 41–50.

Hart, R. (1992) *Children's Participation for Tokenism to Citizenship.* Florence: UNICEF Innocenti Research Centre.

Hayward, P. and Bright, J. (1997) 'Stigma and mental illness: A review and critique.' *Journal of Mental Health 6*, 345–354.

Health Advisory Service (1995) *Child and Adolescent Mental Health: Together We Stand: The Commissioning, Role and Management of Child and Adolescent Mental Health Services.* London: HMSO.

Health Care Commission (2006) *Let's Talk About It: A Review of Healthcare in the Community for Young People who Offend.* London: HMSO.

Hinshaw, S. (2005) 'The stigmatization of mental illness in children and parents: Developmental issues, family concerns, and research needs.' *Journal of Child Psychology and Psychiatry 46*, 714–734.

Hodes, M. (2004) 'Refugee Children in the UK.' In M. Malek and C. Joughin (eds) *Mental Health Services for Minority Ethnic Children and Adolescents.* London: Jessica Kingsley Publishers.

Horwitz, A. (1982) *Social Control of Mental Illness.* New York, NY: Academic Press.

Katz, P. (1982) 'Development of Children's Racial Awareness and Inter-group Attitudes.' In L. Katz (ed) *Current Topics in Early Childhood Education.* Norwood, NJ: Ablex.

Keane, M. (1990) 'Contemporary beliefs about mental illness among medical students: Implications for education and practice.' *Academic Psychiatry 14*, 172–177.

Kendell, R. (2004) 'Why Stigma Matters.' In A. Crisp (ed.) *Every Family in the Land: Understanding Prejudice and Discrimination Against People with Mental Illness.* London: Royal Society of Medicine Press.

Klasen, H. (2000) 'A name, what's in a name? The medicalization of hyperactivity, revisited.' *Harvard Review of Psychiatry 7*, 339–344.

Kurtz, Z. (1996) *Treating Children Well: A Guide to Commissioning and Managing Services for the Mental Health of Children and Young People.* London: Mental Health Foundation.

Laws, S., Armitt, D., Metzendorf, W., Percival, P. and Reisel, J. (1999) *Time to Listen: Young People's Experiences of Mental Health Services.* London: Save the Children.

Link, B. (1987) 'Understanding the labeling effects in the area of mental disorders: An assessment of the effects of expectations of rejection.' *American Sociological Review 52*, 96–112.

Link, B., Struening, E., Neese-Todd, S., Asmussen, S. and Phelan, J. (2001) 'Stigma as barrier to recovery: the consequences of stigma for the self-esteem of people with mental illness.' *Psychiatric Services 5*, 1621–1626.

Lyons, M. and Ziviani, J. (1995) 'Stereotypes, stigma and mental illness: Learning from fieldwork experiences.' *American Journal of Occupational Therapy 49*, 1002–1008.

MacDonald, G. (1993) 'Defining the Goals and Raising the Issues in Mental Health Promotion.' In D. Trent and C. Reed (eds) *Promoting Mental Health: Volume 2.* Aldershot: Averbury.

McDowell, T. (1999) 'Systems consultation and Headstart: An alternative to traditional family therapy.' *Journal of Marital and Family Therapy 25*, 155–168.

Malek, M (2004) 'Understanding Ethnicity and Children's Mental Health.' In M. Malek and C. Joughin (eds) *Mental Health Services for Minority Ethnic Children and Adolescents.* London: Jessica Kingsley Publishers.

Mind (2007) 'Children, Young People and Mental Health.' Available at: www.mind.org.uk/information/factsheets/children, accessed on 14 February 2007.

Page, S. (1995) 'Effects of the mental illness label in 1993: Acceptance and rejection in the community.' *Journal of Mental Health Policy 7*, 61–68.

Penn, D. and Wykes, T. (2003) 'Stigma, discrimination and mental illness.' *Journal of Mental Health 12*, 203–208.

Penn, D., Guynan, K., Daily, T., Spalding, W., Garbin C. and Sullivan, M. (1994) 'Dispelling the stigma of schizophrenia. What sort of information is best?' *Schizophrenia Bulletin 20*, 567–574.

Philo, G., Henderson, L. and McLaughlin, G. (1993) *Mass Media Representations of Mental Health/Illness.* Glasgow: Glasgow University Media Group.

RAMH Education (1996) *The Renfrewshire Experience: School Mental Health Promotion.* Paisley, Renfrewshire: Association for Mental Health.

Roberts, M., Beidleman, W., and Wurtele, S. (1981) 'Children's perceptions of medical and psychological disorders in their peers.' *Journal of Clinical Child Psychology 10*, 76–78.

Roose, G. and John, A. (2003) 'A focus group investigation into young children's understanding of mental health and their views on appropriate services for their age group.' *Child: Care, Health and Development 29*, 545–550.

Sarlin, T. (1967) 'On the futility of the proposition that some people be labelled "mentally ill".' *Journal of Consulting Psychology 31*, 447–453.

Save the Children (2007) 'Child Asylum and Refugee Issues in Scotland: Mental Health Issues: Stigmas, Needs and Definitions.' Available at: www.savethechildren.org.uk/caris/legal, accessed on 14 February 2007.

Scott, S. and Lindsey, C. (2003) 'Therapeutic Approaches in Adoption.' In H. Argent (ed.) *Models of Adoption Support: What Works and What Doesn't.* London: British Association for Adoption & Fostering.

Scheff, T. (1966) *Being Mentally Ill: A Sociological Theory.* Chicago, IL: Aldine Publishing.

Sebuliba, D. and Vostanis, P. (2001) 'Child and adolescent mental health training for primary care staff.' *Clinical Child Psychology and Psychiatry 6*, 191–204.

Sieff, E. (2003) 'Media frames of mental illness: The potential of negative frames.' *Journal of Mental Health 12*, 250–269.

Sigelman, C., Thomas, E. and Whitworth, L. (1986) 'The early development of stigmatising reactions to physical difference.' *Journal of Applied Developmental Psychology 7*, 17–32.

Social Exclusion Unit (2004) *Mental Health and Social Exclusion.* London: ODPM.

Street, C. and Herts, B. (2005) *Putting participation into practice: a guide for practitioners working in services to promote the mental health and well-being of children and young people.* London: Young Minds.

Szasz, T. (1961) *The Myth of Mental Illness.* New York, NY: Hoeber.

Wahl, O. (1995) *Media Madness: Public Images of Mental Illness.* New Brunswick, NJ: Rutgers University Press.

Wahl, O. (1999) 'Mental health consumers' experience of stigma.' *Schizophrenia Bulletin 25*, 467–478.

Wahl, O. (2000) *Stigmatizing Media Images Affect Children.* USA: National Mental Health Association. Available at: www1.nmha.org/newsroom/stigma/wahl/index.fm, accessed on 07 July 2005.

Wahl, O. (2002) 'Children's views of mental illness: A review of the literature.' *Psychiatric Rehabilitation Skills 6*, 134–158.

Wahl, O. (2003) 'Depictions of mental illnesses in children's media.' *Journal of Mental Health 12*, 249–258.

Weiner, B., Magnusson, J. and Perry, R. (1988) 'An attributional analysis of reactions to stigmas.' *Journal of Personality and Social Psychology 55*, 738–748.

Weiss, M. (1980) 'Children's perceptions of stigmatised groups.' *Dissertation Abstracts International 41*, 5.

Weiss, M. (1985) 'Children's attitudes on mental illness as assessed by the opinions about mental illness scale.' *Psychological Reports 57*, 251–258.

Weiss, M. (1986) 'Children's attitudes toward the mentally ill: A developmental analysis.' *Psychological Reports 74*, 11–20.

Weiss, M. (1994) 'Children's attitudes toward the mentally ill: An eight-year follow-up. *Psychological Reports 74*, 51–56.

Welsh Assembly Government (2002) Adult Mental Health Services: A National Service Framework for Wales. Cardiff: Welsh Assembly Government.

Wilkins, J. and Velicer, W. (1980) 'A semantic differential investigation of children's attitudes toward three stigmatised groups.' *Psychology in the Schools 17*, 364–371.

Young Minds (2002) 'Three Surveys Highlighting Distress of Children and Families with Mental Health Problems.' Available at: www.youngminds.org.uk/press/02_10_10.php, accessed on 14 February 2007.

Young Minds (2005) *Minority Voices: A Guide to Good Practice in Planning and Providing Services for the Mental Health of Black and Minority Ethnic Young People.* London: Young Minds.

PART II

Applied Interventions for Vulnerable Children, Young People and their Carers

Interventions for Foster Carers and Adoptive Parents of Children Who Have Experienced Abuse and Trauma

Jeanette Allen

Let Me Be One of You
In a family who
Have a car, have fun, go away,
Eat popcorn in front of the telly.
Laugh and cry without cruelty or abuse
How can I be one of you?
How can you absorb one of me?
What do we need to make it happen?
Please approach with caution
It's not very easy to do.
Let me in then ring-fence your family
So I don't make you become my family.
Allow gradual access, but don't be fooled
For I will not trust you
Unless I see no weakness to exploit,
To make you reject me.
Hold me at a creative distance.
Do not respond to my chaos inducing anxiety.
Do not expect reciprocity.
Take a long view with patience and perspicacity.
Use humour and bribing.

Adapt to ignore the bad and promote the good.
Try every trick in the book and then some more.
Take the best from my family
And with luck, blood sweat and tears,
You will be rewarded with small acts of charity.

> *(Anon, from* Rattle Your Cool, *A collection of poetry and art*
> *by children and young people who are being looked after.*
> *Reproduced by kind permission of Foster Care Associates)*

Evidence and characteristics of needs
Needs of the children
Children come into local authority care for a variety of reasons; however, it is increasingly common that children entering the care system have been the victims of child abuse, neglect, sexual exploitation, and abandonment (Delaney 1998; Quinton *et al.* 1998). Indeed, virtually every foster child has experienced some loss, trauma, or disruption prior to placement in foster care (Delaney 1998). Scholfield *et al.* (2000) in a study of 58 children in long-term foster care, found that 90 per cent of them had a history of abuse or neglect, with 81 per cent having experienced three or more types of abuse.

Research has consistently shown that these children have significantly higher rates of mental health difficulties than children in the general population (McCann *et al.* 1996) and an especially high incidence of disruptive behaviours (Dimigen *et al.* 1999). This rate increases with placement instability, which can in turn contribute to mental health difficulties (Meltzer *et al.* 2003). This cycle can prove difficult to break (Sinclair, Gibbs and Wilson 2005; Ward *et al.* 2003). The risk for children placed as babies (between birth and six months) remains low; however, the risk increases with children being placed at older ages.

Many of the complex and challenging difficulties typically presented by children in substitute care are consistent with attachment difficulties and, indeed, many of these children are diagnosed as suffering a disorder of attachment (Howe and Fearnley 2003). Even in children placed for adoption (typically younger children with less severe needs), a substantial proportion find it difficult to form secure attachments (23%) (Rushton *et al.* 2003).

Impact of abuse and trauma on the developing child
The impact of abuse and trauma on children's psychological development has received growing interest over recent years, both clinically and in the research and academic fields. There is a range of theoretical models which may be useful in providing a framework for understanding how children develop behavioural

strategies which help them to survive situations of abuse and neglect, and how these may persist even when the child has been removed from that environment. (See Golding 2006, pp.200–218, for an outline of theoretical models.)

Childhood is a period of major changes in physical, emotional, social and cognitive development. Developmental models place a particular emphasis on the interaction between the child and their environment in co-determining the child's developmental progress (Stovall and Dozier 1998); in particular, the importance of the social context within which the infant is developing is emphasized in the research. Infants are born with an innate and sophisticated capacity to enter into a relationship (Hobson 1993), and it is the quality of the relationship with their primary caregiver that appears to be the single most influential factor in the child's development. The parent–child relationship is reciprocal and bi-directional, and provides the backdrop for children's development, hence the formation of relationships is the basic starting point for development (Oates 1994).

Within their early care environments, children develop strategies in order to elicit as much care and nurturance as is possible in that context. These strategies are highly adaptive and, in the case of abuse and neglect, are essential for survival. For example, physically abusive and rejecting environments, although highly stressful, are predictable and relatively consistent. Within such environments children learn that their needs are best met when they place very few demands on their carer, as any open expression of need by the child is likely to be met by hostility, rejection, or both. The strategies that children develop in such environments are based around deactivating their attachment behaviour, for example compulsive compliance, suppression, or denial of affect, self-reliance, power, and aggression (Crittendon 1995, 1997). Although this is an insecure (avoidant) pattern in attachment terms, owing to the predictability of such an environment children can organize their behaviour and emotions in an attempt to maximize parental availability and safety. In the case of neglectful environments the situation tends to be less predictable. At the milder end of the spectrum, parents are underinvolved and respond inconsistently to their child's signals of distress. In an environment where distress is responded to some of the time, the most adaptive strategy is to increase distress signals in order to lessen the chances of being abandoned and ignored.

However, many children experience environments in which there is a combination of abuse, neglect, rejection, and danger (Scholfield et al. 2000). These environments are highly unpredictable, therefore it is difficult for children to develop organized strategies to increase feelings of care and protection. Attachment behaviour in infants is a distress signal which serves the function of securing the return of the carer to meet the child's needs, and to reduce levels of anxiety and distress. However, in situations where it is the carer causing the child distress, the child faces an unresolvable conflict. Gaining proximity with the carer may actually increase fear and anxiety, leading to the child experiencing simultaneous feelings of escape and approach which cannot be resolved. In such environments there is no strategy that can increase feelings of care and protection, hence the behaviour is described as disorganized or disorientated. The behaviour of these children reflects high levels of unregulated distress, such as head-banging, repetitive behaviours, hyperactivity, bed-wetting and, particularly as children mature and develop overlays of organization based on other controlling strategies (see Howe *et al.* [1999] for a more detailed discussion on this subject), frantic attempts to control their environment, such as power-sensitive behaviour, compulsive care-giving, physical and verbal aggression. Disorganized attachments in infancy are most commonly seen in children whose parents are physically or sexually abusive, are heavy abusers of drugs or alcohol, are severely neglectful, chronically depressed, or victims of domestic violence, or any combination of these. Stovall and Dozier (1998) believe that although these strategies have helped children to survive in very difficult environments they can also mean that these children are unable to take advantage of new positive experiences in substitute care.

Many children entering into foster and adoptive care will, over time, form satisfactory relationships with their new carers (73%) (Rushton *et al.* 2003); however, for a sizeable minority this can be more difficult. Bowlby (1988) claimed that infants construct internal working models based on their experiences with their earliest attachment figures. Internal working models are theorized to contain core beliefs about the self, others, and relationships, and thus provide templates that set boundaries determining how relationships with other people are perceived and managed. Powerful new care experiences can, in some cases, be sufficient to challenge these internal working models. Nevertheless, as internal working models develop they become automatic, increasingly operating outside conscious awareness. New experiences tend to be assimilated into existing models; hence, children interpret, and therefore can misinterpret, their carers' motives and intentions based on their existing constructs.

Needs of the carers

Over the last decade, there has been a considerable shift in the philosophy and policies regarding the provision of care for children within local authorities in the UK, with a move away from residential care into family placements. Hence some of the most disadvantaged, vulnerable, and disturbed children are now cared for in family placements by foster carers or adoptive parents who often have limited access to professional support, including mental health services. Many studies have recognized the difficulties experienced by carers, and have highlighted the importance of external supports to enable them to continue the task of fostering (Schofield *et al.* 2000; Sinclair, Gibbs and Wilson 2000).

Delaney (1998) describes a cyclical relationship response between the child and their carer. He suggests that the continuing difficulties and conduct of children with a history of abuse and neglect can be confusing and bewildering for carers. Foster carers and adoptive parents then tend to misinterpret the child's behaviour as a sign that they are being rejected rather than understanding it as a communication of the child's anxiety and fear (see also Lieberman 2003). Alternatively, carers may begin to feel that their parenting strategies are ineffective, leading them to doubt their own abilities. Such systematic undermining of the confidence of carers can lead them to emotionally or literally reject the child, thus confirming the internal working models of the child.

A study by Allen and Vostanis (2005) highlighted the emotional impact on carers of caring for children with a history of abuse and neglect. Focus groups with foster carers revealed strong themes of self-doubt and self-blame for the lack of progress made by the child, and a sense of carers feeling rejected by the lack of genuine reciprocal emotion in the child.

> They can be so cruel to their children and so neglectful, but if they [the children] have known their parents for any length of time…[sigh]…. If someone came to him tomorrow and said "get your cases, you're going back to mummy", he'd be in that car and barely bother to wave goodbye. (*Foster carer*)

> I feel like I've failed. (*Foster carer*)

This emotional response among carers and parents of children who are making slow progress is common. In part, the sadness and grief experienced by carers is an understandable reaction to caring for a child who so clearly seems to be struggling and, in many cases, seems to reflect genuine empathy for the child. However, the strong sense of personal failure and self-doubt also seems to reflect a lack of understanding as to why the child's difficulties may persist over time. In addition, there seems to be a, albeit significantly smaller, group of parents and carers who are much more sensitive to interpreting their children's behaviour either as a personal failure or a personal rejection, and the emotional reaction of these carers seems much more intense. Fosha (2000) highlighted the importance of carers' abilities to understand and emotionally attune to the child, in order for the child to be able to face and tolerate intense emotions:

> When attachment figures cannot support the child so that he feels safe in feeling his feeling, affective experiences can threaten to overwhelm the integrity of the self and relationships. When faced alone, they can become unbearable. (Fosha 2000, p.5)

An interesting study by Kaniuk, Steel, and Hodges (2004) explored the development of attachment between a group of 63 late-adopted (age 4–8 years) children with their adopted parents over the first two years of placement. In addition to measuring children's attachment representations, adopters' attachment styles were measured to establish the impact on the children's progress. Although the study found that the control group (48 children placed in infancy) had significantly fewer difficulties than the late-placed children, positive outcomes were also reported for the late-placed children, with 83 per cent showing marked progress in their attachments to their adoptive mothers, and in their overall emotional adjustment, within the first two years of placement. Interestingly, 17 per cent of the late-placed children who failed to make any progress in terms of developing more secure attachment representations to their adoptive mothers were all placed with mothers who had themselves experienced unhappy childhoods and had not been able to process and move on from these experiences and, thus, were all assessed as having an unresolved attachment style at the beginning of the study. These mothers were unable to focus on the children's needs, and more often reported to feel rejected and hurt by their children's behaviour. This striking finding suggests that, although there may well be factors in the child's background that may make it difficult for them to make use of new experiences (e.g. extent of abuse or neglect, age at placement, number of previous placements), a further highly influential factor affecting the child's ability to make progress is the carer's emotional adjustment.

Case vignette

Claire was a 12-year-old girl who had a history of severe physical and sexual abuse. She was removed into local authority care when she was nine years old, when evidence emerged that her mother and father were part of a paedophile ring who had abused countless children, including Claire. Claire was placed with a foster carer and generally the placement was a positive one. The foster carer was very supportive and responded in a very emotionally containing and levelled way to the majority of Claire's behaviours, including sexualized behaviour and self-harm.

However, the foster carer found it incredibly difficult to manage Claire when she told lies. The foster carer tended not to understand this behaviour as reflective of Claire's anxiety and fear, but misinterpreted it as Claire being 'naughty, defiant, and ungrateful'. Claire's placement was at risk of breakdown owing to this issue, with the foster carer stating that unless Claire changed her 'attitude', she would have to go.

The foster carer herself had a 'care history', having lived both in foster care as a young child and later residential care as a teenager. She talked of her experiences of her own birth mother regularly missing contact visits with her, despite promising she would attend, and how devastated she had been when this happened. She referred to her birth mother as a 'bloody liar' and stated she couldn't tolerate 'liars'.

Existing knowledge of effective interventions

Sinclair *et al.* (2000) suggest that the two most common causes of placement breakdown are difficult behaviour of the child and foster carer's lack of confidence to manage the child. Improving the skills and confidence of foster carers to manage the complex difficulties of children in their care has therefore been seen as fundamental to placement stability and positive care outcomes (Hill-Tout, Pithouse, and Lowe 2003). Training for foster carers is seen as an important part of preparing them for and supporting them with the task of fostering (Sellick and Thoburn 1996). However, the value of parent-training programmes with carers and parents of children who have a history of abuse and trauma has not been extensively evaluated.

There have been a number of parent-training programmes developed for birth parents of children displaying problematic behaviours, which have been systematically and comprehensively evaluated as demonstrating positive lasting effects. There is, however, very limited evidence that such training programmes have any such effect on families where there is a risk of abuse (Dadds 1995; Webster-Stratton 1998). This raises fundamental questions about the usefulness of assuming that children's behaviour problems have a common cause, and the effectiveness of applying one model of intervention as standard.

Children who are being cared for by the local authority typically have a history of abuse and trauma, and therefore such parent-training programmes may not be effective for the needs of foster carers and children in their care. The evidence for the generalizability of these parent-training programmes to this population is scarce and that which is available shows mixed results. Minnis and Devine (2001), in a randomized controlled trial of 121 foster families, found no clear evidence of the impact of carer training programmes on foster children's emotional and behavioural functioning. They did, however, report that the training was perceived as a positive experience by foster carers. Similarly, Hill-Tout *et al.* (2003) concluded that, although foster carers reported being highly satisfied with the training, there was no clear evidence that it was effective.

Pallett *et al.* (2002) reported more promising results of a 10-week cognitive behavioural group for foster carers, finding significant improvements in carer–child interaction and in the child's emotional well-being. There was, however, no clear evidence of improvement in the children's conduct problems. Some intensive interventions, such as Treatment Foster Care, have been found to have benefits (Chamberlain 2003), but these treatment programmes target a small number of children with the most severe needs, hence it is difficult to draw conclusions about how useful or indeed practical such interventions would be with the general population of looked-after children or those who have been adopted.

Typically, parent-training programmes have been heavily based on techniques underpinned by social learning theory; however, it is well recognized that traditional parenting skills may need adapting in order to meet the needs of children with attachment difficulties consistent with a history of abuse and trauma (Hughes 1997). Although skill-based training is almost certainly one element towards improving the confidence of carers, and many previous foster care programmes have focused heavily on providing this (Hill-Tout *et al.* 2003), Allen and Vostanis (2005) suggest that perhaps in doing so, such programmes have overlooked other factors contributing to carers' lack of confidence. In their study of a group of carers attending a foster care training programme, they reported that foster carers were, in general, a very experienced, resourceful, and skilled group. However, at the beginning of the programme the carers reported feeling overwhelmed and ill-equipped to deal with the children placed in their care and, when asked what they wanted out of the programme, requested behaviour management strategies. The authors suggested that the carers' lack of confidence in their parenting ability was not necessarily related to their parenting skills, but rather, came primarily from their lack of understanding as to why children's difficulties persist, leading them to ultimately blame themselves and doubt their own ability. Supporting this suggestion is the evidence that interventions which aim to increase carers' understanding and sensitivity to their child have shown positive results in terms of reducing attachment disorganization (Cohen *et al.* 1999; Juffer, Bakermans-Kranenburg, and Van Ijzendoorn 2005).

Golding and Picken (2004) reported on parent-training programmes with foster carers in which the traditional programme was extended and adapted to explore issues relevant to caring for looked-after children, in particular, issues regarding the impact of trauma and of attachment. The evaluation of this foster-care training programme revealed that carers developed a better understanding of children's difficulties and a better relationship with the child in their care. In addition, foster carers reported the child to be less difficult and to be displaying fewer conduct problems.

Recent research provides some, albeit limited, evidence that training for foster carers and adoptive parents primarily from an attachment perspective, which would also incorporate the principles of positive parenting, may be more effective in meeting the needs of foster carers and children in their care, in terms of providing both a conceptual understanding and parenting skills. There are clearly areas of significant overlap between a parent-training programme underpinned by social learning theory and one underpinned by attachment theory. Both approaches would advocate consistent, calm, and sensitive responding, without hostility, to the child's problematic behaviour. The principles relating to a positive parenting approach to behaviour management are, therefore, also likely to foster warmth and attachment between the carer and the child. This may account for the conflicting evidence for the effectiveness of the use of parent-training programmes initially devised for birth parents with foster carers.

How should we adapt parenting interventions for foster carers and adoptive parents?

Interventions with foster carers and adoptive parents need, as in any clinical case-work, to be individualized to the needs of the particular child within that family system, hence based on a comprehensive assessment and formulation.

However, the evidence to date suggests that certain core elements are likely to be common recurring themes. Consequently, interventions with foster carers or adoptive parents of children who have a history of abuse and trauma are likely to need to include the following key areas:

1. A provision of a conceptual framework to help the carer or parent understand the child's difficulties and why these may persist over time.

2. Acknowledgement of the emotional impact on carers or parents of children with traumatic histories, and opportunity for the carers or parents to explore their emotional reactions, which should include their own attachment history.

3. Practical day-to-day parenting advice or strategies.

These areas can, of course, be covered with carers and parents on an individual basis and certainly, in terms of helping carers reflect on their own emotional responses, there are clear benefits to doing this within a safe, contained therapeutic relationship. However, there is also considerable evidence of the value of group work, and many clinicians working in this area have reported that not only is group work an effective use of limited resources, but participants gain a huge amount of support from each other, and from the knowledge that they are not alone in their experiences.

Case vignette

Jayne had adopted Jake, now aged six, when he was two years old. Jake had a history of severe neglect and physical abuse. Although Jake had made significant development progress since living with Jayne, she reported that he remained an independent child and she felt hurt and rejected by his resistance to her nurturance and care. Jayne believed that Jake did not love her, and was wondering if he would be happier if placed with another family. Jayne was on antidepressants and talked about feeling she was a failure as a parent. Following completion of a seven-session group course on the impact of abuse and trauma, Jayne stated that the most useful part of the course for her had been hearing other people's experiences and realizing that she was not alone. She laughingly commented, 'Maybe it isn't my fault after all. Perhaps I am a good mum.'

Jayne felt committed to continuing to work to improve her relationship with Jake and was able to engage in further work with CAMH services.

Practice recommendations

The following practice recommendations are based on clinical experience of facilitating group-based parenting interventions for foster carers and adoptive parents over a number of years. As with all clinical work, the process of reflecting and altering the way we work is a dynamic one, based on current knowledge, experience, and feedback from participants.

Content of the group

As previously outlined, the group content should include the provision of a conceptual framework to help participants understand their child's difficulties and opportunities to reflect on their own emotional response to caring for a child with a traumatic history, as well as more practical issues around day-to-day parenting. The balance between theory and practice is crucial, and the group should not be too academic and theoretical, as this would risk alienating carers and parents whose learning style does not fit with this model. Attachment theory is inherently practical, and it would be a great shame if the essence of this is lost in discussions around the complexities of, for example, the classification of attachment 'styles'. Similarly, the use of the term 'reactive attachment disorder' as a label needs to be used with extreme caution, if it is felt necessary to use it at all. A debate about the usefulness of this as a diagnostic label is beyond the scope of this chapter (but please see *Attachment and Human Development,* Vol. 5, No. 3, 2003 for a discussion on this topic). Clinical experience suggests that this label can detract from the message that the carer's emotional response to the child is crucial, and can serve to further pathologize and alienate the child within the family environment.

Example of group content

A seven-session group intervention programme: the impact of abuse and trauma on the developing child

The training pack was written (Allen 2002) based on the ideas of a number of researchers, authors, and therapists (Schore 1994; Hughes 1997; Delaney 1998; Howe *et al.*1999; Golding 2001).

SESSION 1: IMPACT OF ABUSE AND TRAUMA ON THE CHILD'S VIEW OF THE WORLD

The background to attachment theory as a theory of child development is briefly introduced. The development of different attachment styles is presented as adaptive to early care environments as the child attempts to elicit as much care as is possible from their environment. The concept of internal working models (referred to as 'blueprints') is introduced. Video clips and case material are used to encourage participants to consider how the internal working models of children would differ significantly depending on their early care experiences, and how these children will consequently vary in how they perceive relationships and the intentions and motives of others.

SESSION 2: IMPACT OF ABUSE AND TRAUMA ON CHILD DEVELOPMENT
Child development is covered with an emphasis on the crucial role of the attachment figure in providing experiences necessary for healthy development. Video clips and case material are used to encourage participants to explore how trauma and neglect affect child development, in particular the development of emotional regulation and reflective function.

SESSION 3: EMOTIONAL IMPACT ON THE CARER
Group discussions and exercises are used to encourage the participants to reflect on the emotional impact of caring for children with complex difficulties and how they could manage their own emotional response to the child. Participants are encouraged to reflect of their own experience of being parented, and how this influences their values, beliefs, and expectations as carers or parents.

SESSIONS 4–7: PRACTICAL IMPLICATIONS FOR PARENTING
The model of parenting covered is that suggested by Hughes (1997). The main areas covered are providing a positive family atmosphere, building positive relationships with children in which missed developmental experiences can be provided, responding to difficult behaviour, and managing rage. There is a particular emphasis on emotional attunement. Also stressed is discipline, with empathy and an attitude to parenting that is conducive to the development of secure attachments. A combination of teaching, group exercises, and group discussions are used.

Together or apart?

SHOULD FOSTER CARERS AND ADOPTIVE PARENTS BE PLACED TOGETHER IN A GROUP?
Throughout this chapter, foster carers and adoptive parents have been discussed collectively. However, when delivering group-based parenting interventions it is important to consider the usefulness, or not, of placing foster carers and adoptive parents together in a group. Although there are often clear similarities in terms of the types of children placed in foster care and children released for adoption, and hence many common issues, foster carers and adopters are certainly not a homogenous group, and the differences between them need to be acknowledged.

There is a continuum of 'care' provision from foster carers to adoptive parents. At one end are foster carers who very much see themselves as professional carers and may offer time-limited or task-focused placements, such as parent and child placements or placements preparing children for adoption. The outlook and identity of such carers seems far more closely aligned to other professionals working with looked-after children, such as supervising social workers. At the other end of the continuum are adoptive parents who are, of course, legally the child's parents, but whom also want to be seen as 'normal' parents, and may find it difficult and perhaps even offensive to be grouped with people who view themselves as professional carers. There are also many foster carers and perhaps even some adoptive parents who fall between these two extremes, for example foster carers who have been approved for a particular child, or those who are offering long-term placements and may see themselves as 'parenting' the child.

The issue of participants' identity as either parents or carers is highlighted by the response of participants to offering places on the group to supervising social workers. The model of providing training for foster carers alongside their supervising social workers has been recommended by Hill-Tout *et al.* (2003), and reports by foster carers have been favourable in terms of helping develop a supportive relationship with their supervising social worker and providing a sense of team-working (Allen and Vostanis 2005). This is in stark contrast to the response of many adoptive parents who feel anxious and silenced by the presence of social workers, feeling they are being assessed and judged by them.

Clinical experience suggests that adoptive parents, in particular, seem to benefit far more from group-based parenting interventions when they are not placed with foster carers or other professionals. It seems to be more therapeutic for adopters to be seen as a group of parents. This format can facilitate a greater sense of safety to reflect on the emotional impact on themselves as parents, and to bring up issues such as infertility, loss, and grief, which, although not unique to adoptive parents, are more likely to be salient issues for this group.

Implementation on a day-to-day basis

A major component of any intervention with a carer or parent of a child who has experienced abuse and trauma is the provision of a conceptual framework to help them understand their child's difficulties as reflective of anxiety and fear. Compassion, empathy, and emotional attunement are vital in the development of secure attachments, and without a good understanding of the feelings underlying their child's behaviour, carers or parents are unable to respond sensitively.

Although clear in theory, in practice many group members find these concepts difficult to grasp. This appears to be influenced by both the emotional literacy of carers or parents and also, particularly in the case of foster carers, by previous training experiences. Typically, foster care preparation training includes training on managing challenging behaviour. The shift away from managing behaviours per se to managing emotions can feel like a very significant change, and a lot of work may be needed to help participants understand how this principle may be put into practice. It may well therefore be much more useful to emphasize a general approach to parenting rather than providing absolute behaviour management strategies, which without a clear understanding can be applied inappropriately.

Case vignette

Jean was a foster carer of some 20 years, who had a wealth of experience in terms of the number of children she had cared for. Jean had previously attended training on managing challenging behaviour, where she had been taught to ignore difficult behaviour and to respond positively to appropriate behaviour.

Jean found it difficult to make links between the child's experiences and how that might make them feel. At one stage during the group, she asked the facilitators to write a list of feelings on the flipchart, saying she didn't really know what feelings were. Consequently she tended to interpret all children's difficult behaviour as 'attention-seeking', and managed it by ignoring it.

Following the session on responding to difficult behaviour with empathy, Jean returned to the group the next week and reported, 'I tried that empathy thing and it doesn't work.' When asked to explain, Jean spoke of an incident where the young boy she was caring for was trashing his room following his birth mother failing to attend contact. Jean stated she responded to him by saying 'I know you're angry but I'm not bothered, you won't get a reaction from me by doing that, I'm going to ignore you.' Following this, the boy's behaviour escalated.

One way of encouraging group members to relate the concepts to their own child is through group discussion and exercises, helping them to come up with an individualized formulation for their child. The text below shows how, over a number of sessions, participants can slowly begin to build up the links between their child's past experiences, internal working models, feelings, and behaviours.

Carers' or parents' own emotional reaction to the child

It is important to be clear about the function of this type of group programme in terms of whether it is defined as a training or therapeutic intervention. If the programme is predominantly perceived as educational, then it would be unethical to expect participants to engage in exercises that are personal in nature. Although there are, of course, clear ethical considerations if the programme is defined as a therapeutic intervention, the ongoing involvement of a clinician who can follow up any issues that arise provides more scope to encourage self-reflection in a way that can be appropriately contained. Thought needs to be given as to at what stage clinicians may wish to advise a carer or parent to seek therapeutic help in their own right, and what services would be available should this be required.

Encouraging self-reflection can be done in a variety of ways, such as small group exercises, group discussions, and individual homework tasks (e.g. writing own autobiography). Careful consideration needs to be given to issues such as confidentiality, the number of participants, and the group mix (e.g. many foster carers know each other and are part of the same networks), to ensure that participants feel comfortable about discussing personal information. It is important that participants are aware of what, if anything, they are expected to feed back to the group, that is, content or process, to ensure no-one feels coerced into sharing more than they would have wished to.

Conclusions

Many children entering local authority care have been traumatized within the context of an attachment relationship. Helping such children develop new powerful attachment relationships is therefore a vital component in the resolution of their early experiences, but the needs of both parties in the relationship must be considered. Supporting foster carers and adoptive parents relating to children who resist new relationship experiences is fundamental in helping the children make developmental progress. Providing day-to-day parenting skills is one element of this support, but the needs of carers or parents suggest that support should be more comprehensive, including a conceptual framework to understand the child and an opportunity for carers or parents to reflect on their own emotional issues and their impact on the dyadic relationship.

References

Allen, J. (2002) *The Impact of Abuse and Trauma on the Developing Child – A Training Programme for Foster Carers and Supervising Social Workers.* University of Leicester: CAMH Service.

Allen, J. and Vostanis, P. (2005) 'The impact of abuse and trauma on the developing child: An evaluation of a training programme for foster carers and supervising social workers.' *Adoption and Fostering 29*, 68–81.

Bowlby, J.A. (1988) *A Secure Base: Clinical Applications of Attachment Theory.* London: Routledge.

Chamberlain, P. (2003) 'The Oregon Multidimensional Treatment Foster Care model.' *Cognitive and Behavioural Practice 10*, 303–312.

Cohen, N., Muir E., Partker, C.J., Brown, M., Lojkasek, M., Muir, R. and Barwick, M. (1999) 'Watch, wait and wonder: Testing the effectiveness of a new approach to mother–infant psychotherapy.' *Infant Mental Health Journal 20*, 429–451.

Crittenden, P. (1995) 'Attachment and Psychopathology.' In S. Goldberg, R. Muir and J. Kerr (eds) *Attachment Theory: Social, Developmental and Clinical Perspectives.* Hillsdale, NJ: Analytic Press.

Crittenden, P. (1997). 'Truth, Error, Omission, Distortion and Deception: The Application of Attachment Theory to the Assessment and Treatment of Psychological Disorder.' In S. Dollinger and L. Di Lalla (eds) *Assessment and Intervention Issues Across the Lifespan.* Mahwaeh, NJ: Erlbaum.

Dadds, M. (1995) *Families, Children and the Development of Dysfunction.* Thousand Oaks: Sage.

Delaney, R. (1998) *Fostering Changes: Treating Attachment-disordered Foster Children.* Oklahoma City, OK: Wood and Barnes Publishing.

Dimigen, G., Del Priore, C., Butler, S,. Evans, S., Ferguson, L. and Swan, M. (1999) 'Psychiatric disorder among children at time of entering local authority care: questionnaire survey.' *British Medical Journal 319*, 675.

Fosha, D. (2000) *The Transforming Power of Affect.* New York, NY: Basic Books.

Golding, K. (2001) *Fostering Attachments in Looked After Children: Attachment Theory and Intervention – a Group for Foster Carers.* Unpublished document.

Golding, K. (2006) 'Finding the Light at the End of the Tunnel: Parenting Interventions for Adoptive and Foster Carers.' In K. Golding, H. Dent, R. Nissim and L. Stott (eds) *Thinking Psychologically About Children Who Are Looked-after and Adopted.* Chichester: John Wiley & Sons.

Golding, K. and Picken, W. (2004) 'Group work for foster carers caring for children with complex problems.' *Adoption and Fostering 28*, 25–37.

Hill-Tout, J., Pithouse, A. and Lowe, K. (2003) 'Training foster carers in a preventive approach to children who challenge: mixed messages from research.' *Adoption and Fostering 27*, 47–56.

Hobson, R. (1993) *Autism and the Development of the Mind.* Hove: Lawrence Erlbaum.

Howe, D., Brandon, M., Hinings, D. and Schofield, G. (1999) *Attachment Theory, Child Maltreatment and Family Support: A Practice and Assessment Model.* Basingstoke: Macmillan.

Howe, D. and Fearnley, S. (2003) 'Disorder of attachment in adopted and fostered children: Recognition and treatment.' *Clinical Child Psychology and Psychiatry 8*, 369–387.

Hughes, D. (1997) *Facilitating Developmental Attachment: The Road to Recovery and Behavioural Change in Foster and Adopted Children.* London: Aronson.

Juffer, F., Babermans-Kranenburg M. and Van Ijzendoorn, M. (2005) 'The importance of parenting in the development of disorganized attachment: evidence form a preventative study in adoptive families.' *Journal of Child Psychology and Psychiatry 46*, 263–274.

Kaniuk, J., Steele, M. and Hodges, J. (2004) 'Report on a longitudinal research project exploring the development of attachments between older, hard-to-place children and their adopters over the first two years of placement.' *Adoption and Fostering 28*, 61–67.

Lieberman, A. (2003) 'The treatment of attachment disorder in infancy and early child-hood: Reflections from clinical intervention with later-adopted foster care children.' *Attachment and Human Development 5*, 279–282.

McCann, J., James, A., Wilson, S. and Dunn, G. (1996) 'Prevalence of psychiatric disorders in young people in the care system.' *British Medical Journal 313*, 1529–1530.

Meltzer, H., Gatward R., Corbin, T., Goodman, R. and Ford, T. (2003) *The Mental Health of Young People Looked-after by Local Authorities in England.* London: HMSO.

Minnis, H. and Devine, C. (2001) 'The effect of foster care training on the emotional and behavioural functioning of looked-after children.' *Adoption and Fostering 25*, 44–54.

Oates, J. (1994) *The Foundations of Child Development.* Oxford: Blackwell.

Pallett, C., Scott ,S., Blackeby, K., Yule, W. and Weissman (2002). 'Fostering changes: a cognitive behavioural approach to help foster carers manage their children.' *Adoption and Fostering 26*, 39–48.

Quinton, D., Rushton, A., Dance, C. and Mayes, D. (1998) *Joining New Families: A Study of Adoption and Fostering in Middle Childhood.* Chichester: John Wiley & Sons.

Rushton, A., Mayes, D., Dance, C. and Quinton, D. (2003) 'Parenting late-placed children: the development of new relationships and the challenge of behavioural problems.' *Clinical Child Psychology and Psychiatry 8*, 389–400.

Scholfield, G., Beek, M., Sargent, K. and Thoburn, J. (2000) *Growing Up in Foster Care.* London: British Association for Adoption & Fostering (BAAF).

Schore, A.N. (1994) *Affect Regulation and the Origin of the Self.* Hillsdale, NJ: Lawrence Erlbaum.

Sellick, C. and Thoburn, J. (1996) *What Works in Family Placements?* Barkingside: Barnardo's.

Sinclair, I., Gibbs, I. and Wilson, K. (2000) *Supporting Foster Placements.* Reports 1 and 2, Social Work Research and Development Unit.

Sinclair, I., Wilson, K. and Gibbs, I. (2005) *Foster Placements: Why they Succeed and Why they Fail.* London: Jessica Kingsley Publishers.

Stovall, K. and Dozier, M. (1998) 'Infants in foster care: an attachment theory perspective.' *Adoption Quarterly 12,* 55–88.

Ward, H., Munro, E., Dearden, C. and Nicholson, D. (2003) *Outcomes for Looked-after Children: Life Pathways and Decision-Making for Very Young Children in Care.* Loughborough University: Centre for Child and Family Research.

Webster-Stratton, C. (1998) 'From parent training to community building: families in society.' *Families in Society 78,* 156–171.

Webster-Stratton, C. and Hancock, L. (1998) 'Parent Training for Parents of Young Children with Conduct Problems: Context, Networks and Therapeutic Processes.' In J. Briesmeister and C. Schaefer (eds) *Handbook of Parent Training: Parents as Co-therapists for Children's Behaviour* (2nd ed) Chichester: John Wiley & Sons.

CHAPTER 7

Therapeutic Issues in Working Individually with Vulnerable Children and Young People

Vicki Edwards

Whilst there is a wealth of literature on working therapeutically with children and young people, there is little consideration of the therapeutic issues that may arise when working with vulnerable children and young people. These issues may overlap with children who are not deemed vulnerable, but this chapter will outline some of the issues that are significant to this particular group of children and young people. Pertinent to these children is that therapy does not occur within a stable, supportive family background. The majority of these children have a history of abuse and neglect, and they have experienced multiple placements throughout their childhood. They also frequently face an uncertain and unpredictable future. Therapy with these children must consider this past, present, and future context.

Although the issues considered in this chapter are not related to any one particular type of therapeutic intervention, it is written from a psychodynamic perspective. Psychodynamic theory considers the importance of developmental experiences and how life experiences shape the way that humans relate to one another. Psychodynamic theory provides us with a framework for thinking about and understanding vulnerable children, helping them to make sense of their own lives, past and present, and how their traumatic experiences shape them, and affect their emotional and behavioural world (Stone 2006). Vulnerable children and young people desperately need safe, secure relationships with adults, and psychodynamic theory considers the therapeutic relationship to be central to recovery. However, it is proposed here that the therapeutic issues considered within this chapter can, and should be, considered within any therapeutic model that is used when working with vulnerable children and young people.

This chapter will discuss issues relating to therapeutic engagement, the emotional impact on the therapist, and timing of therapy, followed by issues within the therapeutic process.

Engagement

Therapeutic engagement with children and young people can be fraught with difficulties; children can often be coerced into attending sessions, being delivered to the therapist by a parent or guardian. Children who are vulnerable may already feel so disempowered that they do not feel they can refuse to attend, so they may attend reluctantly; consequently, a reluctant child is a difficult child to engage (Barish 2004). Vulnerable children and young people are most likely to have had very poor past experiences with adults: parents, foster carers, and professionals such as police, social workers, or mental health workers. In addition, the stigma of mental health is great for young people, especially those who may live in residential units where little information is confidential among the other young people and kudos is all-important. Much work needs to be carried out within residential units in general about de-stigmatizing mental health problems.

Children and young people with attachment issues may experience particular difficulties engaging with the therapist, as their early experience of relationships is most likely to have been negative. Relationships with adults are likely to be affected by feelings of mistrust, fear, and unpredictability (Hughes 2004). Vulnerable children and young people often lack a safe, secure base outside the therapeutic relationship, and do not experience containment following sessions. Thereby, they also lack the opportunity to process the content of often emotionally painful sessions external to the therapeutic relationship. They may experience conflicting feelings of wanting to engage with an adult whom they begin to perceive as caring for them, but also fear that they will become too dependent or lose this relationship. This fear of losing a significant relationship may lead to premature ending.

Vulnerable children and young people may feel that they cannot trust another adult, and this trust will be tested regularly during therapy. They may have lengthy hypothetical discussions about what would happen if they disclosed information, they might display a pattern of irregular attendance, or testing of boundaries. Re-enactment of previous abusive relationships may also occur.

There is a need to be creative about engaging these young people. Greater tolerance may be needed for non-attendance, and the usual policy of non-attendance may have to be revised. In addition, the initial stages of engagement may take many months to form, and the therapist may need to meet the young person at their home or residential unit initially. Frequently, young people may attend for several sessions then take a break for a variety of reasons such as intolerance of emotional pain brought about by therapy, life circumstances taking over, or testing of boundaries. The therapist will need to be flexible and progress at the child's pace.

Therefore, there is a need to make use of whatever the child presents with at that time. Banister (2003, p.14) reflects that this is 'the key to successful therapy, even if that means things moved at a slower pace'. Doing this requires that we are flexible, pay close attention to non-verbal communication, and, at times, just be able to be with the child in a stable, containing, and nurturing way. For the child who has experienced so little care and nurturing, we cannot underestimate the power of being attended to just as they are.

Case vignette

Rosie had experienced many placement breakdowns over her 12 years. She had an extremely abusive and neglectful early childhood, and presented as a very detached, self-contained girl. A placement that initially appeared to be going well, and one that within which she had built up a trusting relationship, came to an abrupt end. She attended the following session in a detached, almost unreachable regressed state. This was in contrast to other sessions, during which active consideration of her past had occurred. During this session, I read fairy tales and played quiet games with her. It was a calm subdued session, where I allowed her to be and she lay curled on the chair like a small child. I believe during this session she allowed herself to experience being nurtured. In subsequent sessions, she was able to re-engage more actively, though at times of extreme stress she allowed herself to regress and be nurtured in this way. These periods of quietness seemed to allow her to take respite from her overwhelming emotions and then engage again.

Supporting systems, such as residential units, schools, youth offending services, or social services departments, that the child or young person may be involved with may need to be engaged in the therapeutic process. The initial stages of engagement may require an educational approach to be taken with regard to destigmatizing mental health problems, educating carers about the impact of abuse and trauma, and the management of emotional and behavioural difficulties. Involving other systems and carers will ensure that the child or young person experiences a sense of containment outside the therapeutic session.

Case vignette

Natasha was 15 when she was referred to therapy. After not attending several appointments, her case was closed. However, several months later, a further referral was received. In light of her previous non-attendance, a worker went out to the residential unit where Natasha lived. An informal discussion was held with her regarding her feelings about attending CAMH services. Natasha had had previous contact with the mental health system whilst witnessing her mother being sectioned several times, and she felt that attendance at CAMH services may result in her being sectioned too, or labelled as 'mad' by staff or other residents. Several sessions were spent exploring these views, and this was followed by informal educational sessions to staff and the other young people in the unit about understanding and dealing with mental health problems.

Emotional impact on the therapist

Transference and counter-transference levels are high when working with this group of children and young people. 'Transference' relates to the feelings the client has about the therapist, usually transferred from past relationships. 'Counter-transference' relates to the feelings evoked in the therapist by the client, either because it is a natural reaction to the client and client information, or transferred from another relationship in the therapist's previous experience or current life.

The high degree of counter-transference may be related to the significant levels of both primary and secondary trauma experienced by children in care, rendering them extremely vulnerable. In particular, the frequent experience of loss and abuse by parents, both physically and psychologically, may evoke a parental dynamic between the child and therapist. Counter-transferential feelings of sadness, loss, desire to rescue, disempowerment, and hopelessness may thus arise as part of the therapeutic process (Oaklander 1978). It is important to process these emotions in order to meet the child's needs, and also to protect the therapist's own psychological well-being.

These children in particular carry traumatic experiences which can be difficult for the therapist. The desire to heroically rescue these children when it appears that they have been failed by other systems or services can lead to collusion or avoidance. The therapist may fail to acknowledge all parts of a child, for example avoiding seeing the part of an abused child who abuses or bullies others (Weston 2006). Supervision encourages the therapist to connect with all aspects of a child, and thereby consider the most effective intervention. Pearlman and MacIan (1995) discuss the need to be aware of and avoid vicarious traumatization, whereby the therapist becomes contaminated by the client's material, and begins to experience signs and symptoms of post-traumatic stress themself. This is not an uncommon experience for a therapist working with trauma. Clinical and peer supervision are essential parts of the therapeutic work with this client group.

Supervision also provides an opportunity to review therapeutic progress, to consider the original goals of therapy, and avoid continuous changes in a direction that might arise from external pressures, rather than client-led changes. Pressure may be exerted by other agencies or services that find themselves struggling with immediate crises, such as acute behavioural changes, placement breakdowns, or poor resources. They may attempt to direct therapy in a way that would be helpful to them, but not necessarily in a way that is helpful to the child. Supervision provides an opportunity to reflect on who is directing therapy, since external pressures may be subtle.

Timing of therapy

Placement stability is often thought of as a prerequisite to therapy. Referrals for children whose future is uncertain, whether it is about placing them into care initially, transitions from placement to placement, or dealing with difficult behaviours that are threatening the placement, may often be deemed 'inappropriate'. The therapeutic response is often one that recommends a period of stability first. Therapeutic work can be difficult to undertake when the child has no anchor outside the therapeutic relationship. In addition, the anxiety that uncertainty creates often leaves the child with little space to reflect on their life experiences. Without containment and support, the child may find it difficult to engage in therapy. Referrers often feel that this is a 'Catch 22' situation; unless the child's behaviour improves then the placement will break down.

However, Hunter (2001) suggested that short-term psychoanalytic therapy can be useful in helping children to manage transitional periods. Lanyado (2003) recommended staying with the 'here and now', permitting the child an opportunity to deal with their current anxieties about multiple possible moves and losses. Alternatively, contracts may be agreed upon with foster families, that they will agree to maintain the placement whilst the child is in therapy, thus allowing the opportunity for change within a secure base. Foster carers may require their own ongoing support to tolerate emotional and behavioural difficulties that might occur during the process of therapy (Allen and Vostanis 2005).

When considering the timing of therapy, it is essential to take into account the most apparent needs of the child at that time. It may be more important initially for the child to develop a coherent narrative of their life. Often, vulnerable children have experienced multiple moves or placements and have a fragmented sense of themselves and their lives. Life story work may involve completing a book with the child to provide them with a factual narrative of their life, or it may be a process of 'unravelling confusion and discarding some of the negative baggage' (Connor et al. 1985). This piece of work may need to be undertaken prior to therapy, or considered alongside therapy. The therapist may decide to explore the process of the child's life journey, whilst the child's social worker provides a factual account of their life thus far.

It is imperative that while considering the need for, and timing of, therapy agencies collaborate and provide joint working where necessary. This may be life story work, training, or support. Often, therapy can and should take place alongside other interventions. The commencement of therapy should not lead to other agencies withdrawing or relying on therapy to 'fix' the child. An assessment of a child should clarify expectations of therapy and consider the most appropriate level of intervention and who should deliver this.

Case vignette

Josh was a nine-year-old boy referred to CAMH services to help him deal with past and impending losses. His current foster carers were unsure if they could maintain his placement unless his behaviour improved. The dilemma was that his foster carers wanted his behaviour to improve, which was possible through long-term therapy, but if his behaviour deteriorated, as was possible whilst in therapy, they would probably end the placement. The therapeutic dilemma related to the ethics of starting a process which, although beneficial in the long term, may in the short term cause his placement to break down. It was agreed that in order for Josh to benefit from therapy he would need a secure containing base. A contract was agreed between the foster carers and the Social Services department, that they would maintain the placement for at least one year, even if Josh's behaviour deteriorated at times, whilst therapeutic work was undertaken. It was also agreed that direct work with the foster carers would be undertaken to support them in caring for Josh.

The process of therapy

Issues relating directly to the therapeutic process: confidentiality, setting boundaries, working with defences and endings, are considered below.

Confidentiality

Some children or young people may want their carer or another adult to attend sessions with them. This might only be for the initial part of the therapy or for feedback at the end of the session. Sometimes the young person will want the therapist to feed back issues that have arisen, and act as their advocate with regard to ways of managing their behaviour or dealing with their emotions. Involving others in sessions has implications for confidentiality. Confidentiality becomes three- rather than two-way if the work involves the carer (Golding *et al.* 2006). The issue of confidentiality is of particular importance to this group of children and young people, as, for many of them, much of their history, background, and personal information has been shared among many professionals, and often the child or young person is unaware of who knows what about them. They frequently have an overwhelming sense of their privacy and boundaries being invaded, thus it is of paramount importance to clarify the parameters of confidentiality, including the occasions on which information would be disclosed to a third party.

Setting boundaries

It is important to be clear about the rules that exist within the therapy room, and between the therapist and client, for example that there are no incidents of physical assault, destruction of property, or damage to the room. This can be difficult because this may appear to limit the expression of emotions, but the child needs to have clear boundaries in order to feel safe. Boundaries may also convey to the child that they will be kept safe from harm, and contained too. They will not be allowed to destroy the therapy room or assault another person, as they may have done so many times before, and in the process lost so much and had their negative self-image reinforced.

Case vignette

Katie was a 12-year-old who had experienced several foster care placement breakdowns because she had 'trashed' her and her carers' property, behaved aggressively, and assaulted them at times. She was relieved to know that she would be helped to find other ways of expressing her distress, and our discussion of the rules helped us explore how she might do this. She needed to know that I was strong enough to contain her anger, and not be at risk of losing this relationship through assault or destruction.

Working with defences

When working with defences it is important to note that for many children these have served a purpose and helped them to continue to exist. Without them, many would not have survived. For example, the child who dissociated whilst being sexually abused protected herself, and was not annihilated by the horror of her abuse. Dysfunctional defences may be better than no defences. The therapist should not attempt to break down these defences unless they can be replaced by something more positive. When working with a very resistant child it may be more pertinent to contain their anxiety and use ego-strengthening therapy, such as building their self-esteem, promoting social relationships, or enabling their carers to care for them in a more appropriate way.

A balance is needed between providing a supportive environment, gently challenging the child's resistance, and tentatively testing to see if this resistance is caused by fear of the consequences of loss of defences, or a genuine informed decision that they would prefer to maintain their defences and not explore underlying feelings. To challenge their resistance too aggressively, without forethought of what this may be replaced with, or how the breakdown in defences may manifest and be contained, is unethical and shows a disregard for the child (Casement 1988). It may also compound their previous experiences of feeling powerless. In addition, as discussed earlier, a child who does not wish to attend therapy is unlikely to engage or derive any benefit from attending sessions.

Case vignette

Michael was 16 when he was referred to therapy. His referral was followed by a lengthy telephone discussion with his social worker, who cared very much for Michael. She outlined his appalling history of early neglect and abuse, several foster placement breakdowns, and two adoptive placement breakdowns. During some of these placements, he had experienced further emotional abuse. The social worker felt that, in light of his history, Michael needed therapy and would benefit from it. However, during the initial appointment it became apparent that Michael did not wish to consider his past, or explore his resistance. Unfortunately, I did not pay heed to this at this time, and bowed to the referrer's anxiety. I consequently arranged further sessions with Michael. He attended reluctantly each time and was difficult to engage. After three sessions, Michael said he really did not want to attend therapy, as he felt that his emotional detachment helped him to 'get on with life'. He was attending college, had a small network of friends, and appeared to be functioning adequately. I agreed that he was entitled to make a decision for himself and that I would respect this.

Endings

Endings occur in two parts: the ending of individual sessions, and the final ending of the therapeutic process. Both require careful consideration. With regard to the ending of each session, Rymaszewska and Philpott (2006, p.75) state that 'the venting of emotions must end in order'. Children need to know that the end of the session is imminent. This can be particularly relevant for vulnerable children, as previous endings that they have experienced may have been abrupt, final, or catastrophic. They may believe that they will never see the therapist again, that they have behaved in some way to make the therapist reject them, thus session endings can be fraught with anxiety. Restoring a sense of order to the room can be therapeutic; the child can witness their work being cleared away carefully and mindfully and, if the child chooses, they may wish to be a part of this process.

Case vignette

Jacob had been abandoned as a small child and several placements had abruptly broken down. He attended CAMH services for an assessment, after which it was decided that we would continue to meet for regular therapeutic sessions. It became apparent that he had difficultly believing that he would see me again. He kept asking 'Will I see you here?', 'In this room?', 'What time will it be then?', 'Will it be you again?'. In light of his history, it was clear that a key issue would be containing his anxiety about my abandonment of him and disbelief that relationships can be enduring and, importantly, can end in a positive way when the time comes.

With regard to the ending of therapy as a whole, many issues can arise. Indeed the most common question is likely to be 'When is therapy ended?'. Often the expectation held of therapy, usually by other professionals and occasionally by ourselves, is that the child will end therapy 'cured'. There may be a lack of clarity or agreement about which problems to address (Hawley and Weisz 2003). It is pertinent therefore to be clear and realistic about the expectations held by others and how far these expectations may be met.

Sometimes it may be difficult to be clear when a child or young person is ready to end therapy. There may be many 'false' endings, for example when a child or young person frequently does not attend we may be compelled to consider whether they are ending prematurely because therapy has become too difficult for them, or that they are not ready for their defences to be challenged. It may also be that endings occur prematurely and out of our control, because placements break down and the child is plunged into periods of instability, within which they do not feel safe enough, nor have the containing environment required to endure therapy.

There may be times when we need to consider whether the type of therapy that we are providing is the best approach to offer. Perhaps the child is not ready to engage in interpersonal psychodynamic therapy; they may need to first have a coherent narrative of their past through engaging in life story work, taking part in school-based projects aimed at building their self-esteem, and developing their social skills, so that they are better able to establish and maintain relationships. Work may need to be undertaken with their carers in helping them to understand the child's difficulties and develop ways of managing these in the home environment. What is required of the therapist is the ability to be flexible and reflective, and to remain open to the above considerations.

Often, vulnerable children and young people have experienced such a severe degree of trauma that they will not end therapy fully able to function in all circumstances, with no further reference to the past. Rather, endings may be better viewed as an ending of that period of therapy. One hopes that the positive experience of a safe relationship, and the opportunity to process and reflect on some aspects of the past, may enable the child to re-engage in therapy at a later time, if necessary. An important aspect of ending is for the supporting networks, such as carers and social workers, to continue what has begun in therapy, building on the child's increased ability to form trusting relationships, and it is hoped experience themselves in a more positive and empowered way. One would also hope that they would have acquired some positive coping strategies for managing their own distress and developed useful ways of expressing difficult emotions. 'As a therapist, one fights against sentimentality and fictionally happy endings; real therapy is a ragbag of loose ends and unanswered questions' (Hunter 2001, p.171). This observation captures the essence of endings when working with vulnerable children and young people.

Conclusions

What is apparent is that there are specific issues that need to be considered when working therapeutically with vulnerable children and young people. These children often lack a stable supportive background. They exist within complex health and social care systems. Therefore, there is a need for a high degree of co-operation and collaboration between the agencies that the child or young person is likely to be involved with.

Psychotherapy is often deemed not to be appropriate for many vulnerable children and young people because they are seen to be transient, or their needs are too complex. The evidence suggests that this is not the case, but that specific therapeutic issues must be attended to. Particular attention must be paid to how we engage these children; there is a need for greater flexibility, both individually and as a mental health service. As therapists, we must be clear about the expectations of therapy, and how best we might meet these needs, whether through individual therapeutic work, indirect work with carers, or consideration of other services that may best meet the needs of the child at that time.

Therapeutic work with vulnerable children can engender painful emotions for the therapist, and in order to avoid vicarious trauma, therapists must pay attention to their own psychological needs. Clinical and peer supervision provides an opportunity for reflection and processing of the complex emotions that occur when working with vulnerable children and young people.

References

Allen, J. and Vostanis, P. (2005) 'The impact of abuse and trauma on the developing child: An evaluation of a training programme for foster carers and supervising social workers.' *Adoption and Fostering 29*, 68–81.

Banister, A. (2003) *Creative Therapies with Traumatized Children.* London: Jessica Kingsley Publishers.

Barish, K. (2004) 'What is therapeutic in child therapy? Therapeutic Engagement.' *Psychoanalytic Psychology 21*, 385–401.

Casement. P. (1988) *On Learning From the Patient.* New York, NY: Routledge.

Connor, T., Scare, J., Dunbar, D. and Elliffe, J. (1985) 'Making a life story book.' *Adoption and Fostering 9*, 2–14.

Golding, K., Dent, H., Nissim. R. and Stott. L. (2006) *Thinking Psychologically About Children Who Are Looked After and Adopted: Space for Reflection.* London: John Wiley.

Hawle, K. and Weisz, J. (2003) 'Child, parent and therapist (dis)agreement on target problems in outpatient therapy: The therapist's dilemma and its implications.' *Journal of Consulting and Clinical Psychology 71*, 62–70.

Hughes, D. (2004) 'An attachment-based treatment of maltreated children and young people.' *Attachment and Human Development 6*, 263–278.

Hunter, M. (2001) *Psychotherapy with Young people in Care: Lost and Found.* Hove: Routledge.

Lanyado, M. (2003) 'The emotional tasks of moving from fostering to adoption: Transitions, attachment, separation and loss.' *Clinical Child Psychology and Psychiatry 8*, 337–349.

Oaklander, V. (1978) *Windows to Our Children: A Gestalt Therapy Approach to Children and Adolescents.* New York, NY: Real Press People.

Pearlman, L. and MacIan, P. (1995) 'Vicarious traumatization: An empirical study of the effects of trauma work on trauma therapists.' *Professional Psychology: Research and Practice 26*, 558–565.

Rymaszewska, J. and Philpott, T. (2006) *Reaching the Vulnerable Child: Therapy with Traumatized Children.* London: Jessica Kingsley Publishers.

Stone, J. (2006) 'Seeing and Thinking: Bringing Theory to Practice.' In T. Heineman and D. Ehrensaft (eds) *Building a Home Within: Meeting the Emotional Needs of Children and Youth in Foster Care.* Baltimore, MD: Brookes Publishing.

Weston, R. (2006) 'In Search of the Fuzzy Green Pillow.' In T. Heineman and D. Ehrensaft (eds) *Building a Home Within: Meeting the Emotional Needs of Children and Youth in Foster Care.* Baltimore, MD: Brookes Publishing.

CHAPTER 8

Cognitive-behavioural Interventions for Young Offenders

Ellen Townsend

It is widely acknowledged that young offenders demonstrate high rates of mental health problems (Callaghan *et al.* 2003; Carswell *et al.* 2004) and that they do not receive adequate therapeutic interventions (Chitsabesan *et al.* 2006). This is surprising and of great concern given that it is acknowledged that mental health problems may contribute significantly to offending behaviour (e.g. Dixon, Howie and Starling 2004; Wiesner 2003).

Many cognitive-behavioural therapy (CBT) programmes have been tested in the youth offending population, but most studies in this domain target recidivism and antisocial behaviour rather than mental health problems and outcomes (see Lipsey, Wilson and Cothern (2000) for a review). However, a handful of studies have focused on the mental health problems that are so widespread in this group. Here, interventions that have been developed for this purpose are discussed from a CBT framework.

The focus is on CBT interventions for a number of reasons. First, CBT has a theoretical basis and a robust evidence base in the general mental health literature. Its effectiveness and efficacy have been extensively and rigorously tested in adolescents and children (Southam-Gerow and Kendall 2000). Moreover, mainstay treatments for certain mental health problems in adults, (e.g. antidepressant medication for depression) do not appear to be as beneficial for children (e.g. Hazell *et al.* 2002).

CBT is time-limited and focuses on 'here and now' problems, which many clients find more acceptable than other therapeutic approaches (e.g. Hay *et al.* 2004). As noted above, cognitive-behavioural approaches have been used widely in criminal justice settings to tackle criminal behaviour and recidivism (Cameron and Telfer 2004).

The aims of this chapter are, therefore, to provide an overview of the available evidence on cognitive-behavioural interventions for mental health problems in young offenders and to discuss the practical implications of this evidence in relation to service delivery for young offenders.

CBT for mental health problems in young offenders

This overview includes studies that have developed interventions for young offenders with mental health problems using cognitive-behavioural principles. The studies discussed here are randomized, controlled trials (RCTs) as these give the most reliable and valid estimates of treatment effects (Schulz et al. 1995). RCTs provide the best 'gold standard' evidence because randomization (with adequate concealment of the allocation sequence from triallists) helps to avoid bias. Randomly allocating participants to treatments means that the determinants of the outcome of the trial (both known and unknown) are typically evenly distributed between treatment groups (Khan et al. 2003). The importance of evidence-based research and practice, which is informed by the most robust, highest quality evidence, has been highlighted in recent years (Schulz et al. 1995). Other levels of evidence relating to CBT exist, such as case studies and other descriptive studies, but an evidence-based approach is recommended and adopted here.

The key characteristics of the studies discussed here, in terms of their participants, interventions, settings, and target disorders, may be viewed in Table 8.1. Most of the studies have focused on one specific disorder, such as post-traumatic stress disorder (PTSD) or depression, whereas one employed CBT techniques with young offenders with a range of mental health-related issues and another included all young offenders regardless of their mental health status. All the studies identified here have used a group-based format for the delivery of CBT.

Cognitive processing therapy for PTSD in young offenders

PTSD is rife in offending populations (Ahrens and Rexford 2002; Dixon et al. 2004; Sukhodolsky and Ruchkin 2006), which is perhaps not surprising given the high incidence of violence and trauma in the lives of these young people (Dixon et al. 2004). In young people with behaviour problems it is likely that the symptoms associated with PTSD are overlooked because they tend to be expressed through deviant behaviours (Ovaert et al. 2003).

Ahrens and Rexford (2002) examined the effects of cognitive processing therapy (CPT) for PTSD in incarcerated young male offenders. CPT was developed by Resick and Schnicke (1992) and is theoretically-based on a coping skills approach to the treatment of PTSD that emanates from an information-processing account of this disorder. There are three main elements to CPT:

Table 8.1 Characteristics of CBT intervention studies for young offenders with mental health problems

Study	Participants	Interventions	Setting	Target disorder
Biggam and Power (2002)	n=46 100% male, 0% female Mean age: 19.3 years	Ex: Brief group social problem solving Con: No treatment	Incarcerated, UK	Vulnerable offenders at risk of suicidal behaviour, under protection, or bullied.
Ahrens and Rexford (2002)	n=38 100% male, 0% female Mean age: 16.4 years	Ex: Group cognitive processing therapy Con: Waiting list	Incarcerated, USA	PTSD
Ovaert et al. (2003)	n=45 (12 randomized) 100% male, 0% female Mean age: 15.4 years	Ex: Structured cognitive behavioural group therapy Con: Waiting list	Incarcerated, USA	PTSD
Rohde et al. (2004a)	n=76 100% male, 0% female Mean age: 16.5 years	Ex: Coping course Con: Usual care	Incarcerated, USA	No specific disorder or target group. Residents of the unit took part.
Rohde et al. (2004b); Kaufman et al. (2005)	n=93 55% male, 45% female Mean age: 15.1 years	Ex: Adolescent 'Coping with Depression' course (CWD-A) Con: Life skills training	Community (Juvenile Justice Center), USA	Co-morbid major depressive disorder with conduct disorder
Rohde et al. (2006)	n=114 52% male, 48% female Mean age: 15.2 years	Ex: Adolescent 'Coping with Depression' course (CWD-A) Con: Life skills training	Community (Juvenile Justice Center), USA	Major depressive disorder

Key: Ex – experimental group, Con – control group, PTSD – post-traumatic stress syndrome

- education concerning the symptoms associated with PTSD and information-processing theory
- exposure
- cognitive therapy.

In the education phase, the differentiation between thoughts and feelings, and information-processing theory are discussed. In the exposure phase, clients write and read about an account of the trauma they experienced (this is thought to be less threatening than using imagery about the event). Last, the cognitive component involves development of the skill of identifying thoughts and feelings, and identifying and challenging maladaptive beliefs relating to safety, trust, power, esteem, and intimacy (Ahrens and Rexford 2002).

Ahrens and Rexford (2002) followed the CPT manual to conduct this intervention with their young offenders who met the criteria for PTSD in the *Diagnostic and Statistical Manual of Mental Disorders – Fourth Edition* (DSM-IV) (APA 1994). Many of the participants in this study had seen someone they knew die (often via gang violence). Thirty-eight young offenders were randomized to receive eight, 60-minute sessions of CPT (n=19) or wait-list control (n=19). Four weeks after the end of treatment significant improvements were seen in the CPT group as compared with the control group in terms of PTSD symptoms, depression, and scores on the Impact of Events Scale.

Structured cognitive-behavioural group therapy for PTSD in young offenders
Ovaert *et al.* (2003) conducted a study with 10 groups of incarcerated juveniles (n=45), who completed a 12-session CBT-based intervention (structured group therapy) for PTSD. The CBT intervention here was developed by Ovaert (1998) in consultation with clinical supervisors with the exposure element of the therapy adapted from the CPT intervention described earlier (Resick and Schnicke 1992). Considerable difficulties with recruitment and randomization were reported in this trial. The authors had intended to compare the CBT intervention groups with two wait-list control groups but this was not possible owing to time constraints and the unwillingness of the North Texas Youth Correction facility to allow too much movement of participants from school and living units.

As a result of these difficulties Ovaert *et al.* (2003) present mean change data for a pooled sample of all participants which showed that self-reported symptoms of PTSD decreased post-treatment, and that the intervention seemed to be particularly effective for participants with trauma related to gang and community violence. However, the results of this study must be treated with extreme caution given that, although the authors had intended to run the intervention as an RCT, pragmatic difficulties with recruitment rendered the study an uncontrolled trial.

Problem-solving group therapy for self-harming and other 'at risk' young offenders

Biggam and Power (2002) focused specifically on vulnerable young offenders considered to be 'at risk'. Participants recruited to the study were either:

1. At risk of suicidal behaviour because they had expressed suicide ideation or had self harmed (n=33)

2. In a formal protection hall because they lacked the coping skills to integrate into the routine prison setting (n=6)

3. They had been bullied (deliberately hurt, threatened, or frightened (n=7)) by another inmate whose intention was to intimidate or gain property from the bullying.

Participants were randomized (after balancing for the three vulnerability factors listed above) to receive problem-solving treatment or placed in a no-treatment control group.

Here the problem-solving intervention was delivered in small-group format (four to six individuals per group) and consisted of five 90-minute sessions. The problem-solving intervention used was based on problem-solving training devised for depression (D'Zurilla 1986; Nezu, Nezu, and Perril 1989). The principle techniques focused on instruction, active discussion, reflective listening, and group exercises, as well as extra exercises devised specifically for each group participant. At three-month follow-up, significant improvements were seen in the problem-solving group as compared with the control group on measures of depression and anxiety, and for some (but not all) of the problem-solving sub-scales measured in the study. Thus, the authors conclude that problem-solving treatments are effective in reducing symptoms of psychological distress in young offenders.

Cognitive-behavioural intervention (Coping Course) to enhance problem-solving and coping skills in young offenders

In this pilot-study by Rohde *et al.* (2004a), a cognitive-behavioural intervention that was designed to improve general coping and problem-solving skills was examined with young men incarcerated at a youth correctional facility. Participants were randomly assigned to receive the experimental 'Coping Course' intervention (n=46) or usual care (n=30). An additional source of control data was gathered from participants at a second correctional institution (n=62). Usual care varied, but included sex offender groups, drug and alcohol groups, journals and other writing assignments, or a video-based intervention based on critical thinking skills.

The Coping Course was designed to improve problem-solving and coping skills, to improve behaviour within the facility, and to empower participants to make a successful return to society after incarceration. The Coping Course aimed to provide a set of strategies to reduce distress and self-destructive behaviour, and was a modified version of the Adolescent Coping with Depression (CWD-A) course (Clarke, Lewisohn and Hops 1990). Sixteen sessions were conducted over an eight-week setting in a class-like format, with seven to eight participants in each group. Participants were taught a variety of skills such as problem-solving and cognitive restructuring. Handouts were provided detailing key concepts from the sessions, learning tasks, quizzes, and homework.

A number of significant differences were observed between the Coping Course group and the control group. The Coping Course participants reported significantly fewer 'externalizing behaviours' and less suicidal behaviour. They demonstrated higher scores on three measures of the Life Attitudes Scale, higher self-esteem, increased knowledge of CBT, and they also reported increased feelings of sharing with staff. These results are encouraging, especially in relation to self-destructive behaviour and thoughts, which are known to be significant problems in young offenders. Unlike other studies, participants in this trial were not selected according on the basis of the presence of a mental disorder.

CBT for adolescents with co-morbid major depression and conduct disorder

In this study, which was published in two papers (Rohde et al. 2004b; Kaufman et al. 2005), the effectiveness of the CWD-A course (a CBT-based group intervention) was evaluated in a group of non-incarcerated depressed adolescents with co-morbid conduct disorder, recruited from a county juvenile justice department. Ninety-three participants who met DSM-IV criteria for both major depressive and conduct disorders were randomly assigned to receive CWD-A (n=45) or a control group intervention based on life skills training (n=48).

CWD-A is a group-based intervention which combines cognitive and behavioural strategies to improve the problems and feelings commonly encountered by adolescents with depression. For example, participants are taught how to improve social skills, decrease anxious feelings and depressive cognitions, increase pleasant activities, and improve communication. In the control group participants were educated on basic life skills training (e.g. completing an application for a job, how to rent an apartment) and academic tutoring. The aim being to 'fill in a void' for these young people who are often alienated from society and do not receive parental support and guidance.

For each intervention, mixed-gender groups of approximately 10 adolescents were treated in 16, two-hour sessions over an eight-week period. Participants could also receive up to four brief sessions with the therapist on an individual basis to 'make up' for any lost time in the main intervention groups. At 12-month follow-up, both groups demonstrated improved scores for major depression and conduct disorder, with around two-thirds of the participants in both treatment conditions recovering from the index depressive disorder. In addition, the odds of recovering from a major depressive disorder were significantly higher in the CWD-A group as compared with the control group. Post-treatment recovery rates from a major depressive disorder were 39 per cent in the CWD-A group as compared with 19 per cent in the life skills training control group. This study demonstrates that it possible to treat depression in young people with co-morbid conduct disorder. However, it should be noted that, in past studies of efficacy relating to CWD-A treatment, average attendance rates for therapy were 14 out of 16 sessions, whereas in the present study attendance rates were much lower (8.4 for the CWD-A group and 7.6 for the control group). Nevertheless, this study demonstrates that community-based young offenders will attend psychosocial interventions.

CBT for depressed adolescents from a juvenile justice centre

This report by Rohde et al. (2006) was based on the same study as that just described but in the report the authors focus solely on young offenders with a depressive disorder (rather than young offenders with co-morbid depression and conduct disorder). Thus, 114 depressed adolescents were recruited from a juvenile justice centre in the USA and received either a cognitive-behavioural intervention (CWD-A) (n=56) or a control intervention (life-skills tutoring) (n=58). These interventions have been described in detail above (see Rohde et al. 2004b) and were delivered in a community setting. For both treatment conditions, mixed-gender groups of around 10 young people attended 16 two-hour sessions over a period of eight weeks. Mean attendance at the sessions was 8.4 for the CWD-A group and 7.6 for the control group.

The treatment condition was found to interact with three out of the 19 variables examined in the present study. First, there was an effect of ethnicity, that white participants who received the CWD-A had a median time to recovery of 11 weeks, as compared with white participants in the control group, who had a median time to a recovery of 27 weeks. No advantage of CWD-A was observed for non-white participants. Second, those adolescents who had had two or more episodes of major depressive disorder at intake were faster to recover in the CBT (CWD-A) group than those with this history in the control group (recovery times were six weeks and 38 weeks, respectively). No such effect of intervention was observed for participants experiencing their first episode of major depressive disorder at intake. Third, participants with good coping skills were faster to recover in the CWD-A group as compared with the control group (6 weeks versus 16 weeks, respectively). No treatment effect was observed for participants with poor coping skills.

Discussion and conclusions

This overview highlights a number of important issues in relation to CBT interventions for young offenders. The first observation is the paucity of RCTs investigating the effectiveness of CBT in this group, given the numbers of studies which have provided evidence suggesting high levels of need for mental health problems in young offenders. The limited nature of the evidence in this field has been noted by other authors (e.g. Sukhodolsky and Ruchkin 2006). The lack of randomized studies to evaluate the effectiveness of criminal justice systems in general has been highlighted by Farrington (2003), who argues that individual differences in policy-makers is, rather worryingly, the key factor in determining whether RCT-type studies are promoted and funded (Farrington 2003). As Desai *et al.* (2006) note, CBT-based interventions are extremely well-suited to application in the criminal justice system – especially in secure settings. CBT is short-term, time-limited, and focused on current problems, which is ideal for settings where length of stay is short and outcomes must be highly effective. CBT provides clients with a new set of skills and is both collaborative and empowering. Many CBT interventions are manualized which make them relatively easy to teach to clinicians from a variety of backgrounds.

Indeed, CBT interventions which focus on problem behaviours and reducing recidivism have been researched extensively (Lipsey *et al.* 2000). Sukhodolsky and Ruchkin (2006) note that CBT for 'internalizing disorders' such as mood and anxiety disorders is likely to share techniques with CBT used to tackle aggression and delinquency. This could be a benefit and lead to the development and refinement of interventions for young people with multiple problems. On the other hand, it has also been pointed out that CBT for internalizing disorders may suffer from the limitations of treatments for delinquent behaviour such as possible negative effects of group-based modalities (Dishion, McCord and Poulin 1999). It is noteworthy that all of the studies discussed here used a group-based format to deliver CBT to young offenders. More research is required relating to the effectiveness of group-based CBT treatments as compared to individual treatments in this population.

Unfortunately, many of the trials discussed here suffer from methodological weaknesses such as a lack of information about randomization and blinding procedures, incomplete information about drop-outs, and short follow-up periods. This is unfortunate, given that these factors are known to bias the outcomes of trials (Schulz *et al.* 1995) and that there have been repeated calls in the literature for researchers to report studies in a transparent manner (Moher, Schulz and Altman 2001). Just one of the studies reported here mentioned that it conformed to Consolidated Standards of Reporting Trials (CONSORT) standards, but even in this study the precise method of randomization was not clearly reported (Rohde *et al.* 2006).

Nonetheless, this overview demonstrates the CBT can be used effectively with young offenders with mental health problems in both incarcerated and community settings. To date, most CBT trials for mental health problems in young offenders have been carried out in incarcerated settings (prisons and detention centres) by researchers in the USA (with just one study emanating from the UK). Studies that delivered CBT interventions in the community suffer from lowered attendance rates and thought now must be given to improving attendance. In patient groups where low treatment compliance is a problem, a number of solutions have been explored, including following up non-attendance with letters, telephone calls, and home visits. A flexible approach is undoubtedly required to ensure treatment adherence in in the community. This is especially important, since most young offenders in the UK are managed in the community by youth offending teams (YOTs) and they are known to have high, and largely unmet, mental health needs (Chitsabesan et al. 2006). Moreover, mental health problems in this group tend not to occur in isolation and co-morbidity of disorders is common. This has significant implications for the design and delivery of therapeutic interventions, and effective inter-agency collaboration will be undoubtedly imperative in order to ensure that mental health interventions are successfully delivered in services for young offenders.

It is significant that the majority of studies have examined interventions for mental health problems of male young offenders. Evidence relating to the effectiveness of interventions specifically for female young offenders is extremely sparse. Just three of the reports discussed here (which all emanate from the same study: Rohde et al. 2004b; Kaufman et al. 2005; and Rohde et al. 2006) included females. This undoubtedly reflects the fact that most young offenders are male, but more studies are now required which include both genders. Sub-group analyses may be performed within trials to test for any gender-specific treatment effects.

It should be noted that other types of intervention have been explored in relation to certain mental health problems. For example, a number of trials have demonstrated the effectiveness of multi-systemic therapy for substance abusing young offenders (e.g. Henggeler, Pickrel and Brondino 1999). Another study has explored the effects of muscle relaxation on the psychological well-being of young offenders (Nakaya et al. 2004).

In conclusion, CBT-based interventions for mental health disorders in young offenders demonstrate promising results. Much more research is needed on treatment effectiveness and efficacy to bolster the evidence base, but preliminary data suggest that CBT interventions are ideal for young people with mental health problems in the criminal justice system, both for incarcerated young offenders and those being managed in the community.

Finally, the studies presented here demonstrate that CBT approaches are suitable for, and accepted by, young offenders with mental health problems in both incarcerated and community settings. This has implications for current practice in terms of determining where such interventions could be delivered and by whom. CBT for mental health problems should be delivered by experienced mental health workers who can be from a variety of professional backgrounds. However, current practice in relation to mental health services varies widely between YOTs. Some have designated in-house services, whereas others refer young people with mental health needs to local child and adolescent mental health services. Given the promising results uncovered here in relation to CBT for mental health problems in young offenders, policy-makers may wish to consider the benefits of having a suitably qualified 'in-house' therapist who could lead CBT sessions for young people with mental health problems within the youth justice setting. In community-based settings, this could take place away from the YOT setting in community leisure centres or youth clubs.

Note

This research was supported by the NHS Forensic Mental Health Programme.

References

Ahrens, J. and Rexford, L. (2002) 'Cognitive processing therapy for incarcerated adolescents with PTSD.' In R. Greenwald (ed.) *Trauma and Juvenile Delinquency: Theory, Research and Interventions*. Binghamton, NY: Haworth Press.

American Psychiatric Association (APA) (1994) *Diagnostic and Statistical Manual of Mental Disorders* (4th ed). Washington, DC: American Psychiatric Association.

Biggam, F. and Power. K. (2002) 'A controlled, problem-solving, group-based intervention with vulnerable incarcerated young offenders'. *International Journal of Offender Therapy and Comparative Criminology 46*, 678–698.

Callaghan, J., Pace, F., Young, B., and Vostanis, P. (2003) 'Primary mental health workers within youth offending teams: a new service model.' *Journal of Adolescence 26*, 185–199.

Cameron, H. and Telfer, J. (2004) 'Cognitive-behavioural group work: Its application to specific offender groups.' *The Howard Journal 43*, 1, 47–64.

Carswell, K., Maughan, B., Davis, H., Davenport, F., and Goddard, N. (2004) 'The psychosocial needs of young offenders and adolescents from an inner city area.' *Journal of Adolescence 27*, 415–428.

Chitsabesan, P., Kroll, L., Bailey, S., Kenning., C., Sneider, S., MacDonald, W., and Theodosiou, L. (2006) 'Mental health needs of young offenders in custody and in the community.' *British Journal of Psychiatry 188*, 534–540.

Clarke, G., Lewisohn, P., and Hops, H. (1990) *Adolescent Coping with Depression Course*. Available at: www.kpchr.org/public/acwd/acwe.html, accessed on 10 September 2007.

Desai, R., Goulet, J., Robbins, J., Chapman, J., Migdole, S., and Hoge, M. (2006) 'Mental health care in juvenile detention facilities: A review.' *Journal of the American Academy of Psychiatry and the Law 34*, 204–214.

Dishion, T., McCord, J., and Poulin, F. (1999) 'When interventions harm: Peer groups and problem behaviour.' *American Psychologist 54*, 755–764.

Dixon, A., Howie, P., and Starling, J. (2004) 'Psychopathology in female juvenile offenders.' *Journal of Child Psychology and Psychiatry 45*, 1150–1158.

D'Zurilla, T. (1986) *Problem-Solving Therapy: A Social Competence Approach to Clinical Intervention*. New York, NY: Springer.

Farrington, D. (2003) 'A short history of randomized experiments in criminology: A meagre feast.' *Evaluation Review 27*, 218–227.

Hay, P., Claudino, A., Bentovim, D., and Yong, P. (2004) 'Individual psychotherapy in the outpatient treatment of adults with anorexia nervosa (Cochrane Review).' *Cochrane Library of Systematic Reviews*, Vol. 1. Chichester: Wiley.

Hazell, P., O'Connell, D., Heathcote, D., and Henry, D. (2002) 'Tricyclic drugs for depression in children and adolescents.' *Cochrane Database of Systematic Reviews*, Issue 2.

Henggeler, S., Pickrel, S., and Brondino, M. (1999) 'Multisystemic treatment of substance-abusing and dependent delinquents: outcomes, treatment fidelity, and transportability.' *Mental Health Services Research 1*, 171–184.

Kaufman, N., Rohde, P., Seeley, J., Clarke, G., and Stice, E. (2005) 'Potential mediators of cognitive-behavioural therapy for adolescents with comorbid major depression and conduct disorder.' *Journal of Consulting and Clinical Psychology 73*, 38–46.

Khan, K., Kunz, R., Kleijnen, J., and Antes, G. (2003) *Systematic Reviews to Support Evidence-based Medicine*. London: Royal Society of Medicine Press.

Lipsey, M., Wilson, D., and Cothern, L. (2000) *Effective Intervention for Serious Juvenile Offenders.* Washington, DC: Office of Juvenile Justice and Delinquency Prevention.

Moher, D., Schulz, K., and Altman, D. (2001) 'The CONSORT statement: Revised recommendations for improving the quality of reports of parallel-group randomised trials.' *Lancet 357*, 1191–1194.

Nakaya, N., Kumano, H., Minoda, K., Koguchi, T., Tanouchi, K., and Kanazawa M. (2004) 'Preliminary study: Psychological effects of muscle relaxation on juvenile delinquents.' *International Journal of Behavioral Medicine 11*, 176–180.

Nezu, A., Nezu, C., and Perri, M. (1989) *Problem-Solving Therapy for Depression: Theory, Research and Clinical Guidelines*. New York, NY: Wiley.

Ovaert, L. (1998). 'Posttraumatic stress disorder in adolescents with conduct disorder: Pre- and post-treatment comparison of trauma types.' *Dissertation Abstracts International 58(7-B)*, UMI No. 3931.

Ovaert, L., Cashel, M.. and Sewell, K. (2003) 'Structured group therapy for posttraumatic stress disorder in incarcerated male juveniles.' *American Journal of Orthopsychiatry 73*, 294-301.

Resick, P. and Schnicke, M. (1992) 'Treating symptoms in adult victims of sexual assault.' *Journal of Interpersonal Violence 5*, 488–506.

Rohde, P., Jorgensen, J., Seeley, J., and Mace, D. (2004a) 'Pilot evaluation of the Coping Course: A cognitive-behavioural intervention to enhance coping skills in incarcerated youth.' *Journal of the American Academy of Child and Adolescent Psychiatry 43*, 669–678.

Rohde, P., Clarke, G. , Mace, D., Jorgensen, J., and Seeley, J. (2004b) 'An efficacy/effectiveness study of cognitive-behavioural treatment for adolescents with comorbid major depression and conduct disorder.' *Journal of the American Academy of Child and Adolescent Psychiatry 43*, 660–668.

Rohde, P., Seeley, J., Clarke, G., Kaufman, N., and Stice, E. (2006) 'Predicting time to recovery among depressed adolescents treated in two psychosocial group interventions.' *Journal of Consulting and Clinical Psychology 74*, 80–88.

Schulz, K., Chalmers, I., Hayes, R., and Altman, D. (1995) 'Empirical evidence of bias: Dimensions of methodological quality associated with estimates of treatment effects in controlled trials.' *JAMA 273*, 403–412.

Southam-Gerow, M. and Kendall, P. (2000) 'Cognitive-behaviour therapy with youth: Advances, challenges, and future directions.' *Clinical Psychology and Psychotherapy 7*, 343–366.

Sukhodolsky, D. and Ruchkin, V. (2006) 'Evidence-based psychosocial treatments in the juvenile justice system.' *Child and Adolescent Psychiatric Clinics of North America 15*, 201–216.

Wiesner, M. (2003) 'A longitudinal latent variable analysis of reciprocal relations between depressive symptoms and delinquency during adolescence.' *Journal of Abnormal Psychology 112*, 633–645.

CHAPTER 9

Working Systemically with Vulnerable Children and their Parents or Carers

Maeve McColgan

This chapter will begin with a brief overview of what it means to work systemically and what the evidence is for this approach. Consideration will then be given to a range of issues that may arise when working therapeutically with vulnerable children, and how a systemic approach can prove beneficial. Finally, the focus will move to some of the challenges in working with vulnerable children, and the potential of a systemic approach to meet those challenges.

What is a systemic approach?

A systemic approach refers to the field of systemic psychotherapy, commonly known as *family therapy*. Family therapy is something of a misnomer, as systemic psychotherapy can be utilized with families, couples, individuals, and organizations. The term 'family therapy' is often used as this approach emerged in the 1950s, when a range of developments led practitioners and researchers in different countries to become interested in the impact of working with more than one person (Carr 2000a; Dallos and Draper 2001). Over the years, the range of family therapy models has increased, so that by the early 1990s more than 20 different theoretical models were recognized (Shadish *et al.* 1993). Both the terms 'family therapy' and 'systemic therapy' will be used in this chapter, although not usually interchangeably. Family therapy will be used when describing interventions with families, and systemic therapy will be used when considering applications in other contexts, such as individual therapy and consultations.

Regardless of the increasing number of models, systemic approaches share a common view of problems. Their underlying tenet is that the focus should be on the system (family or otherwise), since difficulties do not arise *within* individuals but in the relationships, interactions, and communication *between* individuals (i.e. problems are *inter*personal rather than intrapersonal). Consequently, it follows that therapeutic interventions should focus on the relationships between people, even during individual therapy. This is reflected in the definition of family therapy as 'any psychotherapeutic endeavour that explicitly focuses on altering the interaction between or among family members, and seeks to improve the functioning of the family as a unit, or its subsystems and/or the functioning of individual members of the family' (Gurman, Kniskern and Pinsof 1986, p.565).

What is the evidence that supports the use of a systemic approach?

Evidence base for a systemic approach

Cottrell and Boston (2002) reviewed a range of family therapy research studies, and concluded that ' there is significant evidence for the effectiveness of systemic therapies' (p.582). Shadish and Baldwin (2003), in a meta-analysis of 20 studies of marital and family therapy, concluded that 'marriage and family therapy is now an empirically supported therapy in the plain English sense of the phrase – it clearly works, both in general and for a variety of specific problems' (p.567). More recently, Stratton (2005) reported on the evidence for systemic therapy and, whilst adding his voice to those who have highlighted the need for further research (Carr 2000a; Corcoran 2000; Cottrell and Boston 2002; Hazelrigg, Cooper and Borduin 1987), he concluded that there ' is strong evidence of both efficacy and effectiveness' (p.14) of family therapy for a range of difficulties.

In general, research indicates that family therapy is an effective type of intervention for child and adult mental health problems and relationship difficulties. The specific child-focused problems include physical child abuse and neglect, conduct problems, substance misuse, emotional difficulties, (including anxiety and grief) eating disorders, and psychosomatic complaints, including toileting difficulties (Asen 2002; Carr 2000a; Carr 2000b; Corcoran 2000; Cottrell and Boston 2002; Fonagy *et al.* 2002).

Children's experiences in family therapy have been the subject of some studies (e.g. Strickland-Clarke, Campbell and Dallos 2000). One conclusion from this research was that children expected to 'feel judged' and 'be reprimanded' (p.337), and they experienced relief when the therapist focused on and acknowledged their strengths, rather than only the difficulties. All of the children highlighted the importance of being listened to and understood by both the therapist and their family.

So how can a systemic approach be used to address those specific issues that arise when working with vulnerable children and their families?

Systemic approaches with vulnerable children
Framework: systems and context

When considering the life circumstances of many of the children who are perceived to be more vulnerable than their peers, some of the historical and current circumstances they may share include chaotic family lives, instability and insecurity, abuse, neglect, or both and multiple moves. Multi-agency working is therefore likely to be a frequent feature of involvement with this client group. Working in this manner fits well with the systemic approach, as it invites practitioners to be interested in the impact of all systems upon the child. These include immediate family, extended family, community, social, and cultural systems along with health, social, and educational services and the criminal justice system. This focus means that a systemic approach has an explicit rationale for practitioners committing to multi-agency working, in a manner that supports the family.

Working systemically allows practitioners to be flexible in relation to which part of the system their intervention is directed. Sessions may involve all family members – an approach associated with traditional family therapy. However, advocates of systemic approaches also state that change in one part of the system inevitably affects other parts of the system, and therefore can effect change across it. In some cases it is appropriate not to engage the entire family, but rather to seek change through therapeutic interventions with one or more family members (e.g. with parents or carers if the child is unable or unwilling to engage therapeutically at that time). In other cases the focus may be on supporting change through consultation with professionals and through indirect, rather than direct, contact with the family. This is considered in more detail below.

Given what has already been highlighted about the life circumstances of many children defined as vulnerable, it is preferable that any therapeutic work undertaken with these children, and their parents or carers, places the presenting difficulties in the context of the child's historical and current circumstances. Systemic approaches, regardless of their differences, share an interest in the contexts in which difficulties arise. This approach encourages therapeutic conversations that explore a range of contexts, including family life, social functioning, education or employment, and the temporal context of changes in the problems between the past and present, and expectations of the future.

Children and their families often are seen by mental health services at the point at which the parents or carers feel overwhelmed by their child's behaviour, and powerless to initiate change. Conversations about the context of the behaviour can promote understanding that leads to different interactions between family members. If, for example, the behaviour of children who are adopted or looked after is placed in the context of their life events prior to care, parents or carers can reflect on the possible meaning and emotions behind the child's current behaviour. Such children may display angry behaviour that parents or carers view as 'impossible' and experience as 'rejecting'. Placing this behaviour in context, and linking it to the child's earlier experiences, may assist the adults to recognize that behind the anger may lie a range of feelings such as fear, distress, or confusion. Such recognition can promote responses from parents or carers that attend to both the behaviour and the possible underlying emotions, which in turn may lead to different reactions from the child. This can contribute to the establishment of a more positive cycle of interactions between family members.

Therapeutic interventions

Children are less powerful than adults in most situations, and it can be difficult for their voice to be heard, particularly if families are experiencing problems. In such instances, ways need to be found to enable the child's voice to be heard within the family and by the other agencies involved in promoting the child's welfare. Family therapy approaches are particularly well-placed to do this by working with all members of the family, and encouraging the expression of different perspectives by family members. This creates a therapeutic space within which everyone has an equal voice. Working in this way enables the practitioner to engage with a child and their birth family, residential worker, foster or adoptive family.

Since the 1980s, researchers and practitioners interested in mental health have increasingly focused on the concept of resilience, and have sought to further their understanding of the range of factors that either assist or work against individuals being able to overcome adversity. Similarly, interest has grown in the significance of resilience for the field of systemic psychotherapy (Rutter 1999; Walsh 1996, 1998, 2002, 2003). Walsh uses the term to refer to a therapeutic focus on family strengths, and explains that a family resilience approach ' fundamentally alters the deficit-based lens from viewing troubled parents and families as damaged and beyond repair, to seeing them as challenged by life's adversities, with potential for fostering healing and growth in all members' (Walsh 2003, pp.2–3).

A 'family resilience' perspective seems likely to be particularly helpful when working with vulnerable children, as my clinical experience suggests that their parents (birth or adoptive) or carers often expect to be criticized, blamed, and judged. Where reflections are offered by a therapist or therapeutic team at the end of an initial session (Andersen 1987), family members often express surprise and relief that workers have been able to recognize positive aspects of their family life and relationships, as well as acknowledging their difficulties. This focus increases the possibility that the referred child will feel less apprehensive at the prospect of returning for further sessions, realizing that the conversation is more than an examination of 'the problem' for which referral has been made. Crucially, if family members feel hopeless about the possibility of change, a family resilience approach can engender hope, giving them a reason to engage and work collaboratively towards change.

Vulnerable children often experience complex family arrangements. They may have siblings and half-siblings who live in different households, and, for those who are looked after or have been adopted, they may have more than one family to which they feel they belong. In addition, some of these children will have professionals who play an important role in their lives, such as residential workers or social workers. A systemic approach enables the importance of all of these relationships to be recognized and brought into the therapeutic conversation, even if working individually with the child.

There is a range of systemic techniques that can be utilized to explore the significant relationships of family members, and consideration will now be given to genograms, family time-lines, sculpts, and circular questions.

GENOGRAMS

Genograms are family tree diagrams that traditionally have been used by family therapists as a succinct means of gathering factual information, usually across three generations, as well as illuminating patterns, including alliances and conflicts. Carr (2000a) and Walsh (2002) both emphasize that, in addition to their usual purposes, genograms can be used to highlight family strengths, and assist family members to focus on stories of past adversities overcome by extended family members. This emphasis can serve to engender hope and enable family members to hold more positive narratives about themselves and each other. Genograms are sufficiently flexible to accommodate reconstituted families and families with fostered or adopted children.

FAMILY TIME-LINES

'Family time-lines' can also be used to capture significant factual information. This therapeutic tool may have particular relevance for children who are in long-term fostering or who are adopted, as their lives began in other families. It may also be valuable for other groups of vulnerable children who have experienced many changes in their family lives. Use of a time-line enables the narratives of family members to be woven together in a manner that acknowledges different experiences, whilst still promoting family cohesion. As with other techniques, hypothetical discussions about family members' ideas of their preferred future time-line can generate hope of change.

SCULPTS

Family members can be invited to create 'sculpts' in which they take turns to position all family members, including themselves, into a tableau that represents their emotional relationships (Walrond Skinner 1976). My clinical experience has demonstrated this often to be a powerful intervention in family sessions. Sculpts can be completed for the past, present, and future (Burnham 1996). Having family members complete their preferred sculpt for an imagined future date helps to engender hope that change is possible. This technique can be adapted using objects rather than people, both in family sessions (Dallos and Draper 2001) and in sessions with children (Wilson 1998). Using objects facilitates the inclusion of a range of people deemed to be significant in the child's life, both past and present, and can be particularly helpful in therapeutic work with children whose family composition has changed, or who have lived with more than one family.

CIRCULAR QUESTIONS

'Circular questions' (Fleuridas, Nelson and Rosenthal 1986; Penn 1982; Selvini-Palazzoli et al. 1980; Tomm 1985) can prove effective, whether in family or individual sessions. These are questions that invite family members to comment on the relationships between other family members. They provide a means of exploring different perspectives, including those relating to relationships, behaviours, emotions, or events. Such questions ensure that space is created for the voice of all family members to be heard. Examples of circular questions include the following.

- Who do you think would agree/disagree with you, that your mum is closest to your youngest sister?

- How do you think your parents' relationship will be different once you have all left home?

- When your mum and sister are arguing, what does your dad do?

- How does your mum react when your dad stays out of the argument between her and your brother?

- Who agrees with dad that the two youngest children are playing together more now than three months ago?

Use of such questions can avoid the sessions being dominated by critical information relating to the referred child. They also enable new information to be released into the family system, as family members share thoughts and ideas that had previously remained unspoken. This new information can be successful in facilitating change. The abstract nature of the questions requires adaptation for use with younger children (Benson, Schindler-Zimmerman and Martin 1991). In addition, circular questions provide a means by which to bring the views of absent individuals into the room, thereby ensuring that significant figures (absent either temporarily or permanently) may be included in the therapeutic conversation, for example:

- If your teacher were here, what would she tell me?
- If your grandfather (deceased) were with us today, what ideas do you each think he would have about this?

Consultation

It is usual for professionals within a range of health and social service settings to offer, and avail of, consultations. Those offered from a systemic perspective (Wynne, McDaniel and Weber 1986) are likely to consider, alongside the usual focus on clinical work, a number of additional issues, including:

- the work context of the consultee
- the systems involved with the consultee, child, and family, including any alliances or conflicts
- how the consultant's role fits with these systems
- the timing of the consultation request and the significance of this
- the dynamics that exist between the consultee, the child, and family; the beliefs the consultee holds about them; do these dynamics and beliefs help or hinder the consultee?
- the impact of the consultee's involvement upon the child and family
- any resonance with the consultee's own experiences of family, either their family of origin or current family
- the therapeutic approach favoured by the consultee and how a systemic perspective may complement this.

These areas merit consideration, alongside an exploration of the specific issues brought for consultation by the practitioner, to ensure that the relevant contextual issues are not overlooked. The significance of this is apparent if considering the example of two practitioners attending for different consultations: a residential worker from a children's home and a worker from the Youth Offending Service (YOS). They work in different contexts, with different systems affecting them, and making demands of them and the children and families they engage with. The residential worker is expected to provide care for the child and promote their welfare in a manner similar to a parent. The worker from the YOS has a more authoritative role, given their involvement alongside the police and the courts. The context and systems relevant to each practitioner need to be considered in order for the consultation to be appropriately tailored to meet their individual professional needs.

Although consultations are primarily offered to professionals, some services also use this format with families. Some systemic approaches that work in this way will follow the family consultation with a therapeutic letter which seeks to capture the ideas that emerged (Street, Downey and Brazier 1991; Street and Downey 1996). A possibility exists, for use in consultations with practitioners, to develop this idea further, whereby the consultant may write a therapeutic letter for the family following a consultation with the practitioner (from any agency) who is involved with them. Provided that these families know that the consultation is taking place, the use of letter-writing can promote further change without direct contact by the consultant. In such cases I have written to the practitioner who has sought consultation. The letter is written, however, on the understanding that it may be shared with the family, and a copy given to them if they wish to have one. This enables family members to receive acknowledgement of their family strengths, and recognition of the changes they have made or continue to work towards (presuming that such information will have been explored during the consultation). It also provides an opportunity for the consultant to share their ideas with the family by making suggestions and asking questions upon which they can reflect.

Having explored some of the specific ways in which a systemic approach can be helpful when working with vulnerable children and their families, what are some of the challenges that may arise?

Challenges

Some families, in which children are perceived to be more vulnerable than their peers, can experience difficulty in attending appointments. Clinical experience, for example, indicates that many families in which children are known to the YOS have significant levels of non-attendance at mental health appointments. For those families experiencing either homelessness, domestic violence, or who are refugees, immediate practical needs and concern for their future may take priority over attending therapeutic appointments. Given the pressures that exist within many services, such families can be viewed as 'resistant', with practitioners reluctant to offer additional appointments that may not be attended. The interest that systemic approaches have in contextual issues encourages practitioners to consider wider issues when thinking about the timing of therapeutic interventions. Rather than families being viewed as 'resistant', the family's non-attendance is viewed as an indication that the service offered is not meeting their needs at that time, encouraging practitioners to consider alternatives. This may take the form of indirect involvement, through consultation to other agencies who are involved with family members. It may also be that further thought is given to who should be involved in the therapeutic work. For example, although a young person known to the YOS may initially refuse to engage, sessions may commence with other family members, which, from a systemic perspective, still makes it possible to facilitate change within the family.

Working systemically with adoptive families raises other challenges. Many adoptive parents are reticent to seek assistance when difficulties arise, because they perceive themselves to have 'failed', and expect to be 'judged' by professionals. This seems to be the case regardless of the extent to which their children had been abused, neglected, or both prior to being placed in their care. If their decision to adopt followed from fertility difficulties, this can re-awaken previous feelings of 'failure'. It is critical that during initial contact the adoptive parents are helped to understand that working systemically with the family does not place responsibility for their children's difficulties with them. Rather, this approach seeks to understand these difficulties in their historical and current context, and using the family resilience model views the family as the child's best resource for resolving their difficulties.

Somewhat different issues may arise for foster carers. Some of those who are caring for a child or young person on a short-term basis and, to a lesser extent, some of those caring long-term, may struggle to understand why their involvement is being sought in family-based therapeutic interventions. The main task in such instances is to offer a rationale that is acceptable to the carers. Even if the child is placed with the carers for a short-term period, he or she experiences living as a member of the foster family during this time. It is important for this to be recognized therapeutically, alongside recognition that the child usually has a sense of belonging to their birth family. Ethical issues also arise in relation to engaging a child or young person therapeutically, especially in the context of historical abuse, neglect, or both, if there are no care-taking adults available to support them fully throughout this process.

Understandably, many children and young people may be reluctant to engage in therapeutic sessions. Given that children who are deemed to be vulnerable have often experienced significant upheaval and multiple changes in their lives, they may not consider any adult as advocating on their behalf. It is therefore particularly important that practitioners persist in attempts to engage them, so that they have opportunities to express themselves, feel listened to, and understood within the families or homes in which they live. Family therapy can contribute significantly to this.

Conclusions

The evidence for systemic approaches confirms their value for practitioners working therapeutically with vulnerable children and their families or carers. This work can often be complex and, as has been outlined, systemic approaches offer a framework that provides a wider lens through which to view the presenting difficulties. This includes consideration of the context in which these difficulties arise, which is central to understanding the types of behaviour often presented by children who are defined as vulnerable. This wider view highlights the need for practitioners to be continuously thoughtful about the impact of other systems and agencies upon the life of the child, and to work with, and alongside, these agencies. Systemic approaches can facilitate the involvement of different combinations of family members and, in addition, members of the professional network, when appropriate. Practitioners may also choose to avail themselves of systemic consultations. These will assist them to consider a range of issues, including significant contextual issues, and the systems which impact on the child and their family or carers, including the impact of the consultee's involvement.

The range of existing systemic approaches highlights the view that one single model is not expected to fit all families; rather, practitioners have the opportunity to draw creatively on a range of systemic ideas to enable them to tailor their interventions to the needs of each particular family. Working systemically, incorporating ideas from a family resilience perspective, enables practitioners to assist families (birth, adoptive, or foster) to recognize and build on their strengths and resources, whilst maintaining hope that change is possible. The ability to engender hope seems particularly important for vulnerable children and their families and carers, given the multitude of challenges they face.

References

Andersen, T. (1987) 'The reflecting team: Dialogue and meta-dialogue in clinical work.' *Family Process 26*, 415–428.

Asen, E. (2002) 'Outcome research in family therapy.' *Advances in Psychiatric Treatment 8*, 230–238.

Benson, M., Schindler-Zimmerman, T. and Martin, D. (1991) 'Accessing children's perceptions of their family: Circular questions revisited.' *Journal of Marital and Family Therapy 17*, 363–372.

Burnham, J. (1996) *Family Therapy*. London: Routledge.

Carr, A. (2000a) *Family Therapy: Concepts, Process and Practice*. Chichester: John Wiley.

Carr, A. (2000b) 'Evidence-based practice in family therapy and systemic consultation: Child focused problems.' *Journal of Family Therapy 22*, 29–60.

Corcoran, J. (2000) *Evidence-Based Social Work Practice with Families: A Lifespan Approach*. New York, NY: Springer.

Cottrell, D. and Boston, P. (2002) 'The effectiveness of systemic family therapy for children and adolescents.' *Journal of Child Psychology and Psychiatry 43*, 573–586.

Dallos, R. and Draper, R. (2001) *An Introduction to Family Therapy: Systemic Theory and Practice.* Buckingham: Open University Press.

Fleuridas, C., Nelson, T. and Rosenthal, D. (1986) 'The evolution of circular questions: Training family therapists.' *Journal of Marital and Family Therapy 12*,113–127.

Fonagy, P., Target, M., Cottrell, D., Phillips, J. and Kurtz, Z. (eds) (2002) *What Works for Whom? A Critical Review of Treatments for Children and Adolescents.* New York, NY: Guildford Press.

Gurman, A., Kniskern, D. and Pinsof, W. (1986) 'Research on the Process and Outcome of Marital and Family Therapy'. In S. Garfield, and A. Bergin (eds) *Handbook of Psychotherapy and Behaviour Change* (3rd ed). New York, NY: John Wiley.

Hazelrigg, M., Cooper, H. and Borduin, C. (1987) 'Evaluating the effectiveness of family therapies: An integrative review and analysis.' *Psychological Bulletin 101*, 428–442.

Penn, P. (1982) 'Circular questioning.' *Family Process 21*, 267–279.

Rutter, M. (1999) 'Resilience concepts and findings: Implications for family therapy.' *Journal of Family Therapy 21*, 119–144.

Selvini-Palazzoli, M., Boscolo, L., Cecchin, G., and Prata, G. (1980) 'Hypothesizing-Circularity-Neutrality: Three guidelines for the conductor of the session.' *Family Process 19*, 3–12.

Shaddish, W., Montgomery, L., Wilson, P., Wilson, M., Bright I., and Okwumabua, T. (1993) 'Effects of family and marital psychotherapies: A meta-analysis.' *Journal of Consulting and Clinical Psychology 61*, 992–1002.

Shaddish, W. and Baldwin, S. (2003) 'Meta-analysis of MFT Interventions.' *Journal of Marital and Family Therapy 29*, 547–570.

Stratton, P. (2005) *Report on the Evidence-Base of Systemic Family Therapy.* London: Association of Family Therapy.

Street, E. and Downey, J. (1996) *Brief Therapeutic Consultations: An Approach to Systemic Counselling.* Chichester: John Wiley.

Street, E., Downey, J., and Brazier, A. (1991) 'The development of therapeutic consultations in child-focused family work.' *Journal of Family Therapy 13*, 311–333.

Strickland-Clarke, L., Campbell, D., and Dallos, R. (2000) 'Children's and adolescents' views on family therapy.' *Journal of Family Therapy 22*, 324–341.

Tomm, K. (1985) 'Circular Interviewing: A Multi-faceted Clinical Tool.' In D. Campbell, and R. Draper (eds) *Applications of Systemic Family Therapy: The Milan Approach.* London: Grune & Stratton.

Walrond Skinner, S. (1976) *Family Therapy: The Treatment of Natural Systems.* London: Routledge & Kegan Paul.

Walsh, F. (1996) 'The concept of family resilience: Crisis and challenge.' *Family Process 35*, 261–281.

Walsh, F. (1998) *Strengthening Family Resilience.* New York, NY: Guildford Press.

Walsh, F. (2002) 'A family resilience framework: Innovative practice applications.' *Family Relations 51*, 130–137.

Walsh, F. (2003) 'Family resilience: A framework for clinical practice.' *Family Process 42*, 1–18.

Wilson, J. (1998) *Child-Focused Practice: A Collaborative Systemic Approach.* London: Karnac Books.

Wynne, L., McDaniel, S., and Weber, T. (eds) (1986) *Systems Consultation: A New Perspective for Family Therapy.* New York, NY: Guildford Press.

CHAPTER 10

Interventions and Services for Refugee and Asylum-seeking Children and Families

Viki Elliott

According to the United Nations (UN), a refugee is someone who:

> Owing to a well-founded fear of being persecuted for reasons of race, religion, nationality, social group or political opinion, is outside the country of his nationality and is unable or, owing to such a fear, is unwilling to avail himself of the protection of that country; or who, not having a nationality and being outside the country of his/her former habitual residence as a result of such event, is unable or, owing to such fear is unwilling to return to it. (UNHCR 1997)

Asylum seekers are:

> people who flee their home country and seek refugee status in another, possibly because of war, oppression or human rights abuse. (UNHCR 1997)

Research suggests that refugee children commonly experience primary trauma, resulting in post-traumatic stress disorder (PTSD), affective, and anxiety disorders (Hodes 2000; Fazel and Stein 2002; Thabet and Vostanis 1999). In addition, they experience social adjustment difficulties related to cultural, language and socio-economic factors. The experiences of this group both before and after their arrival in the country of 'refuge' potentially increase their vulnerability to experiencing mental health problems. There are significant levels of both primary and secondary trauma experienced by child refugees, rendering them extremely vulnerable. In particular, the frequent loss of parents, both physically and psychologically, disturbances in parents' attention towards their children, and other limitations in parental abilities may result in secondary stress for children and young people (Montgomery 2005).

This chapter aims to consider the mental health needs and characteristics of refugee and asylum-seeking children and young people, and to explore issues relating to assessment and engagement within clinical practice. Case vignettes are provided throughout the text to illustrate clinical applications.

Mental health needs of refugee and asylum-seeking children and young people

Mental health presentations

Refugee and asylum-seeking children and young people can present with a wide range of symptoms that may include re-experiencing the traumatic event, attempting to avoid dealing with the emotions associated with this, depression, generalized anxiety, separation anxiety, disrupted behaviour, sleep disturbances, and cognitive changes (Yule, Perrin and Smith 2003). The response of children and young people to trauma will depend on the way in which they have understood an event and the meaning attached to this event (Montgomery 2005).

Children may present in a variety of ways as the result of the experience of fear, helplessness and terror, including disorganized or agitated behaviour, reduced interest in activities, low self-esteem, a sense of hopelessness about the future, and regressive behaviour (Montgomery 2005; Terr 1991). When children are exposed to traumatic events, the developmental process may be disturbed (Pynoos, Steinberg and Wrath 1995). Other commonly reported symptoms include social withdrawal, somatic complaints, sleep problems, difficulties in peer relationships, social withdrawal, and attention problems (Ehntholt and Yule 2006). Additionally, a child's experiences and met or unmet expectations of living in a new and often unfamiliar culture can impact positively or negatively on their mental health. A variety of complex systems need to be negotiated simply in order to meet basic needs.

Risk and resilience

There is a wealth of evidence highlighting the impact of parental mental health problems on children and young people. Their caregiver may be unavailable to them emotionally, their physical needs may be unmet, parenting may be inconsistent, and the children may find themselves in the role of carer. It has been argued that children's responses to trauma are all directly related to the response of the main caregiver; however, research has also clearly demonstrated a direct effect of trauma on children. Whilst identifying that parental reactions in moderating the effects of trauma is important, the degree to which it is important has not yet been established (Yule *et al.* 2003).

Parental risk factors for mental health problems in refugee and asylum-seeking children and young people include parents experiencing PTSD, death or separation from parents, direct observation of the helplessness of parents, underestimation of stress levels in children by parents, and maternal depression. *Child risk factors* include the number of traumatic events either experienced or witnessed, expressive language difficulties, physical health problems from either trauma or malnutrition, and older age. *Environmental factors* include the number of transitions, poverty, time taken for asylum status to be determined, and cultural isolation (McCloskey and Southwick 1996; Realmuto, Masten and Carole 1992; Wood, Halfon and Scarlata 1993; Fazel and Stein 2002). *Protective factors* that enable children at high risk to be more resilient include a supportive family milieu, an external societal agency that reinforces a child's coping efforts, and a positive personality disposition (Fazel and Stein 2002).

Providing children and young people with age-appropriate information will assist them to understand their parents' behaviours and responses. Without this, children are likely to construct their own often-inaccurate explanations (Montgomery 2005). Mixed patterns of communication may present dilemmas for workers, family, and child. Families may openly communicate with their children about traumatic experiences whilst maintaining the notion that they do not talk about traumatic events: 'This discrepancy between what actually takes place in the family (stories lived) and the experience of what takes place (stories told), may result in an ambiguous and unclear situation that may cause massive insecurity in children.' (Montgomery 2004, p.400).

Understanding of trauma and current social context

There can be an assumption that all refugee and asylum-seeking children and young people will be experiencing trauma relating to the primary event. However, whilst they may have experienced war and displacement from their country of origin, not all children remain traumatized by this experience. Often, secondary trauma is the greatest source of distress. Children cite being victims of bullying and racial harassment along with issues of housing, poverty, isolation, difference, and parental bullying, as issues of significant concern. There is a need for services to acknowledge the past trauma and the current social context being experienced, living conditions, and continued anxiety and uncertainty about the future, which can cause considerable stress (Schauer, Neuner and Elbert, 2005).

Case vignette

N was an 8-year-old girl referred to the service via her school owing to mental health concerns. She was reported to have become increasingly withdrawn, isolating herself from her peer group. Her concentration was poor and this was affecting her functioning within school. The staff were concerned that she was traumatized as a result of her experiences in Somalia. N lived with her mother and younger sister. They were in the process of making an application for leave to remain.

Following liaison with her teacher I met N and her mum. Although she had experienced primary trauma, N did not feel significantly traumatized any longer; it was apparent that her main concerns focused on issues relating to the 'here and now' in terms of social adjustment, in particular bullying, both at school and home, housing and poverty, racial harassment, and struggling to negotiate the various systems involved in the asylum process.

I met N and her mum on three occasions. This promoted a clearer understanding of the issues, and through liaison with staff at the school and other community-based voluntary and statutory services, we were able to assist N and her mum to begin to deal with the range of issues that had affected them.

Issues for practitioners and services

Whilst it has been clearly identified that refugee and asylum-seeking children and young people are likely to experience significantly more mental health problems than the general population of the host country (Ehntholt and Yule 2006), PTSD is a diagnosis that has been associated with a great deal of debate. Presentations can be viewed as a representation of mental health problems or as an understandable reaction given the context. Professionals may feel disempowered by the systems within which they work and find themselves bound by rigid diagnostic criteria, which may potentially lead to undue pathologization. It has been suggested in the literature that this may promote an identity with an illness role, as opposed to providing opportunities for rebuilding a way of life (Summerfield 2001). Watters (2001) identified that this may lead to services being characterized as 'service-led' rather than 'user-led', with them orientated towards the labelling of clients. Other literature challenges this notion, identifying PTSD as a pathological consequence of traumatic events occurring in all cultures (Schauer *et al.* 2005).

There appears to be a consensus that it is highly likely for children and young people who have experienced trauma to present with a range of emotional symptoms to varying degrees. Consequently, it is important that their relevant needs are met flexibly by the most appropriate agency (Ethntholt and Yule 2006) alongside psycho-education about symptoms, normalization of the trauma response, and interventions to enhance coping strategies aim to further empower children, young people, and their families. For the assessment process to be valid, clinicians need to gain the perception of the current concerns and difficulties from the child, young person, and the family. Mental health issues may be best viewed on a continuum of emotional difficulties, as well as diagnosable mental health problems, with consideration being given to the impact they are having on an individual's ability to function at any given time.

The diverse range of issues and needs presented by refugee and asylum-seeking children and young people presents a challenge when considering how services should be designed, tailored, and accessed in order to best meet these needs. The complex nature of stressful events and the subsequent needs of refugee children and young people highlights the need for diverse and multi-agency services (Davies and Webb 2000). Appropriate service provision needs to be available and accessible at all levels.

Refugee children have been shown to have limited access to primary and specialist health services (Refugee Council 1994). This may be for a variety of reasons, including mobility, a lack of awareness of local services, cultural differences with respect to perceptions of mental health issues, multiple agency involvement, lack of pathways for access, the current structure of child and adolescent mental health (CAMH) services, and professionals either minimizing the trauma experience or ignoring the impact of social factors. In planning to meet the mental health needs of refugee children, services should target two main areas: the provision of appropriate help for those experiencing psychological difficulties, and the development of primary prevention strategies (Fazel and Stein 2002). Both objectives require collaboration between schools, primary health care, and community child mental health services (Fazel and Stein 2003). As not all aspects of a young person's difficulties may be attributed to trauma, other important factors, such as issues relating to social integration, should not be overlooked.

Case vignette

A is a 13-year-old girl from south Serbia; she left her country with her mum as a result of domestic violence and the political situation. Three other children remain in Serbia, as mum had to leave in a hurry to escape the violence towards herself and A by her husband.

A was referred by her GP because of concerns about nocturnal enuresis and anxiety that were thought to be trauma-based. Through assessment it was clear that the nocturnal enuresis was primary and not connected to trauma. The family were assisted to access the continence service, with which we maintained links. A's anxiety appeared to relate to her experiences in Serbia, as she continued to fear for her safety and felt under constant threat from her father. These were compounded by her struggle to adjust to her new circumstances. The family were experiencing racist abuse at home and felt unsafe. Through links established via a multi-agency forum, I was able to facilitate contact with a community organization which supported families in this situation, and which had established links with the local police force. As the situation improved, the family felt supported and were able to make positive connections with their community.

It was apparent that A struggled with verbal interactions. For this reason, we utilized a variety of non-verbal techniques to assist A to understand, make links, and manage her responses to her intrusive recollections and situations that triggered difficult feelings. Through my work it became increasingly apparent that A had some cognitive impairment. This had been masked for some time owing to English being her second language. A was struggling at school, which was further affecting her self-esteem and ability to adjust. The school had attributed A's difficulties to her traumatic experiences, and consequently no educational support had been considered.

I was able to arrange a cognitive assessment with a clinical psychologist in the team. This identified a range of difficulties, facilitated the statementing process, and appropriate support was put in place for A. It also enabled the therapeutic work to be delivered at a level and pace that suited A. The family were in the appeal phase, having had their application for refugee status rejected. This added obvious limitations to the work. Nevertheless, A reported improvement in her mood, and the family reported feeling a sense of containment as a result of the work, a pervasive sense of feeling more supported, A's needs being appropriately addressed, and having more understanding of the rationale for her symptoms.

Assessment and engagement

Research evidence continues to be lacking with regard to the most effective and appropriate interventions for refugee children and models of delivering them (Hodes 2002; Ehntholt and Yule 2006). There is some disagreement with respect to utilizing a needs-based approach or addressing psychological issues, especially in relation to asylum seekers (George 2002). It is clear that clinicians needed to be open to gaining and hearing the views of children, young people, and families with regard to their symptoms, concerns, and difficulties, and their explanation of the causes of these (Watters 2001). Whilst creating trust, this also allows professionals to gain important insights. Providing due consideration is given to the particular cultural and contextual issues, it seems that the main models of treatment utilized will be the same as those used for the generic population, with adaptations as appropriate. Generally, a holistic approach is required. Given the diversity of issues presented, an array of psychological and psychosocial treatments needs to be available (Melzak 1992; Woodcock 1995).

Many clinicians find themselves using an eclectic approach and practising across the tiers of service.

Trauma counselling aimed at 'working through', often described under the broad term 'debriefing', has become a familiar provision in the UK, but there has been some doubt of its efficacy (Wessely, Rose and Bisson 1998; Mayou, Ehlers and Hobbs 2000; Stallard and Salter 2003). 'Talking' therapy may be considered an alien activity. Summerfield (2001) suggests that a more accepted model for refugees and asylum seekers may be based on a more function- and problem-focused approach, although other authors would challenge this view (Hodes 2002). Children and young people need to be provided with opportunities to talk about issues at their own pace, allowing them to take the lead in defining their difficulties as they see them with respect to past, present, and future (Montgomery 2005). The refugee literature highlights the pivotal role of family and social networks in providing support and nurturing problem-solving strategies. It has been recognized that children may be reluctant to explore their responses to a trauma in front of, or with, a parent because they want to protect them and not add to their burden. This emphasizes the importance of interventions being provided on a variety of levels by those agencies best-placed to address these needs, to enable individual, family, community, health, and social needs to be considered. This can be achieved through multi-agency working, co-ordination, and communication. *The National Service Framework for Children, Young People and Maternity Services* (DoH 2004) highlights that services being provided across the tiers, and accessed at the appropriate level and with effective partnership working, contribute to improved experiences of services and outcomes for children and young people. The challenges of partnership working in relation to issues such as a lack of understanding of the respective roles and responsibilities of differing agencies are acknowledged.

Initially a comprehensive assessment is required in order to identify the nature and range of presenting issues, and to consider which services and agencies are best placed to meet those needs. This process involves gaining information from the various systems with which the young person may be involved, including parents, carers, and school and through collaboration with all these different networks.

Fundamentally, the process of engagement and the therapeutic relationship may be more important than the specific treatment approach used. By establishing therapeutic rapport, trust is promoted, which may facilitate exploration of difficult issues, thus enabling children, young people, and families to find a way to explore their thoughts and feelings, and to facilitate a collaborative approach to care planning. As service providers we have a responsibility to establish flexible arrangements in order to meet the needs of children, young people, and families who may be reluctant to seek help for a variety of reasons, including a lack of trust in statutory services, fear of stigmatization, and perceptions about mental health (DOH 2004).

Planning interventions

There are a range of issues to be considered when planning therapeutic interventions. For example, the scope and focus of the work, is this on the 'here and now', past trauma, or both? The timing of therapeutic work needs to take into account the current context, where people are at in terms of their status, if they have been granted indefinite leave to remain, where they are in the process of appeal following a refusal of their application, and the length of time in their current location. These factors will shape the type and level of therapeutic support offered.

Issues of engagement may relate to cultural perceptions of mental health and ways in which this is understood and managed, where and how services are accessed and promoted, working with defences, and again the importance of considering the current context whilst focusing on the degree to which defences may need to be maintained or challenged. Families from differing cultures may have other ways of understanding symptoms, both in relation to themselves and their children (Montgomery 2005). Readiness to transcend cultural barriers and respectful curiosity are stances that will facilitate the process of engagement and competent practice. The meaning of clinical contact to families must be considered, interviews and therapy may remind children, young people, and their families of past aversive experiences, whilst for others, the different setting and language used by the practitioner may be reassuring, and a reminder of their safety (Hodes 2000).

Refugee and asylum-seeking clients have often established contact and trust with a range of community groups and voluntary agencies. Establishing such links may enable mental health services to be promoted and accessed in a more positive and less threatening manner. Services are likely to be provided in conjunction with other agencies, such as education, social and welfare agencies (Hodes 2000). Forums to promote multi-agency working enable training and education with respect to mental health needs and issues, as well as providing opportunities for consultation and advice, and, if appropriate, referrals and joint working. Involvement of the family and social network within any therapeutic work will enable the young person to feel supported and connected to their own community.

Contacts developed with the education system, from the outset of the project to which the clinical applications within this chapter relate, were key in promoting the service. They also facilitated increased awareness with respect to mental health needs for staff, children, young people, and their families; they removed barriers and improved access to the CAMH service. These contacts also enabled parents to be educated with respect to mental health and at times helped them to access support in their own right to meet their needs.

Schools offer a framework for enhancing resilient behaviour in children and young people, as well as monitoring academic progress, and behavioural and social adaptation (Yule 2000; Williams and Westermeyer 1986; Howard and Hodes 2000). Schools can play a vital part in integration by facilitating not only educational, but also social and emotional development. In addition, they can act as link between the local community for children and parents (Fazel and Stein 2002).

Support networks help to develop children's resilience by enhancing their individual competencies, in turn adding to their self-worth and sense of control over their environment (Lefcourt, Martin and Saleh 1984). Links with the education system enable mental health needs to be identified, training, advice, and consultation to be provided to staff and community workers, and provision of services within a less threatening environment which promotes a positive and acceptable way to access this service. This requires workers to be creative and flexible with respect to how services will be accessed and facilitated to best meet the needs of all concerned.

The age and experiences of children and young people may indicate that their responses to trauma can be difficult to predict, and that they will be affected by the level of exposure to the trauma and their relationship to others affected by the trauma. At times it may be most appropriate for work to be undertaken indirectly with children via their parents or carers. This requires the parent to deal with their own trauma, which may necessitate promoting access to a range of non-statutory or specialist adult services. Parents and carers need to be available to children and young people to enable them to listen and comfort them as required (Osofsky 2004). Parents may require education about the impact of the trauma upon their child, and assist their understanding with respect to the issues associated with both their own and their children's behaviour.

Delivering interventions

Interventions with refugee and asylum-seeking children, young people, and families require a creative and flexible approach focusing on the various layers involved. The presenting issues, current context, both social and psychological, and the individual's aim for accessing the service, will inform the therapeutic approach. It is vital to establish the goals of therapy and intervention and not to make assumptions with respect to needs. The importance of enhancing resilience needs to be promoted. Attention is required with regard to where families are in the process of their application for leave to remain and their social context. These issues will inevitably affect their ability to access work. The ethical considerations associated with undertaking therapeutic work during a period of such potential instability alongside the impact of delaying therapy have to be considered.

The success of an approach based primarily on Western techniques, such as counselling or psychotherapy, is unlikely without consideration of the fundamental issues that may be present. Through liaison with other agencies, clinicians can ensure that basic needs are being addressed and support networks created (Ehntholt and Yule 2006). Factors promoting, enhancing, and impacting on resilience require consideration. Maslow's hierarchy of needs identifies the importance of meeting the needs of food, shelter and safety, before the higher-level needs relating to self-esteem and self-actualization can be considered.

The therapeutic relationship may involve acting as an advocate to assist meeting fundamental needs, including promoting access to legal advice and family tracing programmes; this further facilitates the process of engagement and trust. Professional boundaries need to be maintained but may involve practising outside a rigid, traditional approach (Watters 2001). Legal issues, such as fear of deportation, mobility, and uncertain and changing circumstances, can affect the therapeutic process. Alongside this is the occasional attribution to mental health issues by solicitors and advocates – although well meaning, this could potentially confuse the clinician. Consequently, whilst a flexible approach to practice is beneficial, there is a need for the issues to be clearly identified to enable agencies to work within their roles as appropriate. Clinicians may be required to clarify presenting issues whilst maintaining a degree of distance from these processes. As identified, opportunities for promoting and enhancing resilience are important for children and young people, especially when they are surrounded by adversity. Goldberg and Huxley (1992) defined resilience as being linked to a 'sense of self-esteem and self-confidence; an ability to deal with change and adaptation; and a repertoire of problem solving approaches'. Thus, in order to develop resilience, 'an individual needs experience of secure, stable, affectionate responses and an experience of success and achievement' (Goldberg and Huxley 1992, p.100).

Case vignette

P (13) and A (15) were referred to the child and adolescent mental health (CAMH) service because of concerns about their low mood, apathy, and poor concentration, felt to be related to the trauma they had experienced in the Democratic Republic of the Congo. The boys had been in the UK for five months. They were living with their maternal aunt, with whom they had a positive and supportive relationship. They had witnessed many atrocities, including the killing of their mother.

When I met with them to undertake a mental health assessment at a community organization, they reported feeling increasingly low in mood and this was affecting their ability to function in school and at home. Both boys attributed these feelings to their sense of isolation, lack of contact with their peer group, living away from home and having no access to sports activities that they had previously enjoyed before they fled from the Congo. They had been granted temporary leave to remain until their 18th birthdays. They did not wish to undertake any work around their trauma experiences and losses at this time. We did explore their responses to their experiences, and through psycho-education the boys were able to put these in context, having an increased understanding of their symptoms.

I assisted the boys to become involved in a football team, facilitated by a member of one of the community groups known through a multi-agency forum. The football team was made up of adolescent males from the Democratic Republic of the Congo. They met twice a week, near the boys' housing. They attended for two further appointments a few months apart and both reported a significant improvement in their symptoms. It was agreed that they would be discharged and could re-access the service again if they needed to undertake further work in the future.

Interventions can be provided either directly, through a combination of work with the child or young person individually, with parents or carers, family or group work, and may involve a range of disciplines dependent on the presenting issues, or indirectly, through consultation, advice, liaison, and training with the range of professionals involved in a voluntary, statutory, or private capacity with refugee and asylum-seeking clients.

Case vignette

E was an 11-year-old boy referred via the school with which there were established links. He had been in the UK for three years, the family had fled from Kosovo, where they had experienced and witnessed a variety of traumatic events, including E and his father being taken from the house and tortured on several occasions. They were in the process of appealing against a negative decision with regard to their application for refugee status. School identified concerns with respect to E's increasingly disruptive, aggressive, and hostile behaviour. He was reported to be both physically and verbally aggressive to peers, staff, and property. They had attempted to put in place a variety of strategies to support E, identified via the consultation process; however, the situation continued to deteriorate and E was facing permanent exclusion.

An assessment was initially undertaken at the school with E and his parents. They identified similar concerns with respect to school, but did not feel there were any difficulties in terms of E's presentation at home, with the exception of him continuing to have nightmares on a regular basis. Through regular meetings with E, at school it became apparent that he was misinterpreting the interactions of staff and peers, especially those that involved any degree of challenge or boundary-setting, based on his previous experiences in Kosovo. Thus he quickly responded aggressively in order to protect himself from the danger he perceived he was in.

Work was undertaken with E individually and with the key school staff and E's parents to enable them to understand this response and put in place strategies to address the process of E misinterpreting actions of others based on his early experiences. This was informed by a variety of therapeutic models, including narrative therapy, systemic therapy, cognitive-behavioural therapy, and problem-solving. A constant dilemma existed with regard to how much work should be undertaken around E's established defences, and whether to explore his past trauma, due to the uncertain status of the family. The worker had been liaising with the family lawyer and other relevant agencies and had written numerous letters advising of the extent and apparent triggers of the mental health difficulties being experienced, in support of their claim for indefinite leave to remain; letters from E's father's adult mental health worker accompanied these.

This dilemma had an impact upon the work and the ability of E and his family to achieve a sense of resolution. Sadly, the family were removed from their home and deported; I was informed of this via the school when I arrived at the school to see E for an individual session.

Unaccompanied minors

An unaccompanied asylum-seeking child (UASC) is defined by the United Nations High Commissioner for Refugees (UNHCR) as 'an individual under the age of 18, who is separated from both parents and is not being cared for by an adult who, by law or custom, is responsible for doing so' (UNHCR 1997). This group of children and young people is identified as being particularly vulnerable and, despite evidence of significant resilience and coping strategies, they are likely to display more symptoms of psychological distress than their accompanied peers (Ehntholt and Yule 2006). As with all refugee and asylum-seeking children and young people, unaccompanied minors are likely to have experienced trauma within the country from which they fled, during their journey from this country to the one in which they seek refuge and on arrival in their host country. Issues of loss may be exacerbated by a lack of support systems, such as family and community life, and the associated isolation.

The UK policy *Every Child Matters* (DoH 2003) identified unaccompanied asylum seekers as a particularly vulnerable group in need of protection and highlighted the responsibility of all agencies to work together to ensure their needs are met. A significant challenge when working with this group relates to immigration uncertainty. In the UK, the majority are granted exceptional leave to remain up to the age of 18, when their status is reviewed. This leaves the child with major uncertainties about their future which are likely to significantly affect them psychologically, as well as having consequences for integration and education (Ehntholt and Yule 2006; Fazel and Stein 2002).

Again, multi-agency interventions are required to address issues of isolation, education, foster or residential placements, and to ensure the child's basic needs are met, as well as identifying their emotional and psychological needs, and providing support at the most appropriate level. This may range from befriending schemes and access to activities to promote interaction with peers and reduce isolation to specialist CAMH services involvement. Providing opportunities to enhance resilience and empower young people, especially in relation to decision-making, appears fundamental when working with children and young people who are unaccompanied. Alongside this, work with carers may be required to enable them to increase their understanding of the needs and behaviours of these children and young people.

Cultural implications

Culturally competent practice requires practitioners to be self-reflective: aware of their own values, beliefs, and assumptions based on cultural upbringing. Practitioners need to be aware of the ways in which these notions inform and impact on practice. They relate to cultural issues presented to us in our contact with children, young people, family, and wider systems. However, caution is needed to ensure that practice is not developed within culture-specific frameworks, with clinicians making generalized assumptions on the particular presentation or needs of a family or community, based on rigid criteria. Respectful curiosity will enable us to understand our client's cultural identity and the ways in which this has been constructed and informed over time. Children grow and develop within relationships that are culturally determined. Thus, when children experience trauma, culture provides meaning to their experience (Lewis and Ippen 2004).

In order to better understand the impact of the primary or secondary trauma, we need to be open to understanding the meanings attached to this by the individual and family, and the ways in which these have been informed. We also need to gain valuable insight into the families' perceptions of what level or type of intervention may be beneficial, any fears they may have regarding a treatment approach, as well as understanding views, perceptions, and meaning with respect to mental health problems or difficulties. Clinicians need to familiarize themselves with cultural perspectives of trauma (Morris and Silove 1992). Children may be experiencing the challenge of living within two cultures and trying to negotiate ways to incorporate the 'old and the new'. They may be in a position of acting as advocate for family members because of quickly acquiring new skills such as language. Assessment and treatment planning should be undertaken in collaboration with children, young people, and their families to ensure that these issues are addressed.

As clinicians our approach to practice should be respectful, curious, and non-judgemental within our professional codes, with both ethical and statutory responsibilities. Circumstances may arise which present dilemmas to practitioners with regard to making judgements on values from others countries versus the need to protect children. They may occur, for example, in the context of parenting issues such as physical chastisement. At these times, child protection procedures may need to be initiated. These will obviously be clearly communicated and explained to the family to minimize the impact on the process of engagement.

Therapists undertaking work with clients with such traumatic histories may find themselves feeling overwhelmed by the nature, intensity, and degree of the issues identified and reported (Turner 2000). They may feel deskilled, or at risk of secondary traumatization. There may also be a desire to rescue the client, with workers feeling disempowered by the systems around them and the clients. These feelings may mirror the experiences of the client group and lead to parallel processes within the work. Supervision is a crucial mechanism to enable all these issues to be identified and explored alongside established means of personal support (Ehntholt and Yule 2006).

Group work

The evidence base is limited in relation to the effectiveness of group interventions with refugee and asylum-seeking children and young people. It has been suggested that running groups with a constructive, therapeutic approach can assist individuals to explore and identify coping resources, share feelings and experiences, normalize responses, problem-solve, and achieve a sense of mastery over difficulties (Jones 1998; Yule *et al.* 2003). Therapeutic groups may provide opportunities and challenges, and may diminish the sense of hopelessness (Hodes 2000). However, we also need to consider the constraints of involving fairly diverse groups of children in relation to gender, age, developmental capacity, and traumatic experiences (Yule *et al.* 2003).

Working with interpreters

When working with refugees, a shared language and set of cultural understandings may not exist. Interpreters play an important role in promoting access to services (Tribe and Morrissey 2002). Working with interpreters can present a range of challenges as predictability and consistency are not guaranteed. Thus, each session may involve starting the process of working with a new interpreter. There may also be a lack of suitably trained interpreters, or a lack of those speaking the required language or dialect. There may also be little money available to enable services to be accessed via different statutory or private agencies, or to access translation services for written material. These issues may be further exacerbated with refugee clients as a result of their lack of familiarity with the healthcare systems, or the potential distrust of professionals arising from past traumatic experiences.

Utilizing a collaborative approach with interpreters aims to enhance clinical practice. When using interpreters, consideration should be given to a variety of issues, including booking someone from the appropriate ethnicity, political party, dialect and gender. Ways in which information is shared should be established before sessions to enable the clinician to understand times when the interpreter may be offering their own perception of a situation. Additional time will be required both before and after sessions to enable issues relating to confidentiality and the role of the interpreter, considering issues such as requirements for literal translation, the translation of cultural concepts, and potential transference issues, as well for debriefing after sessions (Ehntholt and Yule 2006).

Where possible, and appropriate, the same interpreter should be used at each appointment to facilitate consistency. Family members, especially children, should not be asked to act as interpreters as this places unreasonable and unrealistic expectations upon them. An additional person within the therapy room adds an additional dynamic to therapeutic work. Preparation is necessary in order to manage issues relating to processes such as working with silence, transference and counter-transference, and boundaries.

Conclusions

Despite the substantial evidence that refugee and asylum-seeking children, young people, and their families present with a variety of mental health needs, there is still limited evidence-based guidance to effective interventions and services. Multi-agency working across the range of statutory, voluntary, and private agencies in contact with refugee and asylum-seeking children and young people will facilitate collaboration and co-ordination, and will address the various needs of this group at the most appropriate level. Providing interventions that promote and enhance resilience, reduce isolation, and are flexible in terms of delivery and environment appears to encourage access to services. Positive relationships with other agencies with differing roles and obligations should promote delivery of services based on individual need, which, in turn, will contribute to the process of engagement and uptake of services by refugee and asylum-seeking children and young people.

The importance of developing therapeutic relationships with our clients and other agencies is fundamental. Reflective practice is essential as part of this process, and as clinicians we must be open to considering the range of values, attitudes, and beliefs bought to clinical practice by ourselves and the others involved in the therapeutic process. It is important to consider the ways in which these assumptions affect our work to enable us to continue to find ways to improve and enhance our practice.

Refugee and asylum-seeking children, young people and their families present with complex needs; it is unlikely that these needs can be met by a single agency. A lack of provision by one service may affect the ability of other services to be effective. Therefore partnership working is an essential requirement of high-quality service provision (DoH 2004).

References

Davies, M. and Webb, E. (2000) 'Promoting the psychological well-being of refugee children.' *Clinical Child Psychology and Psychiatry 5*, 541–554.

Department of Health (DoH) (2003) *Every Child Matters*. London: Stationary Office.

Department of Health (DoH) (2004) *The National Service Framework for Children, Young People and Maternity Services*. London: Stationary Office.

Ehntholt, K. and Yule, W. (2006) 'Assessment and treatment of refugee children and adolescents who have experienced war related trauma.' *Journal of Child Psychology and Psychiatry 47*, 1197–1210.

Fazel, M. and Stein, A. (2002) 'The mental health of refugee children.' *Archives of Disease in Childhood 87*, 366–370.

Fazel M. and Stein A. (2003) 'Mental health of refugee children: Comparative study.' *British Medical Journal 327*, 134.

George, M. (2002) 'Desperately seeking safety.' *Mental Health Today*. February, 8–9.

Goldberg, D. and Huxley, P. (1992) *Common Mental Disorders: A Bio-social Model*. London: Routledge.

Hodes, M. (2000) 'Psychologically distressed refugee children in the United Kingdom.' *Child Psychology and Psychiatry Review 5*, 57–68.

Hodes, M. (2002) 'Three key issues for young refugees' mental health.' *Transcultural Psychiatry 39*, 196–213.

Howard, M. and Hodes, M. (2000) 'Psychopathology, adversity and service utilization of young refugees.' *Journal of the American Academy of Child and Adolescent Psychiatry 39*, 368–377.

Jones, L. (1998) 'Adolescent groups for encamped Bosnian refugees: some problems and solutions.' *Clinical Child Psychology and Psychiatry 3*, 441–551.

Lefcourt, H., Martin, R. and Saleh, E. (1984) 'Locus of control and social support: Interactive moderators of stress.' *Journal of Personal Social Psychology 47*, 378–389.

Lewis, M.L. and Ippen, C.G. (2004) 'Rainbows of Tears, Souls Full of Hope: Cultural Issues Related to Young Children and Trauma.' In J.D. Osofsky (ed.) *Young Children and Trauma. Treatment and Intervention*. New York, NY: Guilford Press.

Mayou, R., Ehlers, A. and Hobbs, M. (2000) 'Psychological debriefing for road traffic victims: Three-year follow-up of a randomized controlled trial.' *British Journal of Psychiatry 176*, 589–593.

McCloskey, L. and Southwick, K. (1996) 'Psychosocial problems in refugee children exposed to war.' *Pediatrics 97*, 394–397.

Melzak, S. (1992) 'Secrecy, privacy, survival, repressive regimes and growing up.' *Bulletin of the Anna Freud Centre 15*, 205–224.

Montgomery, E. (2005) 'Traumatised Refugee Families: The Child's Perspective.' In P. Berliner, G. Arenas, J., and Haagensen, J.O. (eds) *Torture and Organized Violence: Contributions to a Professional Human Rights Response.* Copenhagen: Dansk Psykologisk Forlag.

Montgomery, E. (2004) 'Tortured families: A coordinated management of meaning analysis.' *Family Process 43*, 349–371.

Morris, P. and Silove, D. (1992) 'Cultural Influences in Psychotherapy with Refugee Survivors of Torture and Trauma.' *Hosp Community Psychiatry 43*, 820–824.

Osofsky, J. (ed.) (2004) *Young Children and Trauma Intervention and Treatment.* New York, NY: Guilford Press.

Pynoos, R., Steinberg, A., and Wraith, R. (1995) 'A Developmental Model of Childhood Traumatic Stress.' In D. Cicchetti and D. Cohen (eds) *Developmental Psychopathology.* New York, NY: John Wiley.

Realmuto, G., Masten, A., and Carole, L. (1992) 'Adolescent survivors of massive childhood trauma in Cambodia: Life events and current symptoms.' *Journal of Traumatic Stress 5*, 589–599.

Refugee Council (1994) *The Health of Refugees: NDT Conference Reports.* London: Refugee Council.

Schauer, M. Neuner, F., and Elbert, T. (2005) *Narrative Exposure Therapy: A Short-Term Intervention for Traumatic Stress Disorders after War, Terror or Torture* London: Hogrefe & Huber.

Stallard, P. and Salter, E. (2003) 'Psychological debriefing with children and young people following traumatic events.' *Clinical Child Psychology and Psychiatry 8*, 445–457.

Summerfield, D. (2001) 'Asylum-seekers, refugees and mental health services in the UK.' *Psychiatric Bulletin 25*, 161–163.

Terr, L. (1991) 'Childhood traumas: An outline and overview.' *American Journal of Psychiatry 148*, 10–20.

Thabet, A. and Vostanis, P. (1999) 'Post traumatic stress reactions in children of war.' *Journal of Child Psychology and Psychiatry 40*, 385–391.

Turner, S. (2000) 'Therapeutic Approaches with Survivors of Torture.' In J. Kareem and R. Littlewood (eds) *Intercultural Therapy* (2nd ed) Oxford: Blackwell.

Tribe, R. and Morrissey, J. (2002) 'The Refugee Context and the Role of Interpreters.' In R. Tribe and H. Raval (eds) *Working with Interpreters in Mental Health.* Hove: Brunner–Routledge.

United Nations High Commissioner for Refugees (UNHCR) (1997) *Refugees and Others of Concern to UNHCR.* Geneva: United Nations High Commissioner for Refugees.

Watters C. (2001) 'Emerging paradigms in the mental health care of refugees.' *Social Science and Medicine 52*, 1709–1718.

Wessely, S., Rose S., and Bisson, J. (1998) 'A systematic review of brief psychological interventions (debriefing) for the treatment of immediate trauma related symptoms and the prevention of post traumatic disorder.' *The Cochrane Library*, Issue 2. Update Software: Oxford.

Williams, C. and Wetermeyer, J. (1986) *Refugee Mental Health in Resettlement Countries.* Washington, DC: Hemisphere Publishing Corporation.

Woodcock, J. (1995) 'Healing rituals with families in exile.' *Journal of Family Therapy 17*, 397–409.

Wood, D. Halfon, N., and Scarlata, D. (1993) 'Impact of family relocation on children's growth, development, school function and behavior.' *JAMA 270*, 1334–1338.

Yule, W. (2000) 'From pogroms to "ethnic cleansing": Meeting the needs of war affected children.' *Journal of Child Psychology and Psychiatry 41*, 695–702.

Yule, W., Perrin, S., and Smith, P. (2003) 'Post-traumatic Stress Reactions in Children and Adolescents.' In W. Yule (ed.) *Post-Traumatic Stress Disorders Concepts and Therapy.* Chichester: John Wiley.

CHAPTER 11

Therapeutic Services for Homeless Families and Young People

Panos Vostanis

Children and young people who are homeless broadly fall in two categories: younger children living with parents (usually lone mothers) and single, young, homeless people. These two groups are being discussed separately in this chapter, although it is acknowledged that these are not necessarily homogenous, as reasons and circumstances and pathways leading to homelessness vary. For example, families may become homeless to escape from domestic violence or neighbourhood harassment or, in recent years, at some point during the asylum-seeking process. Single, young, homeless people may have left public care, or found it difficult to hold on to their accommodation because of difficulties such as substance abuse. In reality, a number of such factors are present and inter-related, and are usually explained by longstanding vulnerability rather than solely concentrating on the episode leading to homelessness. Inevitably, many of these children and young people will overlap with groups discussed in other chapters, in particular those who are looked after, victims of domestic violence, refugees and asylum-seekers, or those in contact with the courts and drug and alcohol agencies. Understanding their specific needs and their life pathways is essential in planning and delivering appropriate interventions and services.

Homeless children and families
Extent of the problem
Children and their parents who become homeless have a broad range of complex and inter-related social, educational, and health needs (Haber and Toro 2004; Vostanis and Cumella 1999). For the purposes of this chapter, homeless families are defined as adults and children who are statutorily accepted by

local authorities (housing departments) or equivalent organizations in different countries, and who are usually accommodated for a brief period in voluntary agency, local authority, or housing association hostels. In the UK, approximately 100,000 households live in temporary accommodation at any one time (ODPM 2004), and of these households a significant proportion consists of homeless children and their families. Nineteen per cent of all households in bed and breakfast accommodation are households with dependant children or expectant mothers. Of all households accepted as homeless by UK local authorities, 51 per cent have dependant children, and a further 11 per cent include a pregnant woman. Children constitute 40 per cent of the US homeless population, which has steadily risen to two million during one year (Davey 2004).

Characteristics and needs

The reasons for homelessness are diverse: predominantly domestic violence, relationship breakdowns, and neighbourhood harassment. In an earlier needs analysis, we established high rates of domestic and neighbourhood violence, child abuse, mental health problems among children and parents, special educational needs, lack of community support networks, and lack of access to statutory services (Vostanis et al. 1997; Vostanis 2001). Other studies in the UK and North America identified similar needs. These included family breakdown, child protection, and lack of social supports (Anderson and Rayens 2004), developmental delays, poor nutrition, accidents and injuries (Webb et al. 2001), mental health problems (Buckner et al. 1999), and learning difficulties (Rubin et al. 1996). Children's and parents' difficulties are often associated (Page and Nooe 2002).

With regards to their health needs, homeless children are more likely to have a history of low birth weight, anaemia, dental decay, delayed immunizations, to be of lower height, and have a greater degree of nutritional stress. They are also more likely to suffer accidents, injuries, and burns. Some studies have found that child health problems increase with the duration of homelessness, although this is not a consistent finding. A substantial proportion of homeless children have delayed development compared with the general population of children of a similar chronological age. This includes both specific developmental delays, such as in receptive and expressive language, visual motor and reading skills, as well as general educational status and skills (Page, Ainsworth and Pett 1993; Webb et al. 2001).

Both children and parents are more likely to present with mental health problems, although these are not specific to this group, but rather to the multiple risk factors that they have been exposed to over the years. Previous studies have found high levels of a number of emotional and behavioural problems (Amery, Tomkins and Victor 1995; Vostanis *et al.* 1997). In pre-school and primary school-aged children, behavioural problems include sleep disturbance, feeding problems, aggression, and hyperactivity. These are often concurrent with emotional or developmental problems. Anxiety and post-traumatic stress disorder (PTSD) are often precipitated by life events such as witnessing domestic violence. Children's and mothers' mental health problems (predominantly depression) are often associated, both being predicted by previous family conflict, exposure to violence, and abuse (Bassuk *et al.* 1996; Zima *et al.* 1996). These are likely to continue, even after rehousing, in the absence of intervention (Karim *et al.* 2006; Vostanis, Grattan and Cumella 1998). Although scarce housing can be a key barrier to families' reintegration in the community, lack of social and welfare support, and lack of adaptive coping strategies also largely contribute to further social instability (Lindsey 1998; Tischler and Vostanis 2007). Despite this well-established high level of need, there has been an absence of social care and health services for homeless children and their families, because of their mobility, difficulty in accessing mainstream services, and lack of co-ordination and commissioning of dedicated services.

Access to appropriate services
There are several reasons why homeless children and their families cannot access mainstream health and social care services, despite their high level of need. A major one is their mobility between different health and local authority sectors. As most families will have changed address frequently or urgently, they are less likely than the rest of the population to be registered with a general practitioner (GP) or, in the best of situations, to be registered as temporary patients with a GP covering the hostel residents. This reduces their access to primary and secondary medical care, as well as immunizations and other preventive health procedures (Brooks, Ferguson and Webb 1998). Homeless families therefore tend to rely on accident and emergency departments for medical treatment, and have high rates of hospital admission (Lissauer *et al.* 1993).

The same applies to social services (access teams, family teams, family support units), and other community agencies. In addition, homeless children are more likely to be out of school, as the family could thus be traced by a violent ex-partner, or because of the distance from hostels (particularly in large cities). Parents may wait until they know where they will be rehoused before registering the children with a new nursery or school. Nurseries and primary schools in the proximity of hostels usually have a high pupil turnover, with resulting high costs, and there are often limited vacancies for short periods (Power, Whitty and Youdell 1995). These problems are compounded for refugee children. The outcome is that children miss out on their only source of social stability, that is, their peers, their routines, and a sense of achievement, which are important protective factors. Apart from the organizational problems in accessing services, children may be at increased risk through absence of communication and continuity between agencies, taking into account the frequency of child protection incidents and registrations, as they often move between different parts of the country, and local social services departments may not be aware or be informed in time of their previous history.

These family and service characteristics inevitably affect any potential contact with mental health services. Such issues are less obvious for adults with mental illness, who may be known to local services. However, psychiatric cover of a hostel can be a contentious issue, as residents can be classified as 'non-fixed abode'. The local service may argue that this population substantially increases the number of referrals, thus requiring extra resources. In areas with such additional resources, these usually target the single adult homeless population, as they are more likely to present with severe mental illness (psychotic disorders). It is more difficult to provide cover for parents with depressive or anxiety disorders, self-harm, and substance misuse.

Principles and models of therapeutic and support services for homeless families

Earlier studies showed that homeless children and their parents require a co-ordinated approach by different agencies (Gaubatz 2001). In the UK, there have been a number of recent national policies that acknowledge these principles, predominantly that families need more than rehousing if their placements are to be sustained and break the cycle of homelessness (ODPM 2003).

The nature and complexity of child and family mental health and related needs indicate that plans for the development of a new service should involve key agencies from the beginning, be incorporated in inter-agency policy and commissioning documents, have clear objectives, mechanisms of reviewing the service specifications, and a built-in evaluation process. It is also important that all health and housing organizations have a local strategy for homeless people (children, families, single youths, adults). This framework will ensure that this population no longer slips through the wider service net, or is overlooked for new resources. No single agency can successfully meet families' needs, and a large number of families are likely to fall between existing services. For example, if there are no child protection issues or marked mental health problems, neither social care nor specialist mental health services are likely to be involved.

Because of the diverse and overlapping needs of homeless families, some service models have adopted a predominantly specialist approach, often targeting mental health problems and substance abuse (Holleman et al. 2004; Tischler et al. 2002). Although these services have overcome traditional barriers, such as access and responsiveness, they are not designed to address the whole range of families' needs (Hertlein and Killmer 2004). Similar dilemmas may apply to social work (Stewart and Stewart 1992) or educational interventions (Nabors *et al.* 2003).

Guided by the families' multiple and constantly changing needs, which could thus not be met by any one agency, we have encompassed the overarching model of family support, which we have gradually developed over the years in partnership between housing, health, and social care agencies. The rationale, context, and evaluation findings of this service are summarized below.

Family support service model

Taking into consideration the evidence on the nature of characteristics and needs of homeless families, and their lack of access to and engagement with generic services, a family support service was set up in a UK local authority, jointly financed from housing and health sources. This was initially one family support worker post, whose role was loosely based on previous family support service models (Chaffin, Bonner and Hill 2001; Sanders, Turner and Markie-Dadds 2002) but was adapted to the requirements of this vulnerable and highly mobile client group. The broad objectives of the service were to provide assessment and identification of health and social care needs, liaison with other agencies, parent training and support; help in obtaining education, and accessing primary health care. The initial family support worker post could only provide input to families while they resided at the hostel, but not after their return to the community, when they remained vulnerable. For this reason, the service was subsequently extended to a family support team.

An evaluation of this service suggested that the support provided by the family support team was beneficial to a client group which often felt isolated, although mothers clearly stated that practical help was at least as important to them as counselling and emotional support (Tischler *et al.* 2004; Anderson, Stuttaford and Vostanis 2006). Mothers appreciated equally help in 'showing how to make milk bottles' and 'disciplining the children'; other examples included help with their housing applications, benefits, health, or dental appointments, as well as with their own or their children's emotional difficulties, usually as a result of traumatic experiences ('dealing with the flashbacks'). This was a critical finding which influenced the further development of the service as well as the establishment of further therapeutic interventions. The underpinning philosophy of integrating social care and therapeutic interventions is indeed evident throughout this book.

Consequently, the service evolved by combining aspects of practical support; therapeutic work adapted to the skills of the team, level of service provision and families' needs, and liaison with other agencies during and after the families' stay at the hostel. These components should be fairly balanced. If the worker's role is only to act in an advocate or key working capacity, without active therapeutic input, local mainstream services are unlikely to fill the gap. In contrast, an active role of parenting support can elicit a better response from agencies (such as health visiting, social services, education, or mental health) by ensuring that their specialist skills are used effectively. Although non-statutory services will vary, they also have a valuable role during the families' transition and, more importantly, during their resettlement. These could include drug and alcohol services, youth, or carer support, or action against domestic violence.

Homeless parents have seen different professionals at different times, often in crisis, have frequently changing life circumstances and priorities, and have variable experiences from agencies. Therefore, they may find it difficult to engage with yet another service, particularly if they are concerned about service responses on issues such as child protection and substance use (Swick and Bailey 2004). For these reasons, family support workers require a range of skills and approaches when working therapeutically with families and forming a trusting relationship whilst making difficult decisions in relation to children's safety. Their approach to parenting interventions will also need to differ from similar programmes primarily designed for families living in stability. They will need to overcome anxieties or suspicion about the aims of parent training, adapt traditional programmes (e.g. Webster-Stratton and Hammond 1997), work within time constraints, combine individual and group work, and often run such programmes on the 'back' of more engaging leisure activities such as art and craft.

Despite these constraints there is emerging evidence that such interventions can be effective. Time-limited behavioural therapy or advice given to parents and staff on how to deal with children's aggressive behaviour, bedwetting, or sleep problems was found to lead to positive outcomes among homeless families, which were sustained after rehousing in the community, compared to matched homeless families who received routine care (Tischler *et al.* 2002). Cognitive-behavioural or brief supportive psychotherapy during this family transition may be offered to children who have experienced major trauma, predominantly targeting acute symptomatic presentation (post-traumatic stress reactions), such as nightmares, distressing thoughts and images, or flashbacks. Similar individual interventions can be useful for adults. Family therapy needs to take into consideration the wider systems involved with the family, and incorporate behavioural strategies and crisis interventions if necessary (Hertlein and Killmer 2004; Holleman *et al.* 2004). Parent or family groups can engage a larger number of families in homeless shelters (Davey 2004).

Children and parents with more serious problems or disorders need to have direct access to the local mental health service, with clearly defined care pathways, protocols, and access. In order to best utilize specialist resources, lower-level therapeutic support or counselling may be provided by professionals such as family support workers, although they should be provided with suitable training, supervision, and direct access to the mental health service for consultation and referrals, as appropriate. In many ways, families are most vulnerable on their return to the community, because of difficulties in coping independently or exposure to previous adversities, particularly violence, or both. For this reason there is increasing emphasis for housing departments and related organizations to provide resettlement support in order to help them sustain their placement (Stojanovic *et al.* 1999; Tischler and Gregory 2002). Many agencies have a role to play in strengthening families' reintegration, by helping mothers to break the cycle of violence and homelessness (Walters and East 2001); children to sustain school placements and function adaptively within their peer groups (Nabors *et al.* 2003); and both to become part of their neighbourhood and community (Hill *et al.* 2002). During this process, it is essential that the more needy families are not lost to services, but instead are able to access mental health services without having to go through a new referral episode.

Case vignette

R, a 12-year-old boy, and his mother, suffered harassment from neighbours for several years and found it difficult to cope, which resulted in them moving between different properties, before eventually becoming homeless. An older sister was already living independently and in contact with her family. Whilst at a hostel, R and his mother were anxious and scared of going back to the community, even in a better property. R had nightmares, would not go out on his own, complained of being bullied by other children at the hostel, slept in his mother's bed, and stopped attending school. The child and the parent appeared to reinforce one other's anxieties, that is to say, R's mother was giving him mixed signals each time he attempted to go to school.

Following the first assessment, the mother engaged with the family support worker, and met her individually and jointly with R to understand the origins of their anxieties, and to develop more adaptive behavioural strategies. The family support worker asked the local child psychiatrist to assess R with her, and consult on the short- and long-term plan for the family. Although R did not return to school whilst at the hostel, they both participated more in hostel activities, mixed more with other families, and felt more confident to pursue their housing application. A school placement was arranged for R in the proximity of their new property.

A care package was set up before the family left the hostel. A resettlement worker visited regularly to offer practical support, until the family felt able to live independently. The family support worker arranged a few follow-up meetings, some jointly with the child psychiatrist, to conclude her work with the family, and monitor R's anxiety and reintegration to school. This progressed well for one school term, before R was bullied again. This time, his mother made a quick decision herself to seek a different school for R, who attended regularly and felt settled for the remaining school year. His anxieties gradually subsided, although he still tended to take on adult responsibilities, particularly when his mother worried about finances. There were no further problems with neighbours one year after the family had moved to their new property.

Homeless single young people
Characteristics and needs

This group shares the characteristics and vulnerabilities of adolescents, young people in transition, and young adults, thus making them extremely vulnerable, and likely to fall within a number of services geared for specific age categories or types of mental health problems. In theory, any young people under the age of 16 should be accommodated by local authorities, that is, within public care placements. In reality, there are an alarming number of street children around the world. Even in Western societies it is difficult to establish the real extent and characteristics of homeless young people.

Some figures quote as many as 100 million homeless adolescents worldwide, 40 per cent of whom live in Latin America, 30 per cent in Asia, and 10 per cent in Africa (Ensign and Gittlesohn 1998). In the USA, about 750,000 school-aged children and adolescents are homeless in the course of a year (Buckner and Bassuk 1997) with doubling of this figure when including older teenagers and young adults (Lindsey et al. 2000). Although the numbers of rough sleepers in the UK has decreased to 500 at any given time, one in 30 young people are affected by homelessness at any one time, that is, they lack a secure, safe, and affordable place to live in (Centrepoint 2006). One-third of the total Australian homeless population of approximately 100,000 were young people aged between 12 and 24 years, with 26,000 between 12 and 18 years, and 10,100 aged between 19 and 24 years (Australian Clearinghouse for Youth Studies 2006).

Young, homeless people are believed to be on the increase because of lower income and unemployment, less affordable housing, and restrictions on social care benefits. Certain vulnerable groups are over-represented among the young homeless population, such as care leavers (Craig and Hodson 1998), pregnant young women or young mothers (Webb et al. 2003), and those discharged from state custody or other residential settings (Embry et al. 2000).

Like the previously discussed population of homeless children and their parents, homeless adolescents and young people have a high level of complex and inter-related social, health, and educational needs. Because of their older age they are more likely to present with mental illness and associated serious difficulties, rather than the behavioural and emotional presentations described in younger children. In particular, homeless young people have been found to be at risk for mental health problems and disorders such as self-harm (Tyler *et al.* 2003), depression (Cauce *et al.* 2000; Unger *et al.* 1997), anxiety, PTSD (Whitbeck *et al.* 2004), and alcohol and drug misuse (Ginzler *et al.* 2003; Slesnick and Prestopnik 2005). Also, they are more vulnerable to malnutrition, sexually transmitted, and health diseases (Rotheram-Borus, Koopman and Ernhardt 1991; Sherman 1992). A number of studies in the USA and the UK found that these mental health problems were significantly associated with previous adverse experiences of family breakdown, abuse, residential care, poor educational attainment, and instability of accommodation (Craig and Hodson 1998; Herman *et al.* 1997; Tyler and Cauce 2002; Wrate and Blair 1999). Similar findings are emerging from other countries (e.g. Australia – Kamieniecki [2001]; Spain – Olivan [2002]; Canada – Votta and Manion [2004]).

Many of these problems are likely to persist in the absence of interventions (Deckel, Peled and Spiro 2003). Craig and Hodson (2000) followed up young people one year after they had become homeless. Two-thirds of those with mental health disorders had persistent symptoms, and these were associated with adverse childhood experiences and rough sleeping. Less than half (42%) had satisfactory accommodation, which was predicted by three variables; ethnic minority status, educational achievement, and involvement of a resettlement agency. Offending behaviours and substance misuse were also associated with poor accommodation outcome.

Despite the severity and frequency of mental health problems among young homeless people, research has shown that they cannot easily access mental health services (Commander *et al.* 2002; Pollio, Thompson and North 2000; Wrate and McLoughlin 1997). Reasons for this include lengthy response (waiting lists), young people's mobility and lack of flexibility from services (i.e. moving across different sectors and service boundaries), falling between adolescent and adult services; perceived stigma of mental health services, not fulfilling referral criteria for severe mental illness (particularly for young people with emotional and behavioural difficulties), lack of collaboration between mental health, social, housing, and non-statutory services, and consequently ineffective use of resources (Buckner and Bassuk 1997; Ensign and Gittelsohn 1998). In a study with young people who were homeless or at risk of homelessness, French, Reardon and Smith (2003) identified four barriers to engagement with mental health services: consideration of the young person's multiple life experiences; attractiveness and accessibility of the service; and follow-up offered.

Service models and interventions

In addition to the problems of mobility, and its associated social and mental health needs, young homeless people often fall within adolescent and adult mental health services because of the limited transitional services (Vostanis 2006). Although some mental health service models have been reported and evaluated for adult homeless people (Commander, Odell and Sashadharan 1997; Susser *et al.* 1997), there have been few mental health service initiatives for young homeless people, with described services usually developed by non-statutory (Dickens and Woodfield 2004; Taylor *et al.* 2006) or educational projects (Nabors, Proescher and De Silva 2001).

In a UK survey of homeless shelters for young people, only 27 per cent reported that they had adequate supports, arrangements, or resources to meet young people's mental health needs (Taylor, Stuttaford and Vostanis 2006). A variety of models was adopted, such as use of GP services, internal services, referral to external mental health services, or in-house provision, but these were developed ad hoc, usually as a result of local personal initiatives. Young residents at these shelters had high rates of mental health problems, and long histories of patchy contact with mental health services, but this was not co-ordinated, consequently they were easily lost in the system. Some of these shelters obtained three-year funding to appoint their own specialist mental health professionals, who operated on the interface with local statutory mental health services (Taylor *et al.* 2006). Their service was perceived as engaging by the young people, and supportive by the residential staff, and led to improvement in young people's mental health (Taylor *et al.* 2007). Unfortunately, the organizational model of specialist mental health workers operating in isolation within non-statutory services was not sustainable, as the project was not mainstreamed within a local mental health strategy, and the majority of shelters remained cut off from statutory mental health services (Taylor *et al.* 2006).

The vulnerable nature and high level of needs of this young population suggests that it should not be left to individual managers or units to make arrangements with mental health agencies, but, rather, this should be strategic responsibility of both health and housing organizations. This would ensure the implementation of policies, achievement of high standards, and safeguards that young people 'do not fall through the net'. Shelters and mental health or other therapeutic services should have clear protocols, easy access, and a user-friendly philosophy. The perceived stigma of mental illness and the young people's life circumstances will sooner or later result in dropping out from services if they have to initiate referral and sustain attendance. Instead, an outreach model integrated with youth work and other activities is more likely to be successful. As in the previous section on homeless children and families, there should be a distinction between lower-level supportive therapeutic work (e.g. on improving resilience and self-esteem) and interventions for more severe and complex mental health problems, although the two are not mutually exclusive.

Therapeutic interventions should be adapted to the particular needs and circumstances of young, homeless people. For example, a cognitive-behavioural therapy (CBT) programme was developed for runaway youths in a shelter, and its themes included raising self-consciousness, identifying high-risk situations, and developing coping strategies (Myung-Sun, Hyang-In and Young-Ja 2005). The intervention was effective in reducing depressive symptoms and in improving self-esteem and self-efficacy. Similar components of enhancing young people's strengths have been used in other programmes, such as learning new attitudes and behaviours, learning about themselves, being in relationships with others, obtaining independent skills, and learning from experience (Lindsey *et al.* 2000; Raleigh-DuRoff 2004). Long-term psychodynamic interventions are less likely to engage young people during crisis, but may be more suitable at a later stage, when they feel secure enough to reflect on issues underlying their emotions and behaviours. Tailoring interventions to the young person's needs, feeling involved in the intervention, a trusting relationship with their key worker and therapist (if different), and a flexible approach are important aspects of any therapeutic work (Dickens and Woodfield 2004; Taylor *et al.* 2007).

All direct interventions should be integrated with plans for education and employment, as well as leisure and recreational activities (Gugliano 2004). Youth workers, mentors, advocates, or professional helpers can bridge a gap between the young people and services throughout the transition, in the absence of parents, carers, or supportive networks (Kurtz *et al.* 2000). Throughout this process, close work with shelter staff, including consultation and training, will ensure consistency and co-ordination. A particular challenge for services is to continue their involvement after the young person has left the shelter, in order to help them retain their housing. Taking into consideration the number of agencies potentially involved and young people moving across service boundaries, inter-agency tracking systems and effective exchange of communication will facilitate continuity of care (Pollio *et al.* 2000).

Case vignette

G was a 17-year-old girl who had left local authority care to live in semi-independent accommodation. She had moved between different foster and residential placements for the previous five years, following sexual abuse by a family member. She had been in intermittent contact with the child and adolescent mental health (CAMH) service, predominantly because of self-harm (overdoses and cutting). G would engage for brief periods and respond to behavioural strategies, but usually found it difficult to engage in psychodynamic work, as there were many crises and placement breakdowns. Placements were increasingly difficult to secure, because of G's aggressive outbursts against carers and residential staff. For this reason, the youth offending teams were also involved. G found it difficult to sustain relationships, and hardly attended school in the last two years of secondary education.

Despite the adverse circumstances and the lack of sustainable improvement to a number of agencies, on balance it was decided that the only realistic option was to seek a semi-independent placement with substantive level of support. G initially thrived on the opportunity to live on her own and make choices, and gave positive vibes about pursuing her education. However, she again became overwhelmed by her emotions and social isolation, and her self-harm and externalizing behaviours recurred. G drifted to a local hostel for single homeless adults, where she was extremely vulnerable. A request for individual therapy was not considered realistic at the time. A second intensive care package was negotiated with a more protective placement at a shelter for young women. All agencies drew basic behavioural strategies, adopting a hierarchical approach, with short- and medium-term goals. The mental health worker remained involved, with the main aim being to help sustain the placement, thus enable other components of the care plan to be re-introduced (training, independent skills, recreational activities, mentoring), before moving on to the next level of the plan. This time, G responded for a prolonged period, despite several setbacks of self-harm and behaviour. One year later, it was thought appropriate to try another semi-independent placement. G felt stronger and more able to use new opportunities, but remained vulnerable, particularly through new peer and adult relationships.

References

Amery, J., Tomkins, A., and Victor, C. (1995) 'The prevalence of behavioural problems amongst homeless primary school children in an outer London borough.' *Public Health 109*, 121–124.

Anderson, D., and Rayens, M. (2004) 'Factors influencing homelessness in women.' *Public Health Nursing 21*, 12–23.

Anderson, L., Stuttaford, M., and Vostanis, P. (2006) 'A family support service for homeless children and parents: User and staff perspectives.' *Child and Family Social Work 11*, 119–127.

Australian Clearinghouse for Youth Studies (2006) *Australian Youth Facts and Stats*. Available at: www.youthfacts.com.au, accessed on 10 October 2006.

Bassuk, E., Weinreb, L., Buckner, J., Browne, A., Salomon, A., and Bassuk, S. (1996) 'The characteristics and needs of sheltered homeless and low-income housed mothers.' *JAMMA 276*, 640–646.

Brooks, R., Ferguson, T., and Webb, E. (1998) 'Health services to children resident in domestic violence shelters.' *Ambulatory Child Health 4*, 369–374.

Buckner, J., and Bassuk, E. (1997) 'Mental disorders and service utilization among youths from homeless and low-income housed families.' *Journal of the American Academy of Child and Adolescent Psychiatry 36*, 890–900.

Buckner, J., Bassuk, E., Weinreb, L., and Brooks, M. (1999) 'Homelessness and its relation to the mental health and behaviour of low-income school-age children.' *Developmental Psychology 35*, 246–257.

Cauce, A., Paradise, M., Ginzler, J., Embry, L., Morgan, C., Lohr, Y., and Theofelis, J. (2000) 'The characteristics and mental health of homeless adolescents: age and gender differences.' *Journal of Emotional and Behavioural Disorders 8*, 230–251.

Centrepoint (2006) Available at: www.centrepoint.org.uk, accessed on 10 October 2006.

Chaffin, M., Bonner, B., and Hill, R. (2001) 'Family preservation and family support programs: child maltreatment outcomes across client risk levels and program types.' *Child Abuse and Neglect 25*, 1269–1289.

Commander, M., Davis, A., McCabe, A., and Stanyer, A. (2002) 'A comparison of homeless and domiciled young people.' *Journal of Mental Health 11*, 557–564.

Commander, M., Odell, S., and Sashidharan, S. (1997) 'Birmingham community mental health team for the homeless.' *Psychiatric Bulletin 21*, 74–76.

Craig, T., and Hodson, S. (1998) 'Homeless youth in London: I. Childhood antecedents and psychiatric disorder.' *Psychological Medicine 28*, 1379–1388.

Craig, T., and Hodson, S. (2000) 'Homeless youth in London: II. Accommodation, employment and health outcomes at one year.' *Psychological Medicine 30*, 187–194.

Davey, T. (2004) 'A multiple-family group intervention for homeless families: the weekend retreat.' *Health and Social Work 29*, 326–329.

Deckel, R., Peled, E., and Spiro, S. (2003) 'Shelters for houseless youth: a follow-up evaluation.' *Journal of Adolescence 26*, 201–212.

Dickens, S., and Woodfield, K. (2004) *New Approaches to Youth Homelessness Prevention.* York: Joseph Rowntree Foundation.

Embry, L., Stoep, A.V., Evens, C., Kimberley, R., and Pollock, A. (2000) 'Risk factors for homelessness in adolesents released from psychiatric residential treatment.' *Journal of the American Academy of Child and Adolescent Psychiatry 39*, 1293–1299.

Ensign, J., and Gittelsohn, J. (1998) 'Health and access to care: perspectives of homeless youth in Baltimore City, USA.' *Social Science and Medicine 47*, 2087–2099.

French, R., Reardon, M., and Smith, P. (2003) 'Engaging with a mental health service: perspectives of at-risk youth.' *Child and Adolescent Social Work Journal 20*, 529–548.

Gaubatz, K. (2001) 'Family homelessness in Britain: more than just a housing issue.' *Journal of Children and Poverty 7*, 3–22.

Ginzler, J., Cochran, B., Domenech-Rodriguez, M., Cauce, A., and Whitbeck, L. (2003) 'Sequential progression of substance use among homeless youth: an empirical investigation of the gateway theory.' *Substance Use and Misuse 38*, 725–758.

Guigliano, R. (2004) 'The systemic neglect of New York's young adults with mental illness.' *Psychiatric Services 55*, 451–453.

Haber, M., and Toro, P. (2004) 'Homelessness among families, children and adolescents: An ecological-developmental perspective.' *Clinical Child and Family Psychology Review 7*, 123–164.

Hertlein, K., and Killmer, M. (2004) 'Toward differentiated decision-making: family systems theory with a homeless clinical population.' *American Journal of Family Therapy 32*, 255–270.

Herman, D., Susser, E., Struening, E., and Link, B. (1997) 'Adverse childhood experiences: Are they risk factors for adult homelessness?' *American Journal of Public Health 87*, 249–255.

Hill, M., Dillane, J., Bannister, J., and Scott, S. (2002) 'Everybody needs good neighbours: An evaluation of an intensive project for families facing eviction.' *Child and Family Social Work 7*, 79–89.

Holleman, W., Bray, J., Davis, L., and Holleman, M. (2004) 'Innovative ways to address the mental health and medical needs of marginalized patients.' *American Journal of Orthopsychiatry 74*, 242–252.

Kamieniecki, G. (2001) 'Prevalence of psychological distress and psychiatric disorders among homeless youth in Australia.' *Australian and New Zealand Journal of Psychiatry 35*, 352–358.

Karim, K., Tischler, V., Gregory, P., and Vostanis, P. (2006) 'Homeless children and parents: short-term mental health outcome,' *International Journal of Social Psychiatry 52*, 447–458.

Kurtz, D., Lindsey, E., Jarvis, S., and Nackerud, L. (2000) 'How runaway and homeless youth navigate troubled waters: The role of formal and informal helpers.' *Child and Adolescent Social Work 17*, 381–402.

Lindsey, E. (1998) 'Service providers' perceptions of factors that help or hinder homeless families.' *Families in Society 79*, 160–172.

Lindsey, E., Kurtz, D., Jarvis, S., Williams, N., and Nackerud, L. (2000) 'How runaway and homeless youth navigate through troubled waters.' *Child and Adolescent Social Work Journal 17*, 115–140.

Lissauer, T., Richman, S., Tempia, M., Jenkins, S., and Taylor, B. (1993) 'Influence of homelessness on acute admissions to hospital.' *Archives of Disease in Childhood 69*, 423–429.

Myung-Sun, H., Hyang-In, C.C., and Young-Ja, L. (2005) 'The effect of cognitive-behavioural group therapy on the self-esteem, depression and self-efficacy of runaway adolescents in a shelter in South Korea.' *Applied Nursing Research 18*, 160–166.

Nabors, L., Proescher, E., and De Silva, M. (2001) 'School-based mental health prevention activities for homeless and at-risk youth.' *Child and Youth Care Forum 30*, 3–18.

Nabors, L., Sumajin, I., Zins, J., Rofey, D., Berberich, D., Brown, S., and Weist, M. (2003) 'Evaluation of an intervention for children experiencing homelessness.' *Child and Youth Care Forum 32*, 211–227.

Office of the Deputy Prime Minister (ODPM) (2003) *Supporting People: Guide to Accommodation and Support Options for Homeless Households.* London: Office of the Deputy Prime Minister (Homelessness Directorate).

Office of the Deputy Prime Minister (ODPM) (2004) *Statutory Homelessness: England, Third Quarter 2004.* London: Office of the Deputy Prime Minister (Homelessness Directorate).

Olivan, G. (2002) 'Maltreatment histories and mental health problems are common among runaway adolescents in Spain.' *Acta Pediatrica 91*, 1274–1275.

Page, A., Ainsworth, A., and Pett, M (1993) 'Homeless families and their children's health problems.' *Western Journal of Medicine 158*, 30–35.

Page, T., and Nooe, R. (2002) 'Life experiences and vulnerabilities of homeless women.' *Journal of Social Distress and Homeless 11*, 215–231.

Pollio, D., Thompson, S., and North, C. (2000) 'Agency-based tracking of difficult-to-follow populations: runaway and homeless youth programs in St. Louis, Missouri.' *Community Mental Health Journal 36*, 247–258.

Power, S., Whitty, G., and Youdell, D. (1995) *No Place to Learn.* London: Shelter.

Raleigh-DuRoff, C. (2004) 'Factors that influence homeless adolescents to leave or stay living on the street.' *Child and Adolescent Social Work Journal 21*, 561–572.

Rotheram-Borus, M., Koopman, C., and Ehrhardt, A. (1991) 'Homeless youths and HIV infection.' *American Psychologist 46*, 1188–1197.

Rubin, D., Erickson, C., San Agustin, M., Cleary, S., Allen, J., and Cohen, P. (1996) 'Cognitive and academic functioning of homeless children compared with housed children.' *Pediatrics 97*, 289–294.

Sanders, M., Turner, K., and Markie-Dadds, C. (2002) 'The development and dissemination of the Triple P-Positive Parenting Program: A multilevel, evidence-based system of parenting and family support.' *Prevention Science 3*, 173–189.

Sherman, D. (1992). 'The neglected health care needs of street youth.' *Public Health Reports 107*, 433–440.

Slesnick, N., and Prestopnik, J. (2005) 'Dual and multiple diagnosis among substance using runaway youth.' *American Journal of Drug and Alcohol Abuse 31*, 179–201.

Stewart, G., and Stewart, J. (1992) 'Social work with homeless families.' *British Journal of Social Work 22*, 271–289.

Stojanovic, D., Weitzman, B., Shinn, M., Labay, L., and Williams, N. (1999) 'Tracing the path out of homelessness: the housing patterns of families after exiting shelter.' *Journal of Community Psychology 27*, 199–208.

Susser, E., Valencia, E., Conover, S., Felix, A., Tsai, W., and Wyatt, R. (1997) 'Preventing recurrent homelessness among mentally ill men: A "critical time" intervention after discharge from a shelter.' *American Journal of Public Health 87*, 256–262.

Swick, K., and Bailey, L. (2004) 'Communicating effectively with parents and families who are homeless.' *Early Childhood Education Journal 32*, 211–215.

Taylor, H., Stuttaford, M., Broad, B., and Vostanis, P. (2006) 'Why a "roof" is not enough: the characteristics of young homeless people referred to a designated mental health service. *Journal of Mental Health 15*, 491–501.

Taylor, H., Stuttaford, M., and Vostanis, P. (2006) 'A UK survey into how homeless shelters respond to the mental health needs of homeless young people.' *Housing, Care and Support 9*, 13–18.

Taylor, H., Stuttaford, M., Broad, B., and Vostanis, P. (2007) 'Listening to service users: young homeless people's experiences of a new mental health service.' *Journal of Child Health Care* 11, 221–230.

Thrasher, S., and Mowbray, C. (1995) 'A strengths perspective: An ethnographic study of homeless women with children.' *Health and Social Work Journal 20*, 93–102.

Tischler, V., and Gregory, P. (2002) 'A resettlement service for homeless families.' *Housing, Care and Support 5*, 33–36.

Tischler, V., and Vostanis, P. (2007) 'Homeless mothers: Is there a relationship between coping strategies, mental health and goal achievement?' *Journal of Clinical and Applied Social Psychology 17*, 85–102.

Tischler, V., Karim, K., Rustall, S., Gregory, P., and Vostanis, P. (2004) 'A family support service for homeless children and parents: Users' perspectives and characteristics.' *Health and Social Care in the Community 12*, 327–335.

Tischler, V., Vostanis, P., Bellerby, T., and Cumella, S. (2002) 'Evaluation of a mental health outreach service for homeless families.' *Archives of Disease in Childhood 86*, 158–163.

Tyler, K., and Cauce, A. (2002) 'Perpetrators of early physical and sexual abuse among homeless and runaway adolescents.' *Child Abuse and Neglect 26*, 1261–1274.

Tyler, K., Whitbeck, L., Hoyt, D., and Johnson, K. (2003) 'Self-mutilation and homeless youth: the role of family abuse, street experiences, and mental disorders.' *Journal of Research on Adolescence 13*, 457–468.

Unger, J., Kipke, M., Simon, T., Montgomery, S., and Johnson, C. (1997) 'Homeless youths and young adults in Los Angeles: Prevalence of mental health problems and the relationship between mental health and substance abuse disorders.' *American Journal of Community Psychology 25*, 371–394.

Vostanis, P. (2006). 'Patients as parents and young people approaching adulthood.' *Current Opinion in Psychiatry 18*, 449–454.

Vostanis P. and Cumella S. (eds) (1999) *Homeless Children: Problems and Needs.* London: Jessica Kingsley Publishers.

Vostanis, P., Grattan, E., Cumella, S., and Winchester C. (1997) 'Psychosocial functioning of homeless children.' *Journal of the American Academy of Child and Adolescent Psychiatry 36*, 881–889.

Vostanis P., Grattan E., and Cumella S. (1998) 'Mental health problems of homeless children and families: longitudinal study.' *British Medical Journal 316*, 899–902.

Vostanis, P., Tishler, V., Cumella, S., and Bellerby, T. (2001) 'Mental health problems and social supports among homeless mothers and children victims of domestic and community violence.' *International Journal of Social Psychiatry 47*, 30–40.

Votta, E., and Manion, I. (2004) 'Suicide, high-risk behaviours, and coping style in homeless adolescent males' adjustment.' *Journal of Adolescent Health 34*, 237–243.

Walters, S., and East, L. (2001) 'The cycle of homelessness in the lives of young mothers: the diagnostic phase of an action research project.' *Journal of Clinical Nursing 10*, 171–179.

Webb, D., Culhane, J., Metraux, S., Robbins, J., and Culhane, D. (2003) 'Prevalence of episodic homelessness among adult childbearing women in Philadeplhia, PA.' *American Journal of Public Health 93*, 1895–1896.

Webb, E., Shankleman, J., Evans, M., and Brooks, R. (2001) 'The health of children in refuges for women victims of domestic violence.' *British Medical Journal 323*, 210–213.

Webster-Stratton, C., and Hammond, M. (1997) 'Treating children with early-onset conduct problems: a comparison of child and parent training interventions.' *Journal of Consulting and Clinical Psychology 65*, 93–109.

Whitbeck, L., Johnson, K., Hoyt, D., and Cauce, A. (2004) 'Mental disorder and comorbidity among runaway and homeless adolescents.' *Journal of Adolescent Health 35*, 132–140.

Wrate, R., and Blair, C. (1999) 'Homeless Adolescents.' In P. Vostanis and S. Cumella (eds) *Homeless Children: Problems and Needs.* London: Jessica Kingsley Publishers.

Wrate, R., and McLoughlin, P. (1997) *Feeling Bad: The Troubled Lives and Health of Single Young Homeless People in Edinburgh.* Edinburgh: Lothian Health Authority.

Zima, B., Wells, K., Benjamin, B., and Duan, N. (1996) 'Mental health problems among homeless mothers: Relationship to service use and child mental health problems.' *Archives of General Psychiatry 53*, 332–338.

CHAPTER 12

Helping Families who are Victims of Domestic Abuse

Rachel Brooks and Elspeth Webb

Definition

Domestic violence, known more frequently now as 'domestic abuse' to reflect the broad nature of the abuse experienced, is defined as 'any violent or abusive behaviour (whether physical, sexual, psychological, emotional, verbal, financial) which is used by one person to control and dominate another with whom they have or have had a relationship.' Domestic abuse can occur to men from female partners and within same-sex relationships. However, the majority of domestic abuse is by men towards female partners, and should be seen in the context of global patterns of violence towards women and girls (Watts and Zimmerman 2002).

Prevalence

There are no routine data collected on numbers of children living with domestic abuse, nor on their health and social care needs. We can only draw together data from a variety of sources to gain some impression of the magnitude of the problem.

Women's aid

There were 19,836 women and 24,347 children provided with refuge-based services in England in 2004–2005. Numbers for those using all services (including non-refuge-based outreach, advocacy, and support services) in the same period were 196,205 women and 129,193 children (Williamson 2006).

Police data

In the British Crime Survey 2002–2003, which covered both England and Wales, the number of incidents of reported domestic abuse was 501,000, but how many of these incidents included families with children was not recorded.

Cardiff data

Cardiff has a population of 320,000, of which approximately 65,000 are aged under 16. In a one-year period (2005–2006), 3924 reports of domestic abuse were received by Cardiff Police; of these, 2152 involved children under the age of 17 (Police statistics – Jacqueline Johnson, personal communication). It is one of a few cities in the UK with a one-stop-shop service for domestic abuse – the women's safety unit (WSU). Linked to this is good multi-agency working, which includes multi-agency risk assessment conferences (MARACs) for families at very high risk. The Cardiff WSU and the MARAC process have been the subject of careful evaluation (Robinson 2006), and provide information on both the prevalence and the experience of families affected by domestic abuse. The WSU evaluation ran from mid-December 2001 to the end of January 2003, during which the WSU was accessed by 1150 women and their 1482 children (Robinson 2006). MARACs are held each month; on average there are 30 cases on each MARAC, with about three-quarters of them involving children.

Impact of domestic abuse on children: mechanisms

Living with recurring abuse directed towards a mother will affect a child's physical and emotional health and cognitive development. There are several, often co-existing, mechanisms.

Abuse in pregnancy leading to adverse outcomes

Pregnancy is a time when violence may start or escalate (Burch and Gallup 2004; Jasinski 2004). Abdominal injury can result from falls or from the deliberate targeting of the abdomen as a focus for violence, dangerous to mother and foetus. High alcohol intake and drug misuse affect the foetus through the effect of these on the general health of the mother and directly by their teratogenic affects. Poor engagement with ante-natal services and poor obstetric outcomes, from low birth weight through to foetal and maternal death, are more common in women suffering domestic abuse (Mezey and Bewley 1997). Some pregnancies within an abusing relationship follow rape; vivid procedural memories may be reactivated during labour, affecting the relationship of mother and baby.

Table 12.1 Mental health outcomes of Cardiff Women's Safety Unit clients (n=222)

Mental health problem	Currently experiencing (%)	Ever experienced (%)
Alcohol misuse	2.7	9.0
Drug misuse	0.9	3.2
Depression	38.7	25.7
Anxiety	44.1	26.1
Paranoia	27.5	19.4
Panic attacks	24.8	17.6
Sleeping disorder	23.0	21.6
Agoraphobia	6.8	8.1
Suicidal thoughts	10.8	20.3
Homicidal thoughts	5.0	10.4
Other	1.4	4.1

Poor maternal mental health

Mothers in these families have significantly increased levels of mental health problems, substance abuse and alcohol problems, which post-date the abuse (Stark and Flitcraft 1996); all these difficulties are known to compromise a woman's ability to respond to children's needs (Holden 2003). Table 12.1 shows the mental health of WSU clients in Cardiff.

Social and educational disruption in consequence of fleeing violence

Leaving a violent relationship is dangerous; women run from violence on average seven times before leaving for good (Abraham 1994). As well as disrupting relationships with the extended family, peers, and teachers, and leading to social isolation, frequent moves disrupt access to healthcare and education.

The association of domestic abuse and child abuse

Children exposed to domestic violence are at increased risk of injury, either as a result of direct violence or indirectly as they are caught up in violence directed at

**Table 12.2 Reported behaviours of perpetrators,
Cardiff Women's Safety Unit clients (n=222)**

Abusive behaviour	Current partner (%)	Any partner (%)
Threatened to hurt the children	5.0	10.4
Shouted at the children	16.2	30.6
Abused or threatened to hurt the pets	5.9	16.2
Punished or deprived the children	4.5	11.3
Threatened to take the children away	21.6	26.6
Hit or otherwise hurt the children	5.9	14.0

others. Between 30 per cent and 60 per cent of children exposed to domestic abuse are themselves physically abused (Abraham 1994; Edleson 1999). US studies have shown that male aggression towards partners is correlated with increased aggression by both partners towards their children (Jouriles and Norwood 1995). Fifty-five per cent of children presenting with sexual abuse reported domestic abuse at home (Kellog and Menards 2003). In addition, children may be used to control victims. Table 12.2 shows some of the child-related behaviours reported to the Cardiff WSU evaluation from in-depth interviews with 222 victims.

Impact of domestic abuse on children
Physical health
Low birth weight carries increased risk of adverse health outcomes throughout the life course (Eriksson 2005). Studies of children in refuges, a sub-group of the total population exposed to domestic abuse, have shown poor immunization and surveillance rates: these children are at increased risk of preventable disease, the late diagnosis of conditions picked up by surveillance, and are missing out on the health promotion aspects of the pre-school programme (Webb *et al.* 2001). Continuity of care is difficult for families, many of whom flee without being able to receive appointments, leaving children with chronic conditions without access to specialist services (Berenson, Wiemann and McCombs 2001). In some areas there are real difficulties accessing primary care.

Exposure to domestic abuse is reported to increase health-risking behaviours in adolescent girls (Berenson, Wiemann and McCombs 2001). Studies including domestic abuse as an 'adverse childhood experience' show an increase in high-risk behaviours, and of increased risk of teenage paternity (Anda *et al.* 2002). As well as harm from abuse and neglect associated with domestic abuse, children are 'caught in the crossfire', with bruising, lacerations, fractures, and head injury documented (Christian *et al.* 1997; Fleggon *et al.* 2004); younger children appear to be at greatest risk, although this may be a presentational bias. For some, living with abuse means dying with it, too: domestic abuse has been identified as a risk factor for deaths in serious case reviews of child abuse deaths under Part 8 of 'Working Together' (Saunders 2004). This Women's Aid review of 29 child homicides questions whether the risks these children face are taken seriously either by the professionals involved or by the courts.

Cognitive development and educational achievement

These children have general risk factors for developmental delay, such as maternal depression, child abuse, and homelessness. In addition, exposure to violence in infancy is postulated to affect neuronal connections, and thus concepts and skills acquisition (Hall and Elliman 2004). A longitudinal twin study reported a significant impact on intelligence quotient (IQ) at the age of five years, with a dose–response effect; high levels of domestic abuse resulted in an eight-point reduction in IQ after allowing for other factors, including child maltreatment and genetic influences (Koenen *et al.* 2003). Other researchers have noted high levels of difficulties in school for older children (Abraham 1994). Children affected by domestic violence are more likely to be involved in street or playground violence, bullying, educational failure, and school exclusion (Hall and Lynch 1998).

Mental health

Nearly 75 per cent of children living with domestic violence have witnessed the violence, including 10 per cent witnessing the sexual assault of their mother (Abraham 1994). The mental health of these children will be affected not just by violence, as discussed below, but also by the added risks of poor mental health known to be associated with cognitive limitations, poor school outcomes, and brain injury. Most research in this area supports a link between domestic violence and psychological problems in children, although the findings show a great diversity in the patterns of maladjustment seen (Grych *et al.* 2000); this presumably reflects the difficulty researchers face in attempting to measure its impact in isolation from other co-existing adversities. The severity of maladjustment seems to be affected by the frequency and intensity of the inter-parental violence witnessed (Jouriles *et al.* 1996). Severe episodes of violence sensitize a child to an emotional response which anticipates a repeat of this severity with each subsequent event, even if that subsequent event is minor.

Younger children (aged seven to nine years) are more affected than older children (aged 10–12 years), with children suffering from abuse themselves perceiving the episodes as more threatening (Grych *et al.* 2000).

Clearly, the emotional and behavioural sequelae in the child are a result of their whole experience of family life and parenting. Holden (2003) describes a taxonomy of the psychological sequalae that domestic abuse can cause to children:

- terrorized
- corrupted
- spurned
- denied emotional responsiveness
- isolated
- neglect of health or educational needs.

The range of psychological difficulties in refuge children in the USA has revealed five distinct types (Grych *et al.* 2000). This supports the heterogeneity in the patterns of maladjustment found in the wider literature on domestic violence, but also identifies a considerable number of children who appear to be functioning well, with no apparent distress. A small group of children will have to adjust to the experience of having a parent or sibling killed, sometimes having even witnessed these events, with profound and lasting consequences for their lives (Hendriks, Black and Kaplan 2000).

Multiple jeopardy

Children will rarely present with domestic abuse as an isolated disadvantage, but may be affected by other factors, both intrinsic or extrinsic, that either add to their risk, or interact with the domestic abuse in ways that increase their likelihood or harm.

GENDER

Jaffe *et al.* (1986) showed that boys and girls exposed to domestic violence had similar levels of maladjustment, with perhaps a bias to internalizing problems in girls; but boys showed a greater degree of maladjustment than did girls, in particular related to social competence, when children exposed to violence were compared with control children from non-violent homes. There is also evidence that boys' and girls' experiences within violent families are different; husbands' aggression to wives correlates positively to mothers' and fathers' aggression towards sons, but not daughters (Jouriles and Le Compte 1991), and boys report higher levels of mother-to-child aggression than girls (Grych *et al.* 2000). Numerous studies have also documented a strong association between the development of later violent behaviour and sociality in young adulthood, particularly in males, with various forms of family violence, including family conflict (Felitti *et al.* 1998; US Department of Health and Human Services 2001).

ETHNIC MINORITY GROUP STATUS
Although many US studies include ethnically diverse populations, there do not appear to be any data on the interaction of ethnicity, domestic violence, and maladjustment. In any case, the history, demography, and politics of race in the USA are different to those in the UK, which would preclude any extrapolation of US data to a British context. There are few data from the UK: the Cardiff refuge survey reported lower mental health scores in children from refuges serving minority populations; but as this group was small, and included many highly diverse communities, all one can conclude is that there is a pressing need for research. It is, however, important to consider that for some children the mental health sequelae arising out of their own and their community's experiences of racism and racial disadvantage will greatly add to the risks of adverse outcomes when domestic abuse is added into the equation.

ASYLUM SEEKERS AND REFUGEES
As previously discussed in Chapter 11, children in these groups already have multiple risk factors for their health and welfare (Webb, O'Hare and Ryan 2005), including their mental health status (Davies and Webb 2000), exacerbated by poor access to services. Domestic abuse in this context is highly concerning. First, it adds to the burden of adversity. Second, it is difficult to identify, as victims face even more barriers to reporting their abuse. For example, isolation resulting from the national dispersal scheme, language and cultural barriers, and fear of affecting their asylum claim, may mean that many women keep their abuse secret. Third, there are inadequate policies in place to respond appropriately (Women's Aid 2006).

Interventions

This chapter does not describe therapeutic approaches for children exposed to domestic abuse – there is a wealth of available literature in this area. Instead it will discuss collaborative inter-agency and inter-sectorial interventions with respect to the vital role that child and adolescent mental health (CAMH) services could and should play in such collaborations to provide timely and flexible responses, given the resources and, perhaps even more importantly, the will and commitment to do so. Interventions need to be planned in the context of these three factors.

Families do not access mainstream services effectively
The sub-group which accesses refugees has poor uptake of immunization and surveillance – programmes that are intended to be universal (Webb *et al.* 2001). The reasons for this probably include the isolation and control of women characteristic in domestic abuse and its impact on their mental and emotional health, which is likely to impede a mother's ability to comply with appointments and access services. This same study revealed that concerns about their children's behavioural and emotional well-being were uppermost for many mothers. It provides a good example of Tudor-Hart's 'Inverse Care Law', in which those with most need of care are least served (Webb 1998). It is hypothesized here that the under-resourcing of CAMH services can only exacerbate this; when resources are inadequate to meet the needs of the population as a whole, those best able to access and utilize services are likely to use up what is available. In addition, CAMH services are becoming increasingly medically driven, paralleling adult mental health services in being aimed at the psychiatric end of the spectrum. There needs to be a shift in both the emphasis and the configuration of CAMH services to ensure that these and other vulnerable populations get the care they need.

Many children are left living with violence
In an imperfect world this is often the consequence of the inability or failure of safeguarding agencies to protect these children. Decisions may be made to preserve family cohesion at the expense of child protection when this is deemed to be in the best interests of children, especially in circumstances where the alternative is long-term care. Other children are living in refuges for many months, with uncertainty and instability. In such scenarios, CAMH services may withdraw or postpone engagement, as it is generally accepted wisdom, from a therapeutic perspective, that one should engage in therapy in a secure context, that is, that there will be some predictability about circumstances, and that work can be planned with mutual expectations. The result is that some of the neediest children have no access to specialist mental health services.

The natural history of domestic abuse requires agencies to respond promptly to need when opportunities occur
Ideally, services should prioritize these children rather than see them as marginal to their core work, and they should ensure that children do not spend time on generic CAMH service waiting lists. Although examples of good practice occur, CAMH services do not have a reputation for flexibility, nor in targeting those groups who most need their services, but who are most difficult to engage.

Traditionally, interventions are generally conceptualized as primary, secondary, and tertiary prevention (Mullender 2000):

- *Primary prevention*: working to prevent domestic abuse from happening at all;

- *Secondary prevention*: stopping domestic violence as soon as any agency learns it is happening, and preventing its recurrence;

- *Tertiary prevention*: reducing the harm to those who have already experienced domestic violence, for example direct work with children.

Here, we will also discuss a fourth category: interventions to support children living with domestic abuse.

PRIMARY PREVENTION
Home visiting
There is now good evidence to show that early home visiting prevents domestic abuse (Eckenrode 2000).

School programmes
There is evidence from both the UK (Hester and Westmarland 2005) and the USA (Whitaker *et al.* 2006) that working with school students is effective in raising awareness and challenging attitudes. CAMH service practitioners should have an important role in informing the content of the curriculum. As these are whole-population interventions, it is inevitable that some children will have been affected by domestic abuse, and it would seem reasonable to build into these programmes support for such children.

Integrated approaches
In the USA, there is a move towards incorporating domestic abuse prevention into whole-community interventions to reduce all interpersonal violence (Lubell and Vetter 2006).

SECONDARY PREVENTION
Routine enquiry in health settings
Domestic abuse cannot be tackled if it is hidden. Women are unlikely to disclose abuse if they are not asked about it specifically; repeat enquiry increases the likelihood of disclosure (Koenen *et al.* 2003). These situations require the history-taker to be well trained in domestic abuse and child protection. Given that CAMH service clients are more likely to have been affected by domestic abuse, CAMH services may often be the first to uncover it in a family. They need

to comprehend the real risk to a woman of further violence following disclosure; careful multi-agency decisions need to take place prior to any action.

Child protection services

Where children are involved, domestic abuse should always be seen as a child protection issue and dealt with through recognized child protection procedures. Despite the risk of harm these children face, many are unknown to local child protection services and few are on child protection registers (Josty 2002). Certainly, the number of reviews in which domestic violence has been identified as an important factor suggests that child protection agencies have underestimated the physical risks for children living with domestic abuse (Brandon, Owers and Black 1999). It is the authors' experience that the mental health consequences of domestic abuse are also often underestimated, with other forms of abuse being the main focus of professionals. CAMH service practitioners have a unique knowledge and experience of the long-term impact of domestic abuse, and thus are in a unique position to advocate for the needs of these children within the child protection system. It is important that their views and opinions are included when child protection procedures concern families living with domestic abuse. They themselves should be pro-active in establishing links with local child protection agencies, and advising them of the importance of CAMH services' involvement, rather than working in a more traditional reactive capacity.

Multi-agency working to safeguard women

Domestic abuse is a public health issue that needs statutory and voluntary agencies to work together. In many areas, police attending domestic abuse incidents are undertaking risk assessments and passing on details of any children or pregnancy to local authority children's services and health visitors. Local domestic abuse forums work to raise awareness and combat domestic abuse, and MARACs meet to plan for the safety of woman and children. MARACs are an important innovation in the community and criminal justice response to domestic violence. The multiple and unique needs of victims and their children are recognized in this type of multi-agency approach. The findings presented in a report by Robinson (2006) suggest that MARACs should be continued in the long term, and that a MARAC-type process would benefit any community's response to domestic violence. If the promotion and protection of the mental health of children is to have an appropriate level of priority within these multi-agency domestic abuse initiatives, CAMH service professionals must be central players.

Working with perpetrator

This will not be discussed here, but is an essential component of any multi-agency response to domestic abuse.

Interventions to support children living in situations of domestic abuse

CAMH service practitioners should reflect on what their role is in challenging decisions within the safeguarding system that can leave children exposed to violence. They are well placed to be effective advocates for these children. However, given that there will always be children living with domestic abuse in a world peopled by imperfect parents and imperfect safeguarding structures, there is a need to develop creative responses in order to inform and support those adults who do provide care. These include mothers, teachers, and Women's Aid staff, so that the impact of the abuse is minimized. Women's Aid has already produced a resource manual primarily aimed at children's support workers in refuge projects (Saunders and Humphreys 2002), but such initiatives are likely to be most effective in partnership with local CAMH services, in effect, supporting refuge workers. There is huge scope for consultative work in this area.

'Refuge', another non-statutory agency working with domestic abuse, has reviewed services to pre-schoolers in refuge settings, and concludes that early intervention and support for pre-school children experiencing domestic violence is not recognized, nor is there adequate provision to help these young children overcome the effects of trauma (Refuge 2005). They recommend that under-fives are placed at the centre of all domestic violence policies. For older children it is imperative to avoid victim-blaming, at home or at school. At home the behavioural sequelae of domestic abuse must be seen as the consequences, not the causes, of family dysfunction. Within school, these children may often express their distress as aggression or anti-social behaviour; these behaviours must be recognized for what they represent, and not invoke punitive responses from school staff. CAMH service practitioners have a vital role in helping involved adults to understand the developmental consequences of domestic abuse.

TERTIARY PREVENTION
Interventions to alleviate the effects of domestic abuse once children are no longer exposed to it

Therapeutic interventions for children may be provided on an individual basis (probably the most common approach currently provided in the UK), or to groups of children with a shared experience of domestic violence. Specialist teams within CAMH services providing targeted services to such children are rare despite the need that may be deduced from research findings on prevalence and outcomes. There are also examples of good practice within CAMH services (Tischler *et al.* 2002), but in the main this work is undertaken by an overpressed, under-resourced, and unsupported non-statutory sector. 'We are a long way short of the integrated, comprehensive coverage we need in the UK' (Mullender 2000). The effectiveness of therapeutic interventions for children affected by domestic violence is the subject of a recent review (Rivett, Howarth and Harold 2006).

The need for training

Health professionals, both in CAMH services and other disciplines providing care to children, must understand the nature of domestic abuse; without this insight they cannot safely support a woman and her children. All the professionals working with children have a duty to attend child protection training; it would seem appropriate that local safeguarding partnerships ensure that child protection training includes domestic abuse. Within CAMH services there is an additional need for more focused training on the mental health implications and effective approaches to treatment. CAMH services staff should play a major part in the development, content, and delivery of all such programmes.

Conclusions

Domestic abuse is common, and afflicts the lives of many children with multiple, long-term, severe effects on their health. The implications for child mental health services, and other agencies providing a therapeutic role, include the need to:

- expand the capacity of staff working on the interface with refuges and non-statutory agencies

- develop specialist teams in all areas who will support parents, teachers, primary health professionals, and non-statutory staff providing tier-1 support to children affected by domestic violence, and develop what is a vital, but currently largely unfulfilled, public health role.

References

Abraham, C. (1994) *The Hidden Victims: Children and Domestic Violence.* London: NCH Action for Children.

Anda, R., Chapman D., Felitti, V., Edwards, V., Williamson, D., Croft, J., and Giles, W. (2002) 'Adverse childhood experiences and risk of paternity in teen pregnancy.' *Obstetrics and Gynaecology 100,* 37–45.

Berenson, A., Wiemann, C., and McCombs, S. (2001) 'Exposure to violence and associated health-risk behaviours among adolescent girls.' *Archives of Pediatrics and Adolescent Medicine 155,* 1238–1242.

Brandon, M., Owers, M and Black, J. (1999) *Learning How to Make Children Safer: An Analysis for the Welsh Office of Serious Child Abuse Cases in Wales.* Norwich Social Work Monographs.

Centre for Research on the Child and Family. Available at: www.uea.ac.uk/swk/research/summaries/welsh.htm, accessed on 10 October 2006.

Burch, R., and Gallup G. (2004) 'Pregnancy as a stimulus for domestic violence.' *Journal of Family Violence 19*, 243–253.

Christian, C., Scribano, P., Seidl, T., and Pinto-Martin, J. (1997) 'Pediatric injury resulting from family violence'. *Pediatrics 99*, E8.

Davies, M., and Webb, E. (2000) 'Promoting the psychological well-being of refugee children'. *Clinical Child Psychology and Psychiatry 5*, 541–554.

Edleson, J. (1999) 'The overlap between child maltreatment and woman battering'. *Violence Against Women 5*, 134–154.

Eriksson, J. (2005) 'The fetal origins hypothesis: 10 years on'. *British Medical Journal 330*, 1096–1097.

Eckenrode, J. (2000) 'What Works in Nurse Home Visiting Programmes'. In G. Alexander, P. Curtis, and M. Kluger (eds) *What Works in Child Welfare.* Washington, DC: Child Welfare League of America Inc.

Felitti, V., Anda, R., Nordenberg, D., Williamson D., Spitz A., Edwards V., Koss, M., and Marks, J. (1998) 'Relationship of childhood abuse and household dysfunction to many of the leading causes of death in adults'. *American Journal of Preventive Medicine 14*, 245–258.

Fleggon, A.G., Weimann, M., Brown, C., van As, A.B., Swingler, A.G., and Peter, J.C. (2004) 'Inhuman shields: Children caught in the crossfire of domestic violence'. *South African Medical Journal 94*, 293–296.

Grych, J.H., Jouriles, E.N., Swank, P.R., McDonald, R., and Norwood, W.D. (2000) 'Patterns of adjustment among children of battered women.' *Journal of Consulting and Clinical Psychology 68*, 84–94.

Hall, D., and Elliman, D. (2004) *Health for All Children* (4th ed). Oxford: Oxford University Press.

Hall, D., and Lynch, M. (1998) 'Violence begins at home'. *British Medical Journal 316*, 1551.

Hendriks, J., Black, D., and Kaplan, T. (2000) *When Father Kills Mother: Guiding Children through Trauma and Grief.* London: Routledge.

Hester, M., and Westmarland, N. (2005) *Tackling Domestic Violence: Effective Interventions and Approaches.* London: Home Office Research, Development and Statistics Directorate.

Holden, G. (2003) 'Children exposed to domestic violence and child abuse: terminology and taxonomy'. *Clinical Child and Family Psychology Review 6*, 151–160.

Jaffe, P., Wolfe, D., Wilson, S.K. and Zak, L. 1986) 'Family violence and child adjustment: a comparative analysis of girls' and boys' behavioural symptoms.' *American Journal of Psychiatry 143*, 74–77.

Jasinski, J. (2004) 'Pregnancy and domestic violence: A review of the literature'. *Trauma, Violence and Abuse 5*, 47–64.

Josty, T. (2002) *Are Children in Domestic Violence Refuges Known to Child Protection Agencies?* Unpublished dissertation, University of Cardiff.

Jouriles, E., and Le Compte, S. (1991) 'Husbands' aggression towards wives and mothers, and fathers' aggression toward children: Moderating effects of child gender.' *Journal of Consulting and Clinical Psychology 59*, 190–192.

Jouriles, E., and Norwood, W. (1995) 'Physical aggression towards boys and girls in families characterised by the battering of women.' *Journal of Family Psychology 9*, 69–78.

Jouriles, E., Norwood, W., McDonald, R., Vincent, J., and Mahoney, A. (1996) 'Physical marital violence and other forms of interspousal aggression: Links with children's behaviour problems.' *Journal of Family Psychology 10*, 223–234.

Kellog, N., and Menards, S. (2003) 'Violence among family members of children and adolescents evaluated for sexual abuse.' *Child Abuse and Neglect 27*, 1367–1376.

Koenen K.C., Moffitt T.E., Caspi A., Taylor A., and Purcell, S. (2003) 'Domestic violence is associated with environmental suppression of IQ in young children.' *Development and Psychopathology 15*, 297–311.

Lubell, K., and Vetter, J. (2006) 'Suicide and youth violence prevention: The promise of an integrated approach.' *Aggression and Violent Behaviour 11*, 167–175.

Mezey, G., and Bewley, S. (1997) 'Domestic violence and pregnancy: Risk is greatest after delivery.' *British Medical Journal 314*, 1295.

Mullender, A. (2000) *Reducing Domestic Violence: What Works? Meeting the Needs of Children.* Briefing Note, Crime Reduction Research Series. London: Home Office.

Refuge (2005) *Refuge Assessment and Intervention for Pre-school Children Exposed to Domestic Violence: Under 5s at Significant Risk from Effects of Domestic Violence.* London: Refuge.

Rivett, M., Howarth, E.L., and Harold, G.T. (2006) 'Watching from the stairs': Towards an evidence based practice in work with child witnesses of domestic violence. *Clinical Child Psychology and Psychiatry 11*, 103–125.

Robinson, A.L. (2006) 'Reducing Repeat Victimisation among High-Risk Victims of Domestic Violence: The Benefits of a Coordinated Community Response in Cardiff, Wales'. *Violence Against Women: An International and Interdisciplinary Journal 12 (8)*, 761–788.

Saunders, H. (2004) *Twenty-nine Child Homicides: Lessons still to be Learnt on Domestic Violence and Child Protection.* Bristol: Women's Aid Federation of England (WAFE).

Saunders, H., and Humphreys, C. (2002) *Safe and Sound: A Resource Manual for Working with Children who have Experienced Domestic Violence.* Bristol: Women's Aid *Federation* of England (WAFE).

Stark, E., and Flitcraft, A. (1996) *Women at Risk: Domestic Violence and Women's Health.* London: Sage.

Tischler, V., Vostanis, P., Bellerby, P., and Cumella, S. (2002) 'Evaluation of a mental health outreach service for homeless families.' *Archives of Disease in Childhood 86*, 158–163.

US Department of Health and Human Services (2001) *Youth Violence: A Report of the Surgeon General.* Rockville, MD: US Department of Health and Human Services. Available at: www.surgeongeneral.gov/library/youthviolence/report.html, accessed on 10 October 2006.

Watts, C., and Zimmerman, C. (2002) 'Violence against women: global scope and magnitude.' *Lancet 359*, 1232–1237.

Webb, E. (1998) 'Children and the inverse care law'. *British Medical Journal 316*, 1588–1591.

Webb, E., O'Hare, B., and Ryan, A. (2005) 'Meeting the needs of children newly arrived from abroad'. *Current Paediatrics 15*, 339–346.

Webb, E., Shankleman, J., Evans, M., and Brooks, R. (2001) 'The health of children in refuges for women victims of domestic violence: Cross-sectional descriptive survey'. *British Medical Journal 323*, 210–213.

Whitaker, D., Morrison, S., Lindquist, C., Hawkins, S., O'Neil, J., Nesius, A., Mathew, A., and Reese L. (2006) 'Critical review of interventions for the primary prevention of perpetration of partner violence' *Aggression and Violent Behaviour 11*, 151–166.

Williamson, E. (2006) *Women's Aid Federation of England 2005 Survey of Domestic Violence Services Findings.* Bristol: Womens' Aid Federation of England (WAFE). Available at: www.womensaid.org.uk/downloads/WA_survey_dv_service_findings.pdf, accessed on 10 October 2006.

Womens' Aid Policy Briefing (2006) *National Asylum Support Service Domestic Violence Policy.* Available at: www.womensaid.org.uk/landing_page.asp?section=000100010009000500060001, accessed on 10 October 2006.

Useful Websites

- NSPCC reading list:
www.nspcc.org.uk/inform/resourcesforprofessioanls/readinglists/domesticviolenceandchildren_wda48895.html

- National charity supporting victims: www.womensaid.org.uk
- National charity supporting victims: www.refuge.org.uk
- Website for children and young people affected by domestic abuse: www.thehideout.org.uk
- National charity supporting children and young people: www.youngminds.org.uk

CHAPTER 13

Mental Health Services for Children with an Intellectual Disability

Helen Pote

Mental health services for children with an intellectual disability have a long history, but their provision has often been through idiosyncratic models, with variable provision according to locality and practitioner interest. This client group is particularly vulnerable to developing mental health problems. Epidemiological research suggests four to five times the prevalence of psychiatric disorders compared to clients without intellectual disabilities (Einfeld and Tonge 1996; Rutter, Tizard and Whitmore 1970, both cited in McCarthy and Boyd 2002). The individual clinical need for such services is therefore undeniable. In addition, there is likely to be greater level of need within the family and carer systems owing to factors such as increased economic stress, social isolation, and higher divorce rates (Byrne and Cunningham 1985).

There is a need to consider the needs of these children in particular, in addition to the services offered by generic child and adolescent mental health (CAMH) services. This is for two reasons. First, access to generic CAMH services has often been denied to these children, with rationales ranging from lack of resources to fears about not having the specialist skills thought to be required to work effectively with children with intellectual disabilities. Second, there needs to be specific consideration of the context of the child's mental health problems, both in relation to the interaction with their intellectual disability and other physical or sensory disabilities, and in relation to their family circumstances and other services offering support. Consideration of such contextual issues are important for all children with mental health problems but it is crucial for children with intellectual disabilities whose mental health difficulties are likely to be just a part of the difficulties they face.

The aim of this chapter is to discuss the need for such services and their current forms, before reviewing the historical and policy context for recent work, which has led to the development and implementation of core principles and standards for child mental health services for children with an intellectual disability in the UK (the National Care Pathway for Child Mental Health Services for Children with a Learning Disability) (Pote *et al.* 2006a).

The author has been closely involved as a clinical expert on recent projects to develop and implement the *National Care Pathway*. In addition, ideas and examples are drawn from the author's own practice, as a clinical psychologist with children and adults with and without intellectual disabilities. This practice has been within the voluntary sector, National Health Child Development Services, and CAMS services, as well as joint National Health and local authority Intellectual Disability Services.

Definitions of intellectual disability and mental health

A precise and culturally sensitive definition of intellectual disabilities is the subject of endless debate (Burman 1995; Danforth and Navaro 1998). Traditionally, general intellectual disabilities have been defined using the construct of the intelligence quotient (IQ), alongside some indication of adaptive functioning. The commonly accepted definition of the American Association of Intellectual and Developmental Disabilities relies on an IQ measurement of two standard deviations below the population mean (IQ = 70–75 or below). This has to be accompanied by substantial limitations in present functioning and adaptive skills, such as communication and social skills (Luckasson *et al.* 1992, cited in Emerson *et al.* 1998). It should, however, be noted that IQ has often not been formally measured by services, and that there are somewhat diffuse 'IQ boundaries' in determining who might gain access to services.

The definition of intellectual disability used in this chapter is that outlined in *Valuing People: A New Strategy for Learning Disability for the 21st Century* (2001). Intellectual disability includes the presence of:

- a significantly reduced ability to understand new or complex information, to learn new skills (impaired intelligence)
- a reduced ability to cope independently (impaired social functioning) which started before adulthood, with a lasting effect on development.

It is recognized that children with an intellectual disability are a heterogeneous group. Important variables such as age, gender, ethnicity, and class, as well as cognitive, emotional, linguistic, motor, and sensory abilities all influence a person's views and interactions (Burr 1995). These factors also determine the services that are appropriate for the children.

Children with intellectual disabilities come into contact with mental health and psychological services for a wide variety of reasons, such as behavioural, emotional, and life cycle concerns (Arthur 1999; Gangadharan, Bretherton, and Johnson 2001). The range of behavioural and emotional difficulties has deliberately been left broad in this chapter, and is not confined to mental health categories such as those outlined in the *Diagnostic and Statistical Manual of Mental Disorders – Fourth Edition* (DSM-IV) and the *International Statistical Classification of Diseases and Related Health Problems* (ICD-10) (WHO 1994). The rationale behind this is the difficulty of accurate and specific categorization of mental health problems in children with an intellectual disability.

The present discussion also applies to those children who have difficulties of social communication, such as autism or Asperger Syndrome. This is regardless of their level of intellectual functioning. This is considered necessary because these difficulties have a broad impact on development and functioning which spans social, intellectual and emotional or behavioural domains. There is considerable overlap and debate in defining these social communication difficulties as intellectual or mental health difficulties, or both, and as a consequence they have sometimes fallen between different types of service provision.

Development of mental health services for children with an intellectual disability

There have been many developments in mental health and psychological services for adults and children with intellectual disabilities over the past three decades (DHSS 1971; Mittler and Sinason 1996, cited in Caine, Hatton and Emerson 1998). These have been influenced by a range of models and philosophies, such as normalization (O'Brien 1987; Wolfsenberger 1972, cited in Brown and Smith 1992) and community care (DoH 2001; DHSS 1989). Most of these models emphasized inclusion but assumed an individualized, behavioural, and sometimes medicalized view of the needs of people with intellectual disabilities, and rarely explicitly considered their full psychological needs in context (McIntosh 2002).

Most mental health services for children and adults with intellectual disabilities developed at a time when behaviourism was the predominant psychological model. This shaped the nature of mental health interventions offered (Caine, Hatton and Emerson 1998). It developed into a more ethical behavioural approach during the 1980s, when the individual needs, rights, and wishes of the person with intellectual disabilities were considered (Zarkowska and Clements

1988). However, behaviour modification was still the main psychological intervention offered, and psychotherapeutic services attending to the emotional needs of clients with an intellectual disability and their families were rare.

Indeed, the existence of such emotional needs was often denied, though the clinical need for such services was evident (Arthur 1999; Bender 1993; Sinason 1992; Wright and Digby 1996, cited in Caine *et al.* 1998). Epidemiological research estimates that the rates of mental health problems for people with intellectual disabilities range from 40 per cent to 50 per cent, that is, four to five times the prevalence of psychiatric disorder in clients without intellectual disabilities (Einfeld and Tonge 1996; Rutter *et al.* 1970, both cited in McCarthy and Boyd 2002).

In the late 1980s the influence of normalization led to the development of a broader range of client-focused therapies and services to address the emotional and mental health difficulties of people with intellectual disabilities. Despite this changing philosophical picture, and the obvious clinical need, the provision of psychotherapeutic services offered to this client group remains patchy.

Current UK national service mapping figures suggest that only 45 per cent of child mental health services are accessible to children and young people with intellectual disabilities (CAMHS Mapping 2004). A recent survey of 80 young people defined as showing challenging behaviour or experiencing a psychiatric disorder also found that 64 per cent of them had received no specialist mental healthcare as they entered adult services (McCarthy and Boyd 2002).

Statutory and voluntary sector service structures have developed false dichotomies between intellectual disability and mental health services. Thus, children with intellectual disabilities and mental health needs, of all ages, often fall through gaps in service provision (Gangadharan *et al.* 2001; McCarthy and Boyd 2002). It is clear that currently in the UK children and adolescents with intellectual disabilities are receiving mental health services in a variety of settings, such as traditional CAMH services, community paediatric services, child development centres, specialist intellectual disability services and special needs educational services. The co-ordination of care between these services is very variable nationally.

Recent governmental policy in the UK has tried to tackle these service provision dichotomies, promote inclusion and person-centred planning, and address the clinical need to develop mental health services for children with an intellectual disability (DfES 2003; DoH 2001; Sloper and Statham 2004). These policies have been influenced by the earlier philosophies which advocated inclusion within mainstream services. Thus, for the first time, general child mental health services are being required to ensure access for children with intellectual disabilities. Indeed, this inclusive stance is not just limited to child mental health services, but is being advocated for all child services, across health, social, education, and the voluntary sectors.

Governmental policies and local services are exploring frameworks to help promote and support inter-agency working to address the mental health needs of children with an intellectual disability. For example, the Common Assessment Framework (CAF, updated 2006), is one of the inter-agency tools to help achieve the aims of *Every Child Matters* (DfES 2004). The CAF is intended to change the way that services are delivered, shifting the focus from dealing with the consequences of difficulties in children's lives to preventive strategies. It is a shared assessment tool intended to help practitioners develop a shared understanding of a child's needs, so that they can be met more effectively. One aim is to avoid children and families having to tell and re-tell their story. This is a common experience for families who have a child with multiple needs and intellectual disabilities.

Another UK service development aimed at achieving more co-ordinated services is the re-organization of health services into Children's Trusts. These are likely to play an important role in the coherent and integrated development of services across agency boundaries and may facilitate more ambitious inter-agency working. They may consequently address some of the service dichotomies and inter-agency issues that have affected the delivery of an effective and co-ordinated mental health provision for children with an intellectual disability.

Developing services

Despite these initiatives, a number of obstacles remain to implementing comprehensive child mental health services for children with intellectual disability (Pote, Bureau and Goodban 2006b). These include limited resources (sufficient staff with expertise), limited inter-agency working, and a lack of awareness of other professionals' work. There is also considerable rigidity in service organization in relation to referral criteria and use of language and diagnosis.

One method for developing services and overcoming some of these difficulties is that of care pathway development. The concept of integrated care pathways derives from the USA in the 1980s, when clinicians developed recovery pathways to define delivery of care that focused on the patient rather than the system. Pathways emphasize patient-centred care and are always seeking to improve standards and consistency of care. They aim to set down specific actions planned in sequence for the delivery of care that is appropriate for the patient, based on clinical evidence and acknowledged best practice. Care pathways also provide an accepted framework against which to measure standards and stimulate continuous service improvement. Joint planning is vitally important to the achievement of effective care pathways. Lenton (2005) suggests that 'pathway development, service delivery and quality improvement do not happen spontaneously. The commissioning process cannot be separated from the delivery process, as there needs to be a partnership between all involved'.

The development of pathways has concentrated predominately on surgical procedures and medical conditions with a predictable sequence of events. However, more complex, multi-agency pathways are beginning to emerge. When considering children and young people with intellectual disabilities and mental health difficulties, the concept of a care pathway becomes more complex and challenging. The evidence base is developing. Multi-agency co-operation and teamworking are by no means universal practices. There is diversity in the service models from which these children receive their mental healthcare. Despite these difficulties, a national care pathway for this client group has recently been developed in the UK.

The UK pathway is intended to meet the needs of children with a wide range of intellectual disabilities (mild, moderate, and severe) who are also experiencing emotional and behavioural difficulties. It aims to describe the processes involved in service delivery, for the full range of mental health services provided within the UK, from primary to tertiary care. It is therefore applicable to those planning and providing support for behavioural and emotional difficulties in a variety of non-specialist and specialist services.

Guiding principles for intellectual disability mental health

Currently, no evidence base exists to suggest that a particular service model may be more effective in addressing the needs of children with intellectual disabilities and mental health problems. It is therefore more helpful to outline guiding principles – the underlying philosophies and principles which underpin models of care for this client group. The UK nationally agreed principles are outlined below.

- *Holistic:* The needs of the child with intellectual disability and mental health difficulties are central to any service planning and delivery. The full range of emotional, physical, social, educational, and practical needs should be considered in the context of the family, with special attention paid to the needs of parents or carers and siblings.

- *Child-centred planning:* Service development and delivery should have the child's welfare as paramount (Children Act 1989) (DfES 1989). There should be recognition that 'children are children first', regardless of the level of their intellectual disability and mental health difficulties. The intention should be to develop intervention plans to meet the child's needs rather than reflect service needs. In addition, as in any work with children, their welfare should be paramount, and careful attention should be paid to child protection issues.

- *Developmental framework*: Throughout assessment and intervention, the difficulties presented by the child should be considered within a developmental framework. This should pay attention to both the child's chronological age and developmental level. Children with intellectual disabilities may show a more variable pattern of development than those without leaning disabilities. For example, their verbal skills and emotional understanding may be above what might be expected given their cognitive developmental level.

- *Multi-agency commissioning and consideration of referrals*: For care to be effective, it should be provided across health, social, and educational agencies in a comprehensive and integrated manner. Avoiding duplication of service provision and ensuring effective communication between agencies is essential in offering care which is responsive to the child's and families' needs.

- *Inclusion and equality of access*: Children with an intellectual disability and their families should have equal access to the full range of services that children without intellectual disabilities have in respect of their mental health and other areas of health, social, and educational support. They should be offered appropriate support to access ordinary services where possible, and specialist alternatives where inclusion into ordinary services is not indicated.

- *Pro-active and problem-solving*: Services and individual professionals should take a pro-active and problem-solving approach to addressing the needs of children and their families. They should seek to equip themselves with any necessary knowledge or skills to meet the needs of the child. Working pro-actively will require services to be flexible in several regards: (i) Referrals on to other services should be treated as requests for service provision. Responsibility for care, or liaison with new services, should be retained by the referring service until it is appropriate to transfer responsibility to another service; (ii) It will be important to follow-up with vigour those families who find it difficult to engage with services, recognizing that families may be engaged with several services at once and may find attending appointments difficult. Appointments should be offered in places which are familiar and readily accessible to children and their families, for example school or home; (iii) Clinicians should draw upon other resources and support the co-ordination of care in circumstances where they cannot directly meet the child's needs.

- *Collaborative practice and consent:* Service development and delivery should be committed to collaborative practice, which empowers children, their families, and advocates to overcome their difficulties and gain the support they need from service providers. Children's views should be actively sought throughout the care process, and information should be provided in a child-friendly manner to enable children to be informed about their care and participate in decision-making.

- *Co-operative information sharing and communication:* Issues of consent, confidentiality, and information-sharing require careful consideration for children with complex inter-agency involvement. Information should be shared between service providers to meet the needs of the child, but this should be done collaboratively with children and families. Particular attention will need to be paid to information which may be 'sensitive', and might only be shared to protect the well-being of the child.

- *Encompassing diversity:* Professionals should encompass diversity in their planning of services, and within service delivery and evaluation. Diversity relates to the child's level of disability, as well as any cultural or gender issues. Children from ethnic minority groups who have an intellectual disability may be more likely to face double discrimination in relation to service access.

- *Therapeutic and quality services:* The pathway should enable children to access the best available local service to meet their needs. Such services should be timely, of high quality, and therapeutic for the child and family, offering both comprehensive assessments and interventions. It is recognized that services for children with intellectual disabilities and emotional or behavioural difficulties are currently undergoing considerable expansion. In developing services, we should be mindful of the above guiding principles, and should apply them in the monitoring of service quality.

Key features of services

These principles should translate into a number of key features common to all child mental health services for children with an intellectual disability. First, therapeutic interventions need to be individually tailored to meet the needs of the child and their family. For children with intellectual disabilities, this requires specific consideration of therapeutic adaptations which may be necessary to enable children to access therapeutic interventions according to their cognitive, emotional, and linguistic abilities. This may include a range of process issues: extended engagement; a collaborative versus expert position taken by the therapist; negotiation of therapeutic agendas to follow the concerns of the family; specific therapeutic skills and techniques to concretize the therapeutic process; a slower therapeutic pace; consideration of issues of power; and ritualized endings (see Baum and Lyngaard 2006; Kroese, Dagnan and Loumidis 1997). Given the paucity of outcome research relating specifically to this client group, such clinical decision-making is complex. These issues are discussed further in other chapters.

Second, a networked approach should be taken. It is likely that a child with intellectual disabilities and emotional or behavioural difficulties will have many practitioners and services involved in their care.[1] These will be drawn from health, social care, and voluntary service providers. Mapping this network and liaising with key individuals can be a confusing process for families and practitioners alike. However, this networked approach to care is essential in supporting the delivery of effective mental health services to this client group. It requires knowledge of the network, skills in networking, and time to facilitate liaison.

A networked approach will be appropriate for all children with mental health problems, but it is particularly helpful for children with intellectual disabilities, who utilize a greater range of support services and professionals. Though the knowledge about different networks may be new to some practitioners, networking skills should be familiar, and no different from those developed in working with children without intellectual disabilities. Opportunities for joint working, through individual assessments, interventions, consultation, or training may be particularly helpful in developing network knowledge and skills-sharing between different service providers.

Third, services should include the use of key workers and lead professionals. The key worker or lead professional contributes to the delivery of integrated front-line services, across agencies. They have three main functions which can be carried out by a range of practitioners (and in some cases family members): ensuring that services are co-ordinated, coherent, and achieving intended outcomes; acting as a single point of contact for children being supported by more than one practitioner; and aiming to reduce overlap and inconsistency in services received (DfES 2002; National Service Framework for Children, External Working Group on Disabled Children 2002; Sloper and Statham 2004).

1   The Disabled Child Standard of the Children's NSF (Sloper and Statham 2004) states 'Families of disabled children have contact with an average of 10 different professionals and over 20 visits per year to hospitals and clinics.' Paragraph 39, Section 8.1

Key working can be an intensive role (Greco *et al.* 2005). Some services employ professionals solely in the role of key worker, whereas others ensure that practitioners have a small number of clients to enable them to provide a more intensive and comprehensive service, and play a role in co-ordination. Currently, there is insufficient evidence to advocate one model of key working.

Last, there should be attention to user voices in the planning and delivery of services. Commissioners, managers, and practitioners should be mindful of the key messages from users of services. Primary among these is that effective mental and emotional health support for children with intellectual disabilities relies on strong relationships built on trust and consistency, undertaken by familiar people with sensitive communication skills, and delivered in familiar environments. This kind of support is considered by families, education staff, and young people to be far more important and effective than treatment undertaken solely by specialist professionals who provide appointment-based clinical interventions (Pote *et al.* 2006b).

Quality standards

In developing services, planners should also develop a series of quality standards from which to monitor the delivery and development of services. These outline the minimum quality markers which practitioners and services should be trying to achieve in their delivery of care. The UK has agreed some national quality standards upon which local services can assess themselves. Each phase of care has associated quality standards, as outlined below.

PRE-REFERRAL

- Clear referral criteria and processes should be agreed across provider services to ensure new cases get to the most appropriate service to meet their needs.

- Agreements need to be made within the overlapping agency network about how to deal with children who do not fit current criteria or are at risk of being bounced between services (e.g. CAMH services, child mental health learning disability teams, local authority children's services departments, special schools, challenging behaviour teams).

REFERRAL

- First contact should be made, ideally with both caregivers and referrer, to clarify referral expectations and what is possible (i.e. within team competencies).

- Ideally, contact should take place at home or in a setting relevant to the child (e.g. school or short break care setting).

ASSESSMENT

Assessments should be holistic and consider the child's mental health needs within the context of their intellectual disability and their family's needs. Assessment for mental health difficulties should follow established protocols and good practice (e.g. the National Institute for Clinical Excellence (NICE) Depression and Self-Harm Guidelines, or the National Service Framework for Children in the UK).

INTERVENTION

- Interventions should be individually tailored to meet the mental health needs of the child and their family, taking into account their age, developmental level, and culture.

- Emotional and behavioural interventions should be available at all levels of service delivery (Tiers 1–4) from a variety of psychological models (behavioural, systemic, cognitive, psychodynamic and humanistic) in a variety of formats (direct individual, group or family therapy, and consultation).

- Interventions targeted at mental health issues should be considered within the context of other interventions (social, educational, physical) which the child is receiving. Services should develop effective inter-agency co-ordination to achieve this.

DISCHARGE AND RE-REFERRAL

- Discharge from mental health input should be clearly co-ordinated between agencies, using existing review procedures.

- When considering re-referrals, there should be clear definition of agency roles in relation to new concerns, and an agreed inter-agency action plan.

Conclusions

The current surge of development in mental health services for children with intellectual disabilities is a crucial step in meeting the mental health needs of this vulnerable client group. Given the historical context, using a coherent care pathway model to develop these services is essential. Such pathways should offer effective guiding principles and quality monitoring in order that services develop in a consistent and equitable manner. This chapter has discussed the need for such service development and offered one care pathway model which is being used in the UK to shape service development for this client group. As services develop, further research is necessary to determine the efficacy of these service models, as well as individual therapeutic mental health interventions.

References

American Psychiatric Association (2000) *Diagnostic and Statistical Manual of Mental Disorders* (4th ed). Washington, DC: American Psychiatric Association.

Arthur, A. (1999) 'Emotions and people with learning difficulty: are clinical psychologists doing enough?' *Clinical Psychology Forum 132,* 39–45.

Baum, S., and Lyngaard, H. (2006) *Intellectual Disabilities: A Systemic Approach.* London: Karnac Books.

Bender, M. (1993) 'The unoffered chair: the history of therapeutic disdain towards people with a learning difficulty.' *Clinical Psychology Forum 54,* 7–12.

Brown, H., and Smith, H. (1992) *Normalization: A Reader for the Nineties.* London: Routledge.

Burman, E. (1995) *Deconstructing Developmental Psychology.* London: Routledge.

Burr, V. (1995) *An Introduction to Social Constructionism.* London: Routledge.

Byrne, E., and Cunningham, C. (1985) 'The effects of mentally handicapped children on families: A conceptual review.' *Journal of Child Psychology and Psychiatry 26,* 847–864.

Caine, A., Hatton, C., and Emerson, E. (1998) 'Service Provision.' In E. Emerson, C. Hatton, J. Bromley and A. Caine (eds) *Clinical Psychology and People with Intellectual Disabilities.* Chichester: Wiley.

Common Assessment Framework (CAF) (2006) Available at: www.ecm.gov.uk/caf, accessed on 12 June 2007.

Danforth, S., and Navaro, V. (1998) 'Speech acts: sampling the social construction of mental retardation in everyday life.' *Mental Retardation 36,* 31–43.

Department for Education and Skills (DfES) (1989) *Children Act.* Available at: www.dfes.gov.uk/ publications/childrenactreport, accessed on 12 June 2007.

Department for Education and Skills (DfES) (2002) *The Lead Professional: Managers' and Practitioners' Guides.* Available at: www.dfes.gov.uk/commoncore/docs/CAFGuide.doc, accessed on 12 June 2007.

Department for Education and Skills (DfES) (2004) *Every Child Matters: Change for Children.* London: Department for Education and Skills. Available at: www.everychildmatters.gov.uk, accessed on 12 June 2007.

Department of Health (DoH) (2001) *Valuing People: A New Strategy for Learning Disability for the 21st Century.* London: The Stationary Office.

Department of Health and Social Security (DHSS) (1971) *Better Services for the Mentally Handicapped.* London: HMSO.

Department of Health and Social Security (DHSS) (1989) *Caring for People: Community Care in the Next Decade and Beyond.* London: HMSO.

Einfeld, S., and Tonge, B. (1996) 'Population prevalence of psychopathology in children and adolescents with intellectual disability: II. Epidemiological findings.' *Journal of Intellectual Disability Research 40,* 99–109.

Emerson, E., Hatton, C., Bromley, J., and Caine, A. (1998) *Clinical Psychology and People with Intellectual Disabilities.* Chichester: Wiley.

Gangadharan, S., Bretherton, K., and Johnson, B. (2001) 'Pattern of referral to a child learning disability service.' *British Journal of Developmental Disabilities 47,* 94–104.

Greco, V., Sloper, P., Webb, R., and Beecham, J. (2005) *An Exploration of Different Models of Multi-Agency Partnerships in Key Worker Services for Disabled Children: Effectiveness and Costs.* SPRU Report, York University.

Kroese, B., Dagnan, D., and Loumidis, K. (eds) (1997) *Cognitive-Behaviour Therapy for People with Learning Disabilities.* London: Routledge.

Lenton, S. (2005) *Pathway/Network Thinking: Potential Application to Multi-agency Commissioning, Delivery, Quality Assurance and Inspection of Children's Services.* Available at: www.icwhatsnew.com/bulletin/articles/BACCH1.pdf, accessed on 12 June 2007.

Luckasson, R., Coulter, D., Polloway, E., Reiss, S., Schalock, R., Snell, M., Spitalnik, D., and Stark, J. (1992) *Mental Retardation: Definition, Classification, and Systems of Supports* (9th ed). Washington, DC: American Association of Mental Retardation.

McCarthy, J., and Boyd, J. (2002) 'Mental health services and young people with intellectual disability: is it time to do better?' *Journal of Intellectual Disability Research 46,* 250–256.

McIntosh, P. (2002) 'An archi-texture of learning disability services: the use of Michel Foucault.' *Disability and Society 17,* 65–79.

Mittler, P., and Sinason, V. (eds) (1996) *Changing Policy and Practice for People with Learning Disabilities.* London: Cassell Education.

National Child and Adolescent Mental Health (AMH) Service Mapping Figures (2004) Available at: www.camhsmapping.org.uk, accessed on 12 June 2007.

National Service Framework for Children, External Working Group on Disabled Children (2002) Background Paper on Key Workers. Available at: www.dh.gov.uk/assetRoot/04/11/90/10/04119010.pdf, accessed on 12 June 2007.

Pote, H., Bureau, J., and Goodban, D. (2006b) *Mental Health Services for Children with Learning Disabilities – Developing Local Services: A Resource Pack.* London: CAMHS Publications. Available at: www.camhs.org.uk, accessed on 12 June 2007.

Pote, H., Gale, I., Vostanis, P., and Bureau, J. (2006a) *National Care Pathway for Child Mental Health Services for Children with a Learning Disability.* Available at: www.camhs.org.uk, accessed on 12 June 2007.

Rutter, M., Tizard, J., and Whitmore, K. (1970) *Education, Health and Behaviour.* London: Longman.

Sinason, V. (1992) *Mental Handicap and the Human Condition: New Approaches from the Tavistock.* London: Free Association Books.

Sloper, P., and Statham, J. (2004) *National Service Framework for Children, Young People and Maternity Services: The Mental Health and Psychological Well-being of Children and Young People.* London: Department of Health.

World Health Organization (WHO) (1994) *International Statistical Classification of Diseases and Related Health Problems* (10th ed). Geneva: World Health Organization.

Wright, D., and Digby, A. (1996) *From Idiocy to Mental Deficiency: Historical Perspectives on People with Learning Disabilities.* London: Routledge.

Zarkowska, E., and Clements, J. (1988) *Problem Behaviour in People with Severe Learning Disabilities.* London: Croom Helm.

CHAPTER 14

Children with Physical Illness

Khalid Karim

There is a large population of children who present with mental health problems who have these problems in addition to, or as a consequence of, physical illness. These children can present directly to child and adolescent mental health (CAMH) services through primary care, but often are referred by paediatric medical services. Studies give different estimates of prevalence of children in paediatric services having significantly increased rates of emotional and behavioural problems (Weiland, Pless and Roughmann 1992; Glazebrook *et al.* 2003). As expected, the vast range of physical problems results in a huge range of different presentations, therefore interventions and services need to be available at all the different stages of an illness, from diagnosis to (in some cases) the terminal phase.

Physical illness, in itself, is a significant risk factor for developing mental illness through a multitude of factors. However, it is interesting to note that, despite having physical problems, many children do not develop any mental health difficulties. It is often the interplay of various factors surrounding the child which determines the eventual outcome. This heightens the need to be aware of the development of new problems in children who have previously been mentally healthy.

Specific issues in this group

There are a number of factors that are important to the development of mental health problems which need to be considered when helping these children and their families. The child and the family are susceptible to the normal stressors of any family, but the physical illness can pose additional strains. Before discussing interventions, it is important to understand these factors. The success or failure of treatment may simply depend on the mindset and approach to a young person.

Characteristics of the illness

Certain illnesses such as as neurological conditions have high incidence of co-morbid mental health disorders (Weiland *et al.* 1992). Epilepsy, for example, can have a mental health presentation in the form of behavioural problems or hyperactivity. These problems may be helped by the recognition of their epileptic origin and good pharmacological management. Conditions which affect physical appearance, such as skin disorders, can have a particular impact on certain age groups. Adolescents, who are especially conscious of their self-image, can feel rejected by their peer group, thus affecting their self-esteem and mood.

In general, the severity of the illness itself is associated with increased mental health symptoms. As there is a decline in function, increased treatment regimens, or increased hospitalization, the stress of an illness can affect previously robust children and families. The conditions themselves can run different courses. Some illnesses such as asthma or eczema can be episodic in nature. In these cases, families have to adjust from periods of near normality to times during which the child is more severely affected, including periods of hospital admission. Other illnesses have a more chronic course with a gradual decline in function. Although there is the opportunity to adjust to the changing situation, the constant pressure can affect both the child and family (Pfeffer, Pfeffer and Hodson 2003).

The events surrounding the initial diagnosis can have a significant effect on later coping and functioning. Some conditions are found on routine screening in early years, whereas others may only be diagnosed after repeated presentation to medical services with vague or non-specific symptoms, or after an extensive regimen of tests. Some illnesses have a dramatic and intensive initial presentation, which can leave parents in shock and feeling overwhelmed. All these presentations need to be handled sensitively and, if managed correctly, will foster good relationships between the family and professionals. Any misunderstandings or delays in diagnosis and treatment need to be handled in an open and transparent way. At the time of diagnosis, families often feel overwhelmed by information, but at the same time they need to know the treatment regimen and prognosis of the illness.

Treatment regimens can be as variable as the physical problems themselves. The regimen can be time-consuming and may be considered onerous on a daily basis, for example in cystic fibrosis, or may require intense periods of unpleasant treatment, as in childhood cancer. The treatment may pose a constant stress on already busy lives, and compliance can become problematic. Most illnesses require good engagement with treatment, and poor compliance can be a symptom of possible mental health problems or problems in the family environment. Growing independence in an adolescent may be a source of conflict about taking medication, particularly if the regimen makes the child feel different from their peer group.

All the above factors need to be considered against the age and developmental stage of the young person. Younger children are dependent on their parents for support, both practical and emotional. Changes in hospital systems have resulted in much reduced separations of children from the primary caregiver, and consequently less distress in both groups. The cognitive understanding in a young person may have significant implications on the perception of an illness. Over time, a child will gain an understanding of mortality and the long-term implications of a physical illness. Even in young people unaffected by physical illness, the relationship between maturity and mental health is a strong one.

Family factors

Family and the support available to the child can have a major effect on the way they adapt to a physical illness. The young person is open to all the factors which normally affect their mental health, such as mental health problems in a parent and poor parenting, but has the added stress of the physical problems. As in all families, supportive and containing parenting is a major resilience factor and can protect against other stressors. The stress of having a child with a physical illness can prove a strain on the parents' relationship, and there is a higher incidence of marital break-up (Patterson, McCubbin and Warwick 1990). There is also evidence of increased behavioural problems in siblings, as they may feel ignored and have to compete for attention (Fisman et al. 1996).

Parents may have difficulties adjusting to their child's ongoing stages of development. Increased wish for independence, in particular around adolescence, may cause friction. In some cases, the parents have to encourage the young person to become responsible for their treatment, whereas in others they will have to retain responsibility, despite their child's growth. In conditions such as cystic fibrosis parents have been intensely involved in the treatment regimen for years, and issues of reduced compliance in older children can develop into significant family conflict (Patterson et al. 1990).

Liaison with child mental health services

Although there has been a significant expansion of mental health liaison services for adults in hospitals, this has not been mirrored in the paediatric setting (Klein and Lask 1996; Guthrie 2006; Shaw et al. 2006). Whilst there are good examples of comprehensive paediatric or psychiatry liaison services, mainly in the larger paediatric centres, these are generally less comprehensive and often insufficient.

Specialist CAHM services may be based in the community or in a hospital but whilst they provide mental heath services to the general child population not all offer a more specialized paediatric liaison team (Woodgate and Garralda 2006). Most services, however, do carry out assessments on paediatric patients.

This input is often provided to more specialized areas, such as paediatric intensive care, haematology, oncology, neurology, and surgery, on an ad hoc basis, with no systematic service-level planning. Although virtually all services provide routine outpatient assessments, the level of other input varies. This may include consultation work, inpatient assessments, psychosocial ward rounds, and joint clinics with paediatricians.

In addition to clinical work, mental health professionals may provide training and educational input to clinical staff and students, which can be beneficial in raising awareness of mental health issues in children and teenagers. Rarely, some centres, usually based in teaching hospitals, have large teams consisting of psychiatrists, psychologists, community psychiatric nurses, and social workers, who have specialist roles within the team and perform dedicated tasks. In most places, however, owing to the paucity of staff, the work of the different professionals can be similar, and fulfils whatever role has been locally arranged. Assessment and interventions to young people are mostly provided by consultant psychiatrists and clinical psychologists, usually on a sessional basis; however, it is not uncommon for nursing staff and psychotherapists to be involved from the local CAMH service.

Conflicts may arise from the different expectations of patient care between the medical and mental health teams, with often a poor understanding of the pressures faced by each respective service. Frustration can be expressed if mental health services define their role as diagnosing mental illness rather than dealing with compliance or other such issues. Unfortunately, the provision of mental health services to children with physical illness is often seen as low on the list of priorities in both acute and mental health settings (Shaw *et al.* 2006). Relationships may be fostered by the development of joint clinics, or simple measures such as having all child services based in the same building.

Interventions for children with a physical illness

There are many levels of intervention for these children, which will be related to their specific problem. What can the mental heath professional do? Some examples include:

- help the child and family deal with chronic illness or pain
- advise on the management of painful procedures or problems such as needle phobia
- work with staff and families on treatment compliance
- diagnose and treat underlying mental health problems
- help staff understand staff family dynamics to enable better communication

- help families and staff with bereavement issues
- train staff on mental health awareness and early recognition of mental heath problems in children
- facilitate communication between child, family, and staff.

There are certain issues which need to be addressed in order for the child to get the best care (Ortiz 1997).

Referral process

In hospitals, the child has to be first identified as potentially having a mental health problem by the paediatric staff, which often depends on their experience and training. Some health professionals may feel uncomfortable in discussing mental health concerns with a family, in case the parents or the young person become defensive or even insulted with the suggestion of referral to a mental health service. It is for this reason that introducing the mental health practitioner as a regular member of the paediatric team is important. In some chronic illnesses, the introduction can take place at diagnosis or in early childhood. The timing of the referral can be very important. In the diagnostic period, even if the paediatrician suspects a psychological overlay to a physical illness, the family may be unwilling to discuss this until the diagnosis is clear. If the referral is made after a long duration of the problem, for example family conflict over non-compliance with treatment, problems can become entrenched, thus more difficult to change (Bingley *et al.* 1980).

It is also beneficial if the family are clear and in agreement with the involvement of a mental health worker. It is especially important to obtain consent for older children and adolescents. This can depend on how the referral is framed to the recipient. This can be a routine component of a regular review clinic, or can be presented as a way of helping the family express their feelings. In some conditions, the assessment can be part of an ongoing protocol. Even if the young person or family initially decline referral, the paediatric team can still receive consultation on how they can best manage mental health, family or communication issues.

When referring a child, it is necessary to ascertain the following.

- What are the concerns of the paediatric team?
- What are the expectations of the referral?
- The background to the current situation, for example, the level of physical function, the present treatments, compliance, the timescale of the problem, and any previous interventions offered.

It is therefore important to establish realistic goals at this time. When working with children with a physical illness, it is essential to have a basic understanding of the disease process, the treatment objectives, and the roles of the different members of the multidisciplinary paediatric team.

Mental health assessment

The importance of seeing the child and family together and then, depending on the child's age, interviewing the child and family separately, cannot be underestimated. This will allow the clinician to assess the whole family's view of the problem, but also allow everyone to express their own concerns, feelings, and expectations individually. Parents and teenagers often have opinions that they would not be able to share together. The assessment should not be rushed, as the mental health practitioner may simply gain more insight into a problem by being able to spend a longer period of time on assessment than the paediatric team. In addition to the generic assessment of mental health problems, there are specific aspects which need to be addressed.

The assessment should ascertain the present physical problems and medical state of the young person, in particular levels of pain, breathlessness, loss of function, and the present treatment regimen. If possible, the real level of compliance should be established. It is important to gain an understanding of the child's and family's perspective of the illness, for example their anticipation of the child's future levels of functioning. In some illnesses, such as cystic fibrosis, the adolescent will have to come to terms with reduced life expectancy and other major issues. An appreciation of the child's comprehension of the aetiology and treatment of their condition will help to identify and clarify any misunderstandings about the illness. Previous experience of the illness among relatives or friends will be relevant in considering expectations. Relevant support mechanisms around the family should be discussed.

Getting the parents to describe the illness from its first presentation to the current point enables the clinician to gain an impression of their experience of the condition so far, and of the care they feel they have received. Their level of trust in the health system, or any feelings of guilt, can affect their management of the child. Interviewing parents will also provide an indication of any differences in the way they manage the child's illness, and highlight relationship difficulties. Last, it may be useful to speak to any siblings, who may have a different impression from the rest of the family.

Treatment of underlying mental health problems

After the problem has been identified, a plan should be formulated with the involvement of a member of the paediatric multidisciplinary team. This will ensure that the recommendations are realistic and achievable, and that these can be implemented consistently. It is important to relate the plan clearly to the family and team. An explanation of the aetiology of the mental health problem will facilitate this.

If a mental health diagnosis of a condition such as depression, anxiety, eating disorder, or psychosis is made this should receive the appropriate treatment (MacGuire and Haddeed 2006). Adjustment reactions are commonly found, and these need to be handled sensitively. Although mental health symptoms will often improve over time in response to fluctuating manifestations of the physical condition, children and families can still appreciate the opportunity to discuss their feelings and worries. Although the mental health practitioner may be asked for a 'psychological' opinion, the child's physical symptoms should be controlled as well as possible. For example, pain, nausea, or chronic itching, can all contribute to low mood.

Certain aspects of treatment will require additional attention, and these are discussed below.

COMPLIANCE

Not taking the prescribed medication is a very common problem, estimated at approximately 50 per cent. This can depend on many factors, such as the timing, effect on daytime activities, discomfort, feeling different from peers, or not understanding its medical need. Help is usually sought if the health of the child is being affected, there is an increase in hospital admissions, or there is family conflict over treatment. Non-compliance may have gradually become a 'weapon' for the young person in family disputes.

It is important to work with the child, family, and staff to work out the underlying reasons for non-compliance. If possible, the clinician needs to discover the real level of compliance as a baseline. Although 100 per cent compliance is desirable it is rarely attainable; therefore consensus should be reached on what should be an appropriate level. Education on the indications, benefits, and potential side-effects of treatment can make it more acceptable to the child. Conflict within the family should be addressed without making the compliance the central issue (D'Angelo and Lask 2001).

ANXIETY REACTIONS

Anxiety can be related to the stress of the illness, but can also be a consequence of investigative procedures such as taking blood. This anxiety can interfere with ongoing treatment and can make hospital admissions difficult. During health tests or treatment, pain should be minimized by the use of anaesthetic creams, and distraction can be used in the treatment of younger children. Procedures should be kept to a minimum and, if possible, undertaken by the most experienced staff.

An explanation of the procedure should be given to older children and adolescents, at an appropriate cognitive level, whilst techniques such as play or drawing may be used to convey the same messages to younger children (Jay *et al.* 1985). Cognitive-behavioural therapy (CABT) may help to tackle older children's and adolescents' abnormal thoughts and anxiety reactions (American Academy of Child and Adolescent Psychiatry 2007). In more extreme situations, particularly in older clients, anxiolytic medication can be used with caution.

MOOD CHANGES AND DISORDERS

Mood can be affected in children with both acute and chronic illness, and may present as either an adjustment reaction or a depressive episode. The symptoms of low mood depend on the child's age. In younger children, the presentation can be symptoms such as excessive tearfulness, withdrawal, or worsening behaviour, whereas in older children and adolescents there are expressions of distress, fatigue, and impairment of sleep, appetite or concentration. Self-harm thoughts and related risk should also be assessed.

As stated above, children should be kept as free from unpleasant symptoms as possible. Depressed mood and depressive disorder should be identified early to enable timely intervention. Depending on the situation, individual (usually cognitive) or family therapy can be helpful, but in some cases medication is required. As with all young people the treatment of choice in the UK at the time of writing is fluoxetine, which is generally well tolerated (Sharp and Hellings 2006). Before prescribing, paediatric staff will need to be consulted to avoid drug interactions or symptom exacerbation.

The dying child

Although this chapter is insufficient in covering all aspects of the care of a dying child, this is too important to omit, so this section includes some salient points. The death of a child has a profound effect on all those involved, both family and professionals. The family find the whole experience extremely distressing. For this reason, attention needs to be paid to every stage, such as discussing dying, the terminal phase, and after the death.

As with other aspects of dealing with children with a chronic illness, understanding the child's developmental age is essential, so that discussions are conducted at an appropriate level. Younger children will have a more simplistic understanding, such as going to heaven or seeing a dead relative, whilst older children will have more complex concerns. The mental health practitioner may be able to help facilitate the parents' discussions with their child and help them answer difficult questions. They may also be able to help the child put their thoughts and concerns into words.

During this whole episode, it is extremely important to continually assess for the development of mental health problems, especially mood disorders, which would significantly affect the quality of life. In this respect, the physical care needs to be optimized to minimize any adverse symptoms such as pain (Wolfe, Fribert and Hilden 2002; Hinds *et al.* 2005). The parents' mental health will need some consideration, as they may require support themselves to manage their own distress. Parents should be allowed to be with the child as much as possible, with consideration given to dying at home. Privacy and the allowance of religious practices are necessary (Hinds *et al.* 2005). The belief that everything possible has been done will help the parents through their bereavement process. Apart from the family, the emotional impact on the paediatric or health team will need some consideration. Staff can benefit from debriefing sessions, and may wish to attend the funeral (Dixon *et al.* 2005). The mental health practitioner may be useful in facilitating these meetings.

Conclusions

Providing a service to children with a physical illness can be a challenging but rewarding experience for mental health professionals. The difficulties of working in a hospital environment may seem daunting, but mental health staff will bring a set of skills to the multidisciplinary paediatric team which may enable situations to be viewed from a whole new perspective. This area of practice remains underdeveloped, but as the appreciation of mental health problems in young people continues to expand, interest and services for this young client group should also grow.

References

American Academy of Child and Adolescent Psychiatry (2007) 'Practice parameters for the assessment and treatment of children and adolescents with anxiety disorders.' *Journal of American Academy of Child and Adolescent Psychiatry 46*, 267–283.

Bingley, L., Leonard, J., Hensman, S., Lask, B., and Wolff, O. (1980) 'The comprehensive management of children on a paediatric ward: A family approach.' *Archives of Disease in Childhood 55*, 555–561.

D'Angelo, S., and Lask, B. (2001) 'Approaches to Problems of Adherence.' In M. Bluebond-Langner, D. Angst and B. Lask (eds) *Psychosocial Aspects of Cystic Fibrosis.* London: Arnold.

Dixon, D., Vodde, R., Freeman, M., Higdon, T., and Mathiesen, S. (2005) 'Mechanisms of support: Coping with loss in a major children's hospital.' *Social Work in Health Care 41*, 73–89.

Fisman, S., Wolf, L., Ellison, D., Freeman, T., and Szatmari, P. (1996) 'Risk and protective factors affecting the adjustment of siblings of children with chronic disabilities'. *Journal of the American Academy of Child and Adolescent Psychiatry 35*, 1532–1541.

Glazebrook, C., Hollis, C., Heussler, H., Goodman, R., and Coates, L. (2003) 'Detecting health and behavioural problems in paediatric clinics.' *Child: Care, Health and Development 29*, 141–149.

Guthrie, E. (2006) 'Psychological treatments in liaison psychiatry: The evidence base'. *Clinical Medicine 6*, 544–547.

Hinds, P., Schum, L., Baker, J., and Wolfe, J. (2005) 'Key factors affecting dying children and families.' *Journal of Palliative Medicine 8*, Suppl. 1, S70–S78.

Jay, S., Elliott, C., Ozolins, M., Olson, R., and Pruitt, S. (1985) Behavioural management of children's distress during painful medical procedures. *Behavioural Research and Therapy 23*, 513–520.

Klein, K., and Lask, B. (1996) 'Paediatric Liaison Psychiatry.' In E. Guthrie and F. Creed (eds) *Seminars in Liaison Psychiatry.* London: Gaskell.

MacGuire, P., and Haddeed, P. (1996) 'Psychological Reactions to Physical Illness.' In E. Guthrie and F. Creed (eds) *Seminars in Liaison Psychiatry.* London: Gaskell.

Ortiz, P. (1997) 'General principles in child liaison consultation service: A literature review.' *European Child and Adolescent Psychiatry 6*, 1–6.

Patterson, J., McCubbin, H., and Warwick, W. (1990) 'The impact of family functioning on health changes in children with cystic fibrosis.' *Social Science and Medicine 31*, 159–164.

Pfeffer, P., Pfeffer, J., and Hodson, M. (2003) 'The psychosocial and psychiatric side of cystic fibrosis in adolescents and adults.' *Journal of Cystic Fibrosis 2*, 61–68.

Shaw, R., Wamboldt, M., Bursch, B., and Stuber, M. (2006) 'Practice patterns in paediatric consultation-liaison psychiatry.' *Psychosomatics 47*, 43–49.

Sharp, S., and Hellings, J. (2006) 'Efficacy and safety of Selective Serotonin Reuptake Inhibitors in the treatment of depression in children and adolescents: Practitioner review.' *Clinical Drug Investigation 26*, 247–255.

Weiland, S., Pless, I., and Roughmann, K. (1992) 'Chronic illness and mental health problems in pediatric practice: Results from a survey of primary care providers.' *Pediatrics 89*, Suppl. 3, 445–449.

Wolfe, J., Fribert, S., and Hilden, J. (2002) 'Caring for children with advanced cancer integrating palliative care.' *Pediatric Clinics of North America 49*, 1043–1062.

Woodgate, M., and Garralda, M.E. (2006) 'Paediatric liaison work by child and adolescent mental health services.' *Child and Adolescent Mental Health 11*, 19–24.

CHAPTER 15

The Identification, Prevention, and Treatment of Vulnerabilities among Children of Alcohol- or Drug-dependent Parents

Jeffrey J. Wilson, Lacey Beckmann, and Edward V. Nunes

Many children are exposed to parental alcohol or drug dependence during critical periods of development. The effects of these parental disorders on children directly and indirectly affect children on many levels; that is, children are not only directly exposed to their parents' drug use and related consequences, but they are at risk for multiple parental separations (owing to incapacity or incarceration) physical and emotional abandonment, impoverished circumstances, child welfare placement, child abuse, or chaotic parenting. There is little question that alcohol affects children and drug abuse adversely, but help vis-à-vis preventive and treatment programmes is often relatively unavailable to most of these children. Parental shame, denial, fears of losing their children, neglect, poverty, lack of insurance coverage (in the USA) and the lack of accessible programmes are factors that can prevent these children from receiving desperately needed help. This chapter will explore the developmental psychopathology related to the genetic and environmental consequences of parental drug abuse. Utilizing available scientific and clinical research, developmental trajectories of risk and resilience among these vulnerable children are outlined. A promising body of evidence has demonstrated characteristics of effective preventive programmes that could be implemented in a variety of settings, and the potential benefits of implementing such preventive programmes on the lives of these vulnerable children will be reviewed.

Epidemiology

The high prevalence of drug and alcohol use disorders in the USA and Europe exposes millions of children to parental drug and alcohol use disorders. According to some estimates, there are over 30 million children of alcohol- or drug-addicted parents in the USA (CASA 1999; Cermak and Beckman 1995). In England and Wales, there are 1.3 million children whose parents misuse alcohol, and up to 350,000 children who have a parent with a serious drug problem (DoH 2003).

The adverse effects of parental alcohol abuse on offspring have been well documented over the past several decades. Whilst many studies describe the developmental, social, and overall health risk factors among children of alcohol-abusing parents, relatively little is known about pathways of risk among children of parents addicted to illicit substances. Approximately 20 per cent of individuals in drug and alcohol treatment have a child between the ages of two and 18 years; these families provide opportunities for targeted interventions in the context of parental drug treatment (Stanger *et al.* 1999). Parental alcohol or drug use disorders are associated with increased risks for child abuse, neglect, and other impairments in the parent–child relationship; complicating factors such as co-morbid parent psychopathology and poverty may also contribute to these associations between parental alcohol or drug abuse and increased risk transmitted to offspring (Chilcoat and Anthony 1996; Das Eiden and Leonard 2000; Dishion, Kavanagh and Kiesner 1998; Luthar *et al.* 1998; Nunes *et al.* 1998; Wilson, Bhoopsingh and Nunes 2003a). When compared with children whose parents do not abuse drugs or alcohol, children whose parents abuse drugs and alcohol are nearly three times more likely to be physically or sexually assaulted, and over four times more likely to be neglected (CASA 1999).

Children of substance-abusing parents are at high risk for becoming substance abusers themselves, as well as exhibiting behavioural and mental health problems. Family studies indicate that children of alcohol- or drug-dependent parents have an eight-fold risk of developing substance use disorder (Merikangas *et al.* 1998). In one study, 66 per cent of school-aged and adolescent children of opiate- or cocaine-abusing mothers had at least one psychiatric diagnosis (Luthar *et al.* 1998). In addition, children of drug-dependent parents have a higher risk for both externalizing and internalizing disorders. Child externalizing behaviour can be very difficult for parents to manage, and, in and of itself, can be a daunting stressor in the lives of addicted parents (Luthar *et al.* 1998). For example, child externalizing behaviour has been postulated to increase parental substance use (Pelham *et al.* 1998). Perpetuating the cycle, parental drug use may, in turn, increase the risk of child externalizing and substance use disorders. This can result from specific factors, such as exposure to drugs and parental concordance for drug use, as well as non-specific factors, such as disrupted family functioning resulting from parental substance abuse (Brook *et al.* 1988; Duncan *et al.* 1995; Molina, Chassin, and Curran 1994).

Early developmental risks (pre- peri- and post-natal)

Developmental problems faced by children of alcohol- or drug-dependent parents, or both may include pre-natal exposure to methadone and other substances of abuse, poverty, poor pre-natal care, peri-natal (birth) complications, post-natal deprivation, community violence, parental psychopathology, abuse, abandonment, and neglect (Wasserman *et al.* 1998). Naturalistic research has focused on the effects of pre-natal exposure to drugs of the neonate in utero. Such research shows that pre-natal exposure to cocaine is associated with an assortment of physical problems, including low birth weight and length (Chouteau, Namerow and Leppert 1988), pre-natal haemorrhage (Sparey and Walkinshaw 1995), and childhood impulsivity, inattention, and language irregularities (Mayes and Bornstein 1997). Wasserman *et al.* (1998) note, however, that owing to compounding factors such as inadequate nutrition, economic disadvantage, poor parenting, and potential exposures to other uncontrolled illicit substances (alcohol) it is difficult to control specifically for the effects of the cocaine.

Further studies arrived at similar conclusions. In a study of two-year-old children exposed to methadone in the pre-natal period, researchers found that cumulative risk factors (i.e. maternal communication, sex of child, and social-environmental factors) predicted worse developmental outcome. That is, whereas methadone exposure alone was not enough to negatively affect the children developmentally, these additional factors predicted developmental outcomes only for the methadone group (Bernstein and Hans 1994). Bernstein and Hans (1994) note the critical importance of not oversimplifying these results. It is not that methadone-exposed children develop fundamentally differently from their unexposed counterparts owing solely to the methadone exposure, nor, conversely, does the methadone have no effect. Rather, the importance of auxiliary factors like strengthening family bonds and promoting communication skills between parents and offspring should not be overlooked. Their results emphasize the need for longitudinal research to assess the multitude of environmental risk factors that are likely to interact with individual vulnerabilities.

Several authors have observed that infants pre-natally exposed to heroin are at risk for inattention and poor concentration (Bernstein *et al.* 1984; Regan, Ehrlich and Finnegan 1987; Vorhees and Mollnow 1987). In many cases, poor concentration may lead to poor school performance at a later stage. This association is supported by research showing that children of addicted parents perform less well academically and in terms of social adjustment than control subjects

(Van Baar *et al.* 1994). This, in turn, can lead to delinquent and problematic behaviour during adolescence, including substance abuse. The academic performance and problematic behaviour of these children may be rooted in pre-natal chemical exposure, later parental care, or, most likely, a combination of both. Teasing apart such factors has proved most difficult for researchers in the field.

Results from recent studies further illustrate the need to disentangle risk factors and vulnerabilities among this population. In a review of several studies (Keen and Alison 2001), disadvantages are common among children born to opiate and other substance-addicted mothers. Some of these studies suggest that adequate pre-natal care for substance-dependent women may prove to be a critical factor in determining outcome for their offspring. If treated appropriately, and given access to specially targeted services, such as methadone maintenance, opioid-dependent pregnant women may experience outcomes similar to those enjoyed by their socially matched, non-substance-using counterparts (Broekhuizen, Utrie and Van Mullem 1992). In fact, women maintained on methadone during pregnancy had better outcomes than their untreated heroin-using counterparts (Rosner, Keith and Chasnoff 1982).

Although the studies reviewed in Keen and Alison (2001) illustrate the continuing struggle of researchers to disentangle the efficacy of treatment on pre-natal drug exposure from extensive health and environmental factors, it is clear that health concerns for pregnant substance-using women and their unborn children are paramount. For example, children born to drug-using mothers are at risk for contracting HIV, either via the placental barrier, or through contact with HIV-infected blood during delivery. This risk is especially great on account of the ambivalence towards pursuing active HIV treatment during pregnancy. In researching the safety of antiretroviral therapy during pregnancy, one team found that the use of multiple antiretroviral medications, compared to no therapy or treatment with one medication, was not linked to adverse outcomes (increased rates of pre-term labour, low birth weight, low Apgar scores, and stillbirth) (Tuomala *et al.* 2002). Treating pregnant women with the antiretroviral drug zidovudine (also known as AZT or ZDV) has proved effective in reducing transmission to the offspring by two-thirds in the USA and France (Connor, Barkley and Davis 2000), and one-half to one-third in developing countries, where more simple regimens are used (Dabis, Msellati and Meda 1999; Shaffer, Chuachoowong and Mock 1999; Wiktor, Ekpini and Karon 1999). Overall, studies conducted by the New York State Department of Health have suggested that partial regimens using AZT, initiated during the intrapartum and newborn periods, may significantly reduce the risk of transmission of HIV infection to the child (New York State Department of Health 2007).

A study by Mrus and Tsevat (2004) shows that by offering rapid testing to women in labour who did not receive prior pre-natal care, coupled with antiretroviral prophylaxis for those testing positive, both HIV rates in infants and costs could be decreased. The Department of Health and Human Services in the USA has also put forth a review of the ways in which pregnant women infected with HIV can reduce their risk in a cost-effective manner (DHHS 2006).

Although a great deal of attention has been paid to the pre-natal effects of maternal drug and alcohol abuse, there are peri-natal (risks of being born opioid-dependent, contracting HIV, other infections) and post-natal risks that continue throughout childhood. Hans, Bernstein and Henson (1999) studied 32 children of opiate-dependent mothers (identified pre-natally) and found that pre-natal drug use was associated with negative parenting during early child-hood, but that maternal personality disorders (also identified pre-natally) may have accounted for this association. This suggests that, even with successful drug treatment, risks related to aversive parenting may remain for some women. Bernstein and colleagues (Bernstein and Hans 1994; Bernstein *et al.* 1984) found that methadone-using mothers were less responsive to their infants and less encouraging of their infants' communicative behaviour. One hypothesis is that these negative or neglectful parental behaviours mediate transmission of risk to offspring, as early interactions between infants and their parents are critical in developing normal emotional regulation and communication skills (Siegel 1999). Hence, it is possible that developmental deficits (e.g. behavioural or lin-guistic) may result from such factors secondary to substance abuse, such as other genetic factors or post-natal linguistic deprivation (Mayes and Bornstein 1997; Potter *et al.* 2000; Singer *et al.* 2001; Wilson *et al.* 2003 and 2004).

Beyond the early developmental years, parental substance abuse has been associated with both physical and sexual abuse, as well as neglect (Famularo, Kinshneff and Fenton 1992). A review by Hogan (1998) explored the research beyond pre-natal effects. She delineated three possible methods by which the parental substance abuse may negatively affect children's psychosocial develop-ment. First, parental substance abuse may deprive children of adequate physical care. Recall that children whose parents abuse drugs and alcohol are nearly three times more likely to be physically or sexually assaulted, and over four times more likely to be neglected. Second, the child's socio-emotional and cognitive devel-opment may be impaired. Third, drug-dependent parents may simply influence their young children and adolescents to become drug users themselves. Parental substance use may directly or indirectly affect offspring, that is, parents may introduce children to drugs directly (10% of youths in one study were 'turned on' to drugs by their parents, or parents may model the use of drugs or alcohol for their children) (Survey 2000).

Hogan's (1998) first point, about parental physical care and neglect, may provoke several developmental problems. At first these problems may seem inde-pendent of later adolescent substance abuse, but they may, in fact, increase its risk.

For example, childhood physical and sexual abuse has been shown to be associated with illegal drug use (Heffernan *et al.* 2000). A study by Dube *et al.* (2003) addressed the relationship among several categories of adverse childhood experiences (ACEs). Among the ACEs included were physical, emotional and sexual abuse, physical and emotional neglect, substance-abusing parents, criminal activity in the household, and mental illness. The researchers found that each ACE category was associated with a two-to-four-fold increase in the probability of illicit substance use by age 14. For each ordinal increase in the number of ACEs, the probability of substance use initiation during early adolescent, mid-adolescent, adulthood, or lifetime increased by 40 per cent, 10 per cent, 10 per cent, and 30 per cent, respectively. Also, as anticipated, multiple ACEs tended to co-occur within households. To this end, there is strong evidence showing that the number of ACEs an individual experienced illustrated a robust relationship to the risk of drug initiation from early adolescence into adulthood. In fact, ACEs accounted for one-half to two-thirds of serious problems with drug use.

Further research confirms such effects of neglect on later substance abuse. Dunn *et al.* (2002) reviewed a number of studies in their review on child neglect in substance abuse families, and concluded that maltreatment, especially neglect, has a profound and persistently deleterious impact on children (Cicchetti and Toth 1995; Crouch and Milner 1993; Gaudin 1999). The high rate of childhood abuse and neglect found among adolescents and adults in treatment for substance abuse strongly suggests that this is an especially salient risk factor for the development of substance use disorder (SUD) (Schaefer, Sobieragh and Hollyfield 1988; Toray *et al.* 1991). In as much as the risk for child neglect is augmented by parental SUD (Bays 1990; Famularo *et al.* 1992), children in these families are at higher risk for psychiatric problems and psychosocial dysfunction (West and Prinz 1987), as well as substance abuse and SUD (Chasnoff and Lowder, 1999; Hawkins, Catalano and Miller 1992). Hence, neglect in substance abuse families may coalesce with the child's augmented genetic predisposition to SUD (Cloninger, Bohmann and Sigvardsson 1981; Sigvardsson, Bohmann and Cloninger 1996).

Psychiatric disorders among children of addicted parents

As explored thus far, research on children of substance-abusing parents consistently demonstrates that parental drug use can and will negatively affect children's development in various facets of life. In this section, the relationship between parental substance abuse and child psychopathology will be explored. This is important because of the association of specific psychiatric disorders with child and adolescent substance abuse (Clark *et al.* 2004). A review of studies by Barnard and McKeganey (2004) encompasses a great deal of the research conducted on the psychiatric impact of parental substance abuse on children. The literature included in their review reveals a strong capacity for parental drug use to impede proper parenting, as well as a decrease in ability to provide a nurturing environment. Despite the large scope and urgency of this problem, familial substance abuse interventions are not always widely applicable (non-clinic-based populations are under-represented) and are often not subjected to thorough evaluation.

Among the clinically based studies, however, several interesting results surface. One major study included in the review, by Johnson, Boney and Brown (1991) showed that children raised in families where one or both parents were opioid-dependent had a significantly higher probability of exhibiting depressive symptoms, as well as being anxious, tense, and worried. In addition, these children showed further deficits, as they scored lower on measures of arithmetic. A series of replications find similar results. For example, Nunes *et al.* (1998) found that children of opiate-dependent patients are at potential risk for conduct problems, as well as reduced social and intellectual functioning, and that sons of addicts with depression are at an especially heightened risk. This research team followed up by surveying 78 children of heroin-and/or cocaine-addicted parents and found that 60 per cent of children reported a psychiatric disorder, and 20 per cent reported major depression specifically (Weissman *et al.* 1999). Upon further study of this sample, verbal deficits were found to be related to child disruptive behaviours among some groups of children, consistent with the hypothesis that linguistic deprivation may be related to deficits in behavioural regulation (Tarter *et al.* 1999; Wilson *et al.* 2004).

Although at substantially increased risk for psychiatric disorders and other adaptive dysfunctions, it is noteworthy that most children of substance-dependent parents do not exhibit psychiatric, emotional, or behavioural disorders. It is equally important that we understand which factors within the substance-abusing family unit transmit this risk and which factors increase resiliency among these children (NIDA 2005). Comparing the general population and at-risk samples suggests that family environment plays a large role in predicting conduct problems. 'Family environment' includes aspects such as family communication, problem-solving, affective responsiveness, involvement, and attitudes towards discipline (Gorman-Smith *et al.* 1996; Patterson 1982; Weissman *et al.* 1999). Coercive parent–child interactions have been specifically associated with increased substance abuse in adolescence (Dishion *et al.* 1998).

Family environment has been found to mediate relations between parental substance use and children's outcomes in high-risk samples of youth. Stanger *et al.* (2002) found that both age and gender play important roles in this outcome. Among their sample of 4 to 18-year-old children of drug-dependent parents, they found similar severity of internalizing and externalizing problems for younger (aged 4–11 years) versus older age (aged 12–18 years). Older children, girls specifically, however, showed more deviance and delinquent behaviour than their comparative normative population. Such findings suggest that adolescent daughters of drug-dependent parents may be at distinctive risk of deviance on externalizing problems.

Among the various problematic behaviours exhibited by children of drug-dependent parents are a myriad of disruptive behaviours, including attention deficit/hyperactivity disorder (ADHD) oppositional defiant disorder (ODD) and conduct disorder (CD). Problematic social interactions, including parent–child interactions and peer relations, could be related to adolescent drug use by several mechanisms. These mechanisms may include impaired parent–child communication, reduced parent monitoring, extra-familial social impulsivity (which may promote delinquent peer associations) and impulsive drug use, and/or interactions between several of these factors. In a naturalistic study of children of opioid-dependent parents in methadone maintenance treatment, ongoing parental drug use was strongly associated with child externalizing problems.

ADHD has been associated with parent drug use (Pelham et al. 1998), and has been suggested also to play a role in coercive interactions in the home (Dishion et al. 1998; Patterson 1982). However, in most studies, when controlling for conduct disorder, conduct disorder accounts for most of the variance in this relationship, as 40 per cent of children with ADHD also meet the criteria for conduct disorder (Wilson 2007). Wilson and Levin (2005) address the issues of these often inter-related disorders among children of drug-dependent parents. Children with ADHD followed into adolescence are more likely to have CD, are more likely to have been arrested, and have an earlier age of onset of alcohol dependence (Barkley et al. 2004; Rutter, Giller and Hagel 1998; Weiss, Hechtman and Weiss 1999). Further, these authors report the reciprocal finding that parents of children with ADHD and CD have a greater probability of having cocaine or stimulant dependence. ODD, a developmental prodrome of CD, increases the risk of developing conduct disorder and adolescent substance abuse.

The nature of these psychiatric problems, however, varies based in large part on age and gender of the child. Stanger et al. (2002) calls attention to the fact that very little of the research on substance-abusing families is attuned to gender differences among offspring. Rather, these workers note, much of the research focuses on children of substance-abusing mothers, or sons of substance-addicted fathers, and fail to test both parent and child gender differences. In addressing these issues in their study, Stanger et al. (2002) found that there were indeed significant effects of age and gender. For example, there was a significant relationship between individual parent problems and family problems for mothers, but not for fathers. Additionally, older girls exhibited more deviant behaviour relative to their same age and gender peers than the younger girls and boys. This is likely to be significant because of differences described in studies of children of alcoholics (Hinz 1990; Hussong, Curran and Chassin 1998; Sher *et al.* 1991; Wiers, Seargeant and Gunning. 1994).

Effects of maternal versus paternal psychopathology on children are also likely to be different, given the natures of father–child versus mother–child relationships. Whilst research remains relatively scant about the effects of ongoing maternal substance abuse on children, even less is known about the effects of ongoing paternal substance abuse on children (Luthar *et al.* 1998). Schwartz *et al.* (1990) showed that maternal 'expressed emotion' was associated with a higher risk of depressive disorders as well as substance abuse and CD among her children. In order to understand the contribution of parental substance abuse or other psychopathology to child behaviours, further research needs to consider the possibility of differential effects of variables within different contexts (e.g. effects of maternal versus paternal substance abuse on boys versus girls).

Despite the growing research on the interplay between parental SUD and mental disorders among offspring, it remains unclear whether children with co-morbid mental disorders and SUD themselves are being treated appropriately. Some research suggests that psychopathology is associated with poorer treatment outcomes among substance-abusing adolescents (Grella, Joshi and Hser 2003). Results from Grella *et al.* (2003) add to the great disparity among children with SUD and co-morbid psychiatric disorders. Co-morbid youth had higher rates of drug and alcohol dependence, having ever used a greater number of substances, and initiating alcohol and marijuana use at earlier ages than their non-co-morbid counterparts. As compared to non-co-morbid youths, co-morbid youths were more likely to be white, younger, and to report problems with their family, school, and peers. Furthermore, females were more than twice as likely to have depression, which is notable because adolescents with depression had a greater probability of exhibiting alcohol dependence. This increased likelihood towards alcohol dependence is consistent with Helzer and Pryzbeck (1998) who found co-morbid alcoholism and affective disorders among adults.

Substance use disorder among children of addicted parents

The prevalence of substance abuse has remained relatively stable in the USA over the past few years. In 2005, an estimated 19.7 million Americans aged 12 or older, or approximately eight per cent of the population, were current illicit drug users. The rate of illicit drug use among this demographic in 2005 was similar to the rate in 2004 (7.9%) 2003 (8.2%) and 2002 (8.3%) (SAMHSA 2007). It is not an increase in prevalence, but rather an increase in knowledge of both risk pathways to abuse for children and effective preventive programmes that has driven research forwards in this field.

Kaplow, Curran and Dodge (2002) found a clear difference between pre-adolescent substance users and adolescent-onset users. The pre-adolescent-onset group was characterized by poor child temperament, as well as child psychopathology related to parental behaviours (such as substance abuse and disciplinary practices). The normative, adolescent-onset group was found to be more socially driven by neighbourhood and peer culture. Further, in a prospective study of youth at high risk for alcoholism, Clark, Kirisci and Moss (1998) found that the presence of pre-adolescent CD was a strong predictor of early adolescent cannabis abuse. This study also notes that, in addition to CD and general behavioural dysregulation, children of substance-dependent parents tend to share fundamental deficits in language ability. Such findings reiterate that the development of CD mediates the development of SUDs, especially in these high-risk groups. Overall, early exposure to substances of abuse is correlated with the development of early-onset substance use disorders (Wilson and Levin 2001). Several studies suggest the significance of non-specific factors (e.g. disrupted family functioning resulting from parental substance abuse) in the development of substance use behaviours among offspring. Poor parental control has been associated with drug use among offspring, whereas improvements in behavioural control of offspring and improved parental monitoring have been associated with decreased risk of drug use and delinquency among offspring (Brook *et al.* 1998; Duncan *et al.* 1995; Molina *et al.* 1994). Disruptive behaviours appear to be especially important in the development of early-onset SUD (Tarter *et al.* 1999). In fact, externalizing behaviour disorders, or disruptive, aggressive, or impulsive behaviours, are perhaps the strongest individual risk factors for early-onset drug use disorders. This form of conduct has also been described as 'behavioural disinhibition', which probably indicates a common trait for passing on this risk for early-onset drug abuse.

Highlighting a further risk for childhood and adolescent substance abuse, families with drug-abusing parents have been shown to exhibit less family cohesion, more child psychopathology, and considerably higher rates of drug abuse during early adolescence (Merikangas *et al.* 1998). Among parents with SUD, weakened attachments also seem to mediate the initiation of drug use in offspring (Hoffmann and Su 1998; Keller *et al.* 2002). Weakened attachments prove to be a salient avenue of risk between parents and children. Suchman and Luthar (2000) found that, among a sample of opiate-addicted mothers, dysfunctions in maternal involvement with children could be directly attributed to addiction, and that socio-economic status and mothers' perceptions of their children's maladaptive behaviour may also play a significant role in their parenting. They also noted that socio-demographic factors, such as single marital status and family size, could significantly moderate the relationship between addiction and parenting.

Although this idea that non-specific factors such as stressful family environments and parental psychiatric problems play a significant role in drug involvement, mental health, and behaviour problems for children of parents with substance and alcohol problems, a number of studies have shown that the associations linking drug use to parental alcohol problems are largely specific, and independent of secondary risk factors (Obot, Wagner and Anthony 2001). An earlier study by Obot and Anthony (2000) showed that the existence of parental alcohol problems was closely linked with offspring delinquency, even after controlling for several potentially relevant socio-demographic factors. Biederman *et al.* (2000) also found evidence that exposure to parental SUDs predicted SUDs in offspring. Their study controlled for parental lifetime SUD history, ADHD status, and socio-economic status, solidifying the idea that exposure to parental SUDs predicts offspring SUDs independent of the peripheral risk factors assessed. Overall, such results support the importance of addressing specific familial risk factors in the development of SUDs among children. Moreover, the current evidence regarding treatment of ADHD, though controversial, supports the hypothesis that treating ADHD with stimulants reduces the risk of SUD (Wilens *et al.* 2003; Wilson 2007).

Both direct (modelling of drug use behaviours) and indirect (lack of parental monitoring) factors are likely to play a role in the increased risk conferred to children (Kilpatrick *et al.* 2000). In this case, the modelling effect of familial substance use was specialized, in turn leading to similar types of substance abuse in adolescents. Whilst children of alcohol abusing parents do exhibit various negative consequences, as explored above, there are several reasons to look at children of opiate- and cocaine-addicted parents separately. Fundamentally, at the pharmacological level, behavioural outcomes among substances of abuse differ greatly from one another. At the level of behavioural pharmacology, one would be led to hypothesize that cocaine/amphetamine abuse would be more associated with violent crime than opioid abuse, which would be more associated with domestic crimes related to neglect. Because of the phenomenon of behavioural disinhibition, alcohol would also be associated with an increased risk of violent domestic behaviours (Mack *et al.* 2003). Hogan (1998) addresses further distinct reasons why cocaine and opiate abuse is treated as distinct from alcohol and other drugs. First, she finds that the lifestyle associated with cocaine and opiates is qualitatively different from that of alcohol use. For example, opiate and cocaine users are more likely to comprise a low SocioEconomic Status (SES) population, whereas alcohol and amphetamine users are scattered throughout a range of socio-economic situations. This separates the populations on a sociological dimension, secondary to the substance abuse itself. Second, there is the simplistic fact that drug use is an illegal activity, whereas alcohol consumption is not. The secrecy encapsulating illicit drug use fosters a distinct family dynamic. Not only does it affect the internal workings of the family unit, but carries the risk of outside societal scrutiny, and worse, fear of incarceration.

Developmental pathways to substance use disorder and antisocial personality disorder

From a developmental perspective, the most common occurrence for child neglect peaks during late childhood and remains high throughout adolescence (NRC 1993; Triket and Weinstein 1991). Neglect of adolescents continues to have devastating consequences, as older children and adolescents tend to engage in dangerous health risk behaviours during this time. Moreover, since most parents would have started to use drugs during their own adolescence, they may feel powerless or unable to intercede. Their own guilt regarding their drug use is a particularly problematic aspect of their parenting since it undermines their ability to discipline their children effectively. Specifically, this developmental phase when parental neglect of children is most common coincides with the time in life when children are at high risk for a variety of adverse outcomes such as substance abuse, pregnancy, sexually transmitted disease, and traumatic injury (Kirisci *et al.* 2001). Rates of childhood neglect among adults and adolescents in substance abuse treatment are notably high, which suggests that neglect might indeed be a significant risk factor in the development of SUD (Schaefer *et al.* 1988; Toray *et al.* 1991).

In addition to parental substance abuse and neglect driving the risk of child substance abuse upwards, there is much evidence that shows such maltreatment may additionally lead to the development of disruptive behaviour disorders. Coercive interactions, poor disciplinary practices, poor supervision, and parental yielding to child coercion (negative reinforcement) are all associated with the development of antisocial behaviour during adolescence (Kim, Hetherington and Reiss 1999; Patterson 1982). 'Coercive interactions' stem from Coercion Theory, which states that in the context of hostile, coercive parent–child relationships, non-compliance in early childhood can develop into excessive aggression and persistent antisocial behaviour. Antisocial behaviour in turn increases addictive vulnerability among these children (Dishion *et al.* 1998; Hembree-Kigin and McNeil 1995).

The relationship between SUD and antisocial personality disorder (ASPD) continues the developmental trajectory into adulthood. CD is a necessary prodrome of ASPD. Moreover, a powerful association remains between ASPD and adult substance abuse. It has been noted that overall, SUD patients with ASPD engage in more use of illicit drugs (King *et al.* 2001). In one study to determine whether SUD patients with and without ASPD differed in ways of severity of SUD symptoms, familial SUD, number and type of SUD diagnoses, and extent of SUD treatment, Westermeyer and Thuras (2005) found there were overwhelming *similarities* between the two groups. They did find a few differences, however, including patients with ASPD showing greater risk-taking behaviour in starting alcohol and tobacco use earlier, as well as being more apt to ever use illicit drugs.

Paternal factors were studied specifically as a potential cause for ASPD in patients with SUD. The outcome data, however, are conflicting. One study shows that paternal SUD did not affect the prevalence of ASPD among SUD patients (Moss, Clark and Kirisci 2002). In a separate study by Moss and colleagues, paternal alcoholism was associated with increased rates of conduct disorder in pre-adolescent offspring (Moss *et al.* 2001). In response to this conflict, Westermeyer and Thuras (2005) failed to show a link of ASPD specifically to paternal SUD. However, they did conclude that the sum total of all SUD relatives was significantly greater among the APSD patient population.

Further developmental pathways to ASPD and SUD include ADHD, CD, and ODD. In a review of the relationship between ADHD and SUD, Wilson and Levin (2005) found that ADHD is associated with several factors that may contribute to antisocial behaviour and substance abuse later in development. For example, children with ADHD are more likely to have ODD, anxiety disorders, mood disorders, and learning disorders (Wilson and Levin, 2005). Precursors of antisocial behaviour, such as high impulsivity, low anxiety, low reward dependence, have been observed as early as kindergarten (Tremblay *et al.* 1994). ODD symptoms are highly prevalent among younger children, and many children outgrow these symptoms and do not go on to develop ASPD and SUD. Nonetheless, children with higher levels of aggression and earlier progression to conduct disorder are at dramatically increased risk of ASPD and adolescent substance abuse.

Primary and secondary preventive strategies

Despite the clear public health need for preventive and treatment services among children of substance abusers, actual funding for preventive programmes makes up less than one per cent of the costs of substance abuse in New York City (CASA 1996). One difficulty in prevention programmes for children of addicted parents is the identification of these children, owing to the prohibition of the family secret of a parent's substance abuse (Cermak and Beckman 1995). Parents in recovery are often overwhelmed by their children's behaviour, and lack the parental skills to cope with aggressive and hostile behaviour (whether genetically or environmentally determined). Coupled with the preoccupation of an active addiction or other psychiatric co-morbidity, it seems likely that targeted interventions aimed at reducing these maladaptive interactions may reduce vulnerability among offspring.

Early intervention into these proximal interaction patterns between parents and their disruptive children reduces the risk of aggressive behaviours and disruptive behaviour disorders (Dishion and Andrews 1995; Dishion *et al.* 1998; Rutter *et al.* 1998). Several protective factors have been identified for the children of drug-dependent parents. Such factors include strong bonds with family, parental monitoring (including clear rules of conduct and involvement of parents in their children's lives) success in school performance, strong bonds with pro-social institutions (e.g. school, family, and religious organizations) and adoption of conventional norms about drug use (NIDA 2003). Including both risk and resiliency factors is integral to effective preventative strategies. In their research-based guide to preventing drug use among children and adolescents, the National Institute on Drug Abuse (NIDA) specifies targetable risk and protective factors that may affect individuals in a variety of settings, or 'domains', where interventions may take place (Table 15.1).

The report goes on to explain the relative potency of these factors by developmental stages, as related to Table 15.1. For example, the risk factor of peer pressure is especially powerful during adolescent and teenage years, just as a strong parent–child bond may be more effective in reducing risk during earlier stages of development. Prevention strategies are best executed at these optimal

Table 15.1 Targetable risk and protective factors that may affect individuals in a variety of settings or 'domains' where interventions may take place*

Risk factors	Domain	Protective factors
Early aggressive behaviour	Individual	Self-control
Lack of parental supervision	Family	Parental monitoring
Substance abuse	Peer	Academic competence
Drug availability	School	Anti-drug use policies
Poverty	Community	Strong neighborhood attachment

*Adapted from NIDA (2005)

time windows, and through the most appropriate mediums. That is, where family interventions may want to focus on communication skills, rules enforcement, and discipline styles in the child's earlier years, schools should concentrate on academic skills, enhancing peer relationships, self-control, and explicit drug refusal skills in later childhood and adolescence. School-based prevention programmes optimally should be integrated into the school's academic programme, as school failure is strongly associated with substance abuse (NIDA 2003).

Parental treatment of ongoing substance abuse, to the extent that it reduces substance use and stabilizes it, seems likely to have reciprocal benefits for parents and children. In fact, there appears to be a robust relationship between child externalizing behaviours and parent drug use (Wilson et al. 2000). Little is actually known about the effects of parental substance abuse treatment on these high-risk children. Even less is known about the continuing needs of these children after parental treatment. One of the few studies that examines the effects of parental substance abuse treatment on offspring evaluated 35 women and their 23 children during treatment at a residential treatment facility (Killeen and Brady 2000). In this study, women who completed treatment demonstrated reductions in parental stress and addiction severity, and their children demonstrated improved behavioural and emotional functioning (according to parental reports). Similar changes in child behaviour were reported by Moss et al. (1997). In this retrospective study of a community sample, paternal reports of earlier substance use disorder cessation were associated with lower levels of externalizing and internalizing behaviours. The implications of these studies are promising, but both are somewhat limited by the lack of direct child assessment as well as the lack of any direct assessments of parenting or parent–child interactions.

Studies which do involve direct assessments on parent–child interactions show less promising results for child-centered intervention. In one such study, Catalano et al. (1999) examined whether family-focused interventions would be successful in both reducing parents' drug use and preventing children's onset of drug use. To assess this, they supplemented methadone treatment with 33 family training sessions and nine months of home-based case management. Results show significant positive changes in parent skills, parent drug use, deviant peers, and family management. However, like many studies before, there were few changes in the behaviour and attitude of the children. Programmes that follow this model may prove useful in supplementing treatment programmes in strengthening family bonds and reducing parental substance use.

One study that addresses a potential prevention aimed directly at children was conducted by Kaplow et al. (2002), who found that children with no risk factors for early-onset substance abuse had less than a 10 per cent chance of initiating substance use by age 12, whereas children with two or more risk factors had a more than 50 per cent chance of initiating substance use by this age. 'Risk factors' were deemed as being male, having a substance-abusing parent, having a parent with low levels of verbal reasoning, exhibiting high levels of overactivity, having more thought problems, and displaying greater deficits in social problem-solving skills. The research team concluded that by identifying these specific factors, more precise prevention efforts can focus on this high-risk group in a way that may prove more beneficial than universal interventions that are less focused. By pinpointing specific risk factors, we are given ideas about potential targets of preventative interventions at this stage of development.

Interventions for youth at high risk of sud

Treatment paths for youths at high risk for SUD are not straightforward. Adolescents as a group necessitate a vastly different type of treatment than adults, as the manifestation of SUD occurs during such a distinctive developmental and social phase. Adolescent populations tend to be more impulsive and exhibit greater risk-taking behaviours. Further, as compared to adults, adolescents exhibit greater problems with marijuana and alcohol, higher incidence of binge use, and greater complications due to the many developmental changes they are undergoing (Dennis and Brotman 2003). Additionally, the progression from casual use to dependence can be more rapid in adolescents than in adults (Winters 1999). Attempts to treat adolescent SUD have historically used assessment measures created for adult treatment, and, in light of the striking differences between the two populations, such tools are often not appropriate for use with this younger, less-developed population.

Pinpointing differences between adult and adolescent needs is only half the battle in remedying the fact that adolescent treatment programmes continue to fail. Kaminer (2001) addresses the reasons why adolescent substance abuse treatment programmes prove unsuccessful, and how we can move forwards more effectively. The study cites high rates of early treatment termination and high rates of relapse as two major components of the pitfalls of adolescent substance abuse treatment. The higher rate of relapse, however, is often connected to the higher rates of relapse associated with outpatient therapy in general. Outpatient therapy, notably 12-step programmes, is the most common model used in adolescent treatment (Muck *et al.* 2001).

Treatment programmes, whilst multi-modal in some cases, tend to fall into four main categories: 12-step; cognitive-behavioural; family-based; and therapeutic communities (Muck *et al.* 2001). In the USA, the most prevalent among these modalities is the 12-step model. It is important to note, however, that simple referral *to* a 12-step programme is not considered treatment. In the 12-step model, the first five steps are included in primary care, and steps 6 to 12 are attended to during aftercare (Winters 1999). Winters (1999) also points out that group therapy is a key component in the 12-step model, which can prove to be highly beneficial, as adolescents rely greatly on peer examples and seek approval. Conversely, he notes, it can prove wholly detrimental, as disruptive adolescents can induce bad behaviour in others.

When treating substance abuse, Cognitive-behavioural Therapy (CBT) also known as Relapse Prevention Therapy (RPT) is one of the few evidence-based treatments for adolescent substance abuse. CBT is based on the assumption that drug use is a learned behaviour disorder that develops within a cultural context comprised of family, peers, and social institutions that define drug-related beliefs and behaviours (Bandura 1977; Marlatt and Fordon 1980). Group approaches which follow this model have also been shown to affect both short- and long-term benefits. The ultimate goal of CBT is to minimize the maladaptive beliefs that contribute to drug use, and encourage factors that protect against relapse. Such positive factors include coping skills, drug-free social networks, and academic achievement.

A third common treatment approach to adolescent substance abuse is family-based therapy. The only other evidence-based treatment emphasizes the role familial factors play in the development and maintenance of adolescent drug abuse (Hawkins, Catalano and Miller 1992). Since there are dysfunctional factors that extend beyond the family system, some family-based approaches include adolescent's peers, school, and neighbourhood. Core principles of family therapies include the notions that:

- individual personality traits that influence drug involvement are shaped in large part by observable family relationships and interactions (Latimer et al. 2003);

- the family is viewed as a unit comprised of subsystems, each with a differing role within the family structure (Minuchin 1974); and

- the primary goal is to re-establish parental authority, and improve the relationship between parent and child.

A subsidiary branch of family therapy, pioneered largely by Jose Szapocznik and colleagues, is Brief Strategic Family Therapy (BSFT). Over the past several decades, these research teams have formulated this approach, tuning their focus to the enduring problem of conduct and drug problems among Hispanic and African American youths. This approach has revealed positive results through engaging families into treatment, reducing drug abuse, behaviour problems, emotional distress in children and adolescents, and improving family functioning (Szapocznik and Williams 2000).

Therapeutic communities (TCs) are most often used in the USA to treat youth and adolescents with the most severe substance abuse problems. These are in-patient programmes that tend to last for several consecutive months.

Adolescents who remain in therapeutic communities for the duration of their treatment demonstrate long-term benefits in behaviour, including reductions in substance use, criminal recidivism and adaptive functioning (Wilson 2006). Therapeutic Communities are unique in that they utilize the community itself as therapist and guide, throughout the treatment process (Winters 1999).

Finding a fitting treatment paradigm is a major component in attaining successful adolescent substance abuse treatment, but it is a moot goal if there is no motivation on the part of the adolescent. Muck *et al.* (2001) addressed several key factors in the successful treatment of adolescents, and a vital factor was motivation. Motivation plays a unique role with youths and adolescents, because this population almost unanimously enters treatment through referrals by parents, judges, probation officers, school officials, case workers, etc., rather than through intrinsic motivation on their own behalf. It is further important for treatment to be geared to the individual at hand. Even at a basic level, the response to parental substance abuse manifests drastically differently between males and females. Luthar and Cushing (1999) found that factors that improved outcome for boys can adversely affect outcome for girls and vice-versa.

To address what measures and factors are most needed in adolescent substance abuse treatment, after consulting with the literature and an advisory panel of 22 experts in the field, Brannigan *et al.* (2004) arrived at nine characteristics vital to a successful treatment programme:

1. *Assessment and treatment matching.* Programmes should conduct comprehensive assessments that cover psychiatric, psychological, and medical problems; learning disabilities; family functioning; and other aspects of the adolescent's life. Treatment should then be matched with the needs that have been identified.

2. *Comprehensive, integrated treatment approach.* Programme services should address all aspects of an adolescent's life.

3. *Family involvement in treatment.* Research shows that involving parents in the adolescent's drug treatment produces better outcomes.

4. *Developmentally appropriate programme.* Activities and materials should reflect the developmental differences between adults and adolescents.

5. *Engaging and retaining teens in treatment.* Treatment programmes should build a climate of trust between the adolescent and the therapist.

6. *Qualified staff.* Staff should be trained in adolescent development, co-occurring mental disorders, substance abuse, and addiction.

7. *Gender and cultural competence.* Programmes should address the distinct needs of adolescent boys and girls as well as cultural differences.

8. *Continuing care.* Programmes should include relapse prevention training, aftercare plans, referrals to community resources, and follow-up.

9. *Treatment outcomes.* Rigorous evaluation is required to measure success, target resources, and improve treatment services.

While we are able to gain a general sense of the major components recommended for successful adolescent substance abuse treatment, both Kaminer (2001) and Muck *et al.* (2001) cite the multiple limitations of the existing adolescent substance abuse literature. Such limitations include small sample sizes, lack of adequate controls, non-uniform selection criteria, failure to note compliance and attrition rates, inadequate length of follow up, and failure to document treatment procedures, making it impossible to replicate findings. Due to the lack of uniformity among studies of adolescent substance abuse treatment, universally effective treatment paradigms are still unknown.

While the research and evidence may be limited, it has been found that there are several salient factors that are important for treatment programmes aimed at adolescents with SUD to address. That is, research and treatment appear to be heading in the right direction. Such factors include.

1. the need for programmes to be accessible and provide treatment for a large number of individuals;

2. focus on minimizing and abating treatment drop-out and make efforts to maximize treatment completion;

3. follow-up/aftercare as part of the treatment plan;

4. comprehensive educational, psychological, vocational, recreational, family, and legal services;

5. family therapy as part of treatment; and

6. parent and peer support in the realm of the non-use of substances.

It is also crucial for counsellors to recognize that not all adolescents who currently use drugs are, or will become, dependent (Shedler and Block 1990).

What we see throughout the current research is that the literature on adolescent substance treatment programmes is scarce and lacks consistency. Some studies evaluate outcome at the end of treatment, whereas others focus outcome measures on one or two years post-treatment. Furthermore, studies vary on where 'success' lies on the continuum from baseline use, to reduction, to abstinence. This discord among measurement tactics and lack of uniformity among instruments illustrates the dire need for new, reliable measures to be created.

Access to health care and preventive programes (US/Europe)

In addition to inconsistent research methods, there are several further barriers to proper health care for the substance-abusing population. Such factors include demographics, health status and functional limitations, severity of condition, socio-economic status and employment, patient view of mental illness, acculturation, ethnicity, community support, church participation, provider sensitivity, structural and operating aspects of providers, and a host of economic and/or financial obstacles (Woodward 2004). Woodward notes that, while these external obstacles are prevalent, internal barriers are not to be overlooked. For example, individuals with substance dependency often deny that they need treatment (Metsch *et al.* 2001), or may have an altered perception of their use, leading to avoidance of treatment (Grossman 1993). The demographic of children and adolescents of addicted parents, however, face among the toughest barriers of all, likely due to the parental illness itself impeding the child's access to treatment.

There are various organizations and services that may be called upon to aid in abating substance use among parents and children alike. A model for care in the UK is set forth by Keen and Alison (2001). In their review, targeted at health professionals, they speak of the importance of area child protection committees (ACPCs) to be called upon to play an integral role in ensuring that children of substance-dependent parents are properly assessed. They postulate that committees such as ACPCs should link with adult mental health services to co-ordinate proper action and care for the affected children. The authors also mention the importance of regional drug action teams (DATs) which is a conglomerate of officials from various departments and services including health, social, police, probation, and education. The pairing-up of ACPCs and DATs would be a proactive solution for strategic care of parental substance abuse and its impact on children.

While such a model seems a panacea in theory, the system does not always work so cohesively, both in the USA and Europe. In the USA, for example, treatment for substance abuse varies greatly between states, and many states restrict their services to acute care of substance use problems. At the most basic level, access to treatment for substance abuse is much the same as access to medical or psychiatric care in general. In the end, access to proper care is contingent upon financial and health care insurance barriers. This illustrates a grave deficit in our system, as evidence has shown that substance use requires a comprehensive continuum of care. For adolescents covered by private insurance, a lack of comprehensive substance abuse coverage is a major barrier to accessing treatment (Bennett, Bendersky and Lewis 2002).

Moreover, young populations face significant obstacles in accessing mental health services in addition to substance abuse treatment. Owens *et al.* (2002) posit that parents' perceptions of children's mental illness, as well as their own subsequent parenting difficulties, may serve as an obstruction to mental health services for the children. Equally, parents' own mental health and substance use disorders can impede a child's access to treatment (Cornelius *et al.* 2001). A further obstacle is adopting adult treatment methods that do not consider the adolescent's specific needs (e.g. difficulty comprehending the concept of powerlessness [Riggs and Whitmore 1999]).

Despite these seemingly glaring obstacles, drug use prevention programmes for children and adolescents *are* a feasible reality – we simply need to continue to test them via empirical research. NIDA puts forth a set of principles for preventing drug use among children and adolescents (see Table 15.2). The report is intended to assist parents, educators, and community leaders in delivering research-based prevention programmes at local or community level (NIDA 2005).

The literature illustrates that while there are clear risk factors among children of substance-dependent parents, these risk factors are identifiable and treatable, given the proper resources. Proper resources are born from sound clinical and scientific research, a goal towards which the medical and psychological communities are making strides. Now that the scientific community has identified the multitude of familial environmental risk factors, prominent co-morbid psychiatric disorders, and several barriers to age – and gender – appropriate treatment, successful treatment of these children and adolescents is within reach.

The next step – application of empirical research to practice – is a large and often arduous one, as programme reform (including staff training and treatment model re-organization) is no small endeavour. Alongside widespread education of government agencies, schools, medical establishments, communities, and substance-dependent parents about the vulnerabilities of at-risk children, as well as the effective methods to treat them, will come improved prevention and treatment. Ideally, making this knowledge universal will lift existing barriers such as financial inaccessibility to appropriate and necessary treatment, and promote willingness of substance-using parents to address this issue in terms of the serious implications for their children.

Conclusions

Substance abuse proves to be a widespread and serious problem, and not only for the users themselves. Children of substance-dependent parents are at high risk of developing conduct, oppositional defiant, attention deficit/hyperactivity, anti-social personality disorder, and becoming addicted to a host of substances themselves. Direct insults to children, such as parental neglect while using

Table 15.2 Objectives of preventive programmes

Principle 1 Prevention programmes should enhance protective factors and reverse or reduce risk factors

Principle 2 Prevention programmes should address all forms of drug abuse, alone or in combination, including the under-age use of legal drugs (e.g. tobacco or alcohol); the use of illegal drugs (e.g. marijuana or heroin); and the inappropriate use of legally obtained substances (e.g. inhalants), prescription medications, or over-the-counter drugs

Principle 3 Prevention programmes should address the type of drug abuse problem in the local community, target modifiable risk factors, and strengthen identified protective factors

Principle 4 Prevention programmes should be tailored to address risks specific to population or audience characteristics, such as age, gender, and ethnicity, to improve programme effectiveness

Principle 5 Family-based prevention programmes should enhance family bonding and relationships, and include parenting skills; practice in developing, discussing, and enforcing family policies on substance abuse; and training in drug education and information

Principle 6 Prevention programmes can be designed to intervene as early as pre-school to address risk factors for drug abuse, such as aggressive behaviour, poor social skills, and academic difficulties

Principle 7 Prevention programmes for elementary school children should target improving academic and social-emotional learning to address risk factors for drug abuse, such as early aggression, academic failure, and school drop-out; education should focus on self-control, emotional awareness, communication, social problem-solving, and academic support, especially in reading

Principle 8 Prevention programmes for middle or junior-high and high-school students should increase academic and social competence with the following skills: study habits and academic support; communication; peer relationships; self-efficacy and assertiveness; drug resistance skills; reinforcement of anti-drug attitudes; and strengthening of personal commitments against drug abuse

Principle 9   Prevention programmes aimed at general populations at key transition points, such as the transition to middle school, can produce beneficial effects even among high-risk families and children; such interventions do not single out risk populations and, therefore, reduce labelling and promote bonding to school and community

Principle 10   Community prevention programmes that combine two or more effective programmes, such as family-based and school-based programmes, can be more effective than a single programme alone

Principle 11   Community prevention programmes reaching populations in multiple settings, for example schools, clubs, faith-based organizations, and the media, are most effective when they present consistent, community-wide messages in each setting

Principle 12   When communities adapt programmes to match their needs, community norms, or differing cultural requirements, they should retain core elements of the original research-based intervention which include: structure (how the programme is organized and constructed); content (the information, skills, and strategies of the programme) and delivery (how the programme is adapted, implemented, and evaluated)

Principle 13   Prevention programmes should be long term with repeated interventions (i.e. booster programmes) to reinforce the original prevention goals; research shows that the benefits from middle-school prevention programmes diminish without follow-up programmes in high school

Principle 14   Prevention programmes should include teacher-training on good classroom management practices, such as rewarding appropriate student behaviour. Such techniques help to foster students' positive behaviour, achievement, academic motivation, and school bonding

Principle 15   Prevention programmes are most effective when they employ interactive techniques, such as peer discussion groups and parent role-playing, which allow for active involvement in learning about drug abuse and reinforcing skills

Principle 16   Research-based prevention programmes can be cost-effective; Similar to earlier research, recent research shows that for each dollar invested in prevention, a saving of up to $10 in treatment for alcohol or other substance abuse may be seen

substances themselves and reluctance to seek treatment for their children, perpetuates the cycle of inadequate care for children and adolescents with substance use disorders. Millions of these vulnerable children worldwide are at this increased risk of developing these disorders, although according to current research, it is a problem with potentially modifiable risk if appropriate preventative measures are implemented. It is vital that parents and educators understand the severity and prevalence of problems associated with children of substance-dependent parents, and that they further understand the heightened risk among children with co-morbid psychiatric disorders. While longitudinal studies are needed to provide more comprehensive statistical research findings on these children of addicted parents, the current literature clearly illustrates a desperate call to action to mitigate this transmission of risk to children.

Acknowledgement

Dr Wilson's work is supported by a grant from the National Institute of Health (DA14572).

References

Bandura, A. (1977) *Social Learning Theory.* Englewood Cliffs, NJ: Prentice-Hall.

Barkley, R.A., Fischer, M., Smallish, L., and Fletcher, K. (2004) 'Young adult follow-up of hyperactive children: antisocial activities and drug use.' *Journal of Child Psychology and Psychiatry 45,* 195–211

Barnard, M., and McKeganey, N. (2004) 'The impact of parental problem drug use on children: what is the problem and what can be done to help?' *Addiction 99,* 552–9.

Bays, J. (1990) 'Substance abuse and child abuse: impact of addiction the child.' *Pediatric Clinics of North America 37,* 881–904.

Bennett, D.S., Bendersky, M., and Lewis, M. (2002) 'Children's intellectual and emotional-behavioural adjustment at 4 years as a function of cocaine exposure, maternal characteristics, and environmental risk.' *Developmental Psychology 38,* 648–58.

Bernstein, V., and Hans, S.L. (1994) 'Predicting the developmental outcome of two-year-old children born exposed to methadone: Impact of social environmental risk factors.' *Journal of Clinical Child Psychology 23,* 349–359.

Bernstein, V., Jeremy, R., Hans, S., and Marcus, J. (1984) 'A longitudinal study of offspring born to methadone-maintained women. II. Byadic interaction and infant behaviour at 4 months.' *American Journal of Drug and Alcohol Aubse 10,* 161–193.

Biederman, J., Faraone, S.V., Monuteaux, M.C., and Feighner, J.A. (2000) 'Patterns of alcohol and drug use in adolescents can be predicted by parental substance use disorders.' *Pediatrics 106,* 792–797.

Brannigan, R., Schackman, B., Falco, M., and Millman, R. (2004) 'The quality of highly regarded adolescent substance abuse treatment programs: Results of an in-depth national survey.' *Archives of Pediatric Adolescent Medicine 158,* 904–909.

Broekhuizen, F., Utrie, J., and Van Mullem, V. (1992) 'Drug use or inadequate pre-natal care? Adverse pregnancy outcome in an urban setting.' *American Journal of Obstetrics and Gynaecology 166,* 1747–1756.

Brook, J., Brook, D., De La Rosa, M., Duque, L., Rodriguez, E., Montoya, I., and Whiteman, M. (1998) 'Pathways to marijuana use among adolescents: cultural/ecological, family, peer, and personality influences.' *Journal American Academy of Child and Adolescent Psychiatry 37*, 759–766.

Brook, J.S., Whiteman, M., Nomura, C., Gordon, A.S., and Cohen, P. (1988) 'Personality, family and ecological influences on adolescent drug use: A developmental analysis.' *Journal of Chemical Dependence Treatment 1*, 123–161.

Center for Alcoholism and Substance Abuse (CASA) (1996) *Substance Abuse and Urban America: Its Impact on an American City: New York.* New York, NY: The National Center for Alcoholism and Substance Abuse at Columbia University.

Center for Alcoholism and Substance Abuse (CASA) (1999) *No Safe Haven: Children of Substance-Abusing Parents.* New York, NY: Columbia University.

Catalano, R., Gainey, R., Fleming, C., Haggerty, K., and Johnson, N. (1999) 'An experimental intervention with families of substance abusers: one-year follow-up of the focus on families project.' *Addiction 92*, 241–254.

Cermak, T.L., and Beckman, W. (1995) 'Offspring of Alcoholics and other Addicts.' In R.H. Combs and D. Ziedonis (eds) *Handbook of Drug Abuse Prevention.* Needleham, MA: Allyn & Bacon.

Chasnoff, I., and Lowder, L. (1999) 'Parental Alcohol and Drug Use and Risk for Child Maltreatment: A Timely Approach to Intervention.' In H. Dubowitz (ed.) *Neglected Children, Research, Practice and Policy.* Thousand Oaks, CA: Sage.

Chilcoat, H., and Anthony, J. (1996) 'Impact of parent monitoring on initiation of drug use through late childhood.' *Journal of the American Academy of Child and Adolescent Psychiatry 35*, 91–100.

Chouteau, M., Namerow, P., and Leppert, P. (1988) 'The effect of cocaine abuse on birth weight and gestational age.' *Obstetrics and Gynecology 72*, 351–354.

Cicchetti, D., and Toth, S. (1995) 'A developmental psychopathology perspective on child abuse and neglect.' *Journal of Child and Adolescent Psychiatry 34*, 541–565.

Clark, D., Cornelius, J., Wood, D., and Vanyukov, M. (2004) 'Psychopathology risk transmission in children of parents with substance use disorders.' *American Journal of Psychiatry 161*, 685–691.

Clark, D., Kirisci, L., and Moss, H. (1998) 'Early adolescent gateway drug use in sons of fathers with substance use disorders.' *Addictive Behaviours 23*, 561–566.

Cloninger, C., Bohman, M., and Sigvardsson, S. (1981) 'Inheritance of alcohol abuse: cross-fostering anaysis of adopted men.' *Archives of General Psychiatry 38*, 851–868.

Connor, D.F., Barkley, R.A., and Davis, H.T. (2000) 'A pilot study of methylphenidate, clonidine, or the combination in ADHD co-morbid with aggressive oppositional defiant or conduct disorder.' *Clinical Pediatrics 39*, 15–25.

Cornelius, J., Pringle, J., Jernigan, J., Kirisci, L., and Clark, D. (2001) 'Correlates of mental health service utilization and unmet need among a sample of male adolescents.' *Addictive Behaviours 26*, 11–19.

Crouch, L., and Milner, J. (1993) 'Effects of child neglect on children.' *Criminal Justice and Behavior 20*, 49–65.

Dabis, F., Msellati, P., and Meda, N. (1999) '6-Month efficacy, tolerance, and acceptability fo a short regimen of oral zidovudine to reduce vertical transmission of HIV in breastfed children in Cote d' Ivoire and Burkina Faso: A double-blind placebo-controlled multicentre trial.' *Lancet 353*, 786–792.

Das Eiden, R., and Leonard, K. (2000) 'Paternal alcoholism, parental psychopathology, and aggravation with infants.' *Journal of Substance Abuse 11*, 17–29.

Dennis, T.A., and Brotman, L.M. (2003) 'Effortful control, attention, and aggressive behaviour in preschoolers at risk for conduct problems.' *Annals of the New York Academy of Sciences 1008*, 252–255.

Department of Health (DoH) (2003) *Statistics on Young People and Drug Misuse, England 2002.* London: Department of Health.

Department of Health and Human Services (DHHS) (2006) 'HIV During Pregnancy, Labour and Delivery, and After Birth.' In *AIDS Info,* AIDS info Fact Sheet. Department of Health and Human Services. Available at: http://aidsinfo.nih.gov/ContentFiles/ Perinatal_FS_en.pdf, accessed on 02 November 2007.

Dishion, T., and Andrews, D. (1995) 'Preventing escalation in problem behaviours with high-risk young adolescents: Immediate and 1-year outcomes.' *Journal of Consulting and Clinical Psychology 63,* 538–548.

Dishion, T., Kavanagh, K., and Kiesner, J. (1998) 'Prevention of early adolescent substance abuse among high-risk youth: A multiple gating approach to parent intervention.' *National Institute of Drug Abuse: Research Monograph Series 177,* 208–228.

Dube, S.R., Felitti, V.J., Dong, M., Chapman, D.P., Giles, W.H., Anda, R.F. (2003) 'Childhood Abuse, Neglect, and Household Dysfunction and the Risk of Illicit Drug Use: The Adverse Childhood Experiences Study.' *Pediatrics III,* 564–572.

Duncan, T.E., Duncan, S.C., Hops, H., and Stoolmiller, M. (1995) 'An analysis of the relationship between parent and adolescent marijuana use via generalized estimating equation methodology.' *Multivariate Behaviour Research 30,* 317–339.

Dunn, M.G., Tarter, R.E., Mezzich, A.C., Vanyukov, M., Kirisci, L., Kirillova, G. (2002) 'Origins and consequences of child neglect in substance abuse families.' *Clinical Psychology Review 22,* 1063–1090.

Famularo, R., Kinshneff, R., and Fenton, T. (1992) 'Parental substance abuse and the nature of child maltreatment.' *Child Abuse and Neglect 16,* 475–483.

Gaudin, J. (1999) 'Child Neglect: Short-term and Long-term Outcomes.' In Dubowitz, H. (ed.) *Neglected Children: Research, Practice, and Policy.* Thousand Oaks. Sage.

Gorman-Smith, D., Tolan, P., Zell, I.A., Huesmann, L. (1996) 'The relation of family functioning to violence among inner city minority youths.' *Journal of Family Psychology 10,* 115–129.

Grella, C.E., Joshi, V., and Hser, Y.I. (2003) 'Followup of cocaine-dependent men and women with antisocial personality disorder.' *Journal of Substance Abuse Treatment 25,* 155–164.

Grossman, M. (1993) 'The Economic Analysis of Addictive Behaviour.' In M. Hilton, G. Bloss (eds) *Economics and the Prevention of Alcohol-related Problems.* Bethesda, MD: National Institute on Alcohol Abuse and Alcoholism.

Hans, S., Bernstein, V., and Henson, L. (1999) 'The role of psychopathology in the parenting of drug-dependent women.' *Development and Psychopathology 11,* 957–977.

Hawkins, J., Catalano, R., and Miller, J. (1992) 'Risk and protective factors for alcohol and other drug problems in adolescence and early adutlhood: implications for substance abuse prevention.' *Psychological Bulletin 12,* 64–105.

Heffernan, K., Cloitre, M., Tardiff, K., Marzuk, P., Portera, L., Leon, A. (2000) 'Childhood trauma as a correlate of lifetime opiate use in psychiatric patients.' *Addictive Behaviours 25,* 797–803.

Helzer, J.E. and Pryzbeck, T.R. (1998) 'The co-occurrence of alcholism with other psychiatric disorders in the general population and its impact on treatment.' *J Stud Alcohol 49,* 219–1224.

Hembree-Kigin, T., and McNeil, C. (1995) *Parent–child Interaction Therapy.* New York, NY: Plenum Press.

Hinz, L. (1990) 'College student adult children of alcoholics: psychological resilience or emotional distance?' *Journal of Substance Abuse 2,* 449–457.

Hoffmann, J., and Su, S. (1998) 'Parental substance use disorder, mediating variables and adolescent drug use: a non-recursive model.' *Addiction 93,* 1351–1364.

Hogan, D. (1998) 'Annotation: The psychological development and welfare of children of opiate and cocaine users: Review and research needs.' *Journal of Child Psychology and Psychiatry 39,* 609–620.

Hussong, A., Curran, P., and Chassin, L. (1998) 'Pathways of risk for accelerated heavy alcohol use among adoelscent children of alcoholic parents.' *Journal of Abnormal Child Psychology 26,* 453–466.

Johnson, J., Boney, T., and Brown, B. (1991) 'Evidence of depressive syptoms in children of substance abusers.' *The International Journal of the Addicitons 25*, 465–479.

Kaminer, Y. (2001) 'Adolescent substance abuse treatment: Where do we go from here?' *Psychiatric Services 52*, 147–149.

Kaplow, J., Curran, P., and Dodge, K. (2002) 'Child, parent and peer predictors of early-onset substance use: A multisite longitudinal study.' *Journal of Abnormal Child Psychology 30*, 199.

Keen, J., and Alison, L.H. (2001) 'Drug misusing parents: Key points for health professionals.' *Archives of Disease in Childhood 85*, 296–299.

Keller, T., Catalano, R., Haggerty, K., and Fleming, C. (2002) 'Parent figure transitions and delinquency and drug use among early adolescent children of substance abusers.' *American Journal of Drug and Alcohol Abuse 28*, 399–427.

Killeen, T., and Brady, K. (2000) 'Parental stress and child behavioural outcomes following substance abuse residential treatment: Follow-up at 6 and 12 months.' *Journal of Substance Abuse Treatment 19*, 23–29.

Kilpatrick, D.G., Acierno, R., Saunders, B., Resnick, H.S., Best, C.L., and Schnurr, P.P. (2000) 'Risk factors for adolescent substance abuse and dependence: data from a national sample.' *Journal of Consulting and Clinical Psychology 68*, 19–30.

Kim, J.E., Hetherington, E.M., and Reiss, D. (1999) 'Associations among family relationships, antisocial peers, and adolescents' externalizing behaviours, gender and family type differences.' *Child Development 70*, 1209–1230.

King, V., Kiforf, M., Stoller, K., Carter, J., and Brooner, R. (2001) 'Influence of antisocial personality subtypes on drug abuse treatment response.' *Journal of Nervous and Mental Disorders 189*, 593–601.

Kirisci, L., Dunn, M., Mezzich, A., and Tarter, R. (2001) 'Impact of parental substance use disorder and child neglect severity on substance use involvement in male offspring.' *Prevention Science 2*, 241–255.

Latimer, W.W., Winters, K.C., D'Zurilla, T., and Nichols, M. (2003) 'Integrated family and cognitive-behavioural therapy for adolescent substance abusers: A stage I efficacy study.' *Drug and Alcohol Dependence 71*, 303–317.

Luthar, S.S., Cushing, G., Merikangas, K.R., and Rounsaville, B.J. (1998) 'Multiple jeopardy: Risk and protective factors among addicted mothers' offspring.' *Development and Psychopathology 10*, 117–136.

Mack, A.H., Franklin, J.E., and Frances, R.H. (2003) 'Substance Use Disorders.' In R.E. Hales and S.C. Yudofsky (eds) *The American Psychiatric Publishing Textbook of Clinical Osychiatry – Fourth edition.* Arlington, VA: American Psychiatric Publishing Inc.

Marlatt, G., and Fordon, J. (1980) 'Determinants of Relapse: Implications for the Maintenance of Behaviour Change.' In P. Davidson and D. Sm (eds) *Behavioural Medicine: Changing Health Lifestyles.* New York, NY: Brunner–Mazel.

Mayes, L.C., and Bornstein, M.H. (1997) 'The Development of Children Exposed to Cocaine.' In S.S. Luthar, J.A. Burack, D. Cicchetti, J.R. Weisz (eds) *Developmental psychopathology: Perspectives on adjustment, risk and disorder.* New York, NY: Cambridge University Press.

Merikangas, K.R., Stolar, M., Stevens, D.E., Goulet, J., Preisig, M.A., Fenton, B., Zhang, H., O'Malley, S.S., and Rounsaville, B.J. (1998) 'Familial transmission of substance use disorders.' *Archives of General Psychiatry 55*, 973–979.

Metsch, L.R., Wolfe, H.P., Fewell, R., McCoy, C.B., Elwood, W.N., Wohler-Torres, B., Petersen-Baston, P., and Haskins, H.V. (2001) 'Treating substance-using women and their children in public housing: Preliminary evaluation findings.' *Child Welfare 80*, 199–220.

Minuchin, S. (1974) *Families and Family Therapy.* Cambridge, MA: Harvard University Press.

Molina, B.S., Chassin, L., and Curran, P.J. (1994) 'A comparison of mechanisms underlying substance use for early adolescent children of alcoholics and controls.' *Journal of Stud Alcohol 55*, 269–275.

Moss, H., Baron, D., Hardie, T., and Vanyukov, M. (2001) 'Preadolescent children of substance-dependent fathers with antisocial personality disorder: psychiatric disorders and problem behaviours.' *American Journal on Addictions 10*, 269–278.

Moss, H., Clark, D., and Kirisci, L. (1997) 'Timing of paternal substance use disorder cessation and effects on problem behaviours in sons.' *American Journal on Addictions 6*, 30–37.

Moss, H., Lynch, K., Hardie, T., and Baron, D. (2002) 'Family functioning and peer affiliation in children of fathers with antisocial personality disorder and substance dependence: Associations with problem behaviours.' *American Journal of Psychiatry 159*, 607–614.

Mrus, J., and Tsevat, J. (2004) 'Cost-effectiveness of interventions to reduce vertical HIV transmission from pregnant women who have not received pre-natal care.' *Medical Decision Making 24*, 30–39.

Muck, R., Zempolich, J., Fishman, M., Godley, M., and Schwebel, R. (2001) 'An Overview of the Effectiveness of Adolescent Substance Abuse Treatment Models.' *Youth Society 33*, 143–168.

National Insititute on Drug Abuse (NIDA) (2003) *Preventing Drug Use Among Adolescents.* Bethesda, MD: National Institute of Health.

National Institute on Drug Abuse (NIDA) (2005) *Preventing Drug Abuse among Children and Adolescents. A Research Based Guide for Parents, Educators, and Community Leaders* (2nd ed). Bethesda, MD: National Institute of Health.

National Research Council (NRC) (1993) *Understanding Child Abuse and Neglect.* Washington, DC: National Academy Press.

New York State Department of Health (2007) Peri-natal HIV Prevention Programme (PHPP). New York, NY: New York State Department of Health.

Nunes, E., Weissman, M., Goldstein, R., McAvay, G., Seracini, A., Verdeli, H., and Wickramaratne, P.J. (1998) 'Psychopathology in children of parents with opiate dependence and/or major depression.' *Journal of the American Academy of Child and Adolescent Psychiatry 37*, 1142–1151.

Obot, I., and Anthony, J. (2004) 'Mental health problems in adolescent children of alcohol dependent parents: Epidemiologic research with a nationally representative sample.' *Journal of Child and Adolescent Substance Abuse 13*, 83–96.

Obot, I., Wagner, F., and Anthony, J. (2001) 'Early-onset and recent drug use among children of parents with alcohol problems: Data from a national epidemiologic survey.' *Drug and Alcohol Dependence 65*, 1–8.

Owens, P., Hoagwood, K., Horwitz, S., Leaf, P., Poduska, J., Kellam, S., and Ialongo, N. (2002) 'Barriers to children's mental health services.' *Journal of the American Academy of Child and Adolescent Psychiatry 41*, 731–738.

Patterson, G. (1982) *Coercive Family Process.* Eugene, OR: Castalia.

Pelham, W. Jr., Lang, A., Atkeson, B., Murphy, D., Gnagy, E., Greiner, A.R., Vodde-Hamilton, M., and Greenslade, K.E. (1998) 'Effects of deviant child behaviour on parental alcohol consumption. Stress–induced drinking in parents of ADHD children.' *American Journal on Addictions 7*, 103–114.

Potter, S., Zelazo, P., Stack, D., and Papageorgiou, A. (2000) 'Adverse effects of fetal cocaine exposure on neonatal auditory information processing.' *Pediatrics 105*, 40–52.

Regan, D., Ehrlich, S., and Finnegan, L. (1987) 'Infants of drug addicts: At risk for child abuse, neglect, and placement in foster care.' *Neurotoxocology and Teratology 9*, 315–319.

Riggs, P.D., and Whitmore, E.A. (1999) 'Substance use disorder and disruptive behavior disorders.' In R.L. Hendren (ed.) *Disruptive behavior disorders in children and adolescents.* Washington, DC: American Psychiatric Association. Vol. 18, No.2.

Rosner, M., Keith, L., and Chasnoff, I. (1982) 'Western University dependence program: The impact of intensive pre-natal care on labour and delivery outcomes.' *American Journal of Obststetrics and Gynecology 144*, 23–27.

Rutter, M., Giller, H., and Hagel, A. (1998) *Antisocial Behaviour by Young People.* New York, NY: Cambridge University Press.

Substance Abuse and Mental Health Services Administration (SAMHSA) (2007) *2005 National Survey on Drug Use and Health: National Results*. Rockville, MD: Substance Abuse and Mental Health Services Administration.

Schaefer, M., Sobieragi, K., and Hollyfield, R. (1988) 'Prevalence of child physical abuse in adult male veteran alcoholics.' *Child Abuse and Neglect 12*, 141–150.

Schwartz, C., Dorer, D., Beardslee, W., Lavori, P., and Keller, M. (1990) 'Maternal expressed emotion and parental affective disorder: risk for childhood depressive disorder, substance abuse, or conduct disorder.' *Journal of Psychiatric Research 24*, 231–250.

Shaffer, N., Chuachoowong, R., and Mock, P. (1999) 'Short-course zidovudine for peri-natal HIV-1 transmission in Bankok, Thailand: A randomised controlled trial.' *Lancet 353*, 773–780.

Shedler, J., and Block, J. (1990) 'Adolescent drug use and psychological health. A longitudinal inquiry.' *American Psychologist 45*, 612–630.

Sher, K., Walitzer, K., Wood, P., and Brent, E. (1991) 'Characteristics of children of alcoholics: Putative risk factors, substance use and abuse, and psychopathology.' *Journal of Abnormal Psychology 100*, 427–448.

Siegel, D. (1999) *The Developing Mind*. New York, NY: Guilford Press.

Sigvardsson, S., Bohmann, M., and Cloninger, R. (1996) 'Replication of the Stockholm adoption study of alcoholism: Confirmatory cross-fostering analysis.' *Archives of General Psychiatry 53*, 681–687.

Singer, L., Arendt, R., Minnes, S., Salvator, A., Siegel, A., and Lewis, B. (2001) 'Developing language skills of cocaine-exposed infants.' *Pediatrics 107*, 1057–1064.

Sparey, C., and Walkinshaw, S. (1995) 'Obstetric Problems for Drug Users.' In C. Siney (ed.) *The Pregnant Drug Addict*. Hale: Books for Midwives Press.

Stanger, C., Higgins, S., Bickel, W., Elk, R., Grabowski, J., Schmitz, J., Amass, L., Kirby, K.C., and Seracini, A.M. (1999) 'Behavioural and emotional problems among children of cocaine- and opiate-dependent parents.' *Journal of the American Academy of Child and Adolescent Psychiatry 38*, 421–428.

Stanger, C., Kamon, J., Dumenci, L., Higgins, S.T., Bickel, W.K., Grabowski, J., and Amass, L. (2002) 'Predictors of internalizing and externalizing problems among children of cocaine and opiate-dependent parents.' *Drug and Alcohol Dependence 66*, 199–212.

Suchman, N., and Luthar, S. (2000) 'Maternal addiction, child maladjustment and socio-demographic risks: Implications for parenting behaviours.' *Addiction 95*, 1417–1428.

Survey (2000) 'Survey finds many addicts used drugs with their parents.' *Alcoholism and Drug Abuse Weekly 12*, 2.

Szapocznik, J., and Williams, R. (2000) 'Brief Strategic Family Therapy: Twenty-five years of interplay among theory, research and practice in adolescent behaviour problems and drug abuse.' *Clinical Child and Family Psychology Review 3*, 117–134.

Tarter, R., Vanyukov, M., Giancola, P., Dawes, M., Blackson, T., Mezzich, A., and Clark, D.B. (1999) 'Etiology of early age onset substance use disorder: A maturational perspective.' *Development and Psychopathology 11*, 657–683.

Toray, T., Coughlin, C., Vuchinich, S., and Patricelli, P. (1991) 'Gender differences associated with substance abuse: Comparisons and implications for treament.' *Family Relations 40*, 338–340.

Tremblay, R., Pihl, R., Vitaro, F., and Dobkin, P. (1994) 'Predicting early-onset of male antisocial behaviour from preschool behaviour.' *Archives of General Psychiatry 51*, 732–739.

Triket, P., and Weinstein, R. (1991) 'Physical Abuse of Adolescents.' In R. Lerner, A. Paterson and J. Brooks-Funn (eds) *Encyclopedia of Adolescence*, Vol II. New York, NY: Garland.

Tuomala, R., Shapiro, D., Mofenson, L., Bryson, Y., Culnane, M., Hughes, M., O'Sullivan, M., Scott, G., Stek, A., Wara, D., and Bulterys, M. (2002) 'Antiretroviral therapy during pregnancy and the risk of an adverse outcome' *New England Journal of Medicine 346*, 1863–1870.

Van Baar, A., Soepatmi, S., and Gunning, W. (1994) 'Development after pre-natal exposure to cocaine, heroin, and methadone.' *Acta Paediatrica 83*, 40–46.

Vorhees, C., and Mollnow, E. (1987) 'Behaviour Teratogenesis: Long-term Influneces on Behaviour.' In J. Osofsky (ed.) *Handbook of Infant Development* (2nd vol). New York, NY: Wiley.

Wasserman, G.A., Kline, J.K., Bateman, D.A., Chiriboga, C., Lumey, L.H., Friedlander, H., Melton, L., and Heagarty, M.C. (1998) 'Pre-natal cocaine exposure and school-age intelligence.' *Drug and Alcohol Dependency 50*, 203–10.

Weiss, M., Hechtman, L.T., Weiss, G. (1999) *ADHD in Adulthood*. Baltimore, MD: Johns Hopkins University Press.

Weissman, M., Warner, V., Wickramaratne, P., and Kandel, D. (1999) 'Maternal smoking during pregnancy and psychopathology in offspring followed to adulthood.' *Journal of the American Academy of Child and Adolescent Psychiatry 38*, 892–899.

West, M., and Prinz, R. (1987) 'Parental alcoholism and childhood psychopathology.' *Psychological Bulletin 102*, 204–218.

Westermeyer, J., and Thuras, P. (2005) 'Association of antisocial personality disorder and substance disorder morbidity in a clinical sample.' *American Journal of Drug and Alcohol Abuse 31*, 93–110.

Wiers, R., Sergeant, J., and Gunning, W. (1994) 'Psychological mechanisms of enhanced risk of addiction in children of alcoholics: A dual pathway? *Acta Paediatrica Supplement 404*, 9–13.

Wiktor, S., Ekpini, E., and Karon, J. (1999) 'Short-course oral zidovudine for prevention of mother-to-child transmission of HIV-1 in Abidjan, Cote d'Ivoire: A randomised trial.' *Lancet 353*, 781–785.

Wilens, T.E., Faraone, S.V., Biederman, J., and Gunawardene, S. (2003) 'Does stimulant therapy of attention-deficit/hyperactivity disorder beget later substance abuse? A meta-analytic review of the literature.' *Pediatrics 111*, 179–185.

Wilson, J. (2007) 'ADHD and substance use disorders: Developmental aspects and the impact of stimulant treatment.' *American Journal on Addictions 16*, 5–13.

Wilson, J.J., Bhoopsingh, T., and Nunes, E.V. (2003) 'Emotional availability, parental addiction severity, and child behaviour problems.' Poster presented at *Scientific Proceedings of the College of Problems of Drug Dependence.*

Wilson, J.J., and Levin, F.R. (2001) 'Attention deficit hyperactivity disorder (ADHD) and substance use disorders.' *Current Psychiatry Reports 3*, 497–506.

Wilson, J., and Levin, F. (2005) 'Attention-deficit/hyperactivity disorder and early-onset substance use disorders.' *Journal of Child and Adolescent Psychopharmacology 15*, 751–763.

Wilson, J., Nunes, E., Greenwald, S., and Weissman, M. (2004) 'Verbal deficits and disruptive behaviour disorders among children of opiate-dependent parents.' *American Journal on Addictions 13*, 202–212.

Wilson, J., Nunes, E.V., Weissman, M.M. (2002) 'Parent addiction severity and child externalizing behavior.' Scientific proceedings of the American Academy of Child and Adolescent Psychiatry. New Research Presentation (October). San Francisco, CA.

Wilson, J., Pine, D., Cargan, A., Goldstein, R., Nunes, E., Weissman, M.M. (2003) 'Neurological soft signs and disruptive behaviour among children of opiate-dependent parents.' *Child Psychiatry and Human Development 34*, 19–34.

Winters, K.C. (1999) 'Treating adolescents with substance use disorders: An overview of practice issues and treatment outcome.' *Substance Abuse 20*, 203–225.

Woodward, A. (2004) 'Access to Substance Abuse Treament and Mental Health Services: A Literature Review.' In C. Council (ed) *Health Services Utilization by Individuals with Substance Abuse and Mental Disorders*. Rockville, MD: Substance Abuse and Mental Health Services Administration.

Part III

Applying the Evidence
and Therapeutic Principles
to Different Welfare and Health Systems,
Cultural Contexts
and Social Circumstances

CHAPTER 16

Cultural Diversity Issues in Working with Vulnerable Children

Nisha Dogra

This chapter begins with a consideration of what we mean by the term 'culture', followed by a discussion of the issues we need to consider when working with culturally diverse children and young people. The focus will then be on some issues that warrant further consideration when working with vulnerable children.

The meaning of culture

It is not proposed to engage here in the debate about the different meanings, but rather explain the use and context of related terms. Culture is not a value-free concept, and there are many definitions of this (Edles 2002). The concept of culture, cultural identity, or belonging to a cultural group involves a degree of active engagement by individuals in a dynamic process. Therefore, it is problematic to assign cultural categories externally and based only on certain characteristics such as ethnicity. A suitable definition is that from the Association of American Medical Colleges (AAMC 1999):

> Culture is defined by each person in relationship to the group or groups with whom he or she identifies. An individual's cultural identity may be based on heritage as well as individual circumstances and personal choice. Cultural identity may be affected by such factors as race, ethnicity, age, language, country of origin, acculturation, sexual orientation, gender, socioeconomic status, religious/spiritual beliefs, physical abilities, occupation, among others. These factors may impact on behaviours such as communication styles, diet preferences, health beliefs, family roles, lifestyle, rituals and decision-making processes. All of these beliefs and practices, in turn can influence how patients and heath care professionals perceive health and illness, and how they interact with one another. (AAMC 1999, p.25)

Justification for using this definition is that it is client-centred and may be applied to clinical situations. It suggests that individuals draw upon a range of resources, and that, through the interplay of external and internal meanings, they construct a sense of identity and unique culture. It is also useful because it recognizes that both patients and professionals bring a complex individual self to the consultation.

This definition is preferred over the more sociological ones for reasons that become apparent when those constructs are explored. Edles (2002) states that, despite the plethora of meanings of the term 'culture', the definitions may be divided into three groups. Culture can be used to refer to:

- humanistic refinement and elite artistic activities (classical ballet, opera) (aesthetic)
- an entire way of life of a people or group (ethnographic)
- systems or patterns of shared symbols (symbolic).

Edles (2002) proceeds to state her preference for symbolic notions of culture; that is, culture as systems of shared meanings, which underscores that culture is collective and shared. The *symbolic* definition of culture emphasises that cultural systems are historically linked to specific social groups at specific moments, and intertwined in complex ways with other societal dimensions. Edles (2002) also highlights that this definition is most useful in conjunction with the more general notion that societies are composed of three inter-related components: economic, political, and cultural realms. However, these definitions fail to take into account that people identify themselves in ways that, to them, are so much less abstract than the notion of culture.

What is culturally appropriate care?

In the UK, it has become commonplace to state that professionals need to be culturally competent or culturally capable (DoH 2004). Rarely is it transparent exactly what is being referred to. 'Cultural competence' was a term devised by Cross *et al.* (1989) in the USA. It was at the time a very useful concept because it highlighted that cultural issues are important to the way health, illness, and care are understood. However, it is now used in different ways (Henry J Kaiser Family Foundation 2003; Kleinman and Benson 2006). The problem with the original definition in today's context is that it used a rather simplistic view of culture, and talks about groups of people in non-dominant contexts as though shared ethnicity leads to homogeneity. There is an additional problem that this kind of use also implies that miscommunication only occurs between the majority and minority cultures, as though all minorities or all majority individuals, or both, intrinsically understand each other. Within the concept there is also the implication that cultural competence is a one-off, in the sense that cultural competence may be achieved through a training course. There are those, however, who would argue that to deliver culturally appropriate care requires ongoing development (Dogra 2003; Tervalon and Murray-Garcia 1998).

Delivering care that is culturally appropriate for diverse groups (whether that diversity be related to ethnicity or vulnerability or both) is fundamentally altered, depending on how we view our clients. If we are to deliver care that is relevant to our clients we need to understand the world from their perspective whilst being fully aware of our own perspective. That means we need to be constantly reflecting on how we see the world and how we are influenced by our own experiences (Dogra 2003). It is important to see clients as complex individuals rather than as stereotypes based on their ethnicity or any other single characteristic.

Culturally appropriate care is the care that is right for any particular person at that particular point in time, which takes into account the client and professional perspectives. It is also care or management that the client understands and is comfortable with. If the client does not immediately agree with the healthcare provider, the provider should endeavour to explore the issues. Clients may disagree with a potential approach based on misinformation or fear. It does not necessarily mean that all clients receive the same care, but it should mean that they receive the same options, and the professional does not pre-select options based on assumptions on what the client might want. However, it is important to point out that providing culturally appropriate care is not just about effective communication and negotiation, although that is a significant component. To deliver culturally appropriate care, the provider needs to be constantly aware of the interplay between the external world and what takes place in a consultation.

In the USA, the Institute of Medicine (2001) states that quality care is care that is as follows.

- *Effective:* providing services based on scientific knowledge to all who could benefit, and refraining from providing services to those who are not likely to benefit. For vulnerable children an example of this may be ensuring that a child has physical and emotional safety before expecting them to engage in therapy. Therapy taken in chaos with a lack of security is unlikely to be effective, and indeed may raise the child's anxiety.

- *Safe:* avoiding injuries to clients from the care that is intended to help them. In looked-after children, this may translate into avoiding repeated placements that are damaging to the child. It is usually the child that gets labelled as a problem rather than agencies accepting that they have failed the child. There is also the question of repeated

requests for mental health assessments. In complying with repeated
requests, the damage to the child may be considerable.

- *Timely:* reducing waits and sometimes harmful delays for both those
  who receive and those who give care. In the context of culturally
  appropriate care, healthcare providers need to consider how they
  respond to requests for clients to be reviewed urgently. On what
  basis do they make judgements about who waits and who does not?
  What information do they think they depend on in making such
  judgements and decisions? For vulnerable children, this may mean
  seriously considering how long agencies take to make decisions
  about such children. Agencies may often give repeated opportunities
  for parents to provide evidence that they are able to care for their
  children. The time taken to make a decision may be costly for
  children in terms of their emotional development. When decisions
  are being made about time allocated, the potential benefits need to
  be weighed up against the potential losses.

- *Client-centred:* providing care that is respectful of and responsive to
  individual preferences, needs and values, and ensuring that client
  values guide all clinical decisions. Many cultural competence training
  programmes are contrary to a client-centred approach, as their very
  philosophy of teaching that belonging to a specific group
  automatically brings with it certain characteristics or beliefs. Even
  programmes such as that of the Office of Minority Health (2006),
  which begin by stating that clinicians should avoid stereotyping,
  include statements such as 'learn the preferences of your clients and
  their communities'. This is not a client-centred approach, in that it
  encourages physicians to make assumptions about how people see
  themselves. Dogra (2003) argued that a client-centred approach is
  only possible if the understanding of culture, race, and so on is
  challenged and explored. If clinicians believe that culture is an
  externally subscribed characteristic, the notion of the individual
  being able to define themselves is less important. A client-centred
  approach is somehow assumed if the practitioner and client are
  ethnically or racially the same. Provider assumptions may be
  especially true about vulnerable children. Children ascribed as
  belonging to one vulnerable group often fall into several overlapping
  groups and there may be negative views about and/or assumptions
  about each group. For the child, the assumptions made may be
  cumulative. The mental health needs of vulnerable children are often
  more pronounced and often much more difficult to meet, and

providers may find themselves blaming the child, rather than acknowledging their own helplessness and inability to effect change.

- *Equitable*: providing care that does not vary in quality because of personal characteristics such as gender, ethnicity, geographic location, and socio-economic status. Some of the care received by vulnerable children may be of poorer quality because of prejudices, but there may also be perceived different values on which decisions are made.

- *Efficient*: avoiding waste, including waste of equipment, supplies, ideas, and energy. The inappropriate use of, or not using resources efficiently when they exist, would be contrary to this component. Inadequate screening, which is less costly than treatment, is inefficient as well as unacceptable for other reasons. In the context of cultural competence training, practitioners need to be trained to ask themselves if, for a particular client at a particular time, the most efficient care is being delivered. If not, what are the factors preventing this? The practitioner should consider their own biases on this process. For vulnerable children, often many agencies are involved, yet key issues may remain unaddressed and other issues are dealt with by all agencies. This type of overlap is not only inefficient but also damaging to the child, as each agency is likely to take a different stance, leading to confusion.

Dogra (2005) outlined key educational approaches to teaching cultural competence. Opponents of cultural competence training argue that it is unacceptable for client values (often perceived to be minority) to override those of the majority or the provider. In accepting the client's values, the healthcare provider does not have to give up his or her own values. The process is about exploring and negotiating a position that is acceptable to the client and not unacceptable to the healthcare provider (e.g. that the child is aware of risks involved).

In discussing culturally appropriate service for diverse groups, Dogra *et al.* (2007) review the policies that are in place. The children's National Service Framework in the UK (DoH 2004) highlighted the need for services to provide culturally appropriate care for minority groups. There is considerable debate on whether ethnic and other minority groups (such as homeless, looked-after children, and young offenders) have appropriate access to child and adolescent mental health services (Malek 2004). Key recommendations for mandatory training for all mental health professionals in cultural diversity include *Inside Outside: Improving Mental Health Services for Black and Ethnic Minority Groups in England* (NIHME) (2003) and the recommendation of the inquiry into the death of David

'Rocky' Bennett (DoH 2003). Both advocated mandatory training in cultural competencies for all professional staff working in mental health to try to address current disparities as a priority. In 2004 NIHME and the Sainsbury Centre Mental Health Joint Workforce Support Unit published *The Ten Essential Shared Capabilities: A Framework for the Whole of the Mental Health Workforce*. One of these capabilities is 'respecting diversity'. However, to date there has been little evidence that cultural diversity training makes much, if any, significant change in the quality of service provision (Anderson *et al.* 2003; Beach *et al.* 2005; Dogra and Carter-Pokras 2005).

There is evidence that when people are given information about health beliefs of a group, based on their ethnicity or religion, this type of information is focused on. The warnings not to apply this information stereotypically are less heeded (Culhane-Pera *et al.* 1997; Shapiro, Hollingshead and Morrison 2002). For vulnerable children, the issue may be further complicated, as each agency involved in their care may have different perceptions of culture and the relevance of this. The training that each agency undertakes in this area may affect the care that children receive. Very little research has been undertaken with children who are mixed race (this term is used because rarely is the term 'dual heritage' applied when the parents have the same skin colour). The little work that has been done focused on Afro-Caribbean people. It is of note that, despite how these children define themselves, work on their identity often focuses on their 'blackness' (Tizard and Phoenix 2002).

What are cultural issues or factors?

Before we can consider whether we are providing culturally appropriate care, we also need to think about the following issues:

- the concept of mental health itself (professionals and children may have very different understandings of this)
- understanding symptoms, the way they are described and the meaning they have
- different understanding and views of different treatment or management approaches
- perceptions different people have of children who have mental health problems.

Bhui and Bhugra (2004) argue that when clients who are different present, we need to consider that they may have different explanatory models for mental health and illness. There is also some evidence to suggest that these terms are not as well understood by children and their carers as we might like to believe (Dogra *et al.* 2005). We should be asking all children and their carers some basic key questions which help us establish their understanding. It is only if we are aware of this that we can begin to see whether our perspective makes any sense to them or not. In an excellent paper, Platt *et al.* (2001) write about the key aspects of client-centred interviewing. The key areas that the practitioner needs to know about the child or young person are as follows:

- Who is this child, and what constitutes their life? What are their interests, important relationships, and main concerns?
- What does the child expect from the practitioner? What are his/her values and fears? What does he/she hope to accomplish in the visit or over the longer term?
- How does the child experience their problems?
- What are the child's ideas about the problem?
- What are the child's main feelings about the problem?

This is nothing more than good mental health interviewing, and is all part of a comprehensive assessment. To ensure that the care is culturally appropriate, we need to consider how the responses to the above questions fit in with the wider world and also the practitioner's own perspective.

The issues raised here may be even more pertinent for vulnerable children, whose life experiences may have made them very unsure of who they are and how they see the world. There is no doubt that children in vulnerable groups are less likely to have experienced family cohesion, effective parenting, and effective schooling. However, there is huge variation between individual children. We know that factors such as having particular skills, educational attainment and having a supportive adult protect children from mental health problems (Mortimore 1995). It is therefore important to treat children as individuals in order to establish what sense they have made of their circumstances. Their perceived identity may present with greater problems when vulnerable children become adolescents. For refugee children we may also need to consider specific issues of acculturation and adaptation. The issues for them may be different than for children who face cultural conflict because of different family and personal expectations.

The finding that most vulnerable groups are more likely than the general population to have mental health problems is well established. However, this cannot be generalized to all vulnerable groups. Minority ethnic groups are included as being potentially vulnerable, and yet Chinese and Indian children, especially girls, have high educational attainment, *and* Indian girls show low levels of emotional problems (Green *et al.* 2005), so we need to be careful about assuming that belonging to a vulnerable group automatically leads to mental health problems.

Engaging with diverse populations

As practitioners, it is important we identify our own biases and prejudices regarding vulnerable groups. This is crucial, as this is the 'baggage' we carry into the clinical or consultation context. Our personal perspectives are important, not only because we may give less good care to those towards whom we are prejudicial. We may also overcompensate through guilt, for example if we are uncomfortable dealing with young offenders but do not like to acknowledge this; we may be sympathetic and supportive in a context when the more appropriate response may have been to expect the young person to take some responsibility. In training this is often glossed over as 'awareness'. This needs to be more critical and we need to challenge our own assumptions as routine practice. Working with children is further complicated as many of them will have adults involved in their lives, and this adds another layer and often another perspective that needs to be taken into account.

Issues of engagement and respect are taken as given and not discussed here. There is however, an issue that, in different contexts, respect means different things to different people. Rather than fall back on to stereotypes, this should preferably be negotiated at an individual level. Children who come from families where parents are authoritarian (and this can be from any cultural background), or backgrounds in which children are seen but not heard, may be less forthcoming. Practitioners need to be open to the idea that children may need different levels of coaxing. Just because a child does not say much, it does not mean he or she does not have anything to say.

It is worth paying attention to the contexts. At a workshop, I was recently presented with the issue of how to manage a situation where a Pakistani Muslim father spoke for his female child. The clinician was unsure as to whether it would be appropriate for him, as a male, to offer to see the child alone. Different people I am sure would respond in different ways to this potential dilemma. My view would be to consider with who your primary responsibility lies. I have no doubt that my first duty of care is to the child. I have a responsibility to ensure I hear the parental perspective but my overriding responsibility is to the young person. I would offer to see the child alone and, if neither the child nor parent felt this was appropriate, I would accept the decision unless I felt there were other concerns such as abuse. However, that does not mean one should not explore what worries the parent about the child being seen alone.

Obviously, it is not problematic if one asks, and both the child and the parent agree. If the parent does not wish the child to be seen alone, but the child indicates that they would like to take this option, I feel the child's view is more important, especially the older they are. Some clinicians fear that this will set up tensions in the family; I would argue that the issue in itself is not likely to do so, as it only illustrates what is already happening or what underlies the presentation.

We need to bear in mind that the Convention on the Rights of the Child (CRC) (1989) covers all children in the UK, irrespective of race, ethnicity, or religion. Whether authoritarian parents want their children to have a viewpoint or not is not the point, but rather that children have a right to be heard. We also need to be aware of legislative frameworks that we are obliged to work within (see Chapter 3).

Working with vulnerable children and young people from diverse backgrounds

When working with vulnerable children the approach to assessment needs to be similar, as for a mental health assessment for any young person. However, professionals need to be even more aware that the experiences these children have had may make them even more suspicious of mental health services. They are likely to have experienced stigma associated with their vulnerable status and yet another stigmatizing label may be feared. They may also often be stereotypes about the children and their needs, so that professionals make judgements and assumptions about what is their best interest without asking them.

After introductions have been made, a useful opening question is to ask the young person (and anyone else present) what they anticipate will happen. It is important to explore where they have obtained these ideas from as their sources may be unreliable. Young people need to know that they are not being judged negatively and that they are valued. This may be especially true for vulnerable groups, which may be unfamiliar with being taken seriously or being praised.

As well as clinicians having to address their own assumptions, they may also need to gently unpick the narratives that children from vulnerable groups have created about themselves or had created for them. They may come to accept the labels, such as 'difficult', 'unlovable', and so on, that they may have heard used to describe them. Clinicians need to create an environment of trust and safety before tackling such issues. They also need to understand that when the child is anxious or fearful, they may act out or state that they do not wish to engage. Before complying with a child's request to end the process, the clinician needs to ensure that the child has been presented with a range of acceptable options.

Exploring the meanings of mental health for the child and their family is important as this will reveal so much about their understanding and the work that lies ahead of you. At the same time try to avoid making assumptions or trying to explain things in a way that supports your world view. The framework outlined earlier is adaptable for this audience with the caveats already discussed. It has not yet been formally tested but, at face value, it is an approach that focuses on the needs of the child and acknowledges that the provider is not a neutral being but a real person who is flawed.

Conclusions

In summary, working with children from vulnerable groups may present particular challenges. It is important not to assume that only those from minority ethnic groups have 'cultural needs'. The key to providing culturally appropriate care for vulnerable children is to ensure that the approach is child-centred and practitioners are aware of their own biases and world view, and understand how these influence the choices and care they offer.

References

Anderson, L., Scrimshaw, S., Fullilove, M., Fielding, J., Normand, J., and the Task Force on Community Preventive Services (2003) 'Culturally competent healthcare systems: a systematic review.' *American Journal of Preventative Medicine 24*, (3S), 68–79.

Association of American Medical Colleges (1999) Report III. *Contemporary Issues. in Medicine: Communication in Medicine – Spirituality, Cultural issues and End of Life Care.* Washington, DC: Association of American Medical Colleges.

Beach, M.C., Price, E.G., Gary, T.L., Robinson, K.A., Gozu, A., and Palacio, A. (2005) 'Cultural competence: A systematic review of health care provider educational interventions.' *Medical Care; Medical Care 43*, 4, 356–373.

Bhui, K., and Bhugra, D. (2004) 'Communication with patients from other cultures: The place of explanatory models.' *Advances in Psychiatric Treatment 10*, 474–478.

Convention on the Rights of the Child (CRC) (1989) General Assembly Resolution 44/25, UN Document E.C. 12.1999.10. New York, NY: United Nations.

Cross, T., Bazron, B., Dennis, K., and Isaacs, M. (1989) *Towards a Culturally Competent System of Care, Volume 1.* Washington, DC: Georgetown University Child Development Center, CASSP Technical Assistance Centre.

Culhane-Pera, K., Reif, C., Egli, E., Baker, N., and Kassekert, R. (1997) 'A curriculum for multicultural education in family medicine.' *Family Medicine 29*, 719–23.

Department of Health (DoH) (2003) *Delivering Race Equality: A Framework for Action.* London: Department of Health.

Department of Health (DoH) (2004) *National Service Framework for Children, Young People and Maternity Services: Core Standards.* London: Department of Health.

Dogra, N. (2003) 'Cultural competence or cultural sensibility? A comparison of two ideal type models to teach cultural diversity to medical students.' *International Journal of Medicine 5*, 223–231.

Dogra, N. (2005). 'Cultural diversity teaching in the medical undergraduate curriculum.' *Diversity in Health and Social Care 2*, 233–245.

Dogra, N., and Carter-Pokras, O. (2005) 'Stakeholder views regarding cultural diversity teaching outcomes.' *BMC Medical Education 5*, 37.

Dogra, N., and Karim, K. (2005) 'Training in diversity for psychiatrists.' *Advances in Psychiatric Treatment 11*, 159–167.

Dogra, N., Vostanis, P., Abuateya, H., and Jewson, N. (2007) 'Children's mental health services and ethnic diversity: Gujarati families' perspectives of service provision for mental health problems.' *Transcultural Psychiatry 44*, 275–291.

Dogra, N., Vostanis, P., Jewson, N. and Abuateya, H. (2005) 'Understanding of mental health and mental illness by Gujarati young people and their parents.' *Diversity in Health and Social Care 2*, 91–97.

Edles, L. (2002) *Cultural Sociology in Practice.* Malden, MA: Blackwell.

Green, H., McGinnity, A., Meltzer, H., Ford, T., and Goodman, R. (2005) *Mental Health of Children and Young People in Great Britain.* Basingstoke: Palgrave.

Henry J Kaiser Family Foundation (2003) *Compendium of Cultural Competence Initiatives in Health Care.* Menlo Park, CA: The Henry J Kaiser Family Foundation.

Institute of Medicine (2001) *Crossing the Quality Chasm: A New Health System for the 21st Century.* Washington: Institute of Medicine.

Kleinman, A. and Benson, P. (2006) 'Anthropology in the clinic: the problem of cultural competence and how to fix it.' *PLoS Medicine 3,* 294.

Malek, M. (2004) 'Meeting the needs of minority ethnic groups in the UK.' In M. Malek and C. Joughin (eds) *Mental Health Services for Minority Ethnic Children and Adolescents (Child and Adolescent Mental Health)* London: Jessica Kingsley Publishers.

Mental Health Foundation (2002) *Talkback: Vulnerable Young People.* London: Mental Health Foundation.

Mortimore, P. (1995) 'The Positive Effects of Schooling.' In M. Rutter (ed.) *Psychosocial Disturbances in Young People.* Cambridge: Cambridge University Press.

National Institute of Mental Health in England (NIMHE) (2003) *Inside Outside: Improving Mental Health Services for Black and Minority Ethnic Groups in England.* London: Department of Health.

National Institute of Mental Health in England (NIMHE) and the Sainsbury Centre Mental Health Joint Workforce Support Unit (2004) *The Ten Essential Shared Capabilities: A Framework for the Whole of the Mental Health Workforce.* London: National Institute of Mental Health in England and the Sainsbury Centre Mental Health Joint Workforce Support Unit.

Office of Minority Health (2006) *A Family Physician's Practical Guide to Culturally Competent Care.* Available at: cccm.thinkculturalhealth.org, accessed on 18 December 2006.

Platt, F., Gaspar, D., Coulehan, J., Fox, L., Adler, A., Weston, W., Smith, R., and Stewart, M. (2001) 'Medical writing: Tell me about the patient-centred interview.' *Annals of Internal Medicine 134,* 1079–1085.

Shapiro, J., Hollingshead, J., and Morrison, E. (2002) 'Primary care resident, faculty, and patient views of barriers to cultural competence, and the skills needed to overcome them.' *Medical Education 36,* 749–759.

Tervalon, M., and Murray-Garcia, J. (1998) 'Cultural humility versus cultural competence: A critical distinction in defining physician-training outcomes in multicultural education.' *Journal of Health Care for the Poor and Underserved 9,* 117–125.

Tizard, B. and Phoenix, A. (2002) *Black, White or Mixed Race? Race and Racism in the Lives of Young People of Mixed Parentage.* London: Routledge.

CHAPTER 17

US Perspectives on Interventions for Vulnerable and Underserved Youth

Niranjan S. Karnik, Brenda Krause Eheart, Martha Bauman Power and Hans Steiner

Vulnerable and underserved youth can be understood and defined in multiple ways. For the purposes of this chapter, which seeks to examine the ways that these groups have been addressed in the US's welfare and health care systems, we have opted to examine three subgroups: young offenders; children in foster care; and homeless youth. These three groups are inter-related (Figure 17.1) and often are

Figure 17.1 Inter-relationships of vulnerable youth based in the community or institutions

defined more by the disparate institutions that have responsibility for them, rather than the commonalities that underlie their experience. These are pools of children which channel and cycle through related systems of care.

Vulnerable children differ from other children in health and medical systems. These children are at risk because of predominantly external factors arising out of the social environment, such as poverty, disrupted families or social dislocation. Whilst it is essential to understand and address these factors, vulnerable children also have internal risk factors. The welfare and protective systems of care around these children have long traditions that are accustomed to addressing the needs of these children based on external approaches. We need to acknowledge and address the internal states of these children, and simultaneously address the external or psychosocial context. In this sense, the mind of the child exists within a psychosocial context, and causality can flow in either direction: top–down from the psychosocial world to the individual, or in the opposite direction from the mind to the environmental context (Figure 17.2). This constitutes, in brief, the developmental psychopathological model and a basis for interventions rooted in developmental psychiatry (Steiner 2004).

The top–down causation might best be exemplified by the case of a homeless youth.

Case vignette

Jonathan is a 14-year-old who had done well in school until the past six months. He began to question his sexual orientation about nine months ago, and, as a result, began to have significant arguments with his parents when he revealed his thoughts that he was gay. His father, in particular, took the news very poorly and threatened Jonathan. Fearing for his safety, Jonathan ran away from their home and made his way to the city by hitch-hiking and prostituting himself. After living on the streets and in shelters for several weeks, Jonathan began to display symptoms of depression and anxiety.

In this case, the top–down or external process is evident. Jonathan suffers from discrimination at the hands of his parents, and thereafter feels forced to leave home for his own safety. After months of stress, followed by violence whilst living on the streets of the city, he begins to experience depressive symptoms. Whilst he may have some predisposing factors from his biology, family or developmental history, the majority of stress seems to be driven from the social world and he experiences psychiatric symptoms as a consequence.

Developmental psychiatry: culture, mind and brain

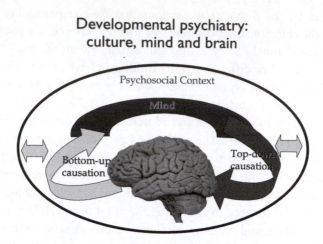

Figure 17.2 The developmental psychopathological model. Reproduced with kind permission from H. Steiner

The bottom–up or internal process can be seen in the case of Amy.

Case vignette

Amy is a 10-year-old girl born to a single mother with a history of substance abuse and bipolar disorder. Owing to the mother's diagnoses, Amy was taken into foster care at birth because it was clear that her mother had little capability or interest in raising this child. She was adopted at the age of two years by a family that had two biological children. Throughout her childhood, Amy had disruptive and aggressive symptoms. She had difficulty with concentration for days or weeks at a time which seemed compounded by profound sleep disturbance. She would sleep little and have surprising energy. These episodes would often happen for a week at a time, which caused her adoptive family great concern since their other children had never experienced symptoms like this before.

Here, the internal quality of these symptoms becomes evident. Amy carries a significant biological risk of bipolar disorder given her mother's history, and there is little evidence from the social situation that might be driving these behaviours. Although social and environmental factors and supports are essential for this family to address this child's needs; she is also experiencing internal symptoms which need to be addressed as well.

In this chapter, the aim is to review interventions from the US experience, and contextualize these within a broader framework for implementing interventions for vulnerable youth. In examining these interventions comprehensiveness has been sacrificed for selectiveness, and tried to highlight promising avenues for further work.

Levels of analysis and intervention

When examining interventions for vulnerable youth, it is not sufficient to take them all in aggregate and simply say that this or that intervention or programme is the way to treat these youths. One of the major lessons when examining the plight of vulnerable youth has been that there is no single formula that can provide for their needs. As a site for the study of interventions, the USA is a large and disparate country. Some health services analysts have taken to describing sub-populations within the country as being the best unit of analysis. Murray and colleagues (2006), in a thoughtful approach, used race in combination with geography to describe what they term the 'Eight Americas', which correspond to socio-cultural-geographic regions that can be used to study health outcomes and disparities.

The study of vulnerable children necessitates a similar approach which takes seriously the socio-economic constraints of the lives of these children and their families. This approach needs to be placed within a developmental psychopathology framework. Children in this sense not only live within the Eight Americas but they also have to face the challenges of progressing through the expected milestones of childhood. Whether due to individual or environmental factors, the degree to which vulnerable youth face stressors within their local contexts is far more significant than non-vulnerable youth. The experience of stress and consequent higher risk of physical and psychiatric morbidity significantly define the lives of vulnerable and underserved youth.

As with most complex psychiatric illnesses, multi-modal approaches are likely to yield the best outcomes (Steiner 2004; Steiner *et al.* 2006a). In order to

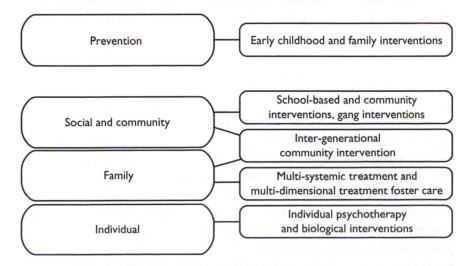

Figure 17.3 Levels of intervention and associated therapy

understand interventions for vulnerable children, we have artificially broken them down by the primary levels of intervention (Figure 17.3). With this in mind, it is important to note that the best interventions are multi-modal and should intervene at multiple levels simultaneously.

Young offenders and juvenile delinquents

Estimates range, but roughly 60–70 per cent of incarcerated juveniles are thought to have one or more psychiatric disorders. Less is known about non-incarcerated offenders, but the rates are likely to be similar or higher, because these youth are in an actively abusing environment. These rates are likely to be context-dependent. But a recent cross-national study of depressive symptoms among urban adolescents found a surprising degree of similarity, with girls having more significant pathology than boys (Ruchkin et al. 2006). Among incarcerated juveniles, a recent comparative study between Austria and the USA found that the morbidity was higher in the Austrian group (Plattner and Steiner 2005). This is likely due to extensive outpatient and diversion programmes that are available in many European countries which continue to sustain a social welfare system, and which are able to address many issues of psychopathology and anti-sociality via means other than incarceration.

One major premise of our work is that the focus on young offenders is best served by shifting from a criminological approach to one that focuses on the treatment of psychopathology. This perspective was formally put forward by August Aichhorn in the 1930s when he, as director of the Vienna Boys Reform School, undertook studies to understand delinquent youth (Aichhorn 1935). His approach was to try to view these delinquents through the lens of psychopathology and to examine the connection between these phenomena and the social environment. The modern understanding of psychopathology has expanded dramatically and now incorporates a developmental perspective (Cicchetti and Cohen 2006). To this perspective it is now possible to include exciting research from the neuroscience of aggression and biological psychiatry. Last, the much-neglected area of social and economic disparity leads us to theorize that a great deal of antisocial behaviour is the result of a lack of interventions on early psychopathology and poor access to care. Even in Western countries with significant resources, there is increasing evidence that social and cultural barriers create situations where children are not given the care they need for early-onset psychiatric phenomena. In aggregate we see multiple strands of research now coming together to feed our knowledge and understanding of young offenders, and it is incumbent on us to try to integrate these rapidly emerging findings to provide the best possible outcomes for these youth (Steiner et al. 2007).

Researchers and clinicians have struggled to develop effective interventions for young offenders. The stakes are high – not only are these attempts to prevent the development of more significant psychopathology but they are also interventions to reduce the morbidity of existing disorders. In addition, reductions in psychopathology can lead to lower rates of recidivism. Finally, antisocial behaviours themselves may be direct objects for therapeutic interventions. A recent consensus panel from the Stanford/Howard/American Association of Child and Adolescent Psychiatry (AACAP) Workgroup on Juvenile Impulsivity and Aggression has comprehensively reviewed interventions and treatments on juvenile maladaptive aggression (Connor *et al.* 2006), which constitutes a much broader area of scholarship and investigation than young offenders. In the present review, we draw on the workgroup's findings and seek to contextualize these interventions within the emerging literature on young offenders and aggression. In doing so we want to bring the overlapping areas of sociology, neuroscience and mental health interventions into alignment (see Figure 17.1), so that we can begin to see the pathways for future interventions and research for young offenders. This is necessarily a selective review of the literature, given the need to focus attention on certain aspects of current research, and also to highlight portions of the literature that are especially promising.

Prevention

Prevention as a strategy requires that providers have knowledge of major clinical issues and public health concerns. It is not sufficient for only specialist providers such as child and adolescent mental health professionals to be aware of the needs of young offenders; primary care providers and general practitioners have an essential role to play in examining risk for children and enabling parents to understand that they have a professional to rely on in helping them prevent their children from entering lives of offending and delinquency.

In this regard, Runyan and colleagues (2005) describe one such intervention programme, created as part of the US National Training Initiation in Injury and Violence Prevention called PREVENT (Preventing Violence Through Education, Networking and Technical Assistance). Although the focus of the training was quite broad, the advantage that it offered was a systemized way for educating professionals about empiric approaches to violence and provided a framework for understanding the nature of violence within a social-ecological model. Such education is a necessary part of creating systems of care and for prevention of the development of environments from which young offenders are likely to emerge.

Calhoun and colleagues (2005) described another different direction for early prevention and intervention in their description of a gun-tracing study in Oakland, California involving 263 juveniles, who were either victims or perpetrators of gun violence over a two-year period. The study was remarkable for the fact that of the 132 guns identified in the study, only 52 of them could be traced, meaning that 80 guns used in violent crimes could not be traced from available data sources. Despite the fact that consensus teams have been unable to show a conclusive correlation between guns and violence (Hahn *et al.* 2005; Task Force on Community Preventive Services 2005), comparative studies have suggested that the presence of guns increases the likelihood of violence (Sloan *et al.* 1988; Sloan *et al.* 1990).

Among the various levels of intervention for young offenders, primary prevention has had the least number of studies, largely owing to the need for long follow-up intervals and large sample sizes. The Workgroup on Juvenile Impulsivity and Aggression identified five programmes that have empirically validated outcomes data (Connor *et al.* 2006). The notable findings for these interventions are that they all had some degree of decreased arrest, delinquency, and aggression in multi-year follow-up, with one as far out as 27 years from the intervention. Only one of the five studies found no difference from control subjects at 10-year follow-up. All these interventions targeted very young children, most under age 4, and only the Chicago Child–Parent Center for children under age nine (Reynolds *et al.* 1998; Reynolds, Temple and Ou 2003; Reynolds, Ou and Topitzes 2004). All of these programmes utilized a combination of family and educational services and supports, as well as parent skills training on a daily or weekly basis. In many respects, we could class the majority of these interventions under the rubric of family interventions, since that is the unit of intervention and the focus is on high-risk children.

Social and community interventions

Interventions at the community and social level have shown some degree of success and are among the most novel and creative areas for further research. This area, which we have termed, 'sociotherapy', marks a major focus on the social and contextual environment around young offenders (Karnik 2004; Steiner 2004).

Gang prevention programmes are one key example in the socio-therapeutic modality. The Gang Violence Prevention Project in Chicago utilized a combination of community mobilization and outreach to youth to help prevent the aggregation of maladaptive and antisocial patterns (Spergel and Grossman 1997). Such interventions are time-consuming and often require large-scale programmes to support them.

Family-based

A significant number of studies have focused on the family as the unit of intervention. Among the most established methods for family intervention is 'multi-systemic treatment' (MST). This form of treatment utilizes a high-intensity case management approach, with specially trained therapists following small numbers of families and having a high degree of availability. Therapists work towards empowering the family and drawing in collateral support from other family members, friends, and community members over several months. Borduin and colleagues have conducted a series of studies on this method in the treatment of young offenders (Borduin 1999; Curtis, Ronan and Borduin 2004; Schaeffer and Borduin 2005). In their long-term follow-up study of 176 youths who were, on average, over 10 years out from the intervention, they found substantially lower rates of recidivism, arrests, and days of confinement. Despite these generally positive results, Littell and colleagues (2005), who conducted a detailed meta-analysis, were unable to establish conclusively that MST was advantageous to standard treatment.

Another intervention at the family level is multi-dimensional treatment foster care (MTFC), which uses an intensive model of foster care to re-parent and re-socialize young offenders. The programme relies on having foster parents who follow a highly structured approach to monitoring and rewarding behaviours from the young offender. The children and their families participate in individual and family therapy during the programme, and also have intensive case management. Foster parents receive additional support through group meetings and programme support (Chamberlain and Weinrott 1990; Chamberlain and Reid 1998; Eddy and Chamberlain 2000; Liddle *et al.* 2001; Leve, Chamberlain and Reid 2005). Such approaches are especially useful when the custodial parents of the child are especially impaired, and perhaps poor candidates for MST. The availability of these two major modalities for treatment at the family level constitutes two empirically based arms of intervention.

Individual

Among all the therapies we have outlined and levels of care we have identified, the research on individual modalities remains the weakest and least clearly explicated for young offenders. We believe that this is the result of the fact that young offenders are embedded in powerful social and family networks, and that these forces are ecologically salient and prevent any single individual-level intervention from yielding a robust result. Nevertheless, in our experience, individual therapy combined judiciously with the use of medication when indicated for co-morbid psychiatric conditions, can lead to reducing triggers in the environment for young offenders (Steiner 1997; Trupin *et al.* 2002; Steiner *et al.* 2007).

The aggregate data on juvenile aggression and conduct disorder indicates that there are two major pathways to delinquency, both of which appear to be differentiated at the neural level (Blair *et al.* under review). Our current focus seems to implicate the amygdala, orbitofrontal cortex, and frontal cortex regions as exhibiting changes which correspond to maladaptive aggression. Such changes are the first steps in understanding the neurobiology of aggression, and as our tools improve we are likely to gain more specificity in targeting regions better. It should be emphasized that our understanding of this biology does not yet indicate a causal source or aetiology. It is likely that some individuals have a genetic risk but, as with most psychiatric disorders, this risk only becomes expressed in relation to certain environmental stimuli and stressors. In the case of young offenders it is important to be mindful of the high rates of trauma exposure at very young ages that have the potential to affect neuronal development. It is also unclear whether these changes are reversible over time and with targeted treatments and interventions.

One path is characterized by reactive, affective, defensive and impulsive (RADI) aggression or what could be summarized as 'hot' aggression. Young offenders with this type of aggression are often unthinking and reactive youth who respond to slights against them. They often show remorse following their acts, and tend to regret what they have done once they have time to think. The second pathway is characterized by pro-active, instrumental, and planned (PIP) aggression. This could also be termed 'cold' aggression. Young offenders who demonstrate PIP patterns are highly sociopathic and tend to show little remorse for their actions. They tend to plan their violence, and are very deliberate in the ways that they use people and violence to achieve their ends. These youth are far fewer than the RADI youth who predominate among youth offenders. Nevertheless, PIP youth are the feared ones, and the ones who are likely to need significant ongoing attention (Steiner and Karnik 2006). We also believe that some subset of these youth exhibit a mixed type, where elements of pro-active and reactive aggression may be discerned.

Our approach to these youth is defined by the predominance of symptoms in one or the other pathway (Karnik and Steiner 2005; Karnik, McMullin and Steiner 2006). We believe that RADI youth often benefit from psychopharmacological and psychotherapeutic strategies that reduce their impulsivity, anxiety and reactivity (Soller, Karnik and Steiner 2006). We know that these children often have high levels of post-traumatic stress disorder (PTSD) (Carrion and Steiner 2000; Plattner *et al.* 2003; Steiner, Garcia and Matthews 1997), and we theorize that this, combined with mood and anxiety symptoms, can place these children in a high state of activation, which potentially leads them to be overly responsive to their environment and aggressively reactive to perceived threats (Edsall, Karnik and Steiner 2005).

With PIP youth, our approach emphasizes the development of moral reasoning and emotional skills development. These are the youths likely to need long-term and concerted systems of care to prevent them from becoming the most problematic and recalcitrant adult offenders. Some of these children will benefit more substantively from highly structured environments and possible residential care which utilizes the therapeutic perspectives we have outlined. Structured environments can create circumstances where these youth can be positively encouraged to develop a better reasoning system, but also enables providers to address with consequences instances of pro-active aggression when they arise.

From a psychotherapeutic perspective it is still unclear which therapeutic modalities are likely to be beneficial to young offenders in either pathway, especially when the sub-typing of aggression is taken into account. The intervention literature shows some benefit from anger management programmes (Lochman 1992; Trupin *et al.* 2002; Zun, Downey and Rosen 2006).

Pharmacologically, we believe that RADI young offenders have the potential to benefit from medication when they are used as part of an integrated treatment strategy which includes individual and family therapy. We have reviewed this topic extensively and will not enumerate all the specific agents here (Soller *et al.* 2006). Two classes of medication do deserve mention here because of their recent and emerging data. Our research indicates that anticonvulsants (Khanzode *et al.* 2006; Rana *et al.* 2005; Saxena *et al.* 2005; Steiner *et al.* 2003) and atypical antipsychotics (Findling *et al.* 2005; Pappadopulos *et al.* 2003; Schur *et al.* 2003) appear to show early efficacy and potential for helping RADI youth to gain better control of their behaviours. Consensus guidelines exist for the use of these agents in the treatment of aggression and conduct disorder (Pappadopulos *et al.* 2003; Steiner 1997; Steiner and Dunne 1997).

Several studies have shown the high rates of psychopathology faced by young offenders. Anecdotally, we know that many of these cases show a pattern of neglect of treatment and intervention for their psychopathology. In the first instance, this is a failure of screening. Second, we know that many of these children have cycled through systems of care repeatedly, and that they once again failed to be identified as needing treatment or they have been poorly treated. In some instances we know that these children received treatment but that it was poorly designed or done without attention to evidence-based techniques. Both of these issues need to be addressed. There is a significant need for accurate and improved screening and detection, which should result in timely referral. And there is also a need for better treatment and focused interventions.

The treatment of young offenders is a rapidly changing field, with new modalities and interventions being implemented constantly. The challenge of the coming years will be to intervene using empirical strategies that are implemented based on the neuroscientific basis of aggression. The new findings emerging concurrently from the fields of neurobiology, developmental psychiatry, and sociology have the potential to change our practices dramatically. They allow us to sub-type young offenders meaningfully, not just for academic purposes, but with the intent and ability to specifically target our interventions to their needs. Professionals in these fields need to be comfortable implementing multi-faceted strategies which make use of the full range of our therapeutic interventions from MST to anticonvulsants. From this point forwards, interventions research must account for the known sub-types of aggression among young offenders, and seek to test which sub-populations their interventions benefit. Only by taking this step will we be able to meaningfully intervene in the lives of these children and prevent their maladaptive trajectory from continuing.

Foster children and youth in care

Another vulnerable population includes children in the foster care system in the USA. These children are comparable with the UK population of children who are 'in care', and have historically been a difficult population to address, given the legal uncertainties surrounding their care. In the USA, 800,000 children spend time in foster care each year, and of these over 100,000 are waiting to be adopted (Children's Defense Fund 2005). Large proportions of these children have emotional or behavioural problems (Bass, Shield and Behrman 2004). In Illinois, for example, over half of all school-aged foster children suffer from a psychiatric disorder or severe behaviour problem (Zinn *et al.* 2006). Nationwide, as many as 80 per cent of children involved with child welfare agencies have conditions indicating they are in need of mental health services (Burns *et al.* 2004). These high numbers reflect Lyons and Rogers' (2004) claim that 'the child welfare system is a de facto behavioural health care system'.

It is difficult to be optimistic about the future of children adrift in this system. In the USA, approximately 20,000 youths 'age out' of the foster care system each year unprepared to make the transition to adulthood. These children, who have spent substantial time in foster care, are much more likely than other children to be unemployed, school drop-outs, on public assistance, involved in drug treatment, parent children at a young age, and become perpetrators or victims of crime (Courtney and Dworsky 2005; Courtney and Heuring 2005).

These vexing social problems affecting foster children show little sign of easing through traditional methods and systems. This is, in part, because conventional programme design tries to target professional interventions to provide just the right skills and resources, to just the right clients, at just the right time. This approach can work when goals are limited and clear, such as increasing reading proficiency. But the most challenging problems lack this specificity. There are actually multiple problems foster children face occurring together within communities, for example poverty, educational failure, mental illness, and delinquency. In addition, too often, the policies and procedures of traditional social service systems are in conflict. Child welfare is mandated to ensure the protection of each child. Medical, legal, and educational systems have their own agendas. Thus, foster children dwell on the boundaries of systems in conflict, each with their own rules and regulations, expectations, and beliefs. Differing factions leave children vulnerable.

What has been missing in addressing the complexity of these social problems affecting children in foster care is recognition of the importance and potential of naturally emergent relationships and lifetime commitments across generations within the community.

Research confirms common knowledge: social relationships are foundational to human well-being (Goleman 2006; Shonkoff, Phillips and National Research Council 2000). Experience shows that, although one-to-one relationships (mentor to mentee, therapist to client, parent to foster child), can often make a difference, their chances of doing so in more challenging situations depend on whether they are situated in a supportive context. The block, the neighbourhood, the community matters. To be successful within this context, foster children must be seen as ordinary kids requiring the same embeddedness in family and community that we would want for our biological children – something that rarely happens once children enter care (Power and Eheart 2001). To have our children moved from one stranger's home to another, often repeatedly, is unconscionable. To have our children at age 18, 28, or even 48, tell someone that they have never known a mother or father or a grandparent is unthinkable.

John Dewey wrote in 1902, 'What the best and wisest parent wants for his own child, that must the community want for all its children.' Once we begin to view each child in the foster care system through this new lens – *as our own son or daughter* – we realize that it is family and community that provide nurturing relationships which serve as the building blocks for healthy development and positive well-being. It is family and community that, for children, help maintain continuity of relationships and of place. And it is through family and community that a strong sense of belonging and commitment can be provided. Professionals simply cannot serve the functions of family and community; they cannot *care* about a child in the way a parent cares about his or her own children. If policymakers, judges, caseworkers, and others would begin to look at foster care service and service delivery through this new lens, change would occur. We would begin wrapping supportive communities around families, including adoptive families, rather than wrapping services around foster children.

In 1994, Generations of Hope, a non-profitable organization licensed and monitored through the Illinois Department of Children and Family Services, took on the challenge of developing a relationship-based programme to address the problem of too many children languishing in foster care. It created Hope Meadows, an intentional inter-generational community, by converting housing on a decommissioned military base to establish a neighbourhood for adoptive families of foster children. It supports 12 families who agree to adopt up to four children, often sibling groups, who would otherwise spend much or all of their childhood in foster care. One parent in each family is an employee of Generations of Hope, receiving a salary, family health insurance, and a home, rent-free. In addition, there are 40 senior households receiving below-market-rate rent in return for six hours a week of volunteer work. On-site staff includes a director, social worker, and therapist who simultaneously address the internal and external contexts of the children's needs.

When this neighbourhood was formed, it was thought its success would be measured by its rate of adoptions of hard-to-place foster children. In its first five years, it achieved a rate of 74.6 per cent in closing child cases (e.g. adoption, return home), compared to the Illinois' rate of 23.7 per cent for the same time period. By 2006, Hope's 12-year rate was 90 per cent. These accomplishments, whilst enormously gratifying, do not, however, represent the single most important achievement of Generations of Hope, which has been Hope Meadows becoming an 'inter-generational community as intervention' (ICI). Unlike traditional social services that intervene in the community, Hope Meadows became the vehicle for action. The community itself became the intervention.

The basic strategy of Hope Meadows as an ICI is to facilitate and support naturally emergent relationships and lifetime commitments across generational lines. ICIs are purposeful, geographically specific inter-generational neighbourhoods, where some residents are struggling with a potentially long-term social challenge around which the entire community organizes. Unlike conventional practice, which delivers a service that is often time-limited and close-ended, behaviourally specific, deficit-oriented, rule-driven, professionally controlled, and provided to, or for, someone, Hope Meadows, as an ICI, generates support that is continuous and open-ended, holistic, asset-based, care-driven, communally controlled, and mutually given and received. Hope Meadows transforms the old-fashioned idea of a cohesive neighbourhood into a purposeful intervention. With a small staff providing support and guidance, the neighbourhood is given the freedom to develop meaningful relationships among neighbours and across generations. Cohesiveness is maintained by the neighbourhood's explicit social purpose, to care for the children who have come to live there.

Hope Meadows has evolved through the years. The cumulative effect arising from complex inter-generational relationships has led to the establishment of a culture of effective care and mutual concern. This 'culture of care' has become the bedrock of this strong, healthy, supportive community, that is, a community able to find solutions to social problems that transcend traditional agency boundaries. Here, foster children are not seen as wards to be managed, but simply as children with the same needs as all children for enduring, caring relationships. Here, child welfare is an entirely different undertaking when a whole neighbourhood, down to the last resident, has explicitly signed on to ensuring the well-being of its children by enfolding them on a daily basis into networks of stable, caring, inter-generational relationships. This community is the intervention in the lives of these children. As an ICI, Hope Meadows is based on ten core principles (Eheart *et al.* 2006), which are shown in brief in Box 17.1.

In conclusion, the purpose of foster care is to keep children safe. For children to flourish they must be safe mentally as well as physically, and feel secure in a nurturing family and community. 'Keeping children safe must be everybody's business. Child protection agencies should partner with families and communities, and use new strategies that protect children and build on family strengths' (Children's Defense Fund 2005). The inter-generational neighbourhood of Hope Meadows is just such a strategy. It is multi-modal and intervenes at multiple levels simultaneously. When the neighbourhood is doing its job, the formal service systems around it are less pressed and more capable of making a difference.

What Generations of Hope has done is taken the ideal of a stable, nurturing community and given it a distinctive twist by creating and organizing the community to address the specific social challenges posed by children adrift in foster care. This is primarily accomplished through the physical and social structure of Hope Meadows. The proximity of the houses to each other, with a community centre at the hub, increases the density of acquaintanceship by providing contexts in which caring relationships can emerge naturally and informally. Here families, seniors, and staff, guided by a shared purpose, live, play, and work together as neighbours, providing the children with a vision of what can be and of what successes are possible. Encouragement, wisdom, insights, and unconditional care and commitment anchor vulnerable children, and buffer them from the uncertainties of everyday life. Over time, a reciprocity of need leads to a reciprocity of care, as the once-vulnerable children share in a spirit of mutual responsibility and sensitivity. They, too, become the intervention.

Homeless and street children in the USA

A little-discussed or noted group of children in the USA are those who live on the streets or are homeless. Unlike young offenders, who have families and a structured environment, or foster children, who have surrogate families, ideally in supportive communities, homeless youth often live far outside these structures and sometimes lack adult supervision or support. Some of these children are ones who have 'aged out' of the foster care system, and many of them cycle through the juvenile justice system on a regular basis. The numbers that make up these groups are unclear, due in large measure to the differing institutions that have

Box 17.1 Principles guiding the Generations of Hope approach to foster care and community intervention

1. Created to address a specific social challenge
An ICI is created to deal directly with a salient social challenge (e.g. foster care, juvenile justice, homelessness) that has potential long-term consequences. These challenges involve persons whose broad range of needs is usually too great to be satisfied solely by family, friends, or neighbourhoods, and for whom formal service systems are often too limited or restrictive.

2. Presence of three or more generations
ICI residents span at least three generations. Families, children, and older adults constitute the right mix for the ICI to develop the necessary level of proficiency in its capacity to care for and support its residents.

3. Older adults are the community's volunteers
Every senior is expected to volunteer on a regular basis in exchange for physical and material support, such as reduced rent and modified housing. Seniors mainly have an identity as givers, not recipients, of service.

4. Requisite diversity
In an ICI the inherent diversity of age is enhanced by the requisite diversity of race, ethnicity, education, income background, life experience, and perspective. Living with differences helps all involved to find creative solutions to complex problems and prepares them for living in a diverse society.

5. Practice grounded in theory and research
Practice in an ICI is empirically grounded in research on human development, specifically child and youth development, and on effective programmes.

6. Evolving programme design/learning from experience
For an ICI to be effective, it cannot be indelibly designed. It must be adaptive and able to respond to the changing needs of members, as well as to insights gained from ongoing research and practice.

7. Professional staff guide but do not govern
The expertise of professional staff is essential for a wide range of managerial and programmatic functions; however, staff practice is most effective when characterized by relationship building and guiding rather than directing.

8. Economic issues are addressed but do not dominate
Whilst economic issues such as job creation and affordable housing are clearly intertwined with other social challenges addressed by the ICI, they must not overshadow the primary reasons for creating the programme.

9. Physical design impacts interpersonal relationships and the ability to age-in-place
A well-functioning ICI designs its facilities to be conducive to the formation and development of inter-generational relationships. Important considerations include the changing needs of people of all ages.

10. Cohesion stops short of insularity
An ICI should look and feel like any other healthy community. The more it blends in with the larger community in which it is situated, the less the stigma associated with the need it serves.

responsibility for these children and the lack of integration of care. Other homeless children live as part of a homeless family unit. Being homeless stresses the family unit significantly but also can provide a method for intervention at the family level.

Most of the literature on homeless youth in the USA has focused on intervention strategies for the prevention of HIV/AIDS and sexually transmitted diseases (Auerswald *et al.* 2006; Kipke *et al.* 1995; Rew 2001; Rotheram-Borus *et al.* 2003; Steele, Ramgoolam and Evans 2003). These programmes focus on expanding street-level care for these youth, and also examine the challenges inherent in providing screening and treatment for a transient and unstable youth population. Many studies of sexual risk have also identified substance use disorders as being co-morbid risks (Booth, Zhang and Kwiatkowski 1999; Ginzler *et al.* 2003; Gleghorn *et al.* 1998; Kral *et al.* 1997). Such studies highlight many of the current challenges faced by children on the street, but they also fail to take a larger holistic view of these children and their lives.

Underscoring the need for multiple levels of intervention and for looking at the family as the unit of analysis, Zima and her colleagues showed a significant connection between maternal psychiatric symptoms and those of the children when homeless (Zima *et al.* 1996). Self-report studies from homeless youth find that they are concerned with sexually transmitted diseases, pregnancy, depression, injuries, and substance use (Ensign and Gittelsohn 1998). These concerns have been reflected in the limited interventions that have been developed for these youth. Nevertheless, interventions for homeless youth also need to account for high rates of suicidal ideation and attempts, and that they are often compounded by past histories of sexual or physical abuse, which tend to increase the likelihood of suicidal behaviour and thoughts (Molnar *et al.* 1998). Among homeless youth, girls face more difficulty in obtaining care (Ensign and Panke 2002).

Interventions for homeless and street youth are at a preliminary stage. Consequently, interventions research in this domain is even less developed than for other populations and more scholarly attention is needed for these children.

Conclusions

Vulnerable and underserved youth face significant risks, but there are also factors that can protect them in the face of adversity. When attempting to intervene in the lives of vulnerable youth, addressing both internal and external factors is important. Traditional systems of care have focused primarily on external factors and even this has been done poorly in some circumstances. In our discussion of Generations of Hope, we trace the ways that good external interventions can be developed, and the need to have interventions at multiple levels of experience. This community makes use of an inter-generation community as intervention to address the needs of foster children by moving them into a stable environment, and simultaneously giving them the resources and support they need to recover from the trauma and dislocation they have faced earlier in their lives. These external interventions are combined with internally focused interventions of psychotherapy and medical care which enable children to have the opportunity to recover.

The focus on external factors is especially evident in care provided for young offenders and juvenile delinquents. As we have argued and documented, the high rates of psychiatric morbidity in this population demand attention to the internal factors while simultaneously building new opportunities to intervene on the

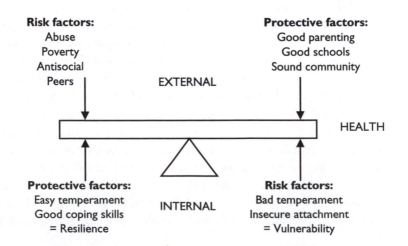

Figure 17.4 Developmental psychopathological model of risk and protection

external factors. To address one aspect of their experience without the other simply sets the stage for a high degree of recidivism.

One model for conceptualizing the lives of vulnerable children is to consider what risk and protective factors they possess (Figure 17.4). Risk factors predispose toward psychopathology, whereas protective factors ameliorate against this process. Poor peer relationships, unstable homes and communities, family history of psychiatric illness, and traumatic events may all be risk factors. Conversely good schools, supportive communities, and integrated healthcare can be protective factors.

As vulnerable children move through their lives, they may experience precipitating factors which heighten risk, especially under particular social, environmental, or biological stress. If this stress resolves, the problematic behaviours may resolve as well because children have a degree of resiliency. But perpetuating factors, such as ongoing familial discord, abuse, or chronic poverty, can push the development or perpetuation of psychiatric disorders.

When behavioural symptoms become evident, it is important to consider what stratum of experience they seem to be emerging from. Has the child changed school, entered into new and problem peer relationships, or has the family encountered a loss in some way? These are environmental and familial changes which require particular interventions at that level. In contrast, do the experiences appear to come from the individual child? Is the child having recurrent nightmares, reporting fears and anxiety which seem disproportionate to the circumstance, and indicating recurrent thoughts of prior abuse or trauma? These experiences seem to come more from the individual stratum and need interventions at that level. Is the child having experiences that cross these boundaries and may need integrated interventions at multiple strata of experience? Finally, if symptoms are evident, it is extremely valuable to obtain consultation early in the process rather than wait until the symptoms escalate. Early interventions have consistently shown better outcomes than later ones. This is to be expected and holds true for almost any illness or pathology.

Addressing the needs of vulnerable and underserved children requires us to reconsider the current structure of care. Only by taking a comprehensive approach, which includes attention to children within their particular context, and utilizing multiple methods of intervention, can we hope to begin to intervene meaningfully in their lives.

References

Aichhorn, A. (1935) *Wayward Youth*. New York, NY: Viking Press.

Auerswald, C.L., Sugano, E., Ellen, J.M. and Klausner, J.D. (2006) 'Street-based STD testing and treatment of homeless youth are feasible, acceptable and effective'. *Journal of Adolescent Health 38*, 208–212.

Bass, S., Shields, M.K. and Behrman, R.E. (2004) 'Children, families, and foster care: Analysis and recommendations.' *Future of Children 14,* 5–29.

Blair, R.J., Coccaro, E.F., Connor, D.F., Ferziger, R., Hutchinson, J., Karnik, N.S., Leibenluft, E., Swann A.C. and Steiner H. (under review) 'Juvenile Maladaptive Aggression: A Review of the Neuroscientific Data.' Working Paper of the AACAP/Stanford/Howard Taskforce on Juvenile Impulsivity and Aggression.

Booth, R.E., Zhang, Y., and Kwiatkowski C.F. (1999) 'The challenge of changing drug and sex risk behaviours of runaway and homeless adolescents.' *Child Abuse and Neglect 23,* 1295–1306.

Borduin, C.M. (1999) 'Multisystemic treatment of criminality and violence in adolescents.' *Journal of the American Academy of Child and Adolescent Psychiatry 38,* 242–249.

Burns, B.J., Phillips, S.D., Wagner, H.R., Barth, R.P., Kolko, D.J. Campbell Y., and Landsverk, J. (2004) 'Mental health need and access to mental health services by youths involved with child welfare: A national survey.' *Journal of the American Academy of Child and Adolescent Psychiatry 43,* 960–970.

Calhoun, D., Dodge, A.C., Journel, C.S. and Zahnd, E. (2005) 'The supply and demand for guns to juveniles: Oakland's gun tracing project.' *Journal of Urban Health 82,* 552–559.

Carrion, V.G. and Steiner, H. (2000) 'Trauma and dissociation in delinquent adolescents.' *Journal of the American Academy of Child and Adolescent Psychiatry 39,* 353–359.

Chamberlain, P. and Reid, J.B. (1998) 'Comparison of two community alternatives to incarceration for chronic juvenile offenders.' *Journal of Consulting and Clinical Psychology 66,* 624–633.

Chamberlain, P. and Weinrott, M. (1990) 'Specialized foster care: Treating seriously emotionally disturbed children.' *Child Today 19,* 24–27.

Children's Defense Fund (2005) *The State of America's Children. Child Welfare: Poverty and Families in Crisis.* Washington, DC: Children's Defense Fund.

Cicchetti, D. and Cohen, D.J. (2006) *Developmental Psychopathology.* Hoboken, NJ: John Wiley & Sons.

Connor, D.F., Carlson, G.A., Chang, K.D., Daniolos, P.T., Ferziger, R., Findling, R.L., Hutchinson, J.G., Malone, R.P., Halperin, J.M., Plattner, B., Post, R.M., Reynolds, D.L., Rogers, K.M., Saxena, K. and Steiner, H. (2006) 'Juvenile maladaptive aggression: A review of prevention, treatment, and service configuration and a proposed research agenda.' *Journal of Clinical Psychiatry 67,* 808–820.

Courtney, M.E. and Dworsky, A. (2005) *Midwest Evaluation of the Adult Functioning of Former Foster Youth: Outcomes at age 19 (executive summary).* Chicago, IL: Chapin Hall Center for Children at the University of Chicago.

Courtney, M.E. and Heuring, D.H. (2005) 'The transition to adulthood for youth "aging out" of the foster care system.' In D. Osgood, E. Foster, C. Flanagan and G. Ruth (eds) *On your Own Without a Net: The Transition to Adulthood for Vulnerable Populations.* Chicago, IL: University of Chicago Press.

Curtis, N.M., Ronan, K.R. and Borduin, C.M. (2004) 'Multisystemic treatment: A meta-analysis of outcome studies.' *Journal of Family Psychology 18,* 411–419.

Eddy, J.M. and Chamberlain, P. (2000) 'Family management and deviant peer association as mediators of the impact of treatment condition on youth antisocial behaviour.' *Journal of Consulting and Clinical Psychology 68,* 857–863.

Edsall, S., Karnik, N.S. and Steiner, H. (2005) 'Childhood trauma.' In W. Klykylo and J. Kay (eds) *Clinical Child Psychiatry,* (2nd ed). Chichester: John Wiley & Sons.

Eheart, B.K., Hopping, D., Power M.B. and Racine, D. (2006) *Intergenerational Community as Intervention: White Paper.* Rantoul, Illinois: Generations of Hope.

Ensign, J. and Gittelsohn, J. (1998) 'Health and access to care: perspectives of homeless youth in Baltimore City, USA.' *Social Science and Medicine 47,* 2087–2099.

Ensign, J. and Panke, A. (2002) 'Barriers and bridges to care: Voices of homeless female adolescent youth in Seattle, Washington, USA.' *Journal of Advanced Nursing 37,* 166–172.

Findling, R.L., Steiner, H. and Weller, E.B. (2005) 'Use of antipsychotics in children and adolescents.' *Journal of Clinical Psychiatry 66*, Suppl. 7, 29–40.

Ginzler, J. A., B. N. Cochran, M. Domenech-Rodriguez, A. M. Cauce and L. B. Whitbeck (2003) 'Sequential progression of substance use among homeless youth: An empirical investigation of the gateway theory.' *Substance Use and Misuse 38*, 725–758.

Gleghorn, A.A., Marx, R., Vittinghoff, E. and Katz, M.H. (1998) 'Association between drug use patterns and HIV risks among homeless, runaway, and street youth in northern California.' *Drug and Alcohol Dependence 51*, 219–227.

Goleman, D. (2006) *Social Intelligence : The New Science of Human Relationships.* New York, NY: Random House.

Hahn, R.A., Bilukha, O., Crosby, A., Fullilove, M.T., Liberman, A., Moscicki, E., Snyder, S., Tuma, F. and Briss, P.A. (2005) 'Firearms laws and the reduction of violence: A systematic review.' *American Journal of Preventive Medicine 28*, Suppl. 1, 40–71.

Karnik, N.S. (2004) 'The social environment.' In H. Steiner (ed.) *Handbook of Mental Health Interventions in Children and Adolescents: An Integrated Developmental Perspective.* San Francisco, CA: Jossey-Bass.

Karnik, N. and Steiner, H. (2005) 'Disruptive behaviour disorders.' In W. Klykylo and J. Kay (eds) *Clinical Child Psychiatry*, (2nd ed). Chichester: John Wiley & Sons.

Karnik, N.S., McMullin, M.A. and Steiner, H. (2006) 'Disruptive behaviours: conduct and oppositional disorders in adolescents.' *Adolescent Medicine Clinics 17*, 97–114.

Khanzode, L.A., Saxena, K., Kraemer, H., Chang, K. and Steiner, H. (2006) 'Efficacy profiles of psychopharmacology: Divalproex sodium in conduct disorder.' *Child Psychiatry and Human Development 37*, 55–64.

Kipke, M.D., O'Connor, S., Palmer, R., and MacKenzie, R.G. (1995) 'Street youth in Los Angeles: Profile of a group at high risk for human immunodeficiency virus infection.' *Archives of Pediatrics and Adolescent Medicine 149*, 513–519.

Kral, A.H., Molnar B.E., Booth, R.E., and Watters J.K. (1997) 'Prevalence of sexual risk behaviour and substance use among runaway and homeless adolescents in San Francisco, Denver and New York City.' *International Journal of STD and AIDS 8*, 109–117.

Leve, L.D., Chamberlain, P., and Reid, J.B. (2005) 'Intervention outcomes for girls referred from juvenile justice: Effects on delinquency.' *Journal of Consulting and Clinical Psychology 73*, 1181–1185.

Liddle, H.A., Dakof, G.A., Parker, K., Diamond, G.S., Barrett, K. and Tejeda, M. (2001) 'Multidimensional family therapy for adolescent drug abuse: Results of a randomized clinical trial.' *American Journal of Drug and Alcohol Abuse 27*, 651–688.

Littell, J.H., Popa, M. and Forsythe, B. (2005) 'Multisystemic therapy for social, emotional, and behavioural problems in youth aged 10–17.' *Cochrane Database Systematic Review 4*, CD004797.

Lochman, J.E. (1992) 'Cognitive-behavioural intervention with aggressive boys: Three-year follow-up and preventive effects.' *Journal of Consulting and Clinical Psychology 60*, 426–432.

Lyons, J.S., and Rogers, L. (2004) 'The US Child Welfare System: A de facto public behavioural health care system.' *Journal of the American Academy of Child and Adolescent Psychiatry 43*, 971–973.

Molnar, B.E., Shade, S.B., Kral, A.H., Booth, R.E. and Watters, J.K. (1998) 'Suicidal behaviour and sexual/physical abuse among street youth.' *Child Abuse and Neglect 22*, 213–222.

Murray, C.J.L., Kulkarni, S.C., Michaud, C., Tomijima, N., Bulzacchelli, M.T., Iandiorio, T.J. and Ezzati, M. (2006) 'Eight Americas: Investigating mortality disparities across races, counties, and race-counties in the United States.' *PLOS Medicine 3*, e260.

Pappadopulos, E., Macintyre Ii, J.C., Crismon, M.L., Findling, R.L., Malone, R.P., Derivan, A., Schooler, N., Sikich, L., Greenhill, L., Schur, S.B., Felton, C.J., Kranzler, H., Rube, D.M., Sverd, J., Finnerty, M., Ketner, S., Siennick, S.E., and Jensen, P.S. (2003) 'Treatment recommendations for the use of antipsychotics for aggressive youth (TRAAY) Part II.' *Journal of the American Academy of Child and Adolescent Psychiatry 42*, 145–161.

Plattner, B., Silvermann, M.A., Redlich, A.D., Carrion, V.G., Feucht, M., Friedrich, M.H. and Steiner, H. (2003) 'Pathways to dissociation: Intrafamilial versus extrafamilial trauma in juvenile delinquents.' *Journal of Nervous and Mental Disease 191*, 781–788.

Plattner, B. and Steiner, H. (2005) Prevalence of Psychopathology among Incarcerated Juveniles in Vienna, Austria. Stanford University Department of Psychiatry Grand Rounds Presentation, 13 October 2005, unpublished.

Power, M.B. and Eheart, B.K. (2001) 'Reflections.' *Children and Youth Services Review 23*, 805–810.

Rana, M., Khanzode, L., Karnik, N., Saxena, K., Chang, K. and Steiner, H. (2005) 'Divalproex sodium in the treatment of pediatric psychiatric disorders.' *Expert Review in Neurotherapeutics 5*, 165–176.

Rew, L. (2001) 'Sexual health practices of homeless youth: a model for intervention.' *Issues in Comprehensive Pediatric Nursing 24*, 1–18.

Reynolds, A.J., Chang, H. and Temple, J.A. (1998) 'Early childhood intervention and juvenile delinquency. An exploratory analysis of the Chicago Child-Parent Centers.' *Evaluation Review 22*, 341–372.

Reynolds, A.J., Ou, S.R. and Topitzes, J.W. (2004) 'Paths of effects of early childhood intervention on educational attainment and delinquency: A confirmatory analysis of the Chicago Child-Parent Centers.' *Child Development 75*, 1299–1328.

Reynolds, A.J., Temple, J.A. and Ou, S.R. (2003) 'School-based early intervention and child well-being in the Chicago Longitudinal Study.' *Child Welfare 82*, 633–656.

Rotheram-Borus, M.J., Song, J., Gwadz, M., Lee, M., Van Rossem, R. and Koopman, C. (2003) 'Reductions in HIV risk among runaway youth.' *Prevention Science 4*, 173–187.

Ruchkin, V., Sukhodolsky, D.G., Vermeiren, R., Koposov, R.A. and Schwab-Stone, M. (2006) 'Depressive symptoms and associated psychopathology in urban adolescents: A cross-cultural study of three countries.' *Journal of Nervous and Mental Disease 194*, 106–113.

Runyan, C.W., Gunther-Mohr, C., Orton, S., Umble, K., Martin, S.L. and Coyne-Beasley, T. (2005) 'PREVENT: A programmeme of the National Training Initiative on Injury and Violence Prevention.' *American Journal of Preventive Medicine 29*, Suppl. 2, 252–258.

Saxena, K., Silverman, M.A., Chang, K., Khanzode, L. and Steiner, H. (2005) 'Baseline predictors of response to divalproex in conduct disorder.' *Journal of Clinical Psychiatry 66*, 1541–1548.

Schaeffer, C.M. and Borduin, C.M. (2005) 'Long-term follow-up to a randomized clinical trial of multisystemic therapy with serious and violent juvenile offenders.' *Journal of Consulting and Clinical Psychology 73*, 445–453.

Schur, S.B., Sikich, L., Findling, R.L., Malone, R.P., Crismon, M.L., Derivan, A., Macintyre Ii, J.C., Pappadopulos, E., Greenhill, L., Schooler, N., Van Orden, K. and Jensen, P.S. (2003) 'Treatment recommendations for the use of antipsychotics for aggressive youth (TRAAY) Part I: A review.' *Journal of the American Academy of Child and Adolescent Psychiatry 42*, 132–144.

Shonkoff, J.P., Phillips, D. and National Research Council (US) Committee on Integrating the Science of Early Childhood Development (2000) *From Neurons to Neighborhoods : The Science of Early Child Development.* Washington, DC: National Academy Press.

Sloan, J.H., Kellermann, A.L., Reay, D.T., Ferris, J.A., Koepsell, T., Rivara, F.P., Rice, C., Gray, L. and LoGerfo, J. (1988) 'Handgun regulations, crime, assaults, and homicide: A tale of two cities.' *New England Journal of Medicine 319*, 1256–1262.

Sloan, J.H., Rivara, F.P., Reay, D.T., Ferris, J.A. and Kellermann, A.L. (1990) 'Firearm regulations and rates of suicide: A comparison of two metropolitan areas.' *New England Journal of Medicine 322*, 369–373.

Soller, M.V., Karnik, N.S. and Steiner, H. (2006) 'Psychopharmacologic treatment in juvenile offenders.' *Child and Adolescent Psychiatry Clinics of North America 15*, 477–499.

Spergel, I.A. and Grossman, S.F. (1997) 'The Little Village Project: A community approach to the gang problem.' *Social Work 42*, 456–470.

Steele, R.W., Ramgoolam, A. and Evans, J. Jr. (2003) 'Health services for homeless adolescents.' *Seminars in Pediatrics Infectious Diseases 14*, 38–42.

Steiner, H. (1997) 'Practice parameters for the assessment and treatment of children and adolescents with conduct disorder.' *Journal of the American Academy of Child and Adolescent Psychiatry 36*, Suppl., 122S–139S.

Steiner, H. (2004) *Handbook of Mental Health Interventions in Children and Adolescents: An Integrated Developmental Approach.* San Francisco, CA, Jossey-Bass.

Steiner, H. and Dunne, J.E. (1997) 'Summary of the practice parameters for the assessment and treatment of children and adolescents with conduct disorder.' *Journal of the American Academy of Child and Adolescent Psychiatry 36*, 1482–1485.

Steiner, H. and Karnik, N.S. (2006) 'New approaches to juvenile delinquency: psychopathology, development, and neuroscience.' *Psychiatric Times*, 15–17.

Steiner, H., Garcia, I.G. and Matthews, Z. (1997) 'Posttraumatic stress disorder in incarcerated juvenile delinquents.' *Journal of the American Academy of Child and Adolescent Psychiatry 36*, 357–365.

Steiner, H., Karnik, N.S., Plattner, B., Silverman, M. and Shaw, R. (2006) 'Neue ansätze zur jugenddelinquenz : Neurowissenschaften und entwicklungspsychiatrie.' In H. Steinhausen and C. Bessler (eds) *Juggenddelinquenz.* Stuttgart: Kohlhammer.

Steiner, H., Petersen, M.L., Saxena, K., Ford, S. and Matthews, Z. (2003) 'Divalproex sodium for the treatment of conduct disorder: A randomized controlled clinical trial.' *Journal of Clinical Psychiatry 64*, 1183–1191.

Steiner, H., Remsing, L. and Work Group on Quality Issues. (2007) 'Practice Parameter for the Assessment and Treatment of Children and Adolescents with Oppositional Defiant Disorder.' *Journal of the American Academy of Child & Adolescent Psychiatry 46*, 126–41.

Task Force on Community Preventive Services (2005) 'Recommendations to reduce violence through early childhood home visitation, therapeutic foster care, and firearms laws.' *American Journal of Preventive Medicine 28*, Suppl. 1, 6–10.

Trupin, E.W., Stewart, D.G., Beach, B. and Boesky, L. (2002) 'Effectiveness of a dialectical behaviour therapy programme for incarcerated female juvenile offenders.' *Child and Adolescent Mental Health 7*, 121–127.

Zima, B.T., Wells, K.B., Benjamin, B. and Duan, N. (1996) 'Mental health problems among homeless mothers: Relationship to service use and child mental health problems.' *Archives of General Psychiatry 53*, 332–338.

Zinn, A., DeCoursey, J., George, R. and Courtney, M. (2006) *A Study of Placement Stability in Illinois.* Chapin Hall Working Paper. Chicago, IL: Chapin Hall Center for Children at the University of Chicago.

Zun, L.S., Downey, L. and Rosen, J. (2006) 'The effectiveness of an ED-based violence prevention programme.' *American Journal of Emergency Medicine 24*, 8–13.

CHAPTER 18

Service Models and Policies in European Countries

Vaya Papageorgiou

Children and young people with good mental health are able to achieve and maintain optimal psychological and social functioning and quality of life. However, the importance of good mental health of this population is not acknowledged universally and young people still represent a population at risk (Wahlbeck 2006). Up to 20 per cent of children and adolescents all over the world are suffering from mental health disorders (WHO 2003), and suicide is the third leading cause of death among adolescents. Moreover, major depressive disorder often has an onset in adolescence and it is associated with substantial social impairment (Weissman *et al.* 1999).

Today, the increasing number of issues and risk factors make attainment of adequate child mental health extremely difficult. Different risk factors, such as poverty, exposure to domestic violence, community and political violence, exposure to accidents, homelessness, and involvement in criminal acts, all affect the overall functioning and threaten the lives of millions of children worldwide each year (Bagchi and Hafez 1995).

Mental health pathology contributes greatly in terms of both death and burden of disease (Shatkin and Belfer 2005; Vostanis 2004). In young people, the burden associated with mental disorders is considerable, and it is made worse by stigma and discrimination. It is acknowledged today that the health sector alone in most cases is a helpless spectator. Children and young people who are at increased risk of developing mental health disorders need a specifically designed network of services. The development of child and adolescent mental health services needs a national policy reflecting the concerns of the population too. National policy is essential for planning, and for developing a national service system consistent with concepts of continuity of care and provision of effective interventions. The absence of policy is a barrier to the development of coherent systems of mental healthcare for children and adolescents, and leads to fragmentation of services and inefficient utilization of resources (WHO 2005).

Today, no country in the world has a clearly defined mental health policy for children and adolescents (Shatkin and Belfer 2005), although the rights of this population, concerning physical and mental health, have been acknowledged by the World Health Organization (WHO) (WHO 1977), the United Nations Convention on the Rights of the Child (UN General Assembly 1989), and the International Association for Child and Adolescent Psychiatry and Allied Professions (IACAPAP 1992). A recent investigation of specific policies for child and adolescent mental health has revealed that across Europe, very few countries have national policies and/or plans focused on the unique mental health problems of this population. Among these countries are the Czech Republic, Denmark, France, Germany, Ireland, the Netherlands, Norway, Portugal, Romania, Serbia /Yugoslavia and the United Kingdom. In other European countries such as Greece, Belgium, and Luxemburg, national policies and/or plans are focused on mental health problems of adults, with some impact upon the mental health of children and adolescents. National policies or plans recognizing the unique mental health problems of children and adolescents have been developed in some countries such as Lithuania, Russia, Slovakia, and Spain, but they do not have a unifying plan of action (Shatkin and Belfer 2005).

This chapter is focused on policies and service models in European countries for specific groups of vulnerable children and adolescents who are at increased risk of developing mental health problems, and are in need of appropriate interventions and services. Although specific topics concerning these groups of young people have been addressed in detail by previous chapters, the aim here is to concentrate and synthesize issues and emerging evidence from policies and research across Europe.

The situation in european countries
Child abuse and neglect

Despite countries' clear human rights obligations to protect all children from all forms of violence, child abuse, and neglect, it is a widespread international problem associated with a variety of negative outcomes. Many abused children suffer from severe and long-lasting emotional and behavioural difficulties, which require specific therapeutic interventions (McMahom and Puett 1999).

Child abuse and neglect is a public health priority, and needs to be considered in the context of contemporary society. Violence against children is least visible and least acknowledged within their families. The family home is the place where violence against children is most prevalent, at least against younger children. Today there are more children in single-parent families who are living in neighbourhoods which are deteriorating and unable to provide support and child care, thus placing further stress on already financially stressed families. Family life is changing dramatically in other ways as well. There is an increase in the rates of divorce and the establishment of new, blended, and extended families, which may be difficult for some parents to cope with.

There are many questions concerning prevention, protection policies, services, and practice in the field of child abuse all over the world. States are obliged to recognize and protect all children from all forms of violence, and to support parenting and consequently, to build an effective protective environment for the child within the family, and to safeguard the child from violence and exploitation outside the family.

The recent WHO initiative on the prevention of child abuse expressed concerns about the lack of community services to uphold the child's right to grow up in a family environment. Furthermore, whilst the number of fostered children is increasing, this is not followed by increase in the number of foster parents (Alpert and Eineen 1992). National child protection policies and legal procedures to rescue children from abuse, neglect, and abandonment have sometimes developed piecemeal strategies for the prevention of abuse and alternative family based care. Thus, in some countries, not enough surrogate family placements are available, so that children may be placed in institutions for long periods. Reports on the *World Perspectives on Child Abuse* between 1998 and 2004 show that in Europe, 38 of the 52 countries have child protection services. However, an EU/WHO survey of official government statistics showed that 43, 842 children aged under three years resided in institutional care within 46 countries (Browne *et al.* 2005; Browne *et al.* 2006).

In different European countries, the child protection system does not have adequate resources to deal with the complex needs of abused children. Other problems, such as the lack of co-ordination at all levels and the deficit of trained professionals, place more strain on an already weakened system. Mental health practitioners working in the area of abuse and neglect have many questions concerning policy statements and guidelines. Our systems need improvement. Abuse cases necessitate the interface of several systems, judicial, social services, and mental health, which hold different methods, objectives, and perspectives. Frequently, these systems are in conflict and conceptualize treatment differently. Their complexity must be taken into account in planning services for prevention and management of children who are victims of abuse and neglect. Every attempt should be made to include professionals, local leaders, and policy-makers when organizing and planning services.

Residential care

Earlier research in the countries of the European Union (EU) that focused on residential and foster care, as well as on their alternatives for young people in need, has revealed some common trends in policy and practice. It was found that, across Europe, there has been a decline of residential child care. Policies were focused on the growth of foster care, whilst residential institutions were becoming the last resort in most European countries. The development of smaller living units was uneven in some countries. The tendency across Europe was to provide temporary, rather than long-term care, with the aim for the child to return home as soon as possible (Colton and Hellinckx 1994).

In some countries, such as Germany and Ireland, small-scale specialized facilities for children and young people with severe behavioural difficulties have been developed, whilst the number of care workers and the level of their training have increased (Colla-Muller 1993). However, the quality of training differed across countries and some countries have made less progress. In Greece, insufficient numbers of staff have been recruited to the state child-care centres, owing to economic constraints and the low political priority given to child care and protection (Agathonos-Georgopoulou 1993). In general, the trends and development have been more advanced in northern rather than southern countries.

A new type of therapeutic or 'specialist' foster care has been developed, with emphasis on greater professionalism in relation to residential care. In western Europe, it has been found that an estimated 0.2–1 per cent of all looked-after children live in foster families or in residential centres (Hukkanen et al. 1998). In the UK, there are currently 41,000 children in family foster care at any one time, with high rates of mental health problems. These have been considered as a high risk population, and it has been suggested that standard child and adolescent mental health (CAMH) services may not be able to address their complex needs (Minnis et al. 2006).

Awareness of the mental health problems of children in care has increased during the last decades throughout Europe. However, the availability of child and adolescent mental health services is limited, and children from multi-problem families often end up in social sector services, even though their mental health problems would need assessment in child or adolescent psychiatric units (Hukkanen et al. 1998). Countries with undeveloped community health and social services are more likely to have higher proportions of institutionalized children.

Although important changes have been made in Europe during the past decade, a recent survey reported overuse of institutional care for young children in need, with and without disabilities (Browne et al. 2005). This form of care for young children is common across the European region, and the overall rate of institutionalization of children aged under three years is 14.4/10,000 (Browne et *al.* 2006). In countries with a high proportion of young children in institutional care, such as Bulgaria, Belgium, and Romania, the development of therapeutic foster care and rehabilitation services is a priority to prevent adverse effects on young people. Training for policy-makers and practitioners on the appropriate care and placement of young children in adversity, and child protection legislation and interventions to deal with abusive and neglectful parents should be developed in all countries in Europe, in parallel with community services and alternative family-based care for children in need (Browne *et al.* 2006).

Immigrants, refugees, and asylum-seekers

In the second half of the past century, Europe changed from an area of emigration into an area of immigration and it has also witnessed an unprecedented inflow of asylum-seekers, mainly from developing countries (Bollini 1997; Muus, 2001). Individuals from problem areas all over the world started to apply for asylum in European countries. This growing trend has been accepted with increasing uneasiness by local populations, especially in a period of rising unemployment and economic hardship (Bollini 1997). Some countries such as Greece were totally unprepared to receive immigrants. Until the 1990s, Greece was a homogeneous society. Since 1990 there has been an inflow of economic refugees and immigrants, mostly from the countries of Central and Eastern Europe. Neither the relevant legislation nor the required social structure and institutions existed (Spinellis and Spinellis 1999) to cope with this. The need for the migration and asylum policies in countries of the EU was necessary after the abolition of internal borders controls, and such attempts have since been made by different EU countries (Kiprianos, Balias and Passas 2003; Muus 2001).

Among refugees and asylum-seekers, physical as well as mental health problems are highly prevalent. Population-based studies on adult refugees and asylum-seekers living in Western countries have reported high prevalence of mental health problems, which mainly concern symptoms of post-traumatic stress disorder (PTSD), depression, and anxiety (Gerritsen *et al.* 2006).

A number of specialized institutions have been created in Europe with the aim of providing interventions to victims of violence, and to ensure proper documentation of torture or ill treatment to support asylum applications. However, it is estimated that the need for adequate treatment, especially of a psychological nature, is far greater than available resources allow (Bollini 1997). In Switzerland, a major difficulty reported by general practitioners was the high diversity of the population of asylum-seekers in respect to place of origin, education and language. The Netherlands and Norway have adopted a clear government policy aimed at transferring the expertise of institutions specialized in the care of victims of organized violence to the regular healthcare sector, by informing general practitioners and primary healthcare workers of the specific health problems of asylum-seekers housed in their municipalities, and providing assistance and advice. In other European countries, expertise on the health consequences of organized violence is concentrated in specialized institutions, without much communication with the regular health sector (Bollini 1997).

Most European countries do not provide comprehensive healthcare for asylum-seekers, with the exception of the UK, where healthcare provided to this population is equivalent to that afforded to British nationals. Some countries limit treatment to cases of acute illness, thereby constituting another striking example of a policy directed at short-term 'survival' instead of long-term care and integration. Thus, reception policies follow different goals than welfare policies (Bank 2000).

In Greece, policies towards immigration and asylum-seeking have been characterized by dilemmas and hesitations of the population concerning the possibility that the immigrants could, in the long term, create problems of national integration. Like other members of the EU, the Greek authorities have tried twice to legalize the previously unauthorized immigrants, and it seems that this is beneficial for both immigrants and Greeks. Since the mid-1990s, there has been a highly visible increase in the number of immigrant children recorded in state schools (Kiprianos *et al.* 2003).

Child refugees are facing a multitude of adversities when seeking protection against violations of their human rights. As children, they have the same vulnerabilities and requirements for special consideration as the general population. As refugees, they have additional experiences and complex needs (Nykanen 2001). The Children's Convention sets forth a legal framework for addressing the concerns of children, including those who are refugees. Despite measures already taken to meet the particular needs of refugee children, considerable work still remains to be done. The gap between the real life of thousands and thousands of child refugees and the legal recognition of their needs is still too long. The Refugee Convention, which applies in principle to all refugees irrespective of their age, has, however, proved inadequate in meeting the needs of child refugees (Nykanen 2001). According to the constitution of the WHO, every person has the right to the highest attainable level of physical and mental health (WHO 2005). The evidence available so far, although not conclusive, indicates that the basic right to health of refugees and asylum-seekers may not be assured in a number of European countries.

Homeless children

Homelessness is an enormous problem in many countries worldwide. It may be seen as an extreme end on a continuum of poverty and residential instability, with the contribution of personal and social factors. The population of homeless children and their families is heterogeneous. Most of them are mothers with young children, whilst adolescents have also been shown to be vulnerable to homelessness. Most children within homeless families, and adolescents who are single homeless, come from poor backgrounds, characterized by domestic violence, relationship breakdown, and neighbourhood harassment (Haber and Toro 2004).

Another group of homeless children, referred to as 'street children', have early adverse life experiences and spend most of their time in the streets. A variety of circumstances such as family breakdown, unemployment, poverty, and abusive background are leading these children and young people to street life. They are either orphaned, abandoned, or have run away from their families. The street has become their home and they use it as the main place of their main daily activities (Altanis and Goddard 2004).

A large-scale study in the UK estimated that 129,000 young people under the age of 16 are running away from their families each year. In Germany, the number of children under 14 years of age living in the streets was in the mid-1990s between 1000 and 2500. Governmental sources estimated the number of street children at 5000 to 7000 (Busch-Geertsema 1996). In the mid-1990s in Greece, the number of children working at traffic lights was about 3500, whereas in 1999 more than 348 children between seven and 18 years of age presented for trial at the Athens Juvenile Court for begging (Altanis and Goddard 2004).

A large body of research confirms the impact of homelessness on children's socio-emotional development (Haber and Toro 2004; Vostanis and Cumella 1999). Increased morbidity among poor and homeless children has been found for psychiatric disorders, as well as academic, health and social problems (Lipman, Hord and Boyle 1996). Children manifest behavioural and emotional problems, general health problems and injuries, learning disabilities, and abuse, while their parents are at high risk for depression and substance misuse (Vostanis and Cumella 1999; Tischler *et al.* 2004). Prevalence rates among homeless adolescents are higher that those found in matched housed groups or the general population. They are at elevated risk for mood disorders and suicide attempts, and often have disrupted families and interrupted or difficult school histories (Cauce *et al.* 2000). Access and use of services through the usual referral routes are limited for homeless children and their families (Tischler *et al.* 2004).

Although a large body of research, especially from the UK and North America, has focused on the needs of homeless children and their families, little research has been conducted on effective interventions and service models (Anderson, Stuttaford and Vostanis 2006; Tischler *et al.* 2004). The impact of homelessness on the children's lives has received limited attention from policy-makers, and homelessness has been seen mainly as a housing problem (Vostanis and Cumelia 1999). In the UK, homelessness policy guarantees temporary housing for families with young children (Gaubatz 2001).

However, homeless families almost always experience significant problems that extend far beyond a lack of decent housing. Homelessness is clearly a complex issue which requires varied policy responses. The rapidly increasing number of homeless families and young people supports the need for culturally sensitive support for families. There is a need for effective mental health interventions as a component of comprehensive and co-ordinated services that can offer homeless families a way out of homelessness, and even out of poverty. There is a need for strategic responsibility from both health and housing organizations to ensure the implementation of such policies.

Young people who offend

Young offenders and appropriate forms of justice and treatment have been for many years the subject of great interest, controversy, and debate internationally. On the one hand, is the concern over children's rights, their well-being, and development, and, on the other, is the perception that young people who offend are given too much attention at the expense of victims and society. Different sources consistently point out that offending among juveniles presents a massive increase during the last decade, with rising similar trends in most European countries (Killias et al. 2004; Papageorgiou and Vostanis 1999). This trend has been attributed to the increase in the actual number of offences, or to changes in registration of offences and intervention practices (Komen 2002).

Across most European countries, children and young people who offend are considered to be developing individuals in need of psycho-educational support. In Scotland, young people who offend are dealt within an integrated system dealing also with young people in need of care and protection, based on the assumption that the difficulties of both groups have similar roots in multiple disadvantage and social adversity (Whyte 2004). In France, the legal jurisdiction for minors is focused on transforming young people, rather than punishing them. Judges are not only responsible for administering the law, they are also charged with promoting the youth's development and/or rehabilitation. The legal system for youth is a specialized approach which includes dealing with young offenders in similar ways as dealing with other youth at risk. For many years, the role of juvenile justice has been based on supporting young offenders in the same manner as they do for youth in care, by protecting them (Blatier 2000). However, with the increase in juvenile delinquency during the last decade, changes in the legal system have been promoted in favour of stiffer sentences and incarceration for juvenile offenders.

Similar trends characterize the Dutch juvenile justice, which is part of a broader welfare system. Judicial intervention may lead to forced use of psychosocial assistance and welfare institutions for juveniles and their families. Juvenile delinquency in the Netherlands has become more serious in recent decades. The law provides for intervention 'in the best interest of the child', and juvenile court officials want to punish less and help more. The wants and the needs of the children and their parents are carefully considered, and joint consultation is a regular aspect of the process (Komen 2002).

In Greece, the minimum age of criminal responsibility is 12 years. Younger children below six years of age are not subjected to Penal Law regulations. From seven to 12 years, they are not considered criminally liable, and they are only subjected to educational or therapeutic measures. Such measures are applied in the case of minors who suffer from certain types of mental or physical illness, or are drug addicts who commit an offence. Adolescents between 13 and 17 years of age do not have criminal responsibility either. However, they can be considered by the court as criminally liable under certain conditions (Spinellis and Spinellis 1999). A penalty of confinement in a correctional institution for adolescents may be imposed to a minor 13–17 years of age, if the court finds, from the circumstances under which the offence was committed and the personality of the perpetrator, that such a penalty is necessary to deter them from the commission of further offences (Pitsela 2000). Nowadays, Greece is meeting new challenges with initiatives stimulated by European or international conventions, and the criminal justice system is undergoing consecutive legislative and structural changes (Spinellis and Spinellis 1999).

Crime rates and processing structures in the former socialist countries display considerable similarities not only in the criminality structures, but also in the 'filtering processes' of these legal systems. However, there are also several differences between these legal systems and those of Western countries. In the West, the large number of suspects is reduced considerably during the later stages of selection to a much smaller number. In the East, a smaller number of suspected offenders enters this process, but tends to remain within it and be sentenced. This could be considered a specific type of criminal justice system (Neubacher *et al.* 1999).

Today there is a growing awareness that young people who offend are at increased risk for psychosocial and health needs. These include mental health problems, increased levels of substance use, poor educational outcomes, and general health problems (Carswell *et al.* 2004; Cocozza and Skowyra 2000). However, the right to treatment of young offenders has not received the attention it deserves, and provision of services for these people remains a challenge (Shelton 2005). The move away from residential care for young people in some European countries has not been met with the development of appropriate community-based health services (Bailey 1993).

The difficulties in serving the complex emotional and behavioural problems of these youth, and high costs and questionable effectiveness associated with these services, result in shifting of responsibility between child service systems (Shelton 2001). Young people move between welfare establishments, and very few are referred to CAMH services. Strategies that appear to be critical in ensuring treatment for young offenders include collaboration across systems, diverting offenders from the juvenile justice system, mental health screening and detailed multimodal assessments, and effective community-based alternatives. Youth offending should lie at the heart of policing programmes. The similar trends in most European countries, suggest the need for research in both the reasons behind the rise of offending, and the systems of dealing with young offenders.

Conclusions

Child and adolescent mental health is an essential part of overall well-being (WHO 2002). Today, the magnitude and burden of disease related to child and adolescent mental disorders is understood by clinicians and parents, but less so by policy-makers and politicians. Young people at risk have a need for specialized networks of health, education, and social services, with clear referral pathways. Both developing and developed countries should focus on child and adolescent mental health national policy for the development of systems of care and specialized services for this population. Legislation that may influence the implementation of policy, political commitment, and close collaboration of other sectors along with the health sector are needed in developing national policy, services, and specific interventions for vulnerable children and young people. The problems associated with poor child and adolescent mental health will grow if countries do not address these problems from a national policy perspective.

References

Agathonos-Georgopoulou, H. (1993) 'Greece.' In M.Colton, and W. Hellinckx (eds) *Child Care in the EC.* Aldershot: Arena.

Alpert, J. and Green, D. (1992) 'Child abuse and neglect: perspectives on a national emergency.' *Journal of Social Distress and the Homeless 1,* 223–236.

Altanis, P. and Goddard, J. (2004) 'Street children in contemporary Greece.' *Children and Society 18,* 299–311.

Anderson, L., Stuttaford, M., and Vostanis, P. (2006) 'A family support service for homeless children and parents: user and staff perspectives.' *Child and Family Social Work 11,* 119–127.

Bagchi, K. and Hafez, G. (1995) 'The state of child health in Eastern Mediterranean countries: a need for a fresh look.' *Eastern Mediterranean Health Journal 1,* 35–37.

Bailey, S. (1993) 'Health in young persons' establishments: treating the damaged and preventing harm.' *Criminal Behaviour and Mental Health 3,* 349–367.

Bank, R. (2000) 'Reception conditions for asylum-seekers in Europe.' *Nordic Journal of International Law 69,* 257–88.

Blatier, C. (2000) 'An analysis of legal intervention concerning minors in France.' *Child and Youth Care Forum 29,* 343–352.

Bollini, P. (1997) 'Asylum-seekers in Europe: entitlements, health status, and human rights issues.' *European Journal of Health Law 4*, 253–265.

Browne, K., Hamilton- Giachritsis, C., Johnson, R., Chou, S., Ostergren, M., and Leth, I. (2005) 'European survey of the number and characteristics of children less than three years old in residential care at risk of harm.' *Adoption and Fostering 29*, 23–33.

Browne, K., Hamilton-Giachritsis, C., Johnson, R., and Ostergren, M. (2006) 'Overuse of institutional care for children in Europe.' *British Medical Journal 332*, 485–487.

Busch-Geertsema, V. (1996) *Youth Homelessness in Germany.* Brussels: FEANTSA.

Cauce, A.. Paradise, M., Ginzler, J. Embry, L., Morgan, C., Lohr,Y., and Theofelis,Y. (2000) 'The characteristics and mental health of homeless adolescents: age and gender differences.' *Journal of Emotional and Behavioural Disorders 8*, 230–239.

Carswell, K., Maughan, B., Davis, H., Davenport, F., and Goddard, N. (2004) 'The psychological needs of young offenders and adolescents from an inner city area.' *Journal of Adolescence 27*, 415–428.

Cocozza, J. and Skowyra, K. (2000) 'Youth with mental health disorders: issues and emerging responses.' *Juvenile Justice Journal 7*, 1–5.

Colla-Muller, H. (1993) 'Germany.' In M. Colton, and W. Hellinckx (eds) *Child Care in the EC.* Aldershot: Arena.

Colton, M. and Hellinckx, W. (1994) 'Residential and foster care in the European Community: current trends in policy and practice.' *British Journal of Social Work 24*, 559–576.

Gaubatz, L. (2001) 'Family homelessness in Britain: more that just a housing issue.' *Journal of Children and Poverty 7*, 3–22.

Gerritsen, A., Bramsen, I., Deville, W., Van Willigen, L., Hovens, J., and Ploeg, H. (2006) 'Physical and mental health of Afghan, Iranian and Somali asylum-seekers and refugees living in the Netherlands.' *Social Psychiatry and Psychiatric Epidemiology 4*, 18–26.

Haber, M. and Toro, P. (2004) 'Homelessness among families, children, and adolescents: An ecological-developmental perspective.' *Clinical Child and Family Psychology Review 7*, 123–159.

Hukkanen, R., Nyquist, L., Sourander, A., Holmberg, M. and Donellan, M. (1998) *Care to Listen? Haluatko Kuunnella? Nos Esforzamos por Escuchar?' A Review of Residential Child Care in Four European Countries by the European Association for Research into Residential Child Care.* Glasgow: The Centre for Residential Child Care.

International Association for Child and Adolescent Psychiatry and Allied Professions (IACAPAP) (1992) *Proclamation: Assuring the Mental Health of Children.* 14 May.

Killias, M., Lucia, S., Lamon, P., and Simonin, M. (2004) 'Juvenile delinquency in Switzerland over 50 years: assessing trends beyond statistics.' *European Journal on Criminal Policy and Research 10*, 111–122.

Kiprianos, P., Balias, S ., and Passas, V. (2003) 'Greek policy towards immigration and immigrants.' *Social Policy and Administration 37*, 148–164.

Komen, M. (2002) 'Dangerous children: juvenile delinquency and judicial intervention in the Netherlands, 1960-1995.' *Crime, Law and Social Change 37*, 379–401.

Lipman, E.L. Offord, D., and Boyle, M. (1996) 'What if we could eliminate child poverty? The theoretical effect on child psychosocial morbidity.' *Social Psychiatry and Psychiatric Epidemiology 31, 303–307.*

McMahom, P., and Puett, R. (1999) 'Child sexual abuse as a public health issue: recommendations of an expert panel.' *Sexual Abuse: A Journal of Research and Treatment 11*, 257–267.

Minnis, H., Everett, K., Pelosi, A., Dunn, J., and Knapp, M. (2006) 'Children in foster care: mental health, service use and costs.' *European Child and Adolescent Psychiatry 15*, 63–70.

Muus, P. (2001) 'International migration and the European Union trends and consequences.' *European Journal of Criminal Policy and Research 9*, 31–49.

Neubacher, F., Walter, M., Valkova, H., and Krajewski, K. (1999) 'Juvenile delinquency in central European cities: A comparison of registration and processing structures in the 1990s.' *European Journal of Criminal Policy and Research 7*, 533–558.

Nykanen, E. (2001) 'Protecting children? The European Convention on Human Rights and Child Asylum-seekers.' *European Journal of Migration and Law 3*, 315–345.

Papageorgiou, V., and Vostanis, P. (1999) 'Psychosocial characteristics of Greek young offenders.' *Journal of Forensic Psychiatry 11*, 390–400.

Pitsela, A. (2000) *Penal Code Interventions for Juvenile Delinquency*, (3rd ed). Athens: Sakkoula Publications.

Shatkin, J., and Belfer, M. (2005) 'The global absence of child and adolescent mental health policy.' *Child and Adolescent Mental Health 9*, 104–108.

Shelton, D. (2001) 'Forensic psychiatric care and juvenile justice.' *Psychiatric Nursing Research Digest 1*, 24–28.

Shelton, D. (2005) 'Patterns of treatment services and costs for young offenders with mental disorders.' *Journal of Child and Adolescent Psychiatric Nursing 18*, 103–112.

Spinellis, D., and Spinellis, C. (1999) *Criminal Justice Systems in Europe and North America*. Athens: European Institute for Crime Prevention and Control, affiliated with the United Nations.

Tischler, V., Karim, K., Rustall, S., Gregory, P., and Vostanis, P. (2004) 'A family support service for homeless children and parents: users' perspectives and characteristics.' *Health and Social Care in the Community 12*, 327–335.

United Nations (1989) *The Convention on the Rights of the Child*. Adopted by the UN General Assembly, 20 November.

Vostanis, P. (2004) 'Refugee and asylum-seeking children: are we missing or overstating the impact of trauma?' *Community Care 7*–13 October, p.47.

Vostanis P., and Cumella S.(eds) (1999) *Homeless Children: Problems and Needs*. London: Jessica Kingsley Publishers.

Wahlbeck, K. (2006) 'Europe's mental health strategy.' *British Medical Journal 333*, 210–211.

Weissman, M., Wolk, S., Goldstein, R., Moreua, D., Adams, P., Greenwald, S., Kliev, C., Ryan, N., Dahl, R. and Wickramartne, P. (1999) 'Depressed adolescents grown up.' *JAMA 281*, 1707–1713.

Whyte, B. (2004) 'Responding to youth crime in Scotland.' *British Journal of Social Work 34*, 395–411.

World Health Organization (WHO) (1977) *Paper No. 623*. Geneva: World Health Organization.

World Health Organization (WHO) (2002) *Reducing Risks, Promoting Healthy Life: The World Health Report 2002*. Geneva: World Health Organization.

World Health Organization (WHO) (2003) *Caring for Children with Mental Disorders: Setting WHO Directions*. Geneva: World Health Organization.

World Health Organization (WHO) (2005) *Mental Health Policy and Service Guidance Package: Child and Adolescent Mental Health Policies and Plans*. Geneva: World Health Organization.

CHAPTER 19

Mental Health Interventions and Services for Vulnerable Children and Young People: The Way Forward

Panos Vostanis

Overview of the challenges ahead

Although child mental health, other therapeutic and welfare services always worked with some groups of vulnerable children, predominantly those in public care, recent years have seen substantial changes in attitudes and policies, and an increase in more systematic provision. The reasons for this vary, including: response to rising numbers of groups such as homeless and asylum-seeking families and youth; more culturally diverse societies and communities; societal and political attitudes towards children, mental health, rights to services, and social inclusion; realization of the importance of prevention (e.g. in reducing offending), hence more favourable and targeted policies; the improvement of such services for the general population, which have enabled the development of designated posts and services for vulnerable young groups; a wealth of experience in various therapies that can be applied to these groups; and evidence in certain areas such as the severity and nature of mental health problems, factors that place children at risk but also protect them from developing mental health problems, and how these interact with other needs that are primarily met by social care, educational, and non-statutory agencies.

All these components are essential for interventions and services to continue to improve in the future, and are thus briefly discussed below.

International, national and local policies

Policies on children and young people, or on specific vulnerable population groups, are often followed by funding streams and opportunities for service development. These are important at international, national, or local levels, and should be equally pursued by shifting public perceptions, lobbying central and local governments, and prioritizing services for children who neither fit in nor benefit from traditional models based on life stability. User groups and charities have a particular and powerful role to play. However, such attempts should have a strategic direction of service implementation and an integrated plan with existing services, as discussed in the next section, rather than aim at securing funding for one organization in isolation from other service provision.

Policies are not necessarily prerequisites to good services, but can also be responsive to well set-up and evaluated service initiatives. In other words, we should not always wait for the right legislation, but rather develop innovative services to also influence policy-makers. Policy and legislative opportunities can then be used to 'move up' our services to the next level, with generalizable and sustainable capacity.

Another important point is that policies do not develop evenly across countries. In Western countries with fairly well developed public health and social care systems, one can anticipate policies focusing more on specific vulnerable groups and therapeutic services. In contrast, international frameworks and broader national policies on child welfare, protection, and health, are more likely to make an impact in countries with more centralized and specialist services, and relatively limited resources. In this category, non-governmental bodies maybe the main drivers for provision to children victims of war, those living in orphanages, or street youth.

We also need to remember that, even in Western countries, the announcement of a policy that does not automatically translate to funding or service implementation. Additional steps and mechanisms are essential for such policies to become meaningful to children. Recent examples in the UK highlight this issue. Policies on looked-after children and young offenders led to the release of new and ring-fenced resources, or the re-prioritization of overall resources for child mental health services, that is, had a 'knock-on' effect, albeit sometimes at the expense of generic services. Both groups of policies were followed by setting measurable service objectives and targets for local authorities and child mental health services. However, their process and implementation differed. In the case of looked-after children and, more recently, adopted children and their families, there was no preferred model, with an initial expansion of posts or small teams ('bottom–up' approach), which are just beginning to cluster into service themes. In contrast, there was an initial organizational model for the mental health input to young offenders, through the establishment of inter-agency youth offending teams (YOTs). This was an advantage, although some services subsequently 'stalled' because of a relatively prescriptive 'top–down' nature, which failed to take into account the substantially different cultures of the youth justice and health system. In contrast to looked-after children and young offenders, there has not been similar extent of services for homeless children and young people, with housing departments being asked to provide local strategies, but without guidance or authority on how to resource and implement them in partnership with health agencies, leaving the initiative to either committed organizations or non-statutory agencies.

Developing integrated and sustainable services

The previously discussed vulnerable groups of children and young people have been in some contact over the years with existing mental health and other therapeutic services. However, there is now substantial evidence that the majority of such children in need are unlikely to access and engage with services, unless their characteristics are understood and taken into consideration when care pathways and interventions are set up. This should not lead to a misinterpretation of one of the key messages of this book. In other words, it does not imply that these children should be seen separately from generic mental health and related services, but rather that they should be approached in a different way. Although it is desirable that resources are protected, otherwise pressures from primary and hospital services can take over, this could happen in integration with existing mental health teams that serve a general population sector. Particularly in rural and semi-urban areas, where the numbers of homeless and refugee children, even young offenders or those in public care, are relatively small, the principles discussed previously can also be applied through designated sessions of generic staff – for example, one day per week working 'differently', that is, directly with children's homes, foster carers, or juvenile services. The components of consultation, assessment, applied interventions, and training for inter-agency staff can be provided at a micro-level. In contrast, inner-city areas may justify, but also be able to attract more resources, including a designated team for vulnerable children.

Despite the increasing policies for vulnerable children, many of these services are initially driven by individual interests, and are time-limited. Securing funding through a variety of sources (e.g. from social care or youth justice rather than health streams), requires imaginative approaches, but within a strategic direction and within a local child mental health strategy. Inter-agency partnerships are important in starting such projects, and conditional in these being successfully mainstreamed and sustained. This is where many of similar interesting initiatives collapse, as they continue to be provided by one organization, without joint agreements or consideration of integrated care pathways and services, in the hope that funding will continue indefinitely. This is often not the case, hence the need for an exit strategy from the planning stage.

Small-scale projects can be a realistic way of kick-starting an important service for vulnerable children. However, even a small service should have an underpinning framework, follow a service model, use resources effectively, and strive for ongoing monitoring and evaluation. It is no longer acceptable to start a service and 'see what happens'. Commissioning bodies, including charities, must ensure that the initiatives they support, are on a solid footing. Almost by definition, most non-governmental agencies may be constrained by their structure, short-term resources, and constant response to new policies and types of funding. Even so, service development can remain responsive rather than opportunistic, in dialogue and integrated with current or evolving statutory services. Where therapeutic services develop within the voluntary sector, clinical supervision, ongoing training, and links with specialist services are paramount.

Application of therapeutic interventions

Compared to the previous generations of practitioners, staff working therapeutically with children and young people are now much better equipped and trained to deliver a range of modalities, rather than follow one particular entity. The main types of therapies have evolved from 'pure' schools to active and applied interventions, with different levels to meet children's needs, as appropriate. This gives more treatment choices and does not constrain therapeutic interventions to specialist child mental health services.

However, there is still often lack of clarity on the underpinning framework, objective of therapies, definition of different therapy levels, and provision of training. For example, the perceptions and expectations of counselling, life story work, play therapy, and psychodynamic psychotherapy vary, even among therapists, depending on their theoretical school and preferred approach. Opportunities for brief training can oversimplify the use of therapeutic components, or there can be over-reliance on one modality for historical reasons. All these issues are important, and should be clearly defined and communicated from the outset of working with a child, young person, or their carers.

The key challenge for the further development of interventions for vulnerable children is their *application* to the characteristics and needs of different client groups which, like previously discussed services, may require the modification and adaptation of therapies predominantly designed for and used with relatively stable groups. The old dilemma of 'how stable before starting therapy?' does not have a simple answer. It rather requires making a judgement between depriving children of help when they most need it, or overwhelming them with therapeutic work on their past experiences, when they are unsafe and their immediate life circumstances and placement are at risk. This is an additional reason for offering different levels of interventions that complement each other, and can prepare the child or carers for more in-depth work. Supportive therapy, counselling or cognitive-behavioural interventions can be valuable in enhancing coping strategies, and helping clients gain some understanding of their experiences and behaviours at times of crisis, whilst the young person may be more ready or equipped for psychodynamic psychotherapy at a later stage. Similar parallels exist between family support and family therapy, and between parenting programmes targeting behaviours (social learning model) and those based on an attachment framework that seek an understanding of the impact of trauma on relationships.

Role of preventive programmes

Specific mention should be made of preventive interventions which, on the whole, have not been well developed for children and young people, but which should expand in future years. *Universal* programmes (i.e. to all children) will be important in addressing risk behaviours such as offending and drug use; in enhancing the acceptance and inclusion of certain groups, such as children with disabilities, refugees, and children in public care, by their peer group, mainstream settings (school, youth, leisure services), and the wider community; reducing the stigma of mental illness; and improving children's and carers' help-seeking from informal supports, non-statutory, and specialist mental health services. Such programmes should be aimed at children, young people, parents or carers, practitioners, and the media.

Targeted programmes (secondary prevention) for high-risk groups are, by definition, the most relevant to children discussed in this text. The substantial evidence on the impact of vulnerability and multiple risk factors in the development and continuation of child mental health problems strongly highlights the importance of early recognition of problems and the initiation of interventions before these become entrenched, and perpetuate the cycle of family or placement breakdowns, school exclusion, and youth justice involvement. Mental health services should thus have good links with all systems and agencies predominantly in contact with vulnerable young populations, and these agencies should be well equipped to detect and manage less complex mental health issues from the outset.

Tertiary prevention for those children and young people who have already developed more severe and complex mental health problems and disorders will target a relatively smaller group, but will often require more intensive, co-ordinated, and resourced levels of support and help from different agencies. Despite the evidence of high allocated costs for children and young people with complex needs (for example, adolescents with self-harm, aggressive, and relationship difficulties), there are substantial gaps in the availability of specialized day or residential units that cross over social care, education, and mental health. Policies, funding and standards should be set at central government level for the development and effective use of skilled and well-resourced services which also bridge the transition to young adult life.

Evidence base: need for evaluation of interventions and services

The research literature on vulnerable children presents a mixed picture, which partly reflects the overall child mental health evidence base, and partly the complex issues surrounding practice and services. We now have a substantial body of findings on the extent and nature of mental health problems, their relationship with other types of needs (social, educational, developmental), the impact of risk factors, and children's psychosocial outcomes in later life. In contrast, we know less on what protects children in the face of adversity, which therapeutic interventions are more effective (particularly in real rather than research settings), and which service models are appropriate in therapeutic and cost terms.

In many ways, the difficulties in carrying out research on what works for vulnerable children is constrained by similar complexities as the development of services. Pure research designs, in particular evaluation based on either pharmacological or disorder-targeting trials, have a number of limitations, including the large number of confounding (mediating) variables; frequently changing circumstances in the child's life; the presence of several mental health problems or disorders; their close association with social care problems; interchangeable psychosocial functioning and environmental factors (such as the child's behaviour placing a foster placement at risk, which in turn exacerbates mental health problems); multiple carers and agencies involved; and ethical and service difficulties in using experimental designs such as allocating a child to a particular treatment or service for research purposes.

Some of these gaps will gradually be addressed by studies adapting to the characteristics of vulnerable children and their supporting agencies, for example by comparing matched services or settings like hostels or children's homes. Qualitative methods and designs are increasingly providing valuable knowledge on issues such as user perspectives and therapeutic process. Economic evaluation is particularly important in informing policy-makers, commissioners, and service providers.

Mental health traning for agencies working with vulnerable children and young people

The recognition that children's mental health is everybody's responsibility has resulted in the development of different levels of training for practitioners working with children and families. These include those working with the groups of children discussed in this book, whose characteristics and needs should be understood, so that training has a service rather than theoretical context. In addition to the generic mental health skills necessary at primary care level, that is, mental health awareness, recognition of common mental health problems, and ability to manage the cases of lesser severity and complexity, there are specific issues that apply to certain agencies.

Training should not aim to develop specialists in different fields. Instead, it should familiarize staff with anxiety-raising behaviours, such as self-harm, which they are likely to encounter in their everyday practice; understand the impact of trauma on children; set up behavioural strategies; and appreciate the importance of their therapeutic role in the child's or young person's care. Agencies in contact with children and young people in public care will, in particular, need knowledge of attachment problems, their (difficult) distinction from developmental delays, and when to use different levels of therapeutic interventions such as life story work, or alternatively seek psychodynamic psychotherapy. Foster and adoptive parents have training needs of their own, both as professionals and as carers. These should be tailored-made and be provided early on following their approval, to prepare them for children's behaviours and expressions of distress, which can otherwise overwhelm them and lead to placement breakdowns a few years later.

Agencies working with young offenders will come across similar presentations, but will be particularly interested in the interface between offending and mental health, which often delays the judicial process because of the perceptions and conceptualization of mental health and mental illness within the youth justice system. Staff in shelters for the homeless will frequently care for family victims of domestic and neighbourhood violence, and will require training on the effect of family and community violence on mothers and children, and on the relationship between the two mechanisms. Basic therapeutic skills should enable them to work individually or jointly, depending on the circumstances. A common theme for practitioners in contact with asylum-seeking and refugee families is the potential link between trauma in the children's country of origin and emerging mental health problems, as well as how the latter can be affected by their adjustment to their new social circumstances. Training in all aspects of child development, how mental health problems are expressed and communicated by children with different developmental delays, and consequently strategies in helping them and their families, will be essential for related agencies.

A cost effective way of providing such training would be its integration and input through existing educational programmes and leading to the required qualifications (e.g. for foster carers or residential social workers). Ideally, and in addition to such 'Level 1' training, practitioners with more specialist roles or those who wish to develop them further, should have access to more in-depth training, in generic child mental health (at certificate, diploma or masters degree level) or different therapeutic modalities.

Conclusions

The recent expansion of interest, service initiatives, and research on vulnerable groups of children and young people is likely to continue and evolve further in the years to come. More targeted, focused, and evidence-based service models will be developed, whilst therapeutic frameworks will become more applied in real settings. The ethos of encompassing diversity within child mental health services is likely to become the norm within a comprehensive provision, rather than merely the reflection of time-limited designated projects. This will be a huge step in the maturation of child mental health services, by achieving equitable access and therapeutic engagement for complex young client groups. Despite the difficulties that this route entails, it is extremely gratifying by having a lasting effect on the mental health and, ultimately, the lives of children and young people who are most in need.

Subject Index

Author Index